PELICAN BOOKS

NEW HORIZONS IN PSYCHOLOGY 1

Born in 1921 and brought up in the Channel Islands, Brian Foss read Mathematics and Physics at Cambridge. After the war he read Psychology at Oxford; from 1948 to 1951 he lectured in Experimental Psychology there, and from 1951 to 1964 at Birkbeck College, University of London. In 1965 he was appointed Professor of Educational Psychology at the Institute of Education, London, then in 1968 Professor of Psychology at Bedford College of London University. He has published articles on imitation, animal behaviour, aesthetics, perceptual illusions, thinking and similar topics, has edited a series of volumes on Determinants of Infant Behaviour, and has broadcast frequently.

NEW HORIZONS IN PSYCHOLOGY

PSYCHOLOGY

1

Edited by Brian M. Foss

Penguin Books

Penguin Books Ltd, Harmondsworth, Middlesex, England
Penguin Books Inc., 7110 Ambassador Road, Baltimore, Maryland 21207, U.S.A.
Penguin Books Australia Ltd, Ringwood, Victoria, Australia

—

First published 1966
Reprinted 1967, 1969
Reprinted as *New Horizons in Psychology I*, 1972
Reprinted 1973

—

Copyright © Penguin Books, 1966

—

Made and printed in Great Britain
by Richard Clay (The Chaucer Press) Ltd,
Bungay, Suffolk
Set in Monotype Times

*The cover design is adapted from a figure
by L. S. Penrose*

CONTENTS

Contents

INTRODUCTION

THIS book is about scientific psychology. In the chapters that follow, it is possible to see the influences of philosophical psychology and of psycho-analysis; nevertheless, the emphasis is on rigorous observation and experiment. The sort of work reported here has been going on for only a few decades. As Professor C. A. Mace once put it, modern psychology has no history, just a past. However, it is not necessarily a shady past, and as Mace has also said, no one has yet shown that better ideas have come out of the laboratory than those which came out of the arm-chair. I am not sure how seriously he intended the remark to be taken, and many experimental psychologists would disagree with it; but to the general public, experimental psychology is still at a testing stage. This book can be regarded as a progress report.

It is intended also to be a guide to what may be some of the exciting developments in the coming years. From this point of view the selection of topics is bound to be personal. There is, for instance, a bias to believing that the study of physiology and animals will continue to provide some of the more important growing points of psychology. Several promising kinds of research have had to be left out on the grounds that it would be necessary to take the reader through an honours degree course in psychology before he would see the point of the problems which the research sets out to solve. The scope of the book has also been narrowed by excluding most of the advances which have been made in applied psychology: there would be so much to report in such little space. Indeed, it will be noticed that authors have rarely drawn attention to the possible applications of the work they report. The editor hopes that readers may be stimulated to thinking of applications for themselves.

The subject matter of psychology is the behaviour of man, and other animals, and this is taken to include man's subjective experience. It is easier to be objective about behaviour which can be observed by others, and measured or classified, but experimenters have made great progress in probing man's experiences.

The first section of the book shows how many techniques there are for investigating the 'internal' worlds of perception, attention and thinking. Some of the results obtained with these techniques might have been anticipated by the non-experimentalist, but many would not. Perhaps what will surprise the general reader even more is the way in which psychologists study every facet of behaviour, using a wide variety of approaches. This variety is often bewildering, and is partly the result of the influence of other scientific disciplines: ideas from engineering have affected psychological ideas of human communication, and of how the nervous system works; ideas from the medical sciences, especially from physiology and neuro-anatomy, are continually being used by psychologists; and social sciences, for instance anthropology, have stimulated new ways of looking at social behaviour and the influences of the group on the individual.

There is, however, another source of variety in techniques and theories. It arises from the fact that psychologists want answers to several different *kinds* of question when they analyse any one facet of behaviour. The following is a list of some of the main explanations used.

Causal. What was the *immediate* cause of the behaviour? A sound like an air-raid siren may cause a sudden twinge of fear. It is the stimulus for the response of fear, and much of 'stimulus–response' psychology (e.g. Pavlov's work – mentioned several times in the book) is concerned with finding causal explanations of this kind.

Historical. The history of the fearful response to the siren is to be found in war-time experiences. Personality is often explained in terms of childhood experiences (both by Freudians and neo-behaviourists; Chapter 18) – a typical historical explanation. But the time interval involved in historical explanations may be very much shorter. It is a matter of months in the case where a driver's faulty use of the gears of his car is explained in terms of 'negative transfer' of training from driving another car with a different gear arrangement. And the interval is a matter of minutes when the way you feel now is explained in terms of what you were doing before you started reading this book. Some kinds of explanation are almost prehistorical rather than historical – for instance, when human behaviour is explained in terms of its evolution from animal ancestors (Chapters 9, 10 and 11).

Purposive. If you ask someone why they are doing what they are, they will usually answer in terms of a purpose or goal. 'I am reading this book to find out what psychology is all about.' Some psychologists use such explanations too. (Freud did, and thought that one's purposes were often unconscious.) Experimental psychologists often talk about the observable goals of behaviour, which is the same kind of explanation in a thinly disguised form.

Rule following. This is a kind of purposive explanation in which the behaviour of someone is explained in terms of the rules laid down by society. We do things in order to conform (see, for instance, parts of Chapters 20 and 21).

Structural. One way of finding out how a clock works is to look inside and observe the structure of its parts. Many psychologists think that this is a sensible approach to human behaviour – to look at the structure of the nervous system and discover the way its various parts relate to each other. One recent development – 'cybernetics' – involves simulating behaviour with machines; by studying the structure and function of machines which are good simulators one may get clues to the structures underlying human behaviour. Several of the chapters in this book are concerned with the physiological structures and functions of man and animals.

Functional. Functional explanations are much used by physiologists ('during emergencies the blood goes from the skin and the large internal organs to the muscles *so that* the person is better prepared to fight or run away') and zoologists ('when a cat fights its hair stands on end *so that* it looks bigger to its adversary'). Psychologists use such explanations sometimes, and so do laymen. 'You must drink your milk because it's good for you.' The first four chapters are often concerned with function, though not always explicitly.

Contingency. Contingency explanations are nothing more than answers to the question 'What goes with what?' If you reinforce (reward) an animal for performing some act, he is likely to perform the act again. It is known that learning of this kind *goes with* reinforcement. 'How' or 'why' is not known. Correlations involve this kind of explanation (or lack of it). Cigarette-smoking correlates with lung cancer. (Again how or why is not known.) Although contingencies and correlations do not give one much insight into behaviour, nevertheless they allow one to make predictions. If you know that someone is a heavy smoker you can predict that his chances of developing cancer are higher than the average. If an animal is deprived of food you can predict that it will search for food – even though you do not know what the underlying mechanism (structure) may be. One kind of psychology (see Chapter 15) is a kind of anti-theory, in that the interest is only in making predictions and not in 'understanding'.

These seven kinds of explanation overlap each other. For instance, S–R psychology is partly causal, partly structural (in that it supposes a reflex arc in the nervous system, or something like one) and partly contingency (in that one is pointing to a relation between stimulus and response). The other thing to notice is that the various explanations are not incompatible with each other. The reaction to the air-raid siren can be explained simply as a contingency, or it can be explained historically, causally, and to some extent in terms of the other categories also. One of the aims of psychology is to explain behaviour from *all* these angles: hence the variety.

The book is divided into five parts, but several of the chapters could have appeared under more than one heading. The first eight papers are concerned with what is sometimes called cognitive psychology – the means of getting to know about the outside world, thinking and reasoning, and language and communication. The second section – 'Origins of Behaviour' – is concerned mainly with 'historical' explanations, in terms of heredity, the beginnings of behaviour in simpler animals, and the effects of learning early in life 'Physiological and Psychological States' deals with motivation and other conditions which are dependent on what goes on within the body rather than outside it. 'Learning and Training' is concerned more with modifications of behaviour through experience. Finally, 'Personality and Social Psychology' presents three selected topics out of a very wide range which would have been possible. There have been very many develop-

Introduction

ments in this field, and those appearing here are chosen simply because the editor finds them particularly stimulating.

Science thrives on controversy. Differences of opinion lead to experiments, and it would be true to say that the traditional sequence of scientific thinking – observation, hypothesis, experimental test – is often replaced by the sequence: difference of opinion, experimental test, convergence of opinion; followed by fresh observation and experiment leading to further controversy. Although the differences of opinion have not often been made explicit in this book, it is to be hoped that the reader will appreciate the implied conflict of opinion where different authors have looked at the same topics, but from different points of view.

I would like to thank all the contributors for their ready response and enthusiasm; and Penguin Books (especially Charles Clark) for the help and advice they have given most generously.

B.M.F.

Note to the 1972 reprint

This book was first published in 1966. It has come to be used as an introductory book for students specializing in psychology, although it remains useful to non-specialists as well. Since the general conception of the book has proved useful, the publishers have decided to base a series of volumes on it. Future books (to be published in the Penguin Education list) will complement this first one and trace the developing horizons of psychology through the years. They will appear every three years. Each will have a new editor who will choose his own contributors. It is because of this development that *New Horizons in Psychology* now appears as *New Horizons in Psychology 1*.

B. M. F.

November 1971

PERCEPTION, THINKING AND COMMUNICATION

This section is about cognition, in the sense of acquiring knowledge. How do we gain information about the world around (perception), and how does the machinery for this sometimes 'go wrong' (illusions)? How is perception affected by attention? The first four chapters in this section are concerned with such problems. Later chapters, on Reasoning and Creativity, are concerned with the way we deal with information once we have got it, in making inferences and arriving at new ideas. Much of the information we acquire is gained from other people, through written and spoken language, and the remaining chapters deal with the psychology of language, and with methods used for dealing with communication in a more general sense.

Until this century, almost the whole of psychology dealt with cognition in one form or another; but with the rise of behaviourism, with the growing evidence for the irrational nature of much of man's thinking and behaviour (evidence from Freud's work for instance) and the growing distrust with the introspective method, psychologists have tended to turn their interest to other aspects of behaviour. However, in the last decade there has been a renewed interest, partly as the result of the use of new objective techniques. The size of this section demonstrates the success of this revival as well as the importance of cognitive psychology in the understanding of behaviour.

PERCEPTION, THOUGHT, AND
COMMUNICATION

1. STUDIES OF THE VISUAL SYSTEM

P. C. DODWELL

For people with normal vision, the eyes with their nervous connexions provide the most important means for obtaining information about the world. The study of the structures involved in seeing, and of the functions of parts of the structures, has interested many different sorts of scientists for centuries. The investigation of almost any optical phenomenon is likely to have a bearing, and it is not surprising to find names such as Kepler, Newton, Maxwell and Sherrington associated with the history of research on vision. Many early studies, particularly in the German laboratories of the late nineteenth century, were concerned with topics like colour perception, the relation between physical measures of intensity of stimulus and the resultant sensation, visual acuity and stereoscopic perception. Professor Dodwell, who has done many experiments on visual perception, shows how recent discoveries are modifying the classical picture.

INTRODUCTION

IT has been estimated that well over ninety per cent of our information about the world is received through the visual sense. Small wonder, then, that a great deal of attention has been focused on its study. Our present picture of the structure and functioning of the visual system is the result of several more or less convergent lines of thought and experiment, which may be listed, approximately, as follows:

(i) Studies of the physical properties of light, its propagation and interaction with matter (reflection, refraction, absorption, etc.).
(ii) Studies of the anatomy and physiology of the eye and its neural connexions with the brain.
(iii) Studies of the relations between physical stimulation and behaviour, where behaviour may be interpreted in a broad sense to include verbal reports of what one perceives.
(iv) Somewhat less obviously, the new science of communication, which has developed over the past twenty years, has already

15

contributed significantly, both in terms of specific hypotheses and – at present more importantly – in terms of a general re-orientation of scientists' systematic conceptions about vision.

In this chapter I shall try to show how advances in the second field, mainly in electrophysiology, have allowed us to delve minutely into the processes in the visual system. The knowledge gained in this way, complementing psychological findings and a theoretical approach which considers the visual apparatus as a special form of communication system, is beginning to reveal a picture of that system, intricate yet wonderfully coordinated, that was scarcely guessed at even ten years ago.

THE VISUAL APPARATUS

The gross functions of the eye itself have been more or less under-stood for a long time. Kepler first correctly explained the role of the pupil and lens in the forming of a sharp image of the external scene on to the thin layer of photosensitive matter at the back of the eyeball called the retina (see Figure 1). It is the same principle of forming an optical image as is used in that 'mechanical eye', the camera; but there the analogy ends, as Dr Dixon's opening remarks make clear (p. 45).

The question now is, how does the image get 'transferred' from the retina to the brain? Even more fundamentally one might ask, how do we know that it must be so transferred? By a variety of procedures such as the tracing of nerve fibres proceeding from the retina, excision of parts of the system and electrical recording in animals, study of visual defects in people who have suffered head injury, etc., we have a rather clear picture of the macro-structure of the visual pathways in man and in higher animals whose nervous systems are basically quite similar to man's. Figure 2 shows this system; put at its simplest, we know that the optical image is transferred to the occipital lobes of the brain because destruction of these areas (by gunshot wounds, for example) destroys the visual sense. Circumscribed lesions in the occipital lobes and else-where in the system lead to partial losses, as shown, for instance, in the work of Teuber, Battersby and Bender (1960).

16

Studies of the Visual System

Some of the biggest advances in knowledge in recent years have had to do with the details of the 'transfer' of the optical image from the retina to the brain. From our general knowledge of neural transmission we know that events on the retina are associated with electro-chemical changes in the optic nerve, which eventually reach the occipital cortex of the brain. For a long time it was thought that some sort of actual spatial representation of the light patterns on the retina were present in the brain when

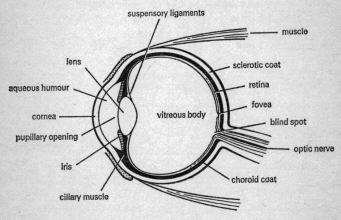

Figure 1. A cross-section of the human eye. Light rays entering the eye pass through the tough glassy cornea, a watery liquid known as the aqueous humour, the pupil and the lens. The pupillary opening varies in size, depending upon the intensity of light. These changes are brought about through reactions of the iris, which thus serves a function comparable with that of the diaphragm on a camera. The curvature of the lens needs to change from time to time. This adjustment, known as accommodation, is carried out reflexly through changes in the ciliary muscle and the suspensory ligaments. After passing through the jelly-like vitreous body, light rays produce an image on the retina. Clearest vision is in the fovea, an especially sensitive depression. Near by is the blind spot, the point at which nerve fibres leave the retina. The walls of the eye comprise the outer tough covering known as the sclerotic coat, an intermediate heavily pigmented layer known as the choroid coat, which keeps out all light except that which comes through the pupil, and the retina, which is an extremely complex photosensitive mechanism for translating photic stimulation into nerve impulses. (From N. L. Munn (1962). *Introduction to Psychology* (4th edn). Boston: Houghton Mifflin.)

17

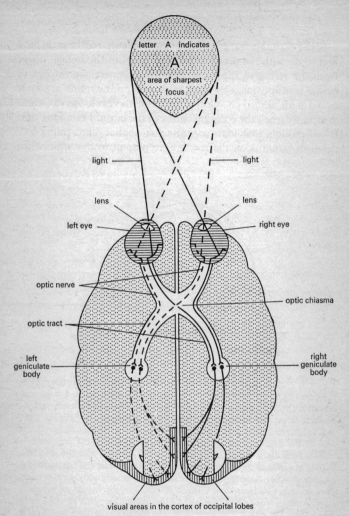

Figure 2. A highly simplified version of the visual apparatus. The area enclosing the letter *A* at the top of the figure represents the centre part of the visual field, and the straight lines marked 'light' indicate that each eye receives a slightly different projection of that field. The smooth and dotted lines tracing the course of optic nerves and optic tracts indicate that the left halves of both retinae project to one side of the brain, the right halves to the

visual perception occurred. In a gross way this is true, since partial defects of vision are known to be topographically related to the sites of brain lesions. (That is, damage in certain specified locations in the cortex always leads to a defect in a specifiable part of the visual field, and damage at neighbouring points usually leads to deficits in neighbouring parts of the visual field.) However, the sort of implicit assumption that all perceptual phenomena are explainable in principle on such a simple 'mirror' model, when the brain mirrors what is on the retina, and the perceiver mirrors what is on the brain, is now known to be both unnecessary and false.

Instead, we shall see that the model now being built up is of an incredibly intricate system, where transformations of the informative spatial patterns focused on the retina occur at many different levels – at the retina itself, within the optic nerve, at the lateral geniculate bodies (see Figure 2) and again at the cerebral cortex. The relations between stimulus and cortical activity turn out in some cases to be surprisingly different from what one would expect on the old 'mirror function' – or isomorphic – view.

Sensory Qualities

Without getting involved in philosophical worries about just how many sensory qualities there may be in the visual mode, and how they should be categorized, we can note that there are a number of obviously different such attributes or qualities. A rough list might be: brightness, colour, contour (edge), extension (surface), shape and depth (the 'solidity' added by the third dimension).

Psychologists are interested in how, if at all, the perceptions of different qualities are correlated with the known activities of the receptor system. Or, as we may say, how the information about a sensory quality is *coded* in the system.

To show how such a problem may be tackled, I shall consider three separate qualities, and describe recent work which, while it does not give a complete answer to the question of how the visual

other. The symbols shown in the geniculate bodies are to indicate that the fibres of the optic tract connect to neurons in the geniculate bodies, and their axons in turn form the connecting links with the visual cortex. (From F. L. Ruch (1953). *Psychology and Life* (4th edn). Chicago: Scott, Foresman.

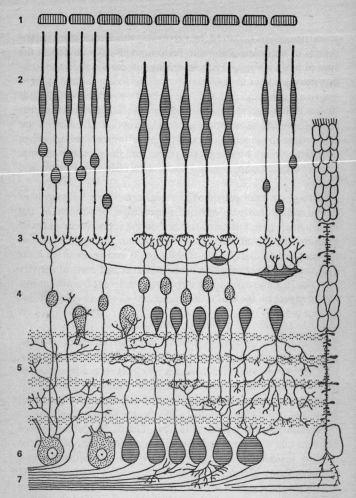

Figure 3. The structure of the human retina (Greeff): 1, pigment layer; 2, rod and cone layer; 3, synapses; 4, bipolar cells; 5, synapses; 6, ganglion cells; 7, optic nerve fibres. Light strikes the retina first at level 7; that is to say, it travels from bottom to top, in terms of this diagram. (From F. E. Cady and H. B. Dates (1928). *Illuminating Engineering* (2nd edn). New York: Wiley.)

system operates in each instance, does indicate the sort of progress now being made and the new prospects which this progress opens up. The three qualities are colour, contour (and shape) and depth.

The Retina

Before asking how colour is perceived, we must take a closer look at the receptor surface of the eye, the retina, where the actual transformation of the physical energy of light into a 'neural signal' occurs. Figure 3 shows diagrammatically a section through a human retina, with its several layers of cells through which light passes before striking the actual photosensitive elements, the rods and cones. These elements 'capture' (absorb) light, and this absorption is a sufficient condition to activate the nerve cell of which the element is a part. Light interacts with single molecules within a rod or cone in discrete packets of energy, called *quanta*, and from detection studies with extremely faint light sources it is estimated that absorption of between two and five *quanta* by a like number of rods is sufficient to cause a sensation of light. The minuteness of the energy involved (about 5×10^{-10} ergs) may be gauged from the fact that, as M. H. Pirenne has pointed out, the energy of a pea falling one inch, converted into light energy, would be sufficient to cause a slight visual sensation in every man that ever lived! The immense ability of the eye to accommodate itself to environmental conditions is indicated by the fact that one's eye can perceive without damage a light that contains hundreds of millions of times more energy than the 'threshold' light, provided that the eye is in a suitable state of 'adaptation'. That is to say, provided it has been exposed for some time (a matter of minutes) to an appropriate level of general illumination.

How can the eye be so versatile? When light is absorbed by the photosensitive elements of the retina the process of absorption itself renders the elements less sensitive to light than they previously were. The details of this process are not completely understood, but we do know that light bleaches rhodopsin, the photosensitive pigment of the rods, and that rhodopsin regenerates spontaneously in the absence of light. The bleached rhodopsin does not absorb light, and partially bleached rhodopsin is only partially absorbent. This reversible photochemical process is the basis of changes in adaptation, yet is not a complete explanation of it; for instance, a very small change in the percentage of bleached rhodopsin leads to a large decrease in sensitivity of the eye, far larger than would be the case if the decreased sensitivity were simply a function of the amount of unbleached rhodopsin available for absorbing light. The explanation of this anomaly will almost certainly be found in the neural organization of the retina, for as Figure 3 suggests, there are rich interconnexions between many of its neighbouring elements, and evidence I shall mention later demonstrates very clearly that interactions between different elements occur.

When a rod or cone has been activated, the neural signal generated must traverse at least two synapses before reaching a ganglion cell (layer 6 in Figure 3) which transmits signals along its axon, which forms part of the optic nerve (Figure 2). The ganglion cells are then, in a sense, the collectors of information about stimulation of the retina by light.

Twilight Vision

In discussing the light-absorbing property of rhodopsin, two important matters were not mentioned. The first is that rhodopsin, which exists mainly, if not exclusively, in the rods, is differentially sensitive to different wavelengths of light. That is to say, it captures light of some colours more readily than others. The second is that the spectral sensitivity of the human eye measured in bright daylight is quite different from the sensitivity when it is measured in dim illumination. The colour that appears brightest in good illumination (so-called photopic vision) is a yellowish-green, of wavelength about 560 millimicrons (mμ), whereas the dark-adapted eye sees best a bluish-green (500 mμ) and is virtually blind to red light (650 mμ and longer). In Figure 4 the spectral sensitivity of the dark-adapted eye is shown, and superimposed on this curve is the 'absorption spectrum' of human rhodopsin, or the capacity of rhodopsin to 'capture' light of different wavelengths.* The remarkable agreement between the two sets of data

* This absorption spectrum is actually found by passing lights of different colours through a solution of rhodopsin extracted from human eyes.

leaves no reasonable room for doubt that rhodopsin is the photo-sensitive substance that mediates twilight – or scotopic – vision.

The spectral sensitivity curve for photopic vision is similar in form to the curve shown in Figure 4, but is shifted to the right; as mentioned above, the maximum sensitivity occurs near 560 mμ rather than 500. One naturally asks, therefore, is there a second visual pigment, like rhodopsin, but having an absorption spec-

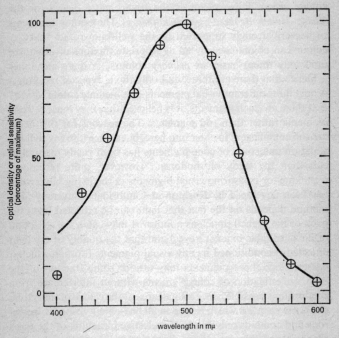

Figure 4. Circles, the spectral sensitivity of the dark-adapted human eye. Curve, the absorption spectrum of human rhodopsin. (From Rushton, W. A. H. (1962). *Visual Pigments in Man.* Liverpool: Liverpool University Press.)

trum closely similar to the sensitivity curve for photopic vision?

The answer to this question is not altogether settled, but it can be stated quite definitely that there is not just one other visual pigment, but several.

Perception, Thinking and Communication

COLOUR VISION

Visual Pigments

Thomas Young, in 1802, concluded that there are three types of
light receptor in the human eye that react with different selectivi-
ties to light according to its wavelength. This assumption is the
basis of the most celebrated, and the most persistent, theory of
colour vision, now known as the trichromatic theory (or the
Young–Helmholtz three-component theory). The assumption seems
to be very strongly supported by the well-known fact that *any*
colour can be matched by an appropriate mixture of just three
(and only three) basic, or *primary* colours. Is there any other
evidence that there are three, and only three, types of receptor –
or just three different visual pigments that mediate colour vision?

If there are such pigments, it is believed that they must be cone
pigments rather than rod pigments. The reasons for this belief
are too complicated to enter into here, but suffice it to say that the
isolation and study of cone pigments has been vastly more difficult than the study of rhodopsin. However, quite recently a
technique for measuring visual pigments in the living human eye
has been developed by Rushton at Cambridge University. The
method depends on the fact that light can be reflected from the
back of the eyeball (much as a motorist may catch the reflection
of his headlights in a cat's eyes) and that the quality of the light
reflected is conditioned by any visual pigments through which it
passes, since those pigments may absorb some fraction of the
light. Investigation of cone pigments without interference from
rhodopsin is possible, since a small area at the centre of the retina,
the *fovea centralis* which is used in all fine-detail vision, is free of
rods and contains only cones. By selective bleaching of the *fovea*
with lights of different colours, Rushton has been able to show the
presence of a green-sensitive * and a red-sensitive pigment, and
by less direct means including inferences from colour-matching
experiments, the probable existence (in very small amounts) of a
blue-sensitive pigment as well. This work is delightfully expounded
in the sixth Sherrington Lecture delivered at Liverpool University
(Rushton, 1962).

* That is to say, a pigment with maximal absorbency for green light.

24

Studies of the Visual System

Even more recently, MacNichol and his associates at Johns Hopkins University have demonstrated the presence of three visual pigments in human cones, and what is more, that a single cone only contains one such pigment, not a mixture of them. These experiments are conceptually very simple, although technically formidable; they involve passing monochromatic light through the photopigment in a single cone (from an excised retina), and measuring the amount of light absorbed by the pigment at different wavelengths. Just three types of photopigment have been identified in cones, a finding in good agreement with Rushton's. This work seems to answer pretty definitively the question of how many 'cone pigments' there may be, although it is still logically possible that other types will be discovered. However, it would be misleading to suggest that we have here a final answer to the problem of how colour coding occurs in the human visual system. The most widely held alternative to the Young–Helmholtz three-components theory (or one of its several variations) was originally propounded by Ewald Hering, a contemporary and rival of Helmholtz. This is the *opponent-process* theory which postulates six colour processes which occur in three opponent-pairs (red–green, blue–yellow, and white–black). A modern version of this theory, proposed by Hurvich and Jameson (1957) gives a coherent quantitative explanation for very many of the facts of colour vision, but lacks support, so far as visual pigments are concerned, of the type afforded by Rushton's and MacNichol's work for the trichromatic theory. However, as we shall see in the next section, a different sort of neurophysiological evidence does indicate very clearly that opponent-colour processes do actually occur in some species, both at the retina and farther back in the visual system.

To conclude this discussion of visual pigments, it may be noted that a great variety of pigments have been extracted and studied from the retinae of fish, birds, reptiles, as well as mammals. Such studies are of great importance for the understanding of the actual photochemistry of the visual receptors, but do not directly shed light on the colour-coding system of the human retina.

Electrophysiology

Some of the most spectacular advances in our understanding of what goes on in the visual system have come through the development of techniques for recording and measuring very small amounts of electrical activity in minute structures. Extremely fine electrodes with a diameter of less than a micron (one-thousandth of a millimetre) can pick up changes in potential which are fractions of a millivolt – the order of change in firing neurons. Thus it is now possible to measure the electrical activity of a single neuron during sensory stimulation.

One of the most extensive, as well as one of the first, series of experiments using this technique was performed by Ragnar Granit and his co-workers in Sweden, to investigate the responses of single ganglion cells and their fibres (Figure 3) in a variety of species including frog, snake, rat, guinea pig and cat. They found that the units from which they recorded could be divided into two quite distinct classes: 'broad-band' receivers, that were activated by light of most wavelengths in the visible spectrum, which they called dominators; and 'narrow-band' receivers (much less common) that fired only for light in a rather narrow band of wavelengths, termed modulators (Figure 5). It was found that the responses really did occur in individual ganglion cells and their optic nerve fibres, thus showing that two separate ways of sending information about light falling on the retina to the brain are involved. In the one case, a rather general signal about 'amount of light', and in the other, more specific signals about its quality (wavelength).

Quite different evidence for colour-coding at the retina has been found recently by another Swedish physiologist, G. Svaetichin, evidence which suggests that in some species of fish the opponent-colour processes first adumbrated by Hering actually occur. His recordings, from deeper in the retina than the ganglion cell layer studied by Granit, were originally claimed to be recordings from the photosensitive elements themselves, in this case, cones. However, it is now known that they are from sites somewhere between the two (see Figure 3). The electrical activity consisted of graded potentials – that is to say slower changes than the all-or-none

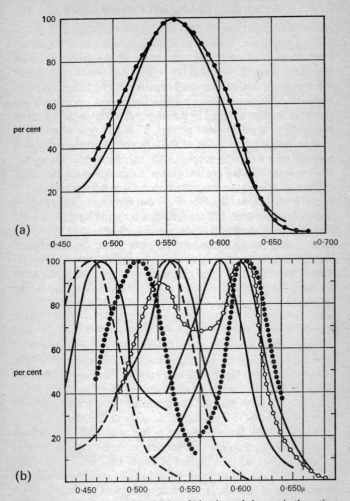

Figure 5. (*a*) Distribution of sensitivity of 'dominator' element in the retina of frog (uninterrupted line) and snake (line interrupted by dots). (*b*) Distribution of sensitivity of 'modulator' elements from eyes of rat (dots), guinea pig (broken line), frog (line in full) and snake (line interrupted by circles). Note that all curves are in percentage of the maximum. (From R. Granit (1943). 'A physiological theory of Colour Perception'. *Nature, 151,* 11–14.)

spikes of constant amplitude typical of nerve discharge – and of varying amplitude. Their most striking feature is that, recording from one and the same point in the retina, change in one direction (increased positive potential) for light of one wavelength, but in the opposite direction (increased negativity) for another, could be obtained. The two opponent-pairs discovered, moreover, are precisely the ones required by the Hering-type theory; a red–green process, and a yellow–blue process. That this type of coding is neither limited to the retina of the fish, nor yet to the retina, has recently been shown by recording the activity of neurons in that staging point between eye and cortex, the lateral geniculate body (Figure 2). De Valois has shown that there are neurons in the lateral geniculate nuclei of monkeys that fire when a green light is shown on the retina, but are inhibited by a red light. Similarly, Hubel (whose work will be discussed further below) has found such colour-specific opponent-type units in the visual cortex of the cat. Thus there is evidence – admittedly of different sorts and from different species – that opponent-type processes occur at all levels of the visual system from the initial receptor surface to the cerebral cortex.

Colour Coding in the Visual System

Nothing has been said here about the world of human *experience* of colour. It might be argued that an analytic dissection of the physiological activities in different parts of the visual system will never enable us to understand the nature of colour and colour-perception. This is like the objections of the German poet and scientist, Goethe, to the analytic methods of the physical optics of his day. Such arguments raise rather profound philosophical questions about the nature and scope of scientific explanation that cannot be tackled here. Suffice it to say that, while knowledge of physiological systems can never be fully *sufficient* to account for why we see particular colours in the way we do, an understanding of such systems is fundamental to an understanding of some of the necessary conditions for colour perception to occur.

From what has been said in previous sections of this chapter, it should be clear that the physiological basis for colour perception is enormously complex, and involves processing at several points in the visual system. Knowledge of the selective light-absorbing properties of visual pigments does not at present help us to understand other processes at the retina completely, such as the opponent-processes. Nor do we know how these processes in turn are related to colour-specific neurons at the lateral geniculate body and cortex. We are obviously still a long way from obtaining a specific and coherent account of colour coding throughout the system even of one species. That such an account will eventually be forthcoming, however, can scarcely be doubted.

CONTOUR AND SHAPE

One of the main puzzles in the psychology of perception is the problem of *stimulus equivalence*. This problem seemed rather intractable under the old 'switchboard' model of the visual system, in which there was thought to be a point-for-point correspondence between receptor units (in vision, the photo-receptors of the retina) and cortical loci which were held to be the final physiological units mediating perception. The problem is most acute in the explanation of shape recognition: how can a square be recognized as such, when it may occur in a variety of sizes, orientations and positions? Different receptor units are activated on different occasions, and yet the square is still seen *as* a square.

The isomorphic theory, mentioned earlier, held that the pattern of stimulation of the retina was more-or-less faithfully reproduced in the cortex, and this pattern was isomorphic with – or congruent with – the shape actually perceived. This theory perpetuates the doctrine of 'the ghost in the machine' (Ryle, 1949), since the theory does not give an account of how the patterns of brain stimulation are themselves recognized as similar to, or different from, one another. Put rather crudely, one might say that to the question, 'How does the perceiver recognize similarities and differences between such patterns?', the isomorphic theorist would have to answer, 'he must inspect them and find out'. Thus the perceiver must be sitting upstairs in the brain observing the brain states, much as the brain 'observes' or records, what is going on in the retina. This pushes the problem of recognition out of the brain, without solving it.

Another way of looking at the problem of equivalence is now prevalent, and it illustrates the impact of ideas from communications engineering on psychology. If one considers any system with a richly variable environment (or as we may say, with a variable 'input'), but which 'reduces' this input in some way, so that the responses of the system to its environment are less variable, or involve fewer categories than the input, then discovery of relations between the 'input class' (sensory stimulation) and the 'output class' (of responses) should tell us something about the 'processing' of the input in the system. Everything depends on being able to establish relations between the two classes (input–output), and, of course, the inferences about the system depend on what precise relationships are discovered. Thus, when we find that, despite variations in size, brightness, colour, etc., people with normal vision can identify certain collections of lines as 'squares', we may ask: how are those lines (contours) processed, so as to give a constant output, or response? Or, as the communications engineer would say, what sort of transformations are done on the variable input, to compute an invariant output?

An important aspect of this new slant on the problem of equivalence of stimuli is its increasing abstractness. Thus it is no longer thought to be important that the final constant physiological state or event 'computed' when a square is in the field of vision should itself have the characteristics of a square, as in the isomorphic theory. What is important is that the internal signal should have an unambiguous one-to-one relation with a certain class of input patterns. Undoubtedly, the acceptance of this view was facilitated by the development of Information Theory (Chapter 5), in which 'information content' is defined and handled independently of its means of expression – whether in words, letters or other symbols (Shannon, 1948), and by the development of computers with several possible modes of information input. The input system enables the computer to 'read' characters. So long as the one-to-one relation between the character and its machine representation is preserved, the computer can perform operations on the character. The exact form of the representation is not important, provided the computer has the right output system (the converse of the input) to inform us of the results of its computation. Such an abstract way of dealing with information, and its transfer and transformation within a system, may seem to be a far cry from the rich, vital world of our perceptions. Yet, astonishing as it may seem, we now know that the visual systems of some species actually do operate in this way.

Receptive Fields

D. H. Hubel and T. N. Wiesel, working at Harvard University, have used a method of inserting a microelectrode into the visual cortex of an anaesthetized cat, from which they can record the activity of individual neurons when the retina is stimulated with a spot of light, or with an illuminated pattern. They find that, typically, such a neuron in the cortex can be activated by the light's falling on a quite circumscribed area of the retina, called its *receptive field*. With a single, small spot of light it is found that some points within the field activate the neuron when the light is turned on, but others cause it to fire when the light is turned off. These two sorts of response are called excitatory and inhibitory, and are naturally antagonistic, in the sense that if the neuron is activated by a spot of light falling in an excitatory area, it can be inhibited – made to cease firing – by a second spot falling in an inhibitory area. What is particularly striking about these receptive fields is the fact that they have quite specific shapes, as shown in Figure 6, *C–G*. The shapes shown in this figure actually map those points on the retina which were found to affect a single cortical neuron, and the different symbols show which areas were excitatory, which inhibitory. The typical field has a narrow band of excitatory points, all lying on a straight line, surrounded by a wider field of inhibitory points, or vice versa. Hubel and Wiesel found that, having mapped such a field with a light spot, they could predict what form of contour would be the 'maximal' stimulus for the neuron concerned. For example, in the field of Figure 6, *C*, it was found that a straight line, falling on the retina so as to coincide with the series of excitatory points, caused the cortical neuron to fire much more intensely than any other stimulus. A contour in the same orientation, but falling slightly to one side, so that inhibitory points are stimulated, would cause a strong off-discharge, or alternatively, strong inhibition of the cortical neuron. Uniform stimulation of the whole field (without contours) leaves the cortical neuron unaffected.

This shows very clearly that the cat's visual system is organized

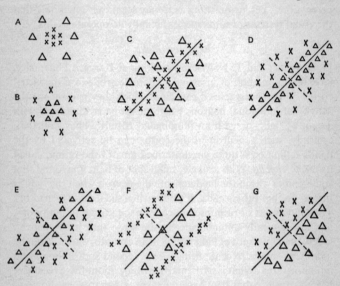

Figure 6. Common arrangements of lateral geniculate and cortical receptive fields. *A.* 'On'-centre geniculate receptive field. *B.* 'Off'-centre geniculate receptive field. *C–G.* Various arrangements of simple cortical receptive fields. X, areas giving excitatory responses ('on' responses); △, areas giving inhibitory responses ('off' responses). Receptive-field axes are shown by continuous lines through field centres; in the figure these are all oblique, but each arrangement occurs in all orientations. (From Hubel, D. H. and Wiesel, T. N. (1962). *J. Physiol. 160*, 106–54.)

specifically for the coding of *contour* information, and that the receptive fields we have so far discussed (called 'simple' fields) are the basis for transmitting information about both the orientation and position of rectilinear contours. Perhaps even more striking was the discovery of 'complex' fields. In this case it was found that some cortical neurons respond *only* to straight contours in a particular orientation (say, horizontal) and not to spots of light; however, they would respond to a contour in the correct orientation even when its position on the retina was changed. Figure 7 shows such a case. On the left is shown the position of the stimulating contour with respect to the receptive field centre,

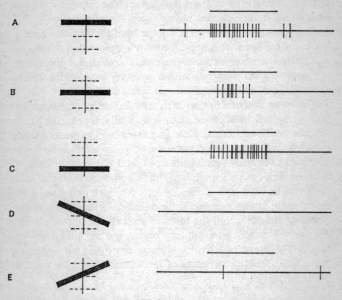

Figure 7. Cell activated only by left (contralateral) eye over a field approximately 5 × 5°. The cell responded best to a black horizontal rectangle, $\frac{1}{3}$ × 6°, placed anywhere in the receptive field (*A–C*). Tilting the stimulus rendered it ineffective (*D–E*). The black bar was introduced against a light background during periods of 1 sec., indicated by the upper line in each record on the right, which shows an 'on' response for this particular unit, (the 'spikes' on the upper three longer horizontal lines on the right). (From Hubel, D. H. and Wiesel, T. N. (1962). *J. Physiol. 160*, 106–54).

and on the right the corresponding neural firing. The information this neuron 'receives' is that a contour in a particular orientation is present, but the actual *position* of the contour is not signalled. In some cases such a 'complex' field can cover quite a large area of the whole retina (Hubel and Wiesel, 1962).

Here, then, is an example of the type of information transmission mentioned earlier; somehow the system transforms the stimulation of the retina by a contour in a particular orientation, but varying in position (variable input) into a constant physiological state (constant output). This constant output shares none of the characteristics of the initial input – the contour – yet in a clear sense is the internal physiological 'representation' of it. Such a relation is almost certainly the basis for stimulus equivalence, for contours. It is not difficult to imagine a still more complex field, where single neurons respond to *collections* of contours – shapes – when they fall within a given area of the retina, although such units have not as yet been identified.*

In a sense this description of receptive field organization has been presented backwards, both historically and so far as the visual system is concerned. Referring again to Figure 6, two fields, *A* and *B*, are shown which are circular. These were recorded for neurons at the lateral geniculate body, and all receptive fields for neurons at this stage are similar. The first work on receptive fields (again in the cat) was Kuffler's, who demonstrated that at the retina itself, single ganglion cells collect information from surrounding elements, and the form of such receptive fields is also circular – typically an excitatory centre and an inhibitory surround. This form of lateral inhibition must play an important part in the selective property of the visual system for contour nformation.

Contour Coding

We can now form a picture of the way in which the system 'transfers' information from the retina to the brain. While the most complete knowledge we have is on the visual system of the cat, there is little doubt that similar principles operate in other species, where investigations are less complete. At the retina, certain ganglion cells are activated by points of light, or by regions of sudden change in illumination level, such as edges and contours. This is so because, as for other receptive fields, uniform stimulation of both excitatory and inhibitory areas causes cancellation

---

* Since this was written, Hubel and Wiesel have reported finding 'hypercomplex fields' which have some of the properties here suggested.

of one by the other and the net effect is zero. These ganglion cells relay to the lateral geniculate bodies via the optic nerve (Figure 2) where single neurons have receptive fields of the same form as those on the retina. However, between the lateral geniculate bodies and cortex another selective process occurs, since the cortical neurons fire maximally for contours in a particular orientation – as if they were organized to receive from certain specific sets of the lateral geniculate body cells, namely, those receiving from retinal units along straight lines in particular orientations. A further selective process occurs between the 'simple' and 'complex' units within the cortex; in this case a given complex unit is apparently organized to receive only from simple units sensitive to one specific orientation, but signalling that orientation for different retinal positions. Finally, we can imagine a still higher selective process, for which only certain *collections* of contours are effective in causing activation. Thus, variable input at the retina is processed through different stages of the visual system to compute an invariant output at a cortical neuron, according to the particular spatial pattern at the retina, but independently of the actual units there activated.

Of course, the details of this process have not all been worked out: for example, the final selective process suggested in the previous paragraph has not been observed in detail (see, however, footnote on p. 34). But we may be reasonably certain that this actually is the basic way in which the pattern on the retina is transferred to the cortex of the brain. One of the most surprising things about this organization is that it seems to be innate. Hubel and Wiesel report that the system is present in all its essentials in kittens as soon as their eyes open. Such a high degree of coordination and organization had previously been thought to be dependent on prolonged perceptual experience and learning.

As a concluding note to this section on contour coding, it may be mentioned that psychologists had arrived independently at concepts of contour and shape recognition quite similar to those demonstrated by Hubel and Wiesel, on the basis of studies of shape discrimination in species such as the rat, squirrel and octopus. The first comprehensive theory along these lines was outlined by Pitts and McCulloch (1947), and the first coding model specific enough to be testable in actual experiments was proposed by J. A. Deutsch (1955). Since then there has been a considerable resurgence of interest in the topic of contour and shape-coding, which had lain dormant for some years following the realization of the inadequacies of the isomorphic theory. An important factor in the renewal of interest was the theoretical formulation of D. O. Hebb (1949).

DEPTH (STEREOPSIS)

The third field to be considered is concerned with depth perception. As in the previous two cases, our consideration will be restricted to rather particular aspects of the field, and in fact to two main questions. The first is: how are the primary cues of binocular parallax (defined below) involved in the perception of the third dimension of visual space? And secondly, what can the integration of two different patterns of spatial information tell us about the organization of the human visual system?

First of all, what is meant by binocular parallax? Suppose one looks at a solid object with one eye, fixing the gaze at one point on the object, and then moves the head a couple of inches to one side while maintaining the same point of fixation: it is clear that the eye sees somewhat different views of the object in the two positions. Parts of the object that were hidden in the first view come into the field of vision, and other parts disappear. If now one imagines the two eyes viewing the object simultaneously from the two positions, each eye receives but one of the two views, and the differences between them are due to 'parallax'. As we know, in normal vision the two fields *fuse*, there is a single perception, and the object is seen *in depth*. This does not allow us to conclude, however, that this perception of depth is due to the binocular parallax. Looking at a familiar scene with one eye, one has quite a vivid impression of depth: people with only one eye or with defective binocular vision perceive depth too, so evidently binocular parallax is not a necessary condition for depth perception. This much has been known more or less explicitly for centuries, but it remained for Wheatstone, in 1838, to demonstrate that binocular parallax *alone* is a *sufficient* condition for causing a depth sensation; this sensation is called stereopsis. Wheatstone demonstrated it by showing simple line drawings, such as the pair shown in Figure 8, in an instrument called a stereoscope, which allows the eyes to superimpose the two images while maintaining a normal line of regard, as if they were viewing a single object. The pair of drawings in Figure 8 so viewed appear as two concentric circles, the smaller one standing out in front of the plane of the larger one.

If one imagines the two large circles perfectly superimposed, when each eye fixates the centre of the larger of the two circles it is looking at, we say that these two circles fall on *corresponding*

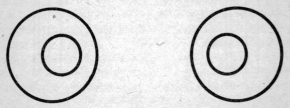

Figure 8. A simple form of stereogram. When the two pairs of circles are viewed in a stereoscope, so that they are visually superimposed, the smaller circle stands out in front of the larger one. (See text.)

points on the two retinae. If the two smaller circles were concentric with the larger ones, they too would fall on corresponding points – and would appear in the same plane as the large circle. However, they are not concentric with the large circles, nor with each other in the superimposed condition, so clearly they fall on non-corresponding points. The horizontal distance (measured on the retinae) between points on one small circle and points on the other is termed *retinal disparity*, and is a particular case of the binocular parallax discussed above. The larger the retinal disparity of the small circles, the more the fused image stands out in depth from the plane of the large circle, up to a certain limit. Beyond this, fusion is no longer possible and the two small circles are seen separated from each other, and – probably – not in depth.

The ability to fuse images on corresponding points of the two retinae is itself a remarkable property of the visual system. Fusion from non-corresponding points is even more extraordinary, especially when we find that this fusion introduces the quite new sensory quality of depth. Wheatstone himself – and Helmholtz after him – realized that if non-corresponding points could fuse to give a single impression, it should be possible to find a situation in which corresponding points did not fuse, i.e. in which images falling on corresponding points on the two retinae appeared to be in *different* parts of the fused image. The search for such a pair of images (or stereogram) went on fruitlessly for a century, and was only successfully concluded by Linschoten (1956).

Figure 9. A stereogram in which corresponding retinal points (see text) appear in different parts of the fused image. (From Linschoten, I. (1956). *Strukturanalyse der binokularen Tiefenwahmemung.* Groningen: Wolters.)

Consider the pair of images in Figure 9. If these are viewed in a stereoscope, and the centre of the right-hand edge of the rectangle is fixated, quite clearly the rectangles fall on corresponding points of the two retinae, when fused. The pair of parallels is arranged in such a way, however, that under this condition of fixation the left-hand parallel in the left-eye image (*a*) is the same distance from the fixation point (on the right-hand edge of the rectangle) as is the right-hand parallel in the right-hand image (*a'*), i.e. *a* and *a'* fall on corresponding sets of points. What happens? Rather than *a* and *a'* fusing, so that three parallels are seen in the fused image, *a* fuses with *c'* and *b* with *a'*, and the two parallel lines are seen in front of the rectangle. Such findings indicate that the binocular fusion system is not bound down to a collection of fixed connexions between corresponding retinal points in the two eyes. The system is flexible, and can integrate images over an (admittedly small) range of disparities from the two retinae, and the process of integration itself somehow gives rise to the sense of depth. Such a degree of lability reminds one of the 'complex field' units of Hubel and Wiesel, and indeed it seems likely that a similar principle of coding exists in the binocular fusion process. It is interesting to note that the great majority of neurons studied by Hubel and Wiesel were binocularly driven; that is to say, could be activated from either eye, and moreover from approximately corresponding areas of the two retinae.

The findings discussed so far suggest that the binocular fusion system might work by matching up contours in the two separate parts of a stereogram, with some flexibility in fusing contours on non-corresponding sets of points, 'interpreting' the disparities in terms of depth. While it is certainly true that the degree of similarity between the two parts of a stereogram is extremely important in achieving fusion (for instance, showing a set of horizontal lines in one eye and vertical lines in the other in a stereoscope never yields fusion; rather one of the images tends to be suppressed so that only one set of lines is seen) it has recently been shown that stereoptic perception can occur when there is *no* pattern or contour recognition in either eye on its own.

In Figure 10 is shown a stereogram consisting of random-dot matrices. Each member of the pair consists of about 10,000 tiny squares (which will be termed dots); the dots in the left-hand member are assigned one of several possible brightness levels on a random basis, which accounts for its uniform, mottled appearance. The right-hand member is identical with it, except that a square array in its centre (about one-quarter of its total area) is displaced horizontally by a distance of four dots. This displacement cannot, of course, ordinarily be perceived. However, if the pair is viewed in a stereoscope, this central square does stand out in depth, and is seen in front of the plane of the rest of the fused image. Such random-dot stereograms were first devised and used to study binocular vision by Bela Julesz of the Bell Telephone Laboratories in the U.S.A. Their importance in the study of binocular vision lies principally in the fact that they give us a 'pure' stereoptic percept, in which monocular pattern recognition plays no part, and other cues to depth such as perspective and relative size are absent. Thus we can be sure that any pattern recognition that occurs (such as perception of the central square of the stereogram of Figure 10) must occur at the point of fusion of the two members, and no earlier. This in turn proves that the binocular fusion system in some sense can compare the fine-grain

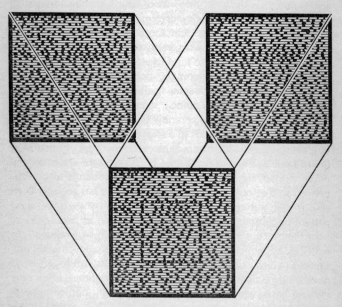

Figure 10. Impression of a random-dot stereogram. When a pair is fused in a stereoscope, a central square stands out in front of the rest of the figure. (See text.)

structures of the two monocular patterns, picking out those parts of the two that are similar and fusing them, but discarding (or suppressing) mis-matches. This is a sort of statistical averaging of the spatial characters of the two patterns. The processes by which such computations on the two monocular inputs might be done are too complex to describe here; instead, I shall mention briefly the application of the stereoptic perception of random-dot stereograms to another area of investigation.

Since we can be sure that perception of depth-patterns with random-dot stereograms depends on central processing in the visual system (that is, in the brain rather than in the retinae and optic nerves), this situation gives us a method of studying central events in the system, which is otherwise difficult in humans. In particular, we can investigate some temporal characteristics of transmission. It has been known for some time that if the two halves of a stereogram are presented very briefly (say for 0·005 second) to the two eyes, stereopsis can occur. Moreover, if the presentations are non-simultaneous the visual system can still integrate the two parts, provided the interval between them is quite small, and of the order of 0·25 second (which depends on the type of stereogram, its brightness and so on). Efron (1957) first studied this phenomenon systematically, although not using dot stereograms, and this work has subsequently been extended in our laboratory. It turns out that the time-integrating characteristics of the binocular fusion system are quite extensive and lawful. While it would be premature to suggest that this work has progressed far enough to give a complete account of the system, it seems likely that important insights into how binocular fusion works will stem from it. For example, it is quite clear that the binocular fusion system is different from the *flicker fusion* system, in which a rapidly flickering light appears as a steady illumination (as in a moving film) since the binocular integration can occur over much longer time periods, and that the 'central representation' of a brief light pulse is not simply related to the duration of that pulse. It has also been found by B. W. White at the Lincoln Laboratories of the Massachusetts Institute of Technology, that the matching process over time is a type of statistical averaging of the properties of the stereograms, since rapid presentation of sets of *different* dot stereograms of the type shown in Figure 10 * results in the perception of a constant and steady three-dimensional figure, the surfaces of which appear to be in constant motion. This motion is due to changes in the brightness of individual points on the figure, as different stereograms are displayed, but

* That is to say, stereograms in which the brightnesses of individual points are not the same from one stereo pair to the next, but which maintain the same disparities in the central square from one pair to the next.

it does not disrupt the steady extraction of information about disparity on which the stereoptic percept depends.

Thus the picture that starts to emerge is of a system capable of statistical averaging and comparing, both over space and over time, extracting information about disparities in the two patterns in such a way as to signal the overall depth relations obtaining in the fused percept.

CONCLUSIONS

If this chapter has done the job it is intended to do, and given the reader something of the flavour of current research into the properties of the visual system, it will also very likely have raised some questions in his mind about the merits of such an approach. Laymen, and I think scientists in other disciplines too, tend to think of psychology as the study of human experience, its development and vicissitudes, so that the psychology of visual perception is expected to be concerned with discussing immediate perceptual experience. This view is represented in psychology too, by the so-called *phenomenological* approach, an approach that has contributed very greatly to the development of scientific psychology. It might be argued that the sorts of experiment I have described are the proper province of the physiologist alone, and that it is a mistake for the psychologist to concern himself too closely with the physiological processes that mediate perception. First of all, it is a mistake, one might argue, because too much enthusiasm about sensory physiology might reduce psychology to a sort of refined but speculative physiology, and secondly, because it is not *necessarily* true that understanding of the physiological system leads to greater insight into the psychology of perception. I hope I have been able to demonstrate that the second of these points is not (at present anyway) valid. It seems that understanding the physiological basis of perception does yield knowledge of importance to psychology. As to the first point, I would say that it is largely true, but not therefore disastrous: psychologists *do* tend to look for explanations of their findings in physiological terms, and do build speculative theories with a physiological bias. This naturally raises the question of the relation between brain and consciousness, or more specifically, between brain processes and perception.

The careful reader may have noticed an ambiguity in the use of the word 'output', when the communications-analysis of the visual system was being discussed earlier. In some cases I used the word 'output' to describe the output of a cortical neuron, or some other physiological unit (for instance, the neurons studied by Hubel and Wiesel), and in others I talked of 'output' in terms of a behavioural response, such as the report of a person of what he perceives. Such a systematic ambiguity could be held to be systematically misleading, covering up, in fact, our ignorance of how neurophysiological 'output' is related to psychological 'output' – perception, or a report of perception. This is a telling point, and should not be ignored or shrugged off, as may all too easily happen.

It is true that we do not know how physiological output is related to perception, although practically every experimental psychologist subscribes to the view that there is a close relationship between the two. One could go further; it is generally accepted that there is a one-to-one relationship, that any one percept must correspond with a unique physiological activity, although this relationship does not require a sort of naïve congruity, such as the isomorphic theory postulated. However, such a perfect correlation between the two sorts of event does not *explain* the conscious experience. Indeed, we do not even know what sort of explanation of this correlation would be possible or adequate. Vague talk of 'higher integrative action' in the brain as the basis of consciousness is not helpful, since it suggests that an explanation of, for instance, perception, is logically possible, if only we knew enough about what actually goes on in the brain.*

I do not wish to end this chapter on too pessimistic or apologetic a note: if we accept the proposition that there is a one-to-one correspondence between physiological 'output' and perception, we can make progress, although this proposition is more an article of faith than a proven factual generalization at present. What we have to recognize, however, is that there are certain

---

* These matters skirt important questions about the logic of psychological explanation too involved to discuss thoroughly here (see Dodwell, 1960).

large questions about 'the nature of experience' or 'consciousness' that experimental psychology is not fitted to answer, any more than is physiology. While this circumscribes our fields of inquiry and endeavour, it does not render them vacuous, as I hope I have been able to show.

2. THE BEGINNINGS OF PERCEPTION

N. F. DIXON

Another way of looking at perception is to study its development in the individual; but in doing this it is useful to know what perception might be like before experience begins to modify it. Is it possible that there is an instinctive element, that the way we see things depends on predispositions which are already there in the newborn child? Dr Dixon reports the evidence for this, and also discusses the possibility that perception is affected by emotion and by unconscious processes, referring to his own well-known experiments on subliminal stimulation.

IT is often helpful when thinking about biological processes to consider some apparently similar yet better understood *non*-biological process. In the case of visual perception an obvious choice would be colour photography. Since in many respects eyes resemble cameras, and percepts photographs, is it not reasonable to assume that perception is a sort of photographic process whereby samples of the external world become spontaneously and accurately reproduced somewhere inside our heads? Unfortunately, the answer must be no. The best that can be said of the photographic analogy is that it points up what perception is not. Beyond this it is superficial and misleading. Four simple experiments should make the matter plain.

In the first a person is asked to match a pair of black and white discs, which are rotating at such a speed as to make them appear uniformly grey. One disc is standing in shadow, the other in bright illumination. By adjusting the ratio of black to white in one of the discs the subject tries to make it look the same as the other. The results show him to be remarkably accurate, for it seems he has made the proportion of black to white in the brightly illuminated disc almost identical with that in the disc which stood in shadow. But there is nothing photographic about his perception, for when the matched discs, still spinning, are photographed, the resulting print shows them to be quite dissimilar in appearance. The disc in shadow is obviously very much darker than the other one. What has happened? Both the camera and the person were accurate, but their criteria differed. One might say that the camera recorded things as they look, and the person things as they are. But the situation is manifestly more complex than this, for the person also recorded things as they look. He did better than the camera because he made them look as they really are. He was not misled by the differences in illumination. He showed perceptual constancy. By reason of an extremely rapid, wholly unconscious piece of computation he received a more accurate record of the external world than could the camera.

In the second experiment a person is asked to match with a colour card the colours of two pictures in dim illumination. One is of a leaf, the other of a donkey. Both are coloured an equal shade of green. In making his match he chooses a much stronger green for the leaf than for the donkey. The leaf evidently *looks* greener than the donkey. The percipient makes a perceptual world compatible with his own experience. It hardly needs saying that cameras lack this versatility.

In the third experiment hungry, thirsty and satiated people are asked to equalize the brightness of pictures depicting food, water and other objects unrelated to hunger or thirst. When the intensities at which they set the pictures are measured it is found that hungry people see pictures relating to food as brighter than the rest (i.e. to equalize the pictures they make the food ones less intense), and thirsty people do likewise with 'drink' pictures. For the satiated group no differences are obtained between the different objects. In other words, perception serves to satisfy needs, not to enrich subjective experience. Unlike a photograph the percept is determined by more than just the stimulus.

The fourth experiment is of a rather different kind. With ears plugged, their eyes beneath translucent goggles and their bodies either encased in cotton wool, or floating naked in water at body temperature, people are deprived for considerable periods of external stimulation. Contrary to what one might expect, however, such circumstances result not in a lack of perceptual experience but rather a surprising change in what is perceived. The subjects in such an experiment begin to see, feel and hear things which bear no more relationship to the immediate external world than does a dream in someone who is asleep. These people are not asleep yet their hallucinations, or so-called 'autistic' perceptions, may be as vivid, if not more so, than any normal percept.*

These four experiments make short work of any theory which attempts to liken the perceptual process to the workings of a simple recording apparatus. If one must use an analogy, then a closer one would be that of the identikit. Like perception, an identikit picture is built up from a given set of parts to resemble a partly unknown external reality. In its build-up a number of factors play a part, actual clues to the real identity, the past experience, needs, attitudes and even prejudices, of those who use it and, last but not least, the range and availability of the kit's component parts. The final product is not so much a reflection of the external world as the best possible match to this world which the user can make with the information available.

One striking difference between perception and the use of an identikit is of course in the time taken: whereas the discriminations, classifications, sortings and integrations which go into the make-up of an identikit picture, may take hours, even days, they occur in perception within the fraction of a second. So rapid is the normal act of perceiving that the underlying stages remain unanalysable except by special methods which have in common the fact that they all involve studying the beginnings of perception.

There are, in fact, three quite different senses in which we can talk about the beginnings of perception:

 (i) In lower forms of life – the phylogenesis of perception.
 (ii) In children – the ontogenesis of perception.
(iii) In the early stages of any normal human adult perceptual act
    – the microgenesis of perception.

The link between these three beginnings is that as an adaptation to changes in the external environment perception has its origin

* For discussion of these and related experiments see Heron (1957) and Brownfield (1964).

in the property of irritability common to all forms of life. Between the simplest example of such irritability in the lowest forms of life and the complex highly efficient adaptive response of the normal human adult many stages in perceptual development have made their gradual appearance. Without subscribing to any general theory of recapitulation it can be said that in many respects they reappear on a much shorter time scale in the early years of human growth.

It is from this triple standpoint that we propose to examine the beginnings of perception. In doing so it is proposed to consider in turn the following stages in perception: the response to light *per se* (i.e. to the intensity characteristics of the stimulus); the response to movement, to form, to colour, to three-dimensionality; and, finally, to meaning. In discussing them, roughly in order of their occurrence, parallels will be drawn where possible between perceptions at adult, child and animal levels.

THE LIGHT INTENSITY RESPONSE

The first stage in visual perception, which is little more than reflex response to light, may be seen in the transparent bodies of genus protozoa. Thus strong light falling on amoeba evokes a series of zig-zag movements which continue until the animal is clear of the stimulus. No less simple, though differing in its end results is the response of other protozoa, those containing chlorophyll, which instead of avoiding light move towards it. Though primitive the response in both cases is of biological value.

Although manifesting the first stage in the beginnings of perception these animals are, however, by human standards, blind. They are light-sensitive but without eyes or brain. At this stage of the perceptual process there is little difference between amoeba and humans for whom the earliest response to light is also reflex, contraction of the iris. This response has even been elicited in the human foetus prior to such development of the brain as would seem to be necessary for any image of external reality.

The Beginnings of Perception

THE CORRELATED IMAGE

Perception can be regarded as the process whereby in order to satisfy its needs an organism gains information about its environment. This being so it is perhaps the *second* stage in the evolution of perception which marks the greatest step forward. This, the level at which mere sensations give way to perception as we know it, depends primarily upon the development of a receptor which can respond to the informative as well as the purely energy characteristics of a light stimulus.

To provide its owner with an image that is in some sense correlated with the external world such a receptor must be able to fixate an object, and respond differentially to variations of brightness within the image so formed.

Space precludes any detailed account of the evolutionary steps whereby these ends have been achieved. Suffice it to say that they involve a progression from general to localized transparency, and from randomly scattered cells carrying light-sensitive pigments to eye spots or clusters of such cells. Such rudimentary eyes, as found in certain worms, consisting as they do of a mosaic of independent receptor cells, provide for crude localization of the stimulus and the basis for subsequent fixation and pattern vision. Functionally, the human eye at birth is in all probability just such a receptor. Certainly it can be said that since a baby less than ten minutes old will turn its eyes towards a sound (Wertheimer, 1961), the earliest beginnings of coordinate spatial localization are present at even this early age.

RESPONSE TO MOVEMENT

At a sub-human level refinements of the eye take several forms. In insects, for example, we find the development of large compound eyes wherein each faceted receptor, or ommatidium, is a complete apparatus for directing light rays upon a neural receptor which feeds into the optic tracts. Such eyes have two characteristics of great biological value and significance for the early stages of perception. They enable a very wide angle of view, and by reason of their mosaic structure are maximally sensitive to a moving stimulus. Though the human eye is very different it is interesting that at a human level the beginnings of perception are also marked by a special sensitivity to a moving stimulus. This is particularly manifest in the case of a stimulus in the outermost edge of the visual field, one falling, in fact, upon the peripheral – and from an evolutionary point of view – oldest part of the retina. There are, of course, other forms of primitive eyes with some capacity for handling information such as that of the mollusc nautilus, wherein an inversion of the retina to form a cup-like structure containing the light-sensitive cells results in a receptor which serves to provide a coarse image in much the same way as does a pinhole camera.

THE RESPONSE TO FORM AND PATTERN

It is, however, with the emergence of the vertebrate refractive eye, using the principle of integration of light rays by means of a lens, that the possibilities of really accurate form and pattern perception may be said to begin. Phylogenetically such an eye reaches the acme of perfection not in humans but in birds of prey.

Compared to the hawk's eye, with its great density of closely packed receptor cells, the human eye, with its much coarser mosaic of retinal receptors, is a poor affair. If hawks could read they could derive information from print so small as to be imperceptible to humans. But the hawk so able at perceiving the distant mouse is none the less, by human standards, a perceptual pigmy for reasons that will become clear later.

In humans there is evidence for the beginnings of form perception within the first few weeks of life. And, according to the results from an ingenious series of experiments by Fantz (1961), sensitivity to patterns within a form is hardly more delayed.

By observing the images reflected from the eyes of a baby confronted with various plain and patterned surfaces he has shown what sort of stimulus best determines the direction of a human infant's gaze (Plates 1 and 2). It seems that not only are patterns discriminated but are also – as something to look at – much preferred to plain surfaces.

The Beginnings of Perception

In this experiment babies also showed a preference for looking at spheres rather than discs of the same diameter. Whether this implies the beginnings of depth perception or merely a liking for greater complexity in the visual stimulus remains, however, a matter for conjecture (Epstein, 1964).

One odd finding from this research was that the human infant does very much better with one eye than when using both together. The implication would seem to be that adult binocular vision, wherein information from the two eyes is integrated into a single perceptual world, depends upon learning or later maturation of the nervous system. For the baby, it seems that what is entering through one eye may very well interfere with what is coming in by the other.

One of the difficulties, of course, in studying the beginnings of perception in young children is that they have few responses to demonstrate, and no language to describe, what, if anything, they *can* perceive. It is largely for this reason that there has been much recent interest in the visual experience of newly sighted adults, i.e. people who blind from birth with congenital cataract are subsequently given sight by the corneal graft operation. Unfortunately, the conclusions to be drawn from the study of such people are less clear-cut than one might think. There are two main reasons for this. In the first place, although possessed of language, these people obviously have had no experience of the relationship between words descriptive of visual space and the attributes of visual space these words describe.

Secondly, there are good grounds for thinking that the first percepts of an adult may in fact be very different from those of a small child. On the one hand, his nervous system, generally, will have matured far beyond that of the newborn infant. On the other, some loss of function may be expected in the visual areas of the brain simply as a result of disuse during the critical growth years. Again, the blind adult, for so long reliant on his other senses, will have acquired a highly complex tactile and auditory perceptual world which may well interfere with his newly acquired visual world. Notwithstanding these difficulties some general conclusions may be drawn. The first is that, though able to make little practical use of their new sensory experience, the newly sighted do possess the capacity for rudimentary form perception. Not only can they see figures against a background but to some extent they can actually locate the objects seen. Though unable to perceive an object clearly and while incapable of saying what it is they can reach out their hands towards it in a manner quite unlike the gropings of someone who is still blind. Things look 'out there' and not 'in the eye'. Along with the work on children described earlier this finding suggests that the capacity for elementary form perception is an inherent attribute of the human nervous system.

From what has been said so far it can be argued that in the first few months of life there is a decidedly 'phylogenetic' flavour about man's perceptual development. But if his inherited capacity for perceptual experiences emerges by the progressive maturation of structures that evolved in roughly the same order, are there not other dimensions of early perceptual experience which lend support to this view? In the case of colour and the perception of depth it would certainly seem so.

THE COLOUR RESPONSE

Although even plants respond differentially to different wavelengths of light, the occurrence of colour perception, that is, the utilization of colour information, hardly counts for much until we come to insects. At this level, however, there is a sensitivity to colour which may be as good as and even, in some respects, better than our own. (Bees, for example, not only display distinct preferences for different colours but are also sensitive to ultraviolet light. They can locate the presence of the sun on those occasions when we would describe it as completely obscured by cloud.) In humans the capacity for colour discrimination is again relatively late in making its appearance.

Thus, though babies under six months show little indication of discriminating a grey from a coloured disc, those above this age display, within their first year of life, a progressive ability to discriminate red, blue, yellow and green. As for adults, it is interesting that when something is brought gradually into view, either because its illumination is increasing, or because the object is being moved in from peripheral to central vision, the presence of the object is experienced considerably earlier than its colour. This order of events is related to the fact mentioned earlier that it is the peripheral and oldest part of the retina which is both the most sensitive to light of low intensity and least sensitive to differences in wavelength.

THE PERCEPTION OF DEPTH

One of the earliest and greatest dangers that threatens the existence of land-based animals is that of falling. Hence, it would not be surprising to find that from the moment they can move about such animals are equipped with the ability to perceive sudden drops in the terrain.

Whether or not they can has been investigated with the help of a novel piece of apparatus designed by Gibson and Walk (1960). Known as the 'visual cliff' it consists of a raised central platform flanked on either side by a horizontal sheet of plate glass. Under the glass, on one side only, there is a large drop to the ground beneath – this is the 'cliff' (Plate 3). The question is, if the surfaces seen through the glass on each side have the same texture (chequered pattern), at what age will different animals, placed on the central platform, move only to the shallow side and shun the 'drop', thus showing that they can perceive the difference in distance to the ground below? From a series of experiments the answer seems pretty clear-cut. In chicks, lambs, goats, cats, monkeys and human babies it does indeed seem to be the case that as soon as it can move (at one day old in the case of chicks and at 6–10 months in the case of babies), an animal will choose the shallow side.

Now, since the distance down from the platform to the glass is the same on either side, this choice must depend on purely visual clues which the animal receives from the surface beneath the glass. There are two such. One is that the chequered pattern seen through the glass on the deeper side, will, because farther away, look smaller than that on the other side. The other clue is that of monocular parallax, whereby with movements of the head, more distant objects appear to move relatively less than objects close to.

From further experiments it seems that while both these clues are used that of parallax is the more important.

From the point of view of survival value this is as it should be, for whereas the size, density or textures of two surfaces may vary in fact, as well as in appearance, parallax effects depend only upon distance and therefore constitute a more reliable guide to a drop in the terrain.

That depth may be inherently frightening as well as merely perceived is suggested by a variant of the experiment in which animals were placed on the glass over the deep side, but with an opaque board in place directly under the transparent surface on which they stood. As long as the board was in position they remained at ease, but with the board removed they immediately showed all the signs of considerable fear. Likewise, babies who could see their mothers across the other side of the 'cliff' became tearful at the conflict engendered by their fear. Could these responses possibly have been learnt? It seems not, for even animals reared in the dark until such age as they could move evinced just as much aversion for the visual cliff as did normally reared animals.

CEREBRAL FACTORS IN PERCEPTION

Along with other points of interest the work on depth perception highlights an important difference between humans and sub-humans: rate of development. The chick achieves in one day what the child takes six months to do. The chick's perceptual performance at birth is very nearly as efficient as it will ever be; the child's, dependent on a much larger and slowly maturing brain, will go on improving in efficiency over a number of years.

When discussing the eye of a hawk it was pointed out that, though in terms of sheer resolving power vastly superior to that of a human, a hawk's perceptual capacity is by our standards severely limited. For perception involves not merely the receipt but also the interpretation of incoming information, and it is in this latter respect that lower forms of animal life are at a disadvantage. So far as information handling is concerned, their eyes have enormously outrun their brains. In a sense the same tendency holds good for man also. Thus it has been calculated that though the human retina can transform light into neural energy at the rate of some million bits a second (see p. 119), only a very small fraction of this information is ever consciously handled.

For humans, however, this discrepancy between what is coming in and what is actually perceived is neither as great nor as wasteful as it may seem, for, with a large brain, having an almost infinite capacity for learning, man can go far beyond the data of his percepts. By reason of stored information, amassed through past experience, he can recognize objects, people, situations, etc., with a minimum of sensory information. Perhaps even more important is the fact that he can select from the vast amount of information supplied by his senses just that which is new or appropriate to his present needs. In terms of news flow, sensitivity to change, cataloguing of and access to past events, and the final emergence of that which is most interesting, most novel and most topical, perception has much in common with running a newspaper. By this analogy it is on the editorial side that humans show the greatest superiority over lower forms of life.

For the latter, limited storage and editing capacity necessitates another and more economical method of adaptation. It is that of instinctive behaviour.

INSTINCT

The phenomena of instinct mark an important stage in the development of perception. They are characterized by an organism 'tuned' from birth to certain crucial stimuli. As they occur these stimuli automatically release behaviour appropriate to the organism's needs. The stimuli may be particular shapes, colours or movements, or combinations of all three. For each, without the necessity, opportunity or capability of learning, there is a resultant pattern of behaviour.

The behaviour though often complex is predictable, unvarying, automatic and stereotyped – the same for all members of the species. All male sticklebacks, for example, will react in the same way to the shape of a pregnant female stickleback. The irrational specificity of this response is shown by the fact that, while a female stickleback, whose swollen abdomen is concealed, will not elicit the mating reaction, a piece of wood having the requisite shape may well succeed in doing so.

By the same token, the female stickleback only indulges in the mating dive which culminates in egg-laying if she perceives the red patch on the male's under-belly. Paint out the red and she remains unmoved, however desirable he may be in other respects.

Instinct has been likened to a system of locks and keys, wherein particular stimuli unlock via apparently fixed connexions (termed innate releasing mechanisms), particular patterns of behaviour. The one other factor involved is that of need. Whether or not a given stimulus meets the criteria demanded by the releasing mechanism will depend upon the need or drive level of the organism. Thus the more sexually deprived an animal the greater the range of evocative stimuli. In the same way a satiated animal will require a supernormal sign stimulus – one literally larger than life – before instinctual responses can be elicited.

In this context it is interesting to find light acting upon the organism both as an information carrier, and in its much earlier role, as a direct agent in the animal's metabolism. It both enables perception of the sign stimuli that will release the appropriate response, and also, by acting upon basal structures of the brain, plays a considerable part in determining the hormone output of the pituitary gland. It is these hormones which in turn, are largely responsible for determining drive level and thereby influencing susceptibility to the sign stimulus. A special case of this reaction is evident in photoperiodism. In fishes, birds and even mammals such internal clocks as govern periodic changes in sexual activity and maternal behaviour may be to some extent retimed by changes in the light regimen to which the creature is subject. *A propos* of this some recent research (Van Brunt *et al.*, 1963), in which light meters were inserted in the brains of dogs and other animals, has shown that these effects may be partly attributed to light affecting the brain directly through the skull. However, that the eye remains, so far as humans are concerned, the main entry for light in both its visual *and* vegetative role, is confirmed by the changes in endocrine activity, water and carbohydrate metabolism which occur in blind people. Nowhere is this more clearly and dramatically portrayed than in Ancient Egyptian pictures of religious functions wherein the traditionally blind harpist is depicted as having, along with his closed eyes, all the physical signs of such endocrine disturbance as is produced by blindness – puffy skin of face and neck, with gross fatty degeneration of the limbs and torso (Johannes Fuchs, 1963).

IMPRINTING

In returning to our main theme it should be pointed out that while instinct and learning represent alternative ways to the same end they are by no means exclusive. Rather is it a case of instinctive responses becoming increasingly modifiable by learning the higher we ascend the phylogenetic scale. However, there is one special case of the early interaction between learning and instinct which is of particular interest. It is that of imprinting. (See also p. 229.)

One of the most important perceptual experiences that the young animal may have is its first visual impression of its parent, for such an experience appears to bring about a long-lasting and strong attachment, or following response, to the object perceived. As an innate predisposition to follow the first large object that is perceived this bond between offspring and parent may be regarded as instinctive, but, as a lasting change in behaviour brought about by a simple experience, it is very clearly a type of perceptual learning. The conditions for this imprinting to take place are merely that the young organism should perceive some large object for a certain minimum period of time at a certain critical period of its life. A classic example has been described by Lorenz (1952). Young jackdaws that had been removed from their real parents became so imprinted upon him as to thereafter prefer his company to that of their own kind. While a later result of this early perceptual experience was that he subsequently became the object not only of their following response but also of other drives, as shown for example by the fact that they insisted on trying to feed him with chopped worms. Whatever the purpose of this behaviour the desire of the birds to feed him was evidently strong, for if he closed his mouth they attempted to push the worms into his ears!

Any consideration of imprinting phenomena raises the very natural question of a possible parallel in human psychology. Are there any stimuli which without prior learning release unique patterns of behaviour in humans? Generally, it would seem unlikely for the very good reason that man's capacity for learning renders instinct unnecessary. Again, if he is innately programmed for adaptive responses to particular stimuli he has little chance to show it before such time as behaviour based on experience takes over anyway. There are, needless to say, some innately determined responses in humans, such as the startle reaction to a sudden strong stimulus or the depth response referred to earlier, but these really lack sufficient specificity or complexity for qualification as instincts.

It is possible, of course, that Fantz's finding of a very early predisposition to look at a drawing of a human face, and the smiling response elicited in infants by a similar stimulus *may* have an instinctual basis but the possibility of learning cannot be ruled out.

Then, again, the strong emotional attachment of the child to its mother and the long-lasting ill effects of maternal deprivation during the critical first few years of life might imply a predisposition for imprinting (see p. 233). Harlow's (1961) finding that orphaned monkeys show an immediate preference for a dummy non-feeding mother made of cloth, as opposed to one made of wire but which gives milk, suggests that the same sort of unlearnt reaction might be expected to occur in human offspring.

The instinctual release of parental behaviour is another possibility worth considering. Lorenz (see Tinbergen, 1951) has drawn attention to the fact that a certain shape of face, short in relation to a large forehead and with protuberant cheeks, appears to release protective and affectionate responses in humans (see Figure 11).

Obviously such a state of affairs would have great survival value for the human baby. It is a device which would ensure protection for the young child without the necessity for learning or reasoning on the part of the parent. It would also, incidentally,

Figure 11. The shapes of head on the left are said to release protective and affectionate responses. (From Tinbergen, N. (1951). *Study of Instinct.* Oxford: Clarendon Press.)

explain the apparent irrationality of the childless woman who while ready to lavish maternal care on an elderly budgerigar or decrepit Pekingese will remain unmoved by a young seagull or greyhound, creatures that, though lacking in years, also lack the essential sign stimuli.

No less controversial than the question of imprinting is that of the possibility of instinctual responses to colour in humans. Has colour, and in particular the colour red, so important as a sign stimulus for many instinctual behaviour patterns in lower animals, any unlearnt significance for humans? Three pieces of evidence are pertinent to the view that it has.

First, it has been known for many years that red, whether present as a meaningless blob in the Rorschach ink blot personality test, or as a background to such meaningful material as words or pictures, tends to evoke an emotional reaction. According to a study by Dreschler (1960), for example, word associations obtained after presentation of a red stimulus show all the signs of emotional disturbance. In another research along the same lines he has found that emotional reactions to a picture of a nude presented at subliminal (not consciously perceived) intensities only occurred when coincident with a supraliminal (consciously perceptible) red stimulus.

Other evidence for a relationship between red light and emotion comes from researches by Kravkov (1941) and Dixon (1960) on the sensitivity for light at the red end of the spectrum. According to the Russian work, drugs which evoke the normal physiological concommitants of emotion decrease sensitivity to red light while increasing sensitivity to green. This finding is consistent with that from an experiment by the author which suggested that the subliminal presentation of emotional words in red light to one eye heightened the threshold for light of the same colour to the other eye. While emotional words in green light produced the opposite effect, neutral words of either colour had relatively no effect upon red/green thresholds. From a subsequent research in which brain rhythm (EEG) changes were recorded during the presentation of emotional and neutral words below the conscious threshold, it seems that while red light *per se* has no immediate effect upon the EEG it will do so if associated with a word that is itself emotional in flavour.

Taken together the results from these various experiments suggest a relationship between redness as a sensory experience and emotion that is best described by saying that red light appears to augment the effect of potentially disturbing meaningful stimuli. Whether this reaction to red is innate or acquired remains, however, a matter for speculation. The nativist could argue that the conventional association between redness and danger is itself the product of some instinctual response to the colour. The notion of an inherently determined response to light at the red end of the spectrum is consistent with the fact that red, more than any other wavelength of light, has a distinct and striking effect upon plants and upon the endocrine systems of animals. Certainly if there is any relationship between, for example, the excessive over-development of gonads in ducks exposed to red light and the emotional responses of humans to light of the same wavelength, then it will hinge upon the fact that both events depend to some extent upon the pituitary gland and basal areas of the brain.

THE LATER STAGES OF PERCEPTION

Leaving aside the controversial issue of instinct it would seem that those stages in perception so far considered, the response to light, to movement, form, pattern and colour, depend very largely upon the maturation of certain innate properties of the nervous system.

What of the later stages? From the experiments described at the beginning of this chapter it would seem that it is in its later stages of identification, recognition and naming that perception is furthest from being in any sense photographic. It is in these stages that the percipient makes the largest contribution to his percep-tions; that past experience, emotion and motivations play their part in determining what is perceived and how it is perceived.

Now it would seem logical to suppose that, if the final percept is, so to speak, the end result of these determining factors, their influence must occur somewhere between receipt of the stimulus and awareness. This being so, how might they be studied? Al-though by their very nature concealed from conscious scrutiny, some insight into the nature of these antecedents to perception has in fact been derived from a number of experiments, whose common denominator is that the stimulus input is greatly reduced. Under such conditions the percipient's contribution to his per-ceptual experience is proportionally greater than the stimulus contribution. Hence we have a better opportunity of studying its nature.

Take first the case of someone who is asked to guess the identity of words which are presented so briefly, or at such low intensity, as to remain to all intents and purposes invisible. According to results from experiments by Werner (1956), McGinnies (1949), Worthington (1962) and Dixon (1956) there is a tendency for the subject to say a word which, though bearing no structural relationship to the stimulus word, does relate to its meaning. Using briefly exposed verbal stimuli Werner found that people tend to respond with words from the same sphere of meaning as the stimulus: e.g. to the word *wind* the subject might respond *air*. McGinnies, on the other hand, has reported a tendency by his subjects to give associated words which appear to imply a definite attitude towards the object associated with the stimulus. Thus, to the word *whore* he obtained names of actual girls. Needless to say his subjects remained unconscious of the significance of the stimulus–response relationship. Worthington and the author found that when told to identify a number which was projected on to a screen at very low intensities subjects tended to give the next highest number. Despite the instructions, and presumably a conscious intent to report what was there, they found themselves saying something associated with what was there. In yet other experiments where tabu- and emotionally-loaded words were presented, either visually or auditorily below threshold, there was a tendency for the responses to be symbolic in the Freudian sense. Thus presentation of the word *penis* below the level of consciousness evoked such responses as *cheroot* or *water pump*.

From these various studies it seems that at some preconscious stage of the perceptual process the meaning of a stimulus determines the class of associates which it evokes. That this occurs at a level of integration below that of normal perceptual awareness gains support from Werner's finding that the kind of response which a normal person gives to a briefly exposed stimulus word is indistinguishable from the verbal responses of certain aphasics. These brain-injured people, though unable to name things correctly, can often respond with a word from the same 'sphere of meaning'. At their best they seem reduced to functioning at a level of perceptual integration which precedes that of correct identification in the normal person. Yet another indication of unconscious classification by meaning is that a person's recognition threshold may be raised or lowered as a function of the emotional significance of the stimulus word. These phenomena of so-called perceptual defence and sensitization imply a sort of unconscious monitoring of the input, as a result of which perception can be facilitated or prevented. As to a possible physiological basis for this monitoring, it has been demonstrated for the central nervous system of many vertebrate species that connexions exist for the alteration of sensory transmission by events further upstream. In man it has also been shown that consciousness of an external stimulus depends not only upon its arrival in the visual area of the brain but also upon coincidental activation of this area by neural impulses from structures within the phylogenetically earlier brain stem. That these physiological arrangements for central control of stimulus input and awareness play some part in perceptual filtering receives support from a research by Dixon and Lear (1963), which showed an inverse relationship between desynchrony of the pre-awareness EEG and the awareness threshold for words. The significance of this finding lies in the fact that EEG desynchrony (or flattening) constitutes a useful measure of cortical activation. Thus emotional words for which the percipient had a raised awareness threshold appeared to delay their arrival in consciousness by inhibition of the normal activation of the visual reception area. It is the author's view that variations in recognition threshold brought about by the meaning of a word exemplify learnt selectiveness, one of the primary characteristics of adult human perception.

Further evidence that meaning determines the organizing processes which precede the conscious percept comes from experiments on the stabilized retinal image. By various techniques involving the use of a contact lens it is possible to keep the image of an external object immovably applied to one part of the retina despite any eye movements which the percipient may make. When this is done two interesting phenomena are reported by the wearer of the lens. First, it seems that the awareness of the object waxes and wanes. After a second or two of seeing whatever is being projected through the lens the image gradually fades only to reappear a few seconds later. It is the nature of the fading and recovery, however, which particularly concerns us here, for it seems that although whatever is being looked at comes and goes a

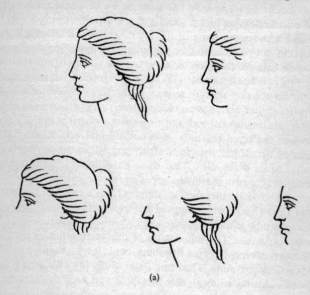

(a)

BEER   **PEER**   **PEEP**

BEE   **BE**

(b)

Figure 12. (*a*) Stabilized images typically fade. The parts of a profile drawing that stay visible are invariably specific features or groups of features such as the front of the face or the top of the head.
(*b*) Words containing other words behave in much the same manner. The subject sees new words made up of letters and parts of letters in the original. (From Pritchard, R. M. (1961). *Sci. Am. 204*, 72–8.)

bit at a time it does so in meaningful units rather than in any random or haphazard fashion. For example, the order of re-appearance of a face might be the nose, an eye, the mouth and not any admixture of parts of these features. Similarly, the letter B, having disappeared, might reappear as P rather than as some meaningless component of the incident stimulus (see Figure 12).

IMPLICATIONS FOR A MODEL FOR PERCEPTION

Like the other phenomena described in this section these, too, imply selection based on meaning. Unlike the lock and key selectivity of instinctual behaviour, wherein inappropriate stimuli play no further part in the perceptual life of the organism, human perception has much in common with the monitoring characteristics of, for example, an early warning radar system in which all signals, including those which meet the criteria for a defensive reaction, will be accepted, judged and filed for future reference. Applying this model to perception it is useful to regard the final product, the conscious percept, as the end result of a succession of appraisals wherein there is a two-way interaction between the incoming information and the schemata, or organized knowledge, of what has gone before. Not only is the meaning of the news interpreted and reacted to in the light of previous experience but itself also becomes a determinant of future perception. This organizational process is not, of course, confined to vision, nor are the after-effects of non-perceived stimulus elements confined to normal waking experiences. As to the first point, an experiment on hearing gives a good illustration of how continuous unconscious monitoring underlies the phenomena of selective attention. When two different streams of information are fed simultaneously, one to one ear and the other to the other, only that with the more meaning for the subject will be consciously perceived. If, however, the listener's name is introduced into the stream of information arriving at the other ear it will be instantly perceived (see p. 109). In other words, even the non-perceived flow of information must have been continuously scanned below the level of consciousness.

The second point, that non-perceived parts of a sensory input play a part in subsequent perceptual experiences of a non-waking kind, is suggested by several researches on the after-effects of briefly exposed pictures. It seems (Fisher, 1954) that those parts of the picture, that were *not* consciously registered at the time, occurred as elements of dreams experienced the following night.

The data from such experiments, which incidentally support the Freudian view that dreams are built from the residue of the previous day's events, are quite consistent with the identikit analogy proposed at the beginning of this chapter. It seems we have a storehouse of potential images which, by processes of selection, matching and integration, help to convert incoming sense data into a meaningful if sometimes biased version of the external world. There are at least three special situations which lend support to this view. The first is where the external supply of sense data has been withdrawn for any length of time, as in sleep, or in the experiments on sensory deprivation. The second is where withdrawal from the external world accompanies psychotic illness. And the third where drugs like mescalin, or direct electrical stimulation of the visual areas of the brain, has disturbed normal cerebral function.

All three situations have one feature in common – the occurrence of hallucinations in the minds of those affected – the spontaneous emergence in consciousness of images which bear at least the hallmark of past perceptual experience.

CONCLUSIONS

This brief review of some of the processes occurring between the receipt of a stimulus and the subsequent elaboration of a percept has carried us from the end of the beginnings to the beginning of the end. A study of its beginnings shows visual perception to be a many-stage process wherein the original outgrowth of the eye from the brain constitutes a parting of the ways regarding the source of limitations on perfect correspondence between inner and outer worlds. As the receptor develops in fineness of structure, and versatility of functions, so more and more about the stimulus, its size, shape, colour, movement, etc., becomes available as data. As the brain develops in size and complexity, so more and more of these data become useful as well as usable.

In what has gone before I have attempted to relate these developments as seen in the phylogenesis of perception to developmental stages in human infancy. In the interests of simplification and brevity, I have purposely glossed over several exceptions to the rule of parallel development. That there are such exceptions derives mainly from the fact of specialization in differing directions by different species. Man's specialization is the capacity to profit from experience and it is this which most clearly distinguishes the higher flights of human perception from that of any sub-human species.

3. VISUAL ILLUSIONS

R. L. GREGORY

Roughly speaking, physiologists have been interested in why we see the world the way it is, while psychologists have been interested in why perception goes wrong. It goes wrong in the sense that we see things differently from the way a camera would 'see' them. Another way of putting it is that the geometry of our vision does not agree with the geometry of the environment, as given by measuring instruments. The so-called optical illusions are famous examples of such occurrences. Some have argued that when perception is thoroughly understood the illusions will be found to be 'special cases'; whereas others have considered them a topic for research in their own right. Mr Gregory presents some famous illusions and some new ones, and relates them to the structure and function of the visual system. In doing this he describes several of the older theories and his own, newly developed.

EXPERIMENTAL psychology was delivered from philosophy by illusions. In the early years of the last century physicists found that the human observer was adversely affected by, for example, sloping cross-lines in the eye-pieces of optical instruments. Quite serious errors were correctly attributed to the eye being upset by simple displays which could be drawn on paper and demonstrated as 'visual illusions'. It was their study and measurement which led to controlled experiments on human beings – to Experimental Psychology. Now, over a hundred years later, we are beginning to understand why these figures are seen as distorted.

We shall be concerned here only with visual distortion illusions, but all the senses can be fooled and can mislead. Fortunately, sensory judgements can usually be checked quite easily (though not while landing an aircraft), and the checks – measurement with comparison scales – serve to measure the amount of the distortion. They may thus be studied quite easily with normal physical methods.

Not all illusions are 'psychological'. There are many *physical* effects which give misleading information to the senses, such as mirages. There are other meteorological illusions: occasionally two suns are seen in the sky, also due to refractive effects; and a stick apparently bent in water is a similar example of an optical illusion.

Some perceptual effects are difficult to classify as 'physical' or 'psychological'. Consider the striking ray figure (Plate 4) studied by Donald MacKay (1961). It produces shimmering, and moving lines appear upon the rays. Now these effects might be due to disturbance of certain brain mechanisms by repeated lines, as suggested by MacKay, or they might perhaps be examples of *moiré* fringes, the rays producing after-images on the retina which with changes of fixation of the eyes give the patterns, which are also produced when a pair of the figures are physically superimposed. It is also possible that the after-images are not on the retina but are due to fatigue of neural systems in the brain representing the rays. But should we call such after-image phenomena – if this is the explanation – 'physical' or 'psychological'? The issue is not entirely trivial; it may be that we will come to call 'psychological' phenomena 'physical' when we understand their origin in detail.

The brain may be thought of as handling information from the sense organs: it is a kind of gigantic computer. This does not mean that it is especially like a man-made computer, but it does essentially the same kind of job. Now when we think of *any* computer, we must distinguish two aspects of its functioning. It is a system of parts forming a machine, and it is guided by and works through a *programme*. The programme specifies the problem of the moment and the strategy required for the solution. It is essentially independent of the particular computer, though it must match its design characteristics to be 'understood'. It controls the steps taken by the machine according to the logic of the problem.

Consider a computer which on some occasions gives distortions of the truth. The errors could occur either because some of the circuits are malfunctioning, or because there is something peculiar or inadequate in its programme or the available information. These are very different possibilities. We may expect to find both kinds of illusion.

For an explanation in terms of brain function, or rather malfunction, we must know how the brain works. For an explanation in terms of its programme and available

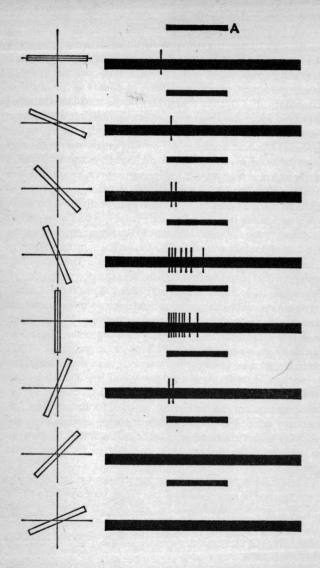

Figure 13. Shows electrical activity recorded from a single cell of the 'visual area' of a cat's brain, while a line is presented at various orientations to its eyes. This cell only fires for one orientation of the line. Other cells

information, we must consider the problem set by perceiving the world.

We know something of how the visual part of the brain works from the American physiologists Hubel and Wiesel (1962)* who have recorded electrical activity from single cells in the visual cortex of cats, and related work of Lettvin *et al.* (1959), on the frog's retina. Figure 13 shows recordings from a single cell of a cat's brain. This cell responds only to lines of a certain orientation presented to the cat's eyes. A given cell will respond to a certain kind of visual characteristic – to orientation, to movement in a given direction or to corners. Evidently, an important part of the secret of how the brain 'recognizes' objects is the way these selective brain circuits respond to characteristic features which define the object. Now we might expect to learn something of these selective brain circuits by studying illusions. It is reasonable to suppose that the circuits are for some reason unable to deal properly with certain kinds of figures, and when this happens we suffer an illusion. It may be that MacKay's ray pattern is an example of this, and it is almost certain that the apparent movement experienced after prolonged stimulation of the eye to movement – the 'waterfall effect' – has this kind of origin, but why should simple line diagrams so upset the system?

There is another possibility – perhaps these figures present the brain with a problem unsuitable to its 'programme'. Perhaps the trouble is not to be found in the brain but rather in the characteristics of the figures themselves. But before we consider this possibility in detail we should look at examples of these illusions, and discuss briefly some of the traditional theories for explaining the distortions.

Visual illusions may be classed as:

(i) 'Impossible objects', figures which cannot be seen as representing a single object lying in space (Figures 14, 15, 16).

(ii) Figures (or objects) which appear distorted. Parts may look too long or too short, or unduly curved or bent (Figure 17).

* Professor Dodwell writes at length on the important work of Hubel and Wiesel on p. 31.

respond to other orientations, or movement in certain directions or to corners. (From Hubel, D. H. and Wiesel, T. N. (1962). *J. Physiol.*, *160*, 106–54.)

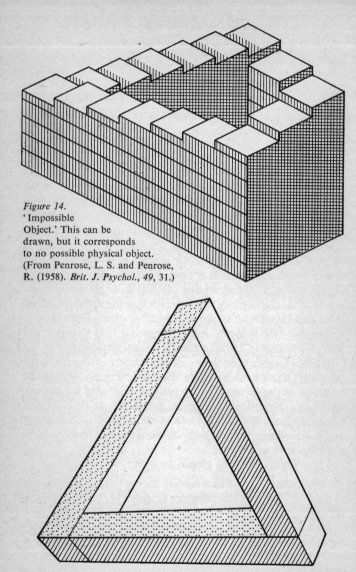

Figure 14.
'Impossible
Object.' This can be
drawn, but it corresponds
to no possible physical object.
(From Penrose, L. S. and Penrose,
R. (1958). *Brit. J. Psychol.*, *49*, 31.)

Figure 15. Another 'impossible object'. This triangle cannot exist. (From Penrose, L. S. and Penrose, R. (1958). *Brit. J. Psychol.*, *49*, 31.)

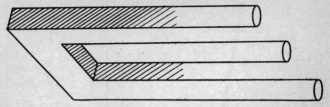

Figure 16. A rather different kind of impossible object – this cannot even be seen! The trouble with all these objects is over the third dimension. The perceptual system has to construct three dimensions from the two given by the image at the eye; here the information is contradictory, and it fails.

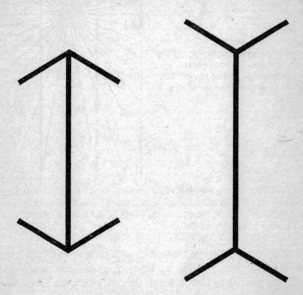

Figure 17. The Muller-Lyer illusion figure. One of the most famous of the distortion-illusions: it is *itself* distorted, while most of the distortions are *produced* on some lines by others.

(iii) Figures (or objects) which *produce* the kinds of distortions noted in (ii) (Figures 18, 19).

(iv) Figures which, when looked at for some time, produce distortions on a second figure looked at immediately after the

73

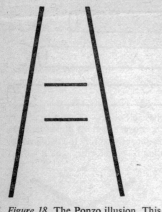

Figure 18. The Ponzo illusion. This also is famous: the upper of the two horizontals appears the longer. The distortion is produced by the converging lines.

Figure 19. The Hering illusion. This striking bending of the verticals is produced by the radiating background lines. (These illusions also occur when they are rotated, the distortions being in the same direction, within the figure, and roughly to the same extent.)

first (Figure 20). These are known as 'figural after-effects'; they build up in time, whereas the other kinds of illusions are virtually unaffected by time, though they may very gradually diminish with experience.

Are such illusions only parlour tricks, or can they be tools for research?

WHAT KIND OF EXPLANATION

In the physical sciences there is general agreement on the kinds of explanations to be accepted as satisfactory, but psychology is very different – psychologists differ greatly over what is an acceptable explanation, and over what is appropriate for deciding between rival theories. Some psychologists give 'mentalistic' explanations, regarding introspective accounts of experience as important, while others concentrate on the nervous system, studied by physiological techniques, using information from

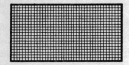

X_1

Figure 20. Figural after-effect. In this example, after fixating X_1 for about half a minute, if X_2 is then fixated, T_1 will appear lower than T_2 (From Köhler, W. and Wallach, H. (1944). *Proc. Am. Phil. Soc., 88*, 269–357.)

lower animals which are disregarded by psycho-analysts and other 'mentalistic' psychologists.

It is known that the distortion illusions which concern us here affect other animals also – such as pigeons – which have some-what similar nervous systems but presumably very different experience, and so we are at once guided away from mentalistic explanations of the illusions. We will, however, start by considering the least implausible mentalistic theory.

TRADITIONAL THEORIES OF THE ILLUSIONS

The 'Empathy' Theory

The idea is that the illusion figures have emotional significance which produces perceptual distortion. It is suggested that we identify ourselves with, say, the arrow figures, and feel 'pulled out' or 'pushed in' by them.

There is indeed some evidence that emotional factors can affect perception; and what we notice may be partly determined by our emotional state. Vague or ambiguous shapes may be seen as frightening objects, such as trees against the night sky being seen as witches' faces, and it has been suggested that size changes can occur as a result of emotional states – in particular, there is evidence suggesting that poor children see coins as larger than do rich children (Bruner and Goodman, 1947). But is it plausible to suppose that the figures we are considering appear distorted through emotional factors? They certainly do not evoke any obvious emotions – except, indeed, in psychologists trying to explain them – and emotions are labile, whereas the illusions are constant for a given individual, and similar in all normal observers. Some differences do occur, but if the cause were emotional we should expect them to fluctuate wildly, and to disappear rapidly with familiarity. It is perhaps difficult to refute this kind of theory, but it lacks any plausibility and one seems safe in abandoning it.

Eye-movement Theories

These suppose that certain features of illusion figures disturb eye movements, thus giving the distortions. Consider the Muller–Lyer arrow figure (Figure 17). It is supposed that the eyes are 'drawn' outwards by the outgoing arrow fins – or alternatively, that the eyes are drawn inwards by them. It is then supposed that the error in the direction of the eyes produces the distortion in length. But there are grave difficulties to this theory. First, it is not at all clear that disturbance of fixation would change the apparent length of a line. Secondly, it is remarkable how constant in length the line appears with apparently free movement of the eyes. Thirdly, and more important, the illusions are still experienced when the figures are presented fixed to the retina. (This may be done by optically stabilizing the retinal image, so that eye movements do not cause a shift of it, or more simply by viewing the figures as after-images, which may easily be done by illuminating them with a short bright flash of light.) The result is that the distortions are still present in the optically stabilized figure, or the after-image (Pritchard, 1958). This rules out any simple eye-movement theory.

The theory may be adapted from *actual* eye movements to *tendency* to eye movements. But if it is said that a tendency to move the eyes to the 'wrong' position produces the distortions we may raise further difficulties. First, the distortions can, and often do, occur in more than one direction, but the eyes cannot move in more than one direction at a time, or presumably, tend to do so. Secondly, if we consider the illusions involving bending of a line, it is extremely difficult to see how a straight line can appear bent because of a tendency to move the eyes. Further, why should only *part* of the figure be affected? There appears to be no evidence to favour an eye-movement theory, while there are such strong objections that we must abandon it.

The Perspective Theory

This theory is very different from those described above, and totally different from the idea that the figures 'confuse' the brain circuits. This theory looks to the figures themselves for the answer, and nearly finds it.

The perspective theory points out that the well-known illusion figures can be regarded as perspective drawings. This is best illustrated with comparison photographs. For example, the Ponzo figure can be thought of as a pair of receding railway lines, with 'sleepers' of equal length. The Muller–Lyer figures are flat projections of corners – the outgoing arrows forming, say, the lines of the ceiling and floor of the inside corner of a room, while the ingoing arrows correspond to the receding lines of an outside corner, perhaps of a tall building or a box. Similarly, the Hering illusion and the rest can all be thought of in this way.

The Perspective Theory goes on to give the following generalization: the features of the illusion figures corresponding to *distant* features of the 3-D world are expanded. We may see this in our examples. Take the Ponzo figure; it is the line near the narrow, converged part of the figure which is expanded. This, by perspective, would be distant, as in Figure 21. In the Muller–Lyer arrows it is the shaft with the outgoing fins, corresponding to an inside corner, in which the shaft would be distant from the ends of the fins, which is expanded. Plate 6 shows an inside corner – the lines of the ceiling and walls, and the floor and walls, are the same

Figure 21. The Ponzo illusion in the real world? The railway lines are the same as in the illusion figure (Figure 18), but here they are clearly perspective lines – parallels converging with distance. The illusion still holds.

as the illusion figure. Plate 7 shows a typical outside corner. They correspond to the most typical, or probable, interpretation of the illusion figures in terms of depth.

From this point the perspective theory goes off the rails. It states that depth is 'suggested' by the perspective features, and this 'suggestion' produces an expansion of the more distant features. But even if we allowed that a 'suggestion' could cause a size change, it would be the wrong way round because distant objects in the real world look *smaller* not *larger*. In each case the traditional perspective theory gives exactly the wrong prediction.

One might at this point be tempted to give up the notion of trying to relate the illusions to depth perception, but there is a good deal of evidence to link them. Indeed, the surprising relation we have already noted suggests some kind of an association.

EVIDENCE FOR LINKING THE DISTORTION ILLUSIONS WITH DEPTH PERCEPTION

There are many illusion figures which are obvious perspective drawings. For example, the men in Figure 22 look larger when

Figure 22. The four men are actually the same size; evidently perspective in some way expands the apparently more distant men. Are all the distortion illusions like this, the perspective being generally less obvious?

perspective indicates greater distance. What we are suggesting is that all the distortion illusions work somewhat like this, though the perspective features are generally less obvious. But we must explain why the obvious ones such as Figure 22 give distortions, the men being actually drawn the same size. And why does the distortion still occur when the perspective is so far from obvious that it has to be pointed out to be seen. And even though the figures appear flat?

It has been found, by several investigators, that people who live in visual environments relatively free of perspective features are hardly afflicted by the distortion illusions. The Zulus live in a 'circular culture' of round huts, with few corners or straight parallel lines, and they see the figures with very little distortion (Segall *et al.*, 1963).

There are more dramatic cases where visual experience is limited or even absent for many years from birth onwards – the rare cases of people who are born blind but gain their sight in adult life through an eye operation (von Senden, 1932). About sixty such cases have been recorded, though only a tenth of that number is sufficient to be of interest. The most recent was studied and described by the author and Miss J. G. Wallace – a man who received corneal grafts at the age of fifty-two, after being blind since the age of ten months (Gregory and Wallace, 1963). We found that after the operation he could name objects by vision which he already knew by touch, but he could make little of drawings or photographs and saw no depth in pictures. Even the ambiguous figures such as the Necker cube (Figure 23), were seen as flat, with no instability. Like the Zulus he saw the illusion figures without distortion. They and he show some distortion for Muller–Lyer arrows, but far less than normal.

Perhaps more direct evidence is to be found in the following experiment on normal observers: Consider any of the illusions where parts of the figure induce distortion in other parts (e.g. the Ponzo, Hering, etc.). Now if the affected lines are displaced in depth from their disturbing background, then the illusion disappears. This is very easily done with a stereoscope. As the affected lines are removed in depth from the background, the distortion is reduced and disappears.

All this suggests that the illusions are in some way related to depth perception. It seems that perspective is especially important and there are many experiments, principally due to the late Adelbert Ames Jr, which show in a very dramatic manner the importance of perspective for determining distance and size (Ittelson, 1952).

If we consider the retinal image in a single eye (or the two identical images from an object lying at considerable distance), it is
clear that the image is infinitely ambiguous. Consider a simple
shape such as the ellipse in Figure 24. Now this could represent
a circular object, lying at such an angle that it gives an elliptical
projection of this eccentricity, or it could be an elliptical object
viewed normally. It could also be an ellipse lying at some angle

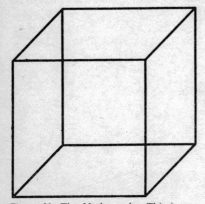

Figure 23. The Necker cube. This is ambiguous in depth – it spontaneously reverses.
There is no information available for deciding which is the nearer and which the farther
face, and the perceptual system entertains
first one hypothesis, then the other.

Figure 24. An Ellipse: Or
is it? It could, as an object,
be a circle, or an ellipse of
any eccentricity with a
given tilt to the observer.

other than normal – there is an infinite range of ellipses, each
lying at a certain angle which would give this shape to the eye.
The same is true for any shape – a straight line image could
'mean' a small and near object or a larger and more distant
object, or it could be short and normal to the observer or tilted
and longer (Figure 25). An image is a flat projection of three-
dimensional space – the brain has the problem of reconstructing
the third dimension from this infinitely ambiguous image. It is
this ambiguity of retinal images (and photographs and drawings)
which sets a particularly difficult problem to the perceptual system.

For objects which lie fairly close to the eyes we have the slight difference of view of the two eyes to locate them in depth. Further, the eyes converge upon objects, and this convergence angle serves, like a range finder, to give distance. But neither of these mechanisms (disparity and convergence) is available for distant objects; for them the views to the eyes are virtually the same and they are effectively parallel. Even when effectively one-eyed, however, we may still see objects in depth, but then we make use of less direct evidence such as perspective.

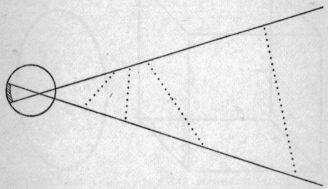

Figure 25. This shows a number of lines of different lengths, distances and orientations all of which give the same retinal image. The brain has to decide what sort of object the image corresponds to in three dimensions.

When all cues to depth are absent, perceptions become highly ambiguous and fluctuate in depth. The best-known example is the skeleton Necker Cube (Figure 23). This changes spontaneously in depth, so that first one face and then another appears nearer. This alternation takes place even when the image is fixed by optical means upon the retina so that there is no change in the stimulation of the eye. The perceptual changes must therefore be 'central', in the brain. It is not hard to see in general terms why this occurs: the figure could equally well be representing a cube lying in either of two positions, and there is no information available for deciding which is the true orientation. There is no unique solution to the problem of interpreting the input information:

first one then the other hypothesis of what the retinal image could represent is entertained in turn, and a decision is never reached. It is curiously difficult to see just what is presented to the eye. The cube is a dozen lines lying on the paper. Arrange the same lines randomly, and that is what one sees (Figure 26), but retinal images are always interpreted as representing objects if at all possible – hence the power of cartoon drawings.

When depth cues are in conflict we may see 'impossible' things. The Necker cube (Figure 23) is an example of a figure which is seen alternatively as one and then another object. 'Impossible objects' are the inverse case: they cannot be seen as any object

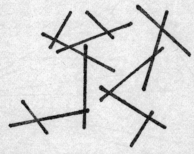

Figure 26. Random arrangement of the lines of a Necker cube (Figure 23). This is not seen as an object, and is not (ambiguously) seen in depth.

which could be realized in space. We may look at the three examples: Figures 14 and 15 show objects which could not be made, and what is Figure 16? In each case the trouble arises over how the two dimensions of the figure could be realized in three-dimensional space.

As we have seen, a drawing is a two-dimensional representation of three dimensions – it is a contraction of three into two dimensions – and so we should not be too surprised that sometimes odd things happen. In fact, what is really surprising is how seldom we are confused about the three-dimensional significance of flat drawings and photographs. They must always be essentially ambiguous, and yet we usually accept only one interpretation – 'reality'.

THE AMES DEMONSTRATIONS

It is possible to construct actual objects which look wrong: illusions are not restricted to figures lying on a flat surface. It is also possible to construct objects, particularly rooms of curious shape, which distort other objects (Ittelson, 1952). These illusions are primarily due to the late Adelbert Ames Jr who started life as a painter, and went on to devise several of the most striking and powerful illusions. What he did was to produce *real objects* which look wrong, and objects – especially rooms of peculiar shape –

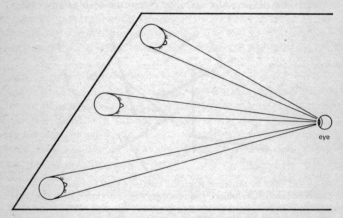

Figure 27. Plan of the Ames room. This shows the actual shape of the room: the men are actually at different distances, and so give different-sized retinal images, or images at the camera. But they are seen as the same distance and wrong size. (Ittelson, 1952.)

which make other objects look wrong. Plate 5 shows Ames's so-called Distorted Room as it appears in a photograph. When the eye is placed in the position of the camera, it looks much the same: *objects placed in the room look the wrong size.* The room itself looks just like any normal room, but in fact it is not. Its true shape is shown, from above, in Figure 27. The room is not in fact rectangular; but it has been so designed that it gives to the eye (or the camera) exactly the same image as a normal rectangular room. Objects in the room look the wrong sizes because their distances are seen wrongly, since they appear to be in a rectangular room which in fact is not rectangular. We refuse to see the room as it really is – non-rectangular – and accept the impossible sizes of the people as given by the sizes of their images at the eye. This could hardly have been anticipated. With no objects in the room it *must* look like a rectangular room, but when there are objects in it the observer has to make a bet on whether it is the room or the objects which are odd. It turns out that the room wins, and the objects within it appear the wrong sizes and at the wrong distances.

However, it is reported that there are exceptions: a wife may refuse to see her husband shrink to the size of a child, and her perceptual system will (sometimes) accept him at his true value, demanding that the environment is at fault while he is normal – so we find a nice moral end to this story.

The effect is less pronounced, even entirely absent, in people unfamiliar with perspective. The tenacity with which the distorting room is seen as rectangular in spite of the implication that a child is taller than a man is extremely strong evidence that, for Western eyes, rectangularity is taken as almost axiomatic in visual perception. We accept – though wrongly – that the room is like other rooms, in which case the people would be the same distance. Making the wrong bet, we see them the wrong size and at the wrong distance. Interestingly enough the effects are different for people living in visual environments almost free of reliable perspective features. Zulus do not see the objects in the room the wrong size – to Zulus the room is non-rectangular and the people normal.

It is important to note that this is *not* a distortion illusion. A given sized retinal image could always represent a large distant object or a nearer small object: there is an infinity of possible distances and sizes for any image. The wrong assumption about the shape of the room has made the perceptual system take the wrong bet on size and distance, *but it has not produced spatial distortion*. The Ames room tells us that perspective is important in estimating distance, and choosing between size and distance, but it does *not* tell us what produces the distortions in the illusion figures, for they are flat, and may be seen as flat. What does cause them?

DISTORTION ILLUSIONS AND
SIZE CONSTANCY

Everyone who has used a camera knows that images shrink with increasing distance of the object. This is also true of retinal images – but we do not see objects as shrinking with distance nearly as much as we would if the eye were only a camera. There is some kind of perceptual process which compensates for changes in retinal image size with distance of objects. The extent of the compensation – 'size constancy' - has been measured many times, notably by Thouless (1931), though there are difficulties in getting reliable measures. Its existence was realized by Descartes in the seventeenth century.

For constancy to operate in the world of normal objects, the more *distant* features must be perceptually *expanded*. But as we have seen, it is also the features representing more *distant* features which are *expanded* in the illusion figures. Suppose then, that perspective depth features can set the constancy directly. It would be inappropriate for the flat figures – and *would produce systematic distortions*. The features indicated as distant would be expanded, which is what happens.

There are several hints in the literature of a connexion between size constancy and illusions (notably Tausch, 1954, and Teuber 1960); but it is odd how little attention it has received, either by discussion or experiment. The idea is worth pushing, even if difficulties should emerge, for it makes the right predictions without our having to introduce *ad hoc* assumptions, or special hypothetical processes. We already know that the size and shapes of retinal images are perceptually modified to give constancy. It is a short and reasonable step to suppose that this known process may go wrong when confronted with depth features on a flat plane – to be set appropriately to the world of three-dimensional objects – and then we should expect just the kind of distortions we observe.

The difficulty with the theory as it stands is that the illusion figures are seen as flat. This is no trivial objection, especially as it is universally believed that constancy always follows apparent depth. If this were so, the theory must be false. Clearly, we must challenge some traditional ways of thinking about constancy.

There are psychologists, notably J. J. Gibson (1950), following in this instance the Gestalt psychologist Koffka (1935), who hold that the third dimension is available to the senses as immediately as the other two spatial dimensions, and that neither depth nor constancy are 'computed'. If this were true, the theory of the illusions to be developed here would be untenable. We must hold that constancy is given by an *active process*, generally mediated by information of depth, which we will call *constancy scaling* (Gregory, 1963).

A famous demonstration allows one to see one's own constancy scaling at work. The method is to 'project' an after-image on to screens at various distances, when it will be seen as almost twice the size for each doubling in distance of the screen. But the area of stimulation on the retina, the effective image, is in fact fixed in size, so what we see is our scaling in action.*

Emmert's Law states that after-images increase linearly with apparent distance. But if this were always true we could not hold that constancy scaling produces the distortions, for the illusion figures are generally seen to be flat, as in fact they are. This is a difficulty which must be resolved if the illusions are to be explained in terms of constancy.

Consider any perspective drawing or photograph. There is something odd about it – it is logically impossible – it lies in both two and three dimensions simultaneously (Gregory, 1965).

Perspective presented on a flat plane presents the eye with two geometries – the flat plane of the paper and the three dimensions of the picture. The picture remains perceptually stuck to its flat background, and yet in a sense it is seen in depth. The perception of depth in a picture is quite unlike the perception of depth in the world of three-dimensional objects: we are not tempted to push

* We must however be careful over this. The area of retinal fatigue will cover a greater area of the background screen with increased distance, and this could make it appear larger apart from any internal scaling. But the observed after-image also changes size with increasing apparent distance when there is *no structured background* (Gregory *et al.*, 1959), which, with other evidence, shows that this change – Emmert's Law – should be thought of in terms of an active scaling process. But it would be a mistake, and a common one, to assume that Emmert's Law tells all there is to know.

our hand through the paper to touch a 'distant' object, and we are not afraid of being poked in the eye by objects in the foreground. Depth is suggested rather than seen; it is paradoxical, impossible, and the amazing thing is that we do see depth through perspective when the picture is on a textured background. There is quite strong evidence that seeing depth in pictures does not come naturally, but depends on years of experience of parallel lines and right-angled corners in the environment, and of perspective pictures. Perspective came very late in the history of art; not until the Italian Renaissance. Its invention may well have followed the first optical instruments, simple lenses and the *camera obscura*. Previously artists never drew objects as they appear at the eye, and with the development of perspective came a host of illusions.

THE INAPPROPRIATE CONSTANCY-SCALING THEORY OF THE DISTORTION ILLUSIONS

We arrive at a possible theory – that the distortion illusions are due to constancy scaling being set by perspective features which are inappropriate, because the figure in fact lies on a flat plane. This involves a kind of constancy which is not accepted in the literature, for it does not simply follow apparent depth, as constancy is supposed to do. But evidently it functions not only when depth is countermanded by background texture, but even more surprising: it is not affected by perceptual reversals in depth. This may be seen in Figure 28, which shows a Necker cube with a straight line drawn across it. The line appears slightly bent at the corner of the cube, and it *looks bent the same way when the cube alternates in depth*. This perspective constancy scaling, then, is not affected by the interpretation of the figure as a whole. It is apparently set systematically by typical perspective depth features, even when non-typical in a given figure. This is seen most clearly in a depth – ambiguous figure, such as the Necker cube, but it is true also of any perspective picture. For example the Muller–Lyer arrows can be seen reversed from their typical perspective depth: the illusion remains unchanged when this occurs.

The constancy scaling which we are supposing produces the distortions cannot be the whole of the scaling giving invariance of size distance in normal three-dimensional space. This is clear because the range over which invariance holds requires scaling of perhaps 1,000 per cent, but illusory distortions are never greater than about thirty per cent. Scaling set by perspective features is

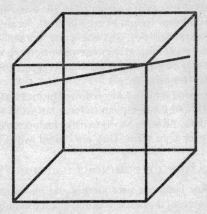

Figure 28. Necker cube with a line drawn across one corner. This is apparently slightly bent, but the direction of bending remains the same whichever way the cube appears to lie (paradoxically) in depth. If this figure is luminous, the direction of bend changes with the way the cube lies in depth.

independent of perceptual organization, and is never large in extent. It seems to occur early on in the perceptual system, though it is not in the retina itself.*

EXPERIMENTS TO TEST AND CHALLENGE THE THEORY

There are many ways open to test the theory. We may first try to attack it by seeking exceptions to the generalization that typical depth perspective always gives expansion. This generalization, pointed out by the old perspective theory, is not as firmly based as one would wish.

One might take a random selection of photographs and judge whether the converging lines and other features giving distortion

* It can be shown quite conclusively that it is not in the retina, but the experiment to show this is somewhat technical. (See Julesz, 1964 and Pappert, 1961.)

really are generally associated with distance. But this would be tedious and not very convincing. Another way is open: we may remove the competing background texture, and literally see what happens.

If the illusion figures are presented to the eye with no visible background: (a) they should be seen in depth according to their perspective characteristics; (b) the parts normally expanded would appear most distant; (c) the distortions should still be present, and may be greater, for we should expect expansion as in Emmert's Law for after-images.*

The background is quite easily removed by making wire models of the figures, and coating them in luminous paint so that they glow in the dark. Another way is to make high-contrast transparencies, and back-light them. They are viewed with a single eye.

OBSERVATION OF LUMINOUS ILLUSION FIGURES

We have made luminous wire models and photographic transparencies of most of the illusion figures, and it certainly does seem that the perspective generalization is supported – the expanded parts look the most distant when the background is removed. The distortions are still present, in the same direction, as we should predict.

Luminous ambiguous figures are interesting. A truly three-dimensional luminous cube will reverse in depth, like the Necker cube, but when it does so it *no longer looks like a cube* – the

---

* Emmert's Law is best demonstrated with after-images, in the following way. If a photographic flash is directed into the eyes, a coloured patch will be seen, which moves with the eyes. This is due to local fatigue of the retina from the bright flash. This area of fatigue remains of constant size; like a photograph stuck on the retina. If the eyes are now directed to a wall, the after-image appears to be on the wall, whatever its distance, but the farther away the wall the larger does the image appear to be, the expansion being proportional to distance. Since it is *physically* constant, there must be a central brain process scaling it, as a function of apparent distance. Actually this is a little too simple, for the area of fatigue will cover a larger area of the wall, since the image of the wall will shrink with increasing distance. Size change is, however, still observed in complete darkness, so though it may be partly set by the relative sizes of the fatigue and wall (or other background), it is at least in part a central size scaling effect. This is most clearly shown with the luminous ambiguous figures which change shape according to apparent distance when there is no background.

apparent front looks too small. A luminous flat cube figure (Necker cube) appears in depth, and will reverse, but the apparently nearer face, whichever this may be, looks smaller than the farther one. When the paradox of the background is removed, constancy functions *simply according to apparent distance*. When the cube is not reversed it appears a true cube, in spite of the farther face giving a smaller retinal image than the nearer one. This means that *size constancy is operating* since the retinal image of the farther face will be smaller than the nearer. We find that in the absence of background texture, size constancy follows apparent distance *even when there are no visual cues to the distance of the various parts of the figure*. In other words, constancy is here being set not direct by depth cues, but by the perceived depth of the figure apart from any cues. Now this is quite different from the setting of constancy scaling by perspective depth. Constancy scaling *can* be set by apparent distance (Emmert's Law) but also it *can* be set directly by depth cues, even when these are countermanded by background texture so that the figure appears flat. We must conclude that constancy scaling occurs in two ways. (1) It can be set directly by depth cues, or (2) it can be set to correspond to apparent depth, even in the absence of specific depth cues. It will then, and only then, change with changing *depth* interpretations of the retinal image.

This double aspect of constancy scaling may seem surprising, but evidently we must accept it, and think of the perceptual system in these terms.

This has taken us quite far, but we have to rely on the verbal reports, the introspections, of observers. Could we perhaps actually measure the depth seen in the illusion figures?

MEASURING VISUAL DEPTH

The trick is to arrange that the observer sees the luminous display with one eye, but sees a reference marker which can be moved along a scale in the third dimension with *both* eyes. If this reference marker is adjusted to the same apparent depth as selected features of the luminous display, seen with one eye, then we shall get a measure of the perceived distance of features in the illusion figures. Indeed, we can measure the depth seen in any kind of

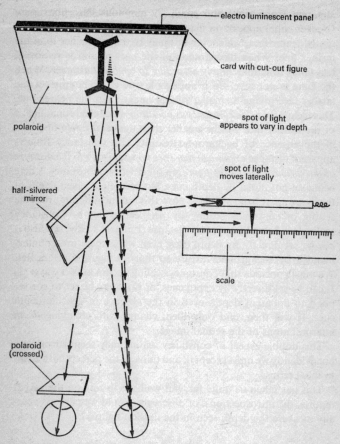

Figure 29. Apparatus for measuring visual depth in pictures. The background is removed by back-illuminating the picture (e.g. an illusion figure), which is seen with only one eye because the light from the picture is polarized, and cross-polarized at one eye. The reference lamp is seen by both eyes (by reflection from the part-reflecting mirror), as lying in the picture. Its distance is adjusted to equal the distance of any selected feature in the picture, giving a plot of visual space in three dimensions.

figure, using range-finder binocular vision to link monocular depth to this physical moving scale.

This presents quite a simple optical problem. First, the light from the luminous display is polarized, and a second polaroid filter is placed over one eye with the angles of polarization crossed at 90° to prevent light from entering this eye. The other eye, however, sees it normally. The reference light is introduced to both eyes. This is a small dim light, optically lying in the display. It is introduced with a part-reflecting mirror, and is seen with both

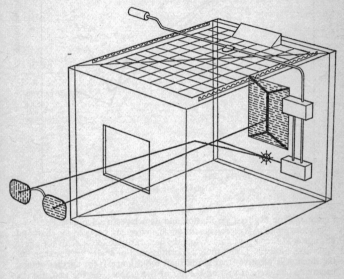

Figure 30. Outside view of apparatus for measuring visual depth.

eyes. It is adjusted in distance, until it lies at the apparent distance of any selected feature of the luminous display. The reference light can be moved around in three dimensions, and so a three-dimensional plot of visual space is obtained. This arrangement is shown in Figures 29 and 30.

If we now plot the visual space for the illusion figures, we can relate apparent depth, measured objectively, with the extent of the illusion also measured objectively. The result is exciting. We find that the luminous figures are indeed plotted as lying in depth, and

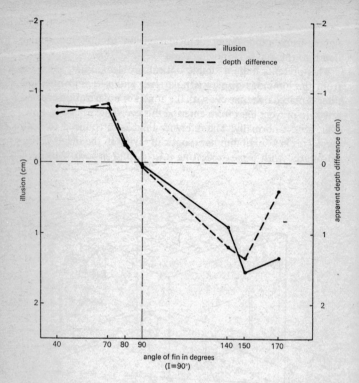

Figure 31. The Muller-Lyer illusion and its perspective depth.

The *horizontal axis* represents the angle, in degrees, between the shaft and fins in the Muller-Lyer figure. When the fins are at 90° to the shaft the figure looks like a capital I, and there is no illusion. For angles greater than 90° the illusion is positive (that is the shaft looks longer); for smaller angles, negative. The *vertical axis on the left* of the graph gives the scale for the extent of the illusion, in terms of error in centimetres, by matching the length of the shaft with a similar, but adjustable, line having no arrow heads. The *solid line* shows how the illusion varies with angle. It was obtained from twenty subjects, each making three judgements at each angle. The shaft of the figure was 10 cm. long and was viewed from half a metre.

The same subjects were used to measure the apparent depth, for the same angles. Here the figures were presented without background texture or other countermanding depth cues. They were shown as back-illuminated transparencies and presented to a single eye. Depth was measured with a comparison light viewed by both eyes, and adjusted in distance to match the apparent distance of the shaft and the ends of the fins.

The *right-hand vertical axis* shows the scale for apparent depth of the figures in centimetres: the *dotted lines* show the apparent depth varying *the greater the depth the greater the illusion.* This is seen in Figure 31 for the Muller-Lyer illusion. Here several different fin angles have been used, to control the amount of the illusion, and the measured illusion is plotted against the measured depth. It will be seen that where the fins are outgoing, the central line, the 'shaft', is recorded as appearing farthest away, and vice versa for the ingoing fins. This justifies the perspective interpretation. The extent of the illusion follows the amount of recorded depth very closely, for both directions. We may regard this result as strong evidence for relating the illusion to perspective depth.

It is worth noting that both the plotted functions lose their linearity at extreme angles of the fins – they break down together at just about the limits of perspective angles which can arise from corners. It seems that the fins are regarded by the perceptual system as indicating depth, and used to adjust constancy appropriate to the indicated depth, even though depth is countermanded by other features, such as background texture. This is a new notion of Constancy, but it does not seem to violate any known facts. We may call it *primary constancy*; and the simple dependence upon apparent distance – shown by Emmert's Law and the size changes in luminous ambiguous figures – *Secondary Constancy*. Their distinguishing features are something like this:

Primary scaling	*Secondary scaling*
1. Does not follow apparent depth in plane figures, for it occurs when figure is seen as flat.	1. Follows apparent distance, as in Emmert's Law.
2. Works only over a small range, about thirty per cent.	2. Works over a very wide range.
3. Is not subject to changes by 'attitude' or 'set'.	3. Is subject to mental 'attitude' or 'set' when there are few depth cues available.
4. Does not change with interpretation of depth in ambiguous figures presented on textured plane.	4. In ambiguous figures, where the retinal image remains constant but the perception changes, the scaling follows the perception of depth.

with fin angle.

The correlation between apparent depth and extent of the Muller-Lyer illusion is better than 0·9. (Experiment by R. L. Gregory and Linda Townes, at M.I.T. 1964.)

It remains to discover what happens in the brain. We do not know the 'electronics' of the scaling mechanisms: this is a problem for electrophysiology. But at least psychological explanations and suggestions from psychological experiments may suggest what to look for in the brain itself. Even without knowing the 'electronics' we do seem to have a theory having explanatory power in its own right. It seems that constancy involves active scaling processes triggered by certain visual features – very reminiscent of ethological 'releasers' (see p. 56). Just as ethologists can discover by behavioural experiments characteristics which elicit certain kinds of behaviour so we can discover, by studying illusions, which features determine how we see the world.

CONCLUSION

Starting with a look at various illusions and perceptual phenomena, we have tried to develop a theory based on an old idea and involving facts already well established – especially size Constancy. We have been forced to extend the usual notion of Constancy, to suppose it set, or adjusted, by typical distance features, even when depth is not seen. This has taken us beyond simply looking at the figures to modifying them by removing their backgrounds, and objectively measuring apparent depth. We find that this correlates highly with the measured illusions. We can look again at the illusion figures and see the subtle compensations which give stability to our experience of the world. Like any other stabilizing or compensating systems it can go dramatically wrong. It can be set inappropriately – even entirely reversed – and then we are in worse trouble than if there were no compensations, no Constancy. So illusions are more than curiosities to amuse children and psychologists, for just as nineteenth-century physicists were concerned about observational errors so are we. In flying, driving and space flight no instrument yet exists to take over completely from human perception. In space, perception is taxed to its limits, for the conditions are just those where illusions occur and are most serious. We must not expect astronauts to rely blindly on mechanisms evolved for our familiar Earth: we must come to understand these mechanisms, and see why they go wrong.

4. HUMAN ATTENTION

ANNE TREISMAN

It is clear from the preceding chapters that perception is influenced by many things apart from the stimulation produced by the thing being perceived. Everyone knows how important attention is in this respect. We can switch attention from looking to listening, or to concentrating on bodily feelings. Even within one sensory mode, say vision, attention fluctuates, and is selective. The topic has been studied by psychologists for a long time, but recently new techniques and ideas have given a new impetus to its study. Dr Treisman describes them. She is an experimental psychologist who has done ingenious experiments in this field.

WHAT do we normally mean by attention? A variety of situations and processes spring to mind: we talk of something catching or attracting our attention – a colourful advertisement, an unusual smell, a loud noise; or of attending in the sense of concentrating on one set of events to the exclusion of others – doing mental arithmetic with the wireless playing popular songs; we talk of the division of attention, of attempting to take in two or more things at once – holding a conversation while driving a car for example; of vigilance and perseverance in tasks like watch-keeping, where we have to watch for intermittent signals over a long period of time – watching a radar screen or a set of dials in industry without missing anything through momentary lapses of attention; finally, of attention in the sense of expectation, where we are 'set' to receive particular stimuli or events – noticing sounds of cooking and smells of food when we are hungry.

We take the ability to attend for granted and are usually unaware how complex a task we set our brains, for instance, at a cocktail party. We are aware simply of deciding to listen to one person, but to do this our ears must analyse an extremely complex sound wave in which many voices are summed together; from this confusion one voice must be extracted, while the remainder are checked for anything relevant and then rejected before they overload our brains. There is some evidence that this ability may break down in certain mental illnesses: McGhie and Chapman (1961) describe some schizophrenic patients who were unable to block out unwanted stimuli, and said things like, 'I can't concentrate. Its diversion of attention that troubles me. I am picking up different conversations all the time.' In contrast an experiment by Hovey (1928) demonstrates how efficient selective attention can be in normal people. He gave subjects an I.Q. test while at the same time trying to distract them with seven electric bells, four buzzers, two organ pipes, a circular metal saw, a flashlight and several peculiarly clothed people walking about carrying strange objects. These subjects did nearly as well on the test as the control group who took it in undisturbed silence.

EARLY RESEARCH

As with much of psychology, most early attempts to explain attention were based on introspection – asking oneself what it feels like to attend in these different ways. Once started, this discussion became voluble but not always very illuminating. A typical comment was, 'the field of inattention seems to resolve itself into an aura, as it were, which aura has now a feel of being fuller and now of being narrower, suggesting that there is something psychic beyond the fields of attention and inattention themselves'. A controversial question was whether things became clearer or more intense as a result of being the centre of attention. Two psychologists of the last century tried to decide the question by playing a musical chord on a harmonium and attending only to the middle note. One thought this made it seem louder, but the other disagreed; the only conclusion could be that there were individual differences between people. As Titchener said in 1908, 'it is true that the discovery of attention by the psychologists did not result in any immediate triumph for the experimental method. It was something like the discovery of a hornets' nest; the first touch brought out a whole swarm of insistent problems.' The main reason for the difficulties was the research method used. It is always possible to disagree about the results of introspection and there is little to be done about this deadlock beyond appealing to the other person's good faith, asking him to try again and making sure he is using words in the same way as the experimenter. Knowledge acquired in this way is knowledge only so long as no one tries to contradict it; it is difficult to establish in a more permanent and public form. As a result the topic of attention fell into disrepute and little research was done on it until the last decade.

RECENT APPROACHES

Recently, however, there has been a great revival of interest, partly arising from the urgent practical need, with increasing automation and the greater complexity of control problems in industry, to know the characteristics of human beings as links in industrial or traffic control systems. Increasingly we have to deal with information and make decisions rather than use our muscular energy. We need to know the limits imposed by our capacity to attend to several competing inputs in order to avoid inefficiency and accidents. Instead of trying to get access to some mysterious entity or faculty called attention, as such, we can investigate the many forms of behaviour normally called attentive, most of which are quite amenable to experiment. To do this we need to use a new type of theoretical description. Subjective language like 'increased clearness' or 'focalization of consciousness' has been abandoned, since introspection is no longer used as a source of explanation but only to provide one type of data among many others. Instead, we use the results of our objective experiments to map out the functional stages in which the brain must select or reject information from the senses, analyse and store it or organize it to determine our overt behaviour. The descriptive model which emerges is so far mainly qualitative rather than quantitative, and the evidence is used to find out what goes on in dynamic terms rather than the actual mechanisms which carry it out. In this way we hope that our everyday questions about attention will take on a new meaning in terms of a scientific model predicting further results and giving coherence to past findings. In this chapter, I shall try to illustrate this with some examples.

SPAN OF ATTENTION

We might start with the age-old question: how much can we attend to at once, what are the limits to our attention? Some of the earliest experiments were on the so-called 'span of attention', which was thought to be a measure of how much a person could take in at any one moment of time. Jevons in 1871 threw handfuls of beans on to a tray and examined how many he could take in at a single glance. He found that with numbers higher than eight he tended to make errors. His experiment has since been elaborated and repeated in a variety of forms, using the tachistoscope, an instrument for presenting visual stimuli for brief durations. His finding has been confirmed: there appears to be a definite and low limit to the number of items which can be reliably reported under these conditions, although it varies a little with the stimuli used. For instance, more letters can be reported if they form a word than if they are chosen at random.

So far it was assumed that this technique measured all the information available to the subject at the moment the stimulus was seen. But recent and ingenious experiments by Averbach and Sperling (1960), show that this is wrong. They thought the explanation for the low limit was that the later items were disappearing from memory during the time it took to identify and report the first ones. If one could find a way to measure what was available immediately on the exposure, one might find that subjects take in considerably more than the size of the span indicates. To test this, they invented a sampling technique. For instance, they showed a subject three rows of letters and immediately afterwards indicated which one of the three he was to recall. Since subjects did not know in advance which row would be required, their report of the one row allowed an estimate of the total information available at that moment. If they recalled two-thirds of it, one could assume that they had taken in two-thirds of the whole display. This experiment revealed that subjects have a much larger span of attention than had been thought – up to two or three times as much. It also showed the interesting fact that this information decays very rapidly: if subjects were told which row was required as soon as one second after the exposure, they did no better than normal. It was not the immediate intake of information by the senses which was limited, but rather the time it took to identify the stimuli and report them, and the time for which they could be stored. Visual intake is rapid and a large number of items can be stored briefly before they decay and disappear. The central 'read-out' procedure is much slower and probably handles the items successively. This experiment parallels our everyday experience of glimpsing something which promptly slips out of our memory, although we are convinced we saw it at the time.

LIMITS OF ATTENTION: 'THE COCKTAIL PARTY PROBLEM'

Extending this attention span in time, the question becomes how many sequences of stimuli can we take in at once? Can we listen to two conversations at a cocktail party? Can we read a book and listen to the wireless at the same time? Is there such a thing as dividing attention? Since we could correctly report four letters when these were presented tachistoscopically for a single, brief moment, can we watch for signals on four different display screens for a long period? We find that we can attend to two familiar and expected sequences fairly well – a favourite radio soap opera and a familiar road along which we are driving – but if the stimuli become at all complex or unpredictable, we can either take in one complete set and nothing of the other, or alternatively about half of each.

Mowbray (1953) gave subjects two different passages of prose, one to read, and at the same time one to listen to; he then asked them questions about both stories to see how much they had heard. With easy passages they did quite well on both, but with more difficult ones they absorbed considerably less when hearing and reading them at the same time than if they could read one first and then listen to the other later. Cherry in 1953 did an experiment which has led to much further research: he played subjects two passages of prose over headphones, one to each ear, and asked them to repeat one of the two continuously as they heard it – a kind of auditory reading aloud which he called 'shadowing'. He then asked what they had noticed about the other passage, which he varied in a number of ways. He found that they could tell him nothing at all about its verbal content. They noticed if it was a man's or woman's voice or a pure tone, but often did not notice if the passage changed from English to German or to speech played backwards on the tape-recorder, which normally sounds very different and quite meaningless. His subjects seemed to have blocked out one whole stream of words, noticing only the general characteristics of the messages as sounds.

Why should this be necessary? Since the brain consists of a finite number of nerve cells or neurons, its capacity for dealing with incoming signals must be limited. But if we ask subjects to repeat a familiar nursery rhyme played to one ear, or a passage of prose played much more slowly than usual, we find that they can hear a good deal of what is said in the other ear. The limit to our capacity is due not just to the number of words reaching our ears, nor the number of voices, but rather to the unpredictability of the words or signals, the number of different possibilities we have to expect at each point. Experiments have shown that the main limit is one of information content in the mathematical sense (see Chapter 5); the rate at which we can take decisions rather than the amount of energy needed or the number of stimuli as such. This limit in our capacity for handling information explains why we needed to develop the system of selectivity we call attention.

GENERAL MODEL OF ATTENTION

Cherry's experiment suggests that we deal with messages reaching our ears in at least two stages: the first can handle several messages at once. Their general physical features are identified – such as where they come from, whether a man or woman is speaking and how loudly or softly. The second stage can normally deal with only one message at a time. Here the verbal content of the message is analysed to discover what words or sentences were spoken. Between these two stages there must be some selective system which passes only one of a number of competing sensory messages and rejects others. Broadbent (1958) called this system a 'filter'

selecting between the different 'input channels', by analogy with
the mechanical communication systems of engineering. The word
'channel' usually implies a physical system with defined properties, along which information is passed; an example would be a
telephone link. It might also be used to describe different sensory
pathways like those from ear or eye to brain. However, we find
that people can attend selectively not only to sights while ignoring
sounds but also to one class of sounds or sights, while ignoring
another. They can listen for words spoken by a man rather than
a woman, words coming from the left rather than from the right,

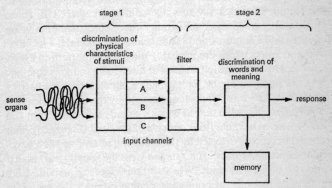

Figure 32. Broadbent's filter model for selective attention.

words that are either a little louder or a little softer than their com-
petitors and so on. Psychologists have extended the use of the
word 'channel' to cover these cases, so that in the context of
attention a channel is defined as carrying any class of sensory
messages which can be selectively attended to or ignored. Figure
32 shows the main elements of the brain's system for selective
attention, as they have emerged so far. The filter blocks sounds on
channels *A* and *C* and passes only those on *B* for further analysis
of words and meaning.

The filter can reject and select on the basis of any features
identified at the first stage, since the brain has already used these
features to separate out the sounds. On the other hand, it should
not be able so easily to pick out one of two messages on the basis

103

of its meaning or even of the language in which it is spoken, if the two do not differ in any general physical characteristics. Experiments show that with two messages in different languages, if the subject understands both, he does hardly better than with two recordings in the same language (Treisman, 1961).

INPUT CHANNELS

This still leaves the important question of how at Stage 1 the brain distinguishes different messages in the single complex sound reaching the ears. Presumably, the method differs according to the feature in which the messages differ, whether it is voice, localization, loudness or some other cue. Some attempt is being made to find a solution, and I shall select two examples – localization and voice, which are probably the most important in everyday life. How can one tell from what direction a sound is coming? It is not done simply by looking, since blind people can be very good at it. The most important cue used by the brain is the very small difference in the time at which a sound reaches the right and left ears when it comes from one side of the head (Figure 33). This small difference is detected by the brain and interpreted as a particular direction in space. If it gets too large the sound 'tears apart' into two different sounds. When two messages are arriving from different directions the brain must compare closely the sounds at the two ears to decide which of them match and should be heard together and which do not. It must compare the sound at one ear with all the sounds arriving at the other ear either before or after it, over a range of a few milliseconds. When the two messages are coming from different directions it will find that half the sounds match best at one interval and half at another. The small time differences between the ears can thus be used to separate the two messages, so that one can be selected for attention and the other rejected.

What is it that makes one voice different from another? We are conscious of a difference in pitch between a man's and a woman's voice as well as a number of subtler differences. The easiest way to decide what is crucial is to experiment with artificial speech, specially constructed by machine, so that we can control all the different features. Speech sounds consist of vibrations of the air at a number of different frequencies coming in bursts or pulses at another much lower frequency, which is produced by the larynx or vocal chords. Any one speaker will produce sounds of several different frequencies at once, but they will all be pulsed

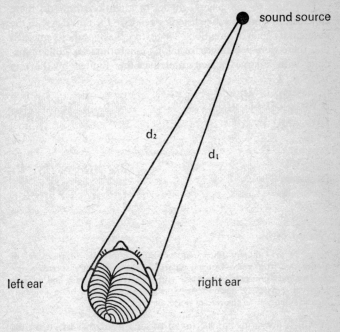

sound reaches right ear slightly sooner than left, since distance d_1 is a little shorter than d_2

Figure 33. Auditory localization of single sound source.

at the same rate. Broadbent and Ladefoged (1957) experimented using sounds at two different frequencies which were pulsed either at the same or at different rates. When the pulse rates were the same, listeners heard the sounds as coming from one source, even when the two frequencies were played one to each ear. But if the pulse rates were different they heard two sounds, even if the same frequency was being pulsed at the two different rates or the same ear was receiving the sounds. This pulse rate, which we hear as the pitch of the voice, seems, then, to be an important feature which the brain can use to separate out messages spoken by two different voices (Figure 34).

To return to the general model of attention: how do these conclusions from selective listening relate to the findings with the momentary span of attention? There, too, the hypothesis emerged that there were two stages for taking in information – one imme-diate with a large capacity and the other limited by the rate

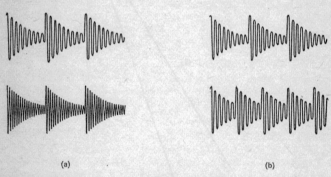

(a)   (b)

Figure 34. (*a*) Different filter frequencies but same rate of pulsation or modulation from voice. Listener reports he hears one vowel sound.
(*b*) Two pulsation rates, combined with same filter frequency and fed into each ear separately, produce two distinct sounds. The brain evidently focuses attention on the rate of pulsation.

at which decisions can be taken to identify items. In vision the main physical dimensions of stimuli are location, colour, size, brightness and shape. The fact that subjects could pick out the letters in one of the three rows shows that in vision the spatial location of items is identified at the first stage. On the other hand, they could not pick out the letters from an array of letters and numbers in the same efficient way. If one could show that subjects can pick out the red letters from a display including red, green and blue letters, or the small letters from an array in which letters differed in size, the parallel with the auditory research would be complete.

SHORT TERM MEMORY

Sperling's experiments also showed that the first stage has a memory store which can hold items for a short time. Is there any parallel in the auditory tasks with a sequence of signals presented in succession? We are all familiar with the 'double-take' experience: we hear someone speaking without registering what he is saying; then one or two seconds later the meaning dawns. It is as if we had kept a copy of the sounds in our memory for a short time before identifying them as words. An experiment by Broadbent (1954) has thrown more light on this experience. He was trying to test whether subjects could remember anything of the items presented on a channel to which they could not attend immediately. He gave his subjects three pairs of simultaneous digits, one of each pair to each ear, and asked them to recall as many digits as they could. His subjects were quite able to recall all six digits, but they repeated back first all those on one ear and then all those on the other. They found it impossible to alternate between the ears in the order in which the digits were arriving, when these were presented faster than one digit per ear per second. In order to be able to repeat the second set of three digits, they must have stored them during the time they were identifying the first set from the other ear. But when given six pairs, so that they had to recall six digits from one ear before switching to the other, subjects forgot the digits from the second ear. This experiment reveals that there is a short-term store for information lying between the two stages of recognition of auditory messages, like that found by Sperling in his visual experiments. Does the same occur when attention has to alternate between vision and hearing? Broadbent (1956) repeated his digit experiment presenting half to the ears and half to the eyes and got the same result. It seems to be a general feature of human perception. Clearly this buffer storage would be very useful when a number of important signals are arriving at once, if it is true that we can deal with items only in sequence rather than simultaneously.

This short-term memory store holds items which have not yet received attention; we can think of it as keeping a record of raw sensory data, still awaiting recognition. It would be interesting to compare its properties with normal short-term memory for material which has already been recognized. We need some test which requires us in one condition to remember things we have attended to and in the other to remember things to which we paid no attention at the time. One way of doing this is to play the same passage of prose independently to each ear of a subject with the two recordings out of step by a few seconds, and to ask him to attend to and shadow one of them. When the message he is attending to is ahead of the other by about ten seconds, he has no idea what the other message is about. If we then reduce the interval gradually, at about five or six seconds the subject breaks off to say, 'Oh, they are both the same.' To do this he must have kept a record of the message he had been attending to for five or six seconds, so that he could then compare it with the second message arriving on the other ear. If we reverse the recordings and play the unattended message ahead of the other, we find that the interval has to be reduced to only one or two seconds before subjects notice that they are the same. In this case, of course, the unattended message is being stored, and we find that the time for which it survives is considerably shorter (Treisman, 1961). This suggests that raw data are stored for a shorter period and probably in a different place from material which has been recognized.

SWITCHING OF ATTENTION

Broadbent's experiment with the digits on both ears revealed another point of interest. His subjects were unable to alternate between the ears at fast speeds, but could do so when he slowed up the rate of the digits. This must imply that it takes time to shift one's attention – to reset the selective system or 'filter' for a new input channel. Another way of showing this limit to the speed of shifting from one source to another is to listen to a recording which is switched alternately from ear to ear as we listen. Cherry and Taylor (1954) showed that when speech is switched at a rate of three to five cycles per second, it becomes very difficult to understand. As they put it, 'at a certain rate one might expect the mental and the acoustic switching to become out of phase, so that no recognition takes place', and this is what seems to happen.

Their method allows us to measure the time taken for one shift of attention: it seems to be about one-sixth of a second. In an environment where a great deal is happening at once – watching a crowded stage at the opera, or working in an air traffic control tower – this switching time for attention will impose an additional limit on what we can perceive.

ATTENTION: ABSOLUTE OR RELATIVE

So far we have assumed that the selective filter acts in an all-or-nothing fashion, blocking any sounds or sights that are not receiving attention, so that nothing can be known about them unless it has already been analysed at some earlier stage. This gave a satisfactory account of most of the evidence when Broadbent suggested it, but some recent findings are a little difficult to reconcile with this picture. One was a laboratory test by Moray (1959) of a familiar experience – that of hearing one's own name in a conversation to which one is not listening, even though one picks up nothing else of what is said. Moray also showed how exceptional this recognition of one's own name is. He used Cherry's technique of playing two passages of speech, one to each ear and asking subjects to shadow one of the two. When he played repeated lists of words to the unattended ear, the subjects could not afterwards recognize any at all. But when he included the subject's own name in the passage, it was heard by at least half the people. In another experiment two passages were changed round from one ear to the other halfway through (Treisman, 1960). At the point of change the word coming to the attended ear no longer fitted what had gone before, while the word on the other ear fitted perfectly. The right ear might hear, '. . . *sitting at a mahogany / three possibilities* . . .', while the left heard, '. . . *let us look at these / table with her head* . . .'. Under these conditions subjects occasionally heard the word '*table*' from the unattended ear instead of the word '*three*' on the ear to which they were listening.

We have also seen that subjects can become aware of what is said on the ear to which they are not attending when both ears receive the same message, but it is out of step by a few seconds.

It might be that the brain is simply comparing sounds rather than words, since both recordings are identical. This can be tested by keeping the meaning the same but making the sounds different, by using two different voices to read the same passage or by using passages in different languages but with the same meaning and playing these to subjects fluent in both languages. In both cases subjects can still notice what is coming to the unattended ear (Treisman, 1961). This shows that the two messages are compared at a late stage of recognition depending on knowledge of words and meaning.

To explain these results we must conclude that unattended signals are not blocked completely. Instead, the filter only damps them down – attenuates them or makes them in some way less likely to get through to recognition. But how can we reconcile this with the complete loss of information about neutral unattended messages? The answer to this must depend on the system used by the brain to identify words.

WORD RECOGNITION

What would be the essentials of such a system? There would have to be a stored memory of all known words against which to match incoming signals, since they could not otherwise be recognized. We need some kind of dictionary in the brain with units corresponding to words or phrases. How would the incoming sounds select their appropriate units? Each might be paired with each unit in turn to see whether or not it matched, but this would take far too long. Since the features which distinguish different speech units are limited in number (Jakobson, *et al.* (1951) has suggested that with twelve pairs of features one can classify all the basic, relevant, speech sounds), it might be more economical for the brain to carry out a series of tests for these criterial attributes, asking for instance, 'Is it a vowel or a consonant?'; then, if it is a vowel, asking, 'Is it an open or closed vowel?' and so on until the correct unit is pinpointed. The basic units of analysis could be words or phrases rather than single speech sounds, but the same principle would apply. In this way each word would be identified by a series of answers to the test questions.

How does this relate to our problems of selective attention? One needs to make a further, plausible assumption – either that we can select which tests to make on the basis of our expectations or interest, or that the tests can be biased in favour of particular answers which are relevant or important to us, so that if we have just heard the words, '*I sang a . . .*', we are ready to accept less evidence from the incoming sound to decide that it is a one syllable word, starting with *s*, containing the vowel *o* and ending with *ng* than to make any other decisions. This would mean that we should hear these important or expected words even when they are much softer than neutral words or when they are masked by noises. This in fact happens: unlikely words like *giraffe* coming after '*I sang a . . .*' need to be much louder than *song*, and a little louder than *carol* or *ditty*, to be heard correctly. Now earlier we supposed that the selective system would have just this effect, reducing the intensity of unattended signals in the brain. This would mean that neutral words would not be recognized because there would be little evidence in their favour, but expected or important words would get through because of the bias of the tests in their favour. This system would also be economical for the brain. The filter only has to distinguish messages by general features like voice, position and so on; the system for word recognition can concentrate on attended messages, and ask only a few questions about the others – 'Is it one of these four or five words or phrases?', instead of 'Which word is it from the thousands I know?'.

The model assumes that two factors determine whether or not we see or hear a signal: how clear or intense it is, which will depend both on the external signal and on what happens to it in the brain, and how strict or how lenient we are in making up our minds about it, in other words, our own internal standard or criterion. The second depends both on how likely the signal is and on whether we will be rewarded or punished for being right or wrong. If we are in the jungle or the zoo we will be quicker to believe our eyes when we see a lion than if we are in a London street; if we are in the jungle we will accept less evidence before making up our minds than if we are seeing an animal in the distance safely caged at the zoo. If we change our criterion because any error is highly unlikely, we should not as a result make more mistakes in the form of false positives (that is seeing it when it is not in fact there); but if we change our criterion because the signal is important to us we shall also inevitably see more imaginary lions when there are only moving leaves, since we need less evidence to be convinced. These suggestions sound like common sense, but were difficult to prove. However, a recently developed mathematical technique from signal detection theory (Tanner and Swets, 1954) allows us to measure the two factors independently, and so to discover which is determining what we see or hear at any particular time. Using this method, Broadbent and Gregory (1963) have tested this account of selective attention and their results so far are consistent with the theory.

TWO KINDS OF ATTENTION

We have shown that selective attention to one source or channel can be accounted for by a filter which attenuates material from other sources, and that changes in the internal criterion for decision can compensate for this attenuation in certain cases. Can the state of this internal criterion also be used to determine selective attention not to one of several channels but to one of several classes of signals which are not distinguished by any single physical characteristics? For instance, can we attend to names of food and reject names of colours, or select words which make up one coherent sequence of speech versus words which make up another, when these are all presented in the same voice and on the same tape? We have a number of experiments paralleling those on attention to different channels. The first was by Cherry in 1953: he was interested in testing whether we can pick out one sequence of words when two are jumbled together by being recorded on the same tape. He found that we can do this, with considerable effort and after a number of trials, provided that the two messages are coherent passages of prose. He suggested that in this case we use the transition probabilities between words – the fact that some words are much more likely to follow a certain preceding sequence than others. He tested this by presenting his subjects with peculiar passages made up of clichés from newspapers strung together at random, sounding rather similar to some typical election speeches. For example: '*I am happy to be here today to talk to the man in the street. Gentlemen, the time has come to stop beating about the bush – we are on the brink of ruin and the welfare of the workers and the great majority of the people is imperilled.*' Here the transition probabilities are high within clichés and low between them. As expected, his subjects often switched to the wrong passages at the breaks, although they usually repeated the phrases between the breaks correctly.

If this is a true case of attentive selection between words rather than channels, we might expect to find other parallels to the previous experiments. One example is shifting of attention: does it also take time to shift our attention from one class of words to another, as it did to shift from ear to ear or from ear to eye? If we present three digits and three names of colours at a fairly rapid rate, it should be easier to recall them if they are presented three by three ('*four, eight, seven, red, green, blue*') than if they are presented alternately ('*four, red, eight, green, seven, blue*'). This in fact happens (Broadbent and Gregory, 1964). It should also be harder to recall items channel by channel if this involves alternating between classes of words, and easier to alternate between channels if this allows one to keep to one class of words; and this also occurs (Yntema and Trask, 1963).

These results reveal some close parallels between the two kinds of attention. However, selection between classes of words is very much less efficient than selection between different sources of sounds. This would be expected, since the criteria at decision points determine much more complex and varying features than the earlier filter. Even when a subject attends to a message in English and rejects one in French, there is no single physical feature which he can use to separate the sounds of the two messages into distinct groups. The criteria he raises to exclude French words must be those determining decisions at a late stage in the identification of words.

EFFECTS OF MOTIVATION

If attention can be determined by changes in our internal criterion, another prediction follows: we should be more likely to see or hear important or rewarding signals than signals which are neutral or unpleasant. Dodwell (1964) found that if he presented pairs of words, equated for probability, of which one was 'good' (like '*butter, truth, flower, Bible, study, light*') and one was '*bad*' (like '*hate, steal, crooked, scorching, putrid*') subjects tended to hear the 'good' ones. This might be an example of the much

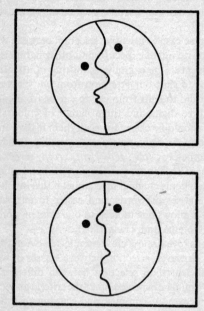

Figure 35. Ambiguous figures composed of four profiles.

discussed phenomenon called 'perceptual defence': the fact that we may be less likely to see or hear threatening or 'taboo' words than other words at the same intensity. The experiments are difficult to control, since subjects may see the words but be shy about reporting them, or so surprised that they decide they must have been wrong. However, some experiments have probably succeeded in avoiding these snags and demonstrated the effect quite convincingly (Dixon and Haider, 1961). It could plausibly be explained by supposing that subjects apply a much stricter criterion for perception of these emotional words than for neutral ones.

A rather different method of revealing personal and emotional determinants of attention is the use of ambiguous pictures, such as those in Figure 35. Schafer and Murphy (1943) tried the effect of reward and punishment associated with different views of the pictures. They showed subjects the four profiles separately; two profiles they associated with a reward of money and two with the punishment of a loss of money. They then showed the combined profiles with neither reward nor punishment and found that their subjects reported seeing the rewarded aspect much more often than the other.

NOVELTY

Expectancy and motivation play an important part in determining attention. A third very important factor in catching our attention is novelty either of the stimulus itself, or novelty to the subject in the sense that he has not recently paid attention to it. External novelty may take the form of any change in the surroundings, a movement, a new appearance or even the cessation of some sound. We sometimes notice the clock stopping when we had been unaware of it while it was ticking. Anyone who has watched a baby will know how easily its attention can be caught and absorbed by a new and complex object; similarly, it has been shown that rats will learn their way through a maze simply for the reward of having a new area to explore at the end. It seems that the filter has a built-in bias to select signals that change or are new rather than others.

A signal may also be novel in the sense that it has been rejected from a subject's attention for some time, although physically present. After one aspect of the stimulus has been attended to for some time, there will be a tendency either to stop reacting to it at all or to shift to something else. If one looks at an ambiguous figure like the Necker cube in Figure 23 it tends to turn inside out from time to time, the rate of alternation increasing as you go on watching it. This change in attention can take place at the level of channels and filters, as, for instance, when a new voice outside the room distracts one from listening to a lecturer who has been speaking for some time. Or it may happen at a later stage – in the recognition of word or meaning, and reveal itself as a change in the identification made of the same sound. If you play a single word over and over again on a tape-recorder, after some time you begin to hear it as a number of new words (Warren, 1961). *Trice* may change to *choice*, *Esther*, *Joyce*, *toys*, *twice*, *dress*, *florist*, *price* or *twice*. It has also been claimed that if one listens to a single note for long enough, it begins to sound like a tune.

VIGILANCE AND HABITUATION

An important example of continued attention to one source or type of signal is the typical vigilance task in which a man must watch for occasional events over long periods of time, usually in a monotonous environment. A factory worker watching for rare defective examples on a moving belt of articles, or a man watching a radar screen for occasional important signals are carrying out tasks requiring vigilance. Performance usually begins efficiently and gradually declines over the course of time. Various reasons for this decline have been suggested. One is that people tend to get less alert and more sleepy in boring surroundings with little happening and so tend to miss more signals as time passes. There is some support for this view from physiological measures of arousal which often decline in these vigilance tasks. Another suggestion is that people know how rare the signals are, so that those that do occur are unexpected and may go unnoticed. This, too, has experimental support: the more a subject expects a signal the more likely he is to see it (Colquhoun, 1961). A third possibility put forward by Broadbent (1958) was that subjects get distracted by other things, and in his terminology they tend to shift to a new channel. The last suggestion (also by Broadbent and Gregory, 1963a) is that the decline is caused by a change in the subject's criterion for the detection of signals, such that he requires more evidence to believe his ears or eyes as time passes. These last two alternatives can also be tested experimentally. Instead of asking subjects simply to respond when they see a signal, as in the usual vigilance task, one asks them to rate their confidence about seeing or hearing the signal on a scale running from, 'quite sure there was a signal' through 'perhaps there was', 'uncertain', 'perhaps there was not', and 'quite sure there was not'. The somewhat surprising result is that subjects do not miss more signals as time passes; they simply get less confident about them (Broadbent and Gregory, 1963b). This suggests that the decline in performance is not due primarily to shifts of attention to a new channel, which would affect the number of signals detected, but to a change in criterion, which might be explained in a number of ways: it might be due to a change in motivation, subjects being eager to please at the beginning so that they try to avoid missing signals by setting a low criterion, which gradually rises as they get bored. Or it might be the effect of a change in arousal. Finally, the criterion should be affected by the subject's level of expectancy, if he is behaving rationally, since he can afford to accept less evidence for a signal he knows is bound to come soon.

CONCLUSIONS

In this chapter I have attempted to sketch in new horizons in the study of human attention. We have come a long way since the two psychologists playing their chord on the harmonium. The horizon has shifted rapidly, and in the last few years has been accelerating its advance as interest and research have increased. There remains a great deal to discover and even more to explain. Little or nothing has so far been said about the output or response side of the human system of selective attention. How far can we divide our attention between two different responses to a single stimulus? This is now being tested and we may hope to fill in more stages of the general model at this end of the chain. Further advances in theory may come from other fields, as the concepts of channel and filter came from telecommunication engineers, and those of signal strength and decision criterion from the mathematical theory of signal detection. Perhaps the most exciting goal is to link our psychological models and flow diagrams with the underlying physiology of the nervous system, in whose study great advances are now being made.

5. INFORMATION THEORY

JOHN BROWN

During the last decade Information Theory has had a considerable impact on many kinds of psychological work. Basically it provides a system of measurement dependent on a definition of amount of information. The definition is such that the nature of the information is irrelevant. Professor Brown compares the concept of amount of information with that of the weight of an object.

This new method of measurement has made possible all kinds of discoveries not only with regard to our communication with the outside world (through perception and language) but also in memory. Professor Brown, who has used Information Theory in his own experiments on memory, describes some of these findings. It is impossible to do such a presentation justice without giving some of the basic argument, and that involves mathematics. However, the mathematics does not require more than some knowledge of logarithms and of ideas about probability.

INFORMATION THEORY, also known as Communication Theory, arose out of the efforts of engineers to assess the performance of radio and telephone communication systems. The theory had a long period of gestation and finally became coherent in 1948 with the publication of two papers by C. E. Shannon and of a book by N. Wiener. It involves precise definitions of concepts important in communication engineering and a theorem, due to Shannon, stating an upper limit to the rate at which information can be transmitted over any given communication channel. The most important definitions concern amount of *information*, *redundancy* and *channel capacity*. The theory quickly excited the interest of psychologists. It provides something approaching a universal language in terms of which man's capacities can be described. One point over which there has been considerable confusion is that Information Theory, as applied to psychology, is not really a theory but a system of measurement. It makes possible the statement of theories in terms of information, but it does not prescribe what those theories should be.

Information Theory

The plan of this chapter is to introduce the concepts of the theory one by one and to illustrate how each has been applied in psychology. As originally defined, these concepts concern properties of long series of events or messages. However, they are defined below primarily in relation to particular events. This greatly simplifies the exposition. Moreover, psychologists do often apply the concepts to individual events or short sequences of events.

AMOUNT OF INFORMATION

Amount of information is defined in such a way that the nature of the information is irrelevant – just as weight is defined in such a way that the nature of the object is irrelevant. Thus any event can be considered to contain information, irrespective of whether the information is important. For example, the event of a coin falling 'heads' contains information, and so does the event of throwing a 'six' with a die. How much information is contained in each of these events? Some progress can be made towards answering this question if one accepts that, in one sense at least, information is *that which removes prior uncertainty*. Receiving a telegram does not yield information if one knows in advance what its contents will be; it yields some information, but not very much, if it merely confirms a strong prior expectation; and it contains a great deal of information if its contents are extraordinary. Now with the die, uncertainty as to the outcome is greater than with the coin, since a die can fall in more ways than a coin. Consequently, the occurrence of 'six' removes more uncertainty than the occurrence of 'heads' and therefore contains more information.

If the number of possible events is n and the events are equally likely, then the prior probability of any particular event is $1/n$. For example, when a coin is thrown, the prior probability of either possible outcome is 1/2, provided the coin has no bias. The information content of such an event is defined as $\log_2 n$ 'bits', where the 'bit' is the unit of information. (Note that ordinary log tables are for $\log_{10} n$ and that $\log_2 n$ is the same as $3 \cdot 32 \times \log_{10} n$. Thus the choice of the base merely determines the size of the unit.) The name 'bit' is a contraction for 'binary digit'.

The two binary digits are 0 and 1. When both digits are equally likely, a binary digit conveys exactly one 'bit' of information. The following table illustrates how the number of 'bits' varies with n:

n	2	4	8	16	32
'bits'	1	2	3	4	5

It will be seen that each time n is doubled, the amount of information rises by one 'bit'. For values of n intermediate between those shown, the number of 'bits' will not be a whole number, e.g. there are 2·58 'bits' when n is 6.

The definition just given applies when the event is one of a number of equally likely events. In general the amount of information in an event is defined as $\log_2 (1/p)$ 'bits', where p is the prior probability of the event. For example, if the probability of 'heads' with a biased coin is 0·53, then $1/p$ is 1·89. A fall of 'heads' therefore contains $\log_2 1·89$ or 0·92 'bits'. (Note that $\log_2 (1/p)$ can also be written as $-\log_2 p$.)

The reader may wonder why amount of information is defined as $\log (1/p)$ units instead of $(1/p)$ units. Consider two throws of a die. There are six equally likely outcomes on each throw. If the two throws are considered together, there are 6×6 equally likely outcomes. Thus, on the $1/p$ definition, each throw contains six units of information yet the two throws considered together contain thirty-six units of information. This paradox is avoided on the logarithmic definition since $\log (6 \times 6) = \log 6 + \log 6$.

In the following applications of the definition of amount of information the psychological difficulty of various tasks is studied as a function of the information content of the stimulus (or stimulus series). With certain tasks one of the simple relationships shown in Figure 36 may hold. Consider the relationship represented by line *A*. This has three features: (1) the difficulty can always be predicted from the stimulus information; (2) the relationship is linear, i.e. is represented by a straight line; (3) when the stimulus information is zero, the difficulty is zero. The relationship represented by line *B* also has the first two features, but not the third: with line *B* difficulty is not zero when stimulus information is zero, indicating that the stimulus information is not the only cause of difficulty. The relationship represented by line *C* can arise if the task is too easy. Here difficulty is zero unless the amount of stimulus information exceeds the value indicated by the arrow.

One of the relationships shown in Figure 36 holds in two out of the three applications described below. It would be surprising

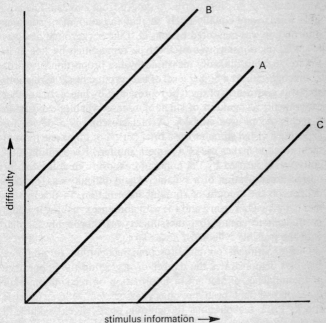

Figure 36. Some possible relationships between the amount of stimulus information and the difficulty of a task.

if such simple relationships were to hold universally. Firstly, the shape of the relationship may depend on how difficulty is measured. Secondly, the way a given amount of information is coded is likely to be important – just as the difficulty of handling a physical object depends not only on its weight but also on its shape and size. Thirdly, other factors may affect difficulty. For example, performance may be affected by anxiety when stimulus information is high.

Recognition. An interesting hypothesis is that the difficulty of recognizing (identifying) a stimulus is proportional to its information content. The results of a number of experiments have tended to support this hypothesis. In an early experiment, recognition of spoken words partially masked by background hiss was studied. The number of possible words (n) ranged from 2 to 256. The possible words were equally likely so that the amount of stimulus information was measured by $\log_2 n$. If the background hiss was low, the relationship was of the type represented by line C in Figure 36, with difficulty measured by the proportion of words not recognized. At a higher level of background hiss, the relationship was very nearly of the type represented by line A. In another experiment, recognition of single nonsense syllables exposed in a tachistoscope was studied. (A tachistoscope is a device for exposing a visual stimulus for a brief period of time: one form of tachistoscope makes use of a camera shutter.) Recognition difficulty was measured by the minimum exposure time needed for correct identification of a syllable. Again difficulty was found to depend on the amount of stimulus information. In this experiment, n varied between 2 and 15: with nonsense syllables, it would be difficult to ensure that the subject was thoroughly familiar with the possible syllables if n was large.

One experiment on tachistoscopic recognition of nonsense syllables demonstrates the danger of neglecting the importance of the influence of amount of information on recognition. Half the syllables had been previously associated with an electric shock. Prior to conscious recognition of a 'shock' syllable, a change in skin resistance, indicating emotional anxiety, was often detected. This was interpreted to mean that unconscious recognition of a syllable can occur before conscious recognition, as might be expected on psycho-analytic theory. However, only one 'bit' of information is needed to recognize a stimulus as coming into one of two categories ('shock' or 'non-shock') whereas 3·32 'bits' are needed to identify which of ten syllables is shown (this was the number of syllables). Thus unconscious recognition of syllables by a super-sensitive detection system need not be postulated in order to explain the results of this experiment.

Span of Immediate Memory. If a sequence of stimuli is presented to a subject one by one and he is asked to reproduce it as soon as presentation is complete, he will be certain to reproduce it correctly if it is very short and certain to reproduce it incorrectly if it is very long. The memory span is defined as that length of sequence which has a 50 : 50 chance of being reproduced correctly. Does the memory span vary with the information content of the stimuli? The answer is 'only slightly'. For example, the span for a random sequence of decimal digits, such as 0944621, is not much lower than the span for a random sequence of binary digits, such as 1000101: it is often around seven digits in both cases. Yet each decimal digit contains 3·32 'bits', whereas each binary digit contains only one 'bit'. The span for words is noticeably smaller – around five words. Yet five randomly chosen words contain many more 'bits' than seven decimal digits, since each word must contain at least ten 'bits'. The conclusion is that the span is much closer to being a constant number of stimulus items than to being a constant number of 'bits'. This conclusion can also be expressed by saying that the size of the span, measured in 'bits', depends largely on the way the information is coded.

Some individuals have an exceptionally large span for a particular type of item. For example, spans of over twenty for decimal digits are found. It seems likely that such individuals are able to code several items as a single unit. So-called 'lightning calculators' tend to be familiar with quite large numbers as single units and to have large spans for decimal digits. One advantage of a reduction in the effective number of units should be that confusions of order are less likely to occur. Indeed, an analytic approach to certain problems in psychology, including that of the memory span, requires a definition of amount of order-information. Communication engineers have little use for such a concept: for example, it is virtually impossible for two signals sent over a radio link to arrive in the wrong order.

Choice Reaction Times. It often seems to be assumed that the reaction time (R T) is constant for a given individual. For example, one reads of a comparison between the R T of a famous racing driver with the R T of the average man. In fact, however, the R T for a given individual varies widely with circumstances. One important determinant of reaction time is the number of choices.

In a typical experiment on choice R T, the subject sits in front of a number of small electric lamps. Associated with each lamp is a button. When a particular lamp lights up, he presses the appropriate button as quickly as possible. Here the R T can be regarded as a measure of the difficulty of choosing the correct button. We will consider first the case where the n possible stimuli are equally likely, so that the amount of stimulus information is measured by $\log_2 n$. A relation of the type represented by line B, in Figure 36, is usually obtained. The R T rises steadily with the information content of the stimulus. Note that the R T is not zero when the stimulus information is zero: it takes time to respond even when there is only one possible stimulus.

An interesting theory to account for this relation between R T and stimulus information is that the nervous system identifies a stimulus by a process of successive classification, as in the following word game. One player selects a word at random in a dictionary containing n words. The second player has to discover the word by asking as few questions as possible: the answer to each question is limited to 'yes' and 'no'. Only $\log_2 n$ questions are needed if the following strategy is followed. (This means for example, that fifteen questions will identify any word in a 30,000-word dictionary.) The player first selects a word in the middle of the dictionary and asks, 'Is it after this word?' This classifies the word as belonging either to the first or to the second half of the dictionary. He then selects a word in the middle of the appropriate half and repeats the question. This shows in which quarter of the dictionary the word lies. This process of successive classification is repeated in the same manner until the word is finally identified. If the number of questions needed is $\log_2 n$, then the time taken for identification will be proportional to $\log_2 n$. If the nervous system proceeds by an analogous process of classification, then the relationship represented by line B in Figure 36, will be obtained, provided the R T consists of the time taken to identify the stimulus plus a constant. The constant is simply the R T when $n = 1$.

If this theory is correct at all, it does not seem to be correct all the time. For in some circumstances choice time does not increase much with the information content of the stimulus. In one experiment the stimulus was administered via a vibrator attached to the finger required to make the response. The choice time when there were eight choices was no higher than when there were only two choices. Here the relation (or code) between stimulus and response is a very simple one. It is possible that the choice time depends on the information content only when the relation is more complex. However, even when the relation is more complex, a very extensive period of practice can reduce the effect of the number of choices on choice time.

So far we have been considering choice reaction times when the possible stimuli are equally likely. When they are not equally likely, a relationship of the type represented by line *B* in Figure 36, again tends to be obtained. The relationship, however, is between *average* RT and *average* amount of information per stimulus rather than between the RT to an individual stimulus and its information content. The average information per stimulus is highest when the stimuli are equally probable and falls as variation in the probabilities of the stimuli increases: this is what one expects intuitively because the more probable stimuli, which contain less information, occur more often than the less probable stimuli, which contain more information.

AMOUNT OF SHARED INFORMATION

In a choice reaction time experiment all the stimulus information reappears in the response when no errors are made. If errors are made, then the stimulus cannot be inferred with certainty from a knowledge of what response occurred. The amount of information shared between stimulus and response, which can also be described as the amount of information transmitted from stimulus to response, then depends on the *extent* to which the stimulus can be inferred from the response. The concept of shared information not only enables us to evaluate the relation between stimuli and responses, as in a choice time experiment, but also enables us to measure the extent to which successive stimuli repeat the same information (see section on Redundancy). The actual way shared information is calculated is basically quite simple, although apt to be confusing. It is given below, but is not essential to a general understanding of the remainder of this chapter.

Suppose a stimulus *A* evokes a response *B*. If $p(A)$ is the probability of *A*, then $-\log_2 p(A)$ measures the total amount of stimulus information. The amount of stimulus information remaining when the response is known is $-\log_2 p(A:B)$, if $p(A:B)$ is the probability of *A* given that *B* has been the response. This represents the amount of stimulus information *not* shared between *A* and *B*. The amount of shared information, which will be denoted by *R*, can be defined as:

The total stimulus information) —

        (The stimulus information not shared by the response)

So $R = [-\log_2 p(A)] - [-\log_2 p(A:B)]$ 'bits'

If $p(A:B)$ is the same as $p(A)$, then *R* is zero. If $p(A:B)$ is unity, then *R* is the same as the information content of *A*, since $\log 1 = 0$. If $p(A:B)$ is higher than $p(A)$, then *R* will be a positive quantity greater than zero. If $p(A:B)$ is less than $p(A)$, then *R* will be a negative quantity. This last statement is apt to be rather startling. How can shared information be negative? However, the possibility of negative shared information is no more paradoxical than the possibility of a negative bank balance. The information shared between stimulus and response is negative when an unlikely response is made to the stimulus: when this happens, the response gives misleading information regarding the stimulus. For a long series of stimuli and responses, the *average* amount of shared information is always zero or positive.

An alternative formula to the one given above for *R* can be obtained by deducting the information unique to *B* from the total information content of *B*. The formulae apply whether *A* and *B* are successive or simultaneous events. In practice, the estimation of shared information is apt to be formidable. For example, in a reaction time experiment with four stimuli and four responses, sixteen stimulus–response combinations are possible so that sixteen probabilities corresponding to $p(A:B)$ above have to be estimated.

Information Theory

Some Applications

Choice Reaction Times. In an experiment on choice reaction times, the subject is usually instructed to make his responses as quickly as possible, but to avoid making more than occasional errors. It is interesting, however, to observe the effect of instructing subjects not to bother about errors but to concentrate on making responses as quickly as possible. Reaction times are now shorter, but the occurrence of errors means that not all the stimulus information is transmitted. If the horizontal axis in Figure 36 is labelled 'stimulus information transmitted' instead of just 'stimulus information', line *B* still represents the relationship found. The implication is that the rate at which information passes through the subject stays constant whether all or some of the information is transmitted.

Absolute Judgements. If a person is asked to judge a stimulus on its own rather than to compare it with other stimuli, he is said to be making an absolute judgement. Usually some form of rating is required. For example, a series of tones of constant frequency but differing in loudness may be presented. If there are four levels of loudness, the subject may be asked to indicate the loudness of each tone by giving a number between one and four. In this experiment there are four stimulus categories and four response categories. Surprisingly, not more than about four response categories can be used consistently when only a single aspect of the stimulus (such as the loudness of a tone) is judged. If four categories are appropriate equally often, then consistent use of these categories will transmit two 'bits' of information per stimulus. The interesting question is whether the amount transmitted rises, falls or stays the same when the number of categories is increased and errors are made in their use. It is usually found that the amount transmitted at first rises slightly and then remains constant at some limiting value between two and three 'bits'. Thus the relation between stimulus information and amount of information transmitted is of the type shown in Figure 37: here the dotted line shows the amount which would be transmitted if no errors were made. One unexpected finding is that the amount transmitted is not much affected by the range of stimulus values used.

For example, with judgements of pitch, one might suppose that if five notes selected from a single octave can be categorized more or less consistently, then ten notes selected from two octaves could be categorized with equal consistency. This is not found to be the case. In one experiment the amount of information

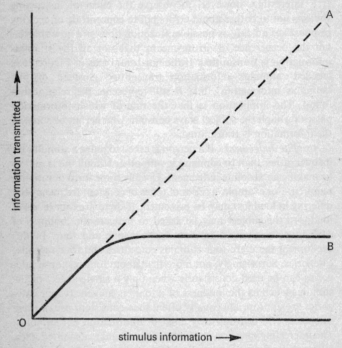

Figure 37. Relation between the amount of stimulus information and the amount of information transmitted by an absolute judgement.

transmitted increased by only ten per cent when the range of pitches was more than doubled. This implies that the accuracy of judging pitch over a given range deteriorates if the range of possible pitches is extended.

What happens when more than one aspect of the stimulus is to be judged? If it is worth using five categories for judgements of the pitch of a sound and five for its loudness, then it would be worth using 5×5 categories for judgements of both pitch and loudness, if the two aspects can be judged independently. In practice, it is found that having to judge pitch adversely affects simultaneous judgements of loudness and vice versa, although a judgement about both pitch and loudness will contain considerably more information than a judgement about one of these aspects alone. An interesting problem is how it is possible to recognize a face (a form of absolute judgement) when there are millions of possible faces. Here the number of usable categories is obviously very large. Now a face has many separable aspects. They include: the sizes of the nose, mouth, eyes and ears; their shapes (and shape itself has more than one separable aspect); the heights of the forehead and cheekbones, etc. If there are only twenty-two separable aspects and each can be reliably placed in one of two categories, then they can form the basis for recognizing any one of about fifty million faces. One remarkable fact is the speed with which the recognition of a face can occur. Part of the reason is that recognition usually takes place when the face is in one of a very limited number of contexts: the face of the butcher seen on a cross-channel steamer can be surprisingly difficult to identify. (Mere recognition that a face is familiar involves comparatively little information – cf. the case of recognizing 'shock' syllables discussed earlier.)

CHANNEL CAPACITY

There is a theoretical upper limit to the rate at which information can be transmitted over any physical communication system. In the case of radio communication, this limit is set largely by the signal : noise ratio. The extent to which the theoretical limit can be approached depends on the way the information is coded. The concept of channel capacity is important to the communication engineer because it enables him to assess whether a channel is being used efficiently. Applications of the concept in psychology tend to be of dubious validity.

Possible Applications

Absolute Judgements. The limit to the amount of information which can be transmitted by an absolute judgement is sometimes called the channel capacity for absolute judgement. There are several points to notice here. First, channel capacity is normally measured in terms of bits per second: in the case of absolute judgement, it is measured in terms of bits per stimulus. Secondly, the capacity depends on how many aspects of the stimulus are involved. Thirdly, the limit is empirical – not one computed from a knowledge of the physical constraints on information transmission.

Serial Tasks. In a task such as typing, performance can be measured in terms of the rate at which information is transmitted from stimuli to responses. In performing any particular serial task, there is an upper limit to the transmission rate. The maximum rate varies from task to task. The highest rate found is sometimes taken to be an indication of the channel capacity of man when he is functioning as a communication channel. When typing random sequences of letters, the maximum rate is about fifteen 'bits' per second. When playing random sequences of notes on a piano, it is about twenty-two 'bits' per second. (These values apply to experts only.) The limit to the transmission rate may often lie in the difficulty of selecting and executing the appropriate responses quickly enough, especially in tasks which are not highly practised. Significantly, the rate at which information can be absorbed in silent reading appears to be as high as forty-four 'bits' per second.

REDUNDANCY

Messages sent over a communication channel are said to exhibit redundancy if they contain less information than they could contain. The basic implication is that shorter messages, using the same range of possible symbols, could contain the same amount of information. In general, sequences of events contain the maximum possible amount of information and are therefore non-redundant if (*a*) the events are independent of one another, and (*b*) the possible events are equally likely. For example, the sequence of events obtained from throws of a die are non-redundant: throws do not influence one another and the six possible outcomes of each throw are equally likely. The sequences of letters and spaces in printed English provide a good example of redundant sequences. Some letters such as *b* are more likely than other letters such as *z*. Moreover, successive letters are not independent: *u* is more likely following *q* than following *t*. Shannon estimated that printed English is seventy-five per cent redundant (though other estimates have been somewhat lower). This implies that the same amount of information could be conveyed by using only twenty-five per cent as many letters and spaces, a space being in effect a symbol. Quite a good way of recoding written English without much loss of information is simply to miss out the vowels and spaces. This approximately halves the number of symbols required. It has been found that over ninety per cent of the missing letters can be guessed successfully. For example: btthtsksfrlyhrd. The redundancy of English is not without its advantages: it makes bad handwriting easier to read, for example. The redundancy of a language such as German is even higher, as any translator from German into English can attest.

The *average* redundancy of sequences generated in a certain way is always zero or positive. However, individual sequences can exhibit either positive or negative redundancy. A sequence exhibits positive redundancy if its parts are so related that knowledge of one part makes it easier to guess another part, as is usually the case with a sentence. With such a sequence, the parts share information in common and the sequence as a whole contains less information than it would contain if its parts were independent. A sequence will exhibit negative redundancy if knowledge of one part makes it harder to guess another part: such a sequence will be composed of parts which are unlikely to occur together. The fact that the redundancy of individual sequences can be either positive or negative emphasizes the danger of taking an individual sequence generated in a certain way as typical of the average – a danger which is often overlooked.

Perception, Thinking and Communication

Some Applications

Recognition. It is possible to construct sequences having varying degrees of resemblance to the sequences of letters occurring in printed English and, as a result, varying degrees of redundancy. To construct a sequence with what is called zero-order redundancy (no redundancy), successive letters are chosen independently and each letter is selected randomly from the twenty-six letters of the alphabet. To construct a sequence with first-order redundancy, successive letters are again chosen independently, but the relative probabilities of the letters are the same as in English text: such a sequence can be obtained by choosing letters at random from a text and has about fifteen per cent redundancy. To construct a sequence with second-order redundancy, the choice of each letter is made to depend on the immediately preceding letter, so that the relative probabilities of successive pairs of letters are the same as in text: here the redundancy is about twenty-nine per cent. And so on. In one experiment, eight-letter sequences were exposed tachistoscopically. For a given exposure time, the number of letters correctly recognized increased with the percentage redundancy. However, when allowance was made for the percentage redundancy, the amount recognized was no greater for sequences with high redundancy than for sequences with low or zero redundancy. Thus, for a given exposure time, recognition was variable in terms of number of letters identified, but not in terms of amount of information gained.

Short-term Memory. We saw earlier that the memory span for items of high information content (such as words) is not very much lower than for items of low information content (such as binary digits). However, the efficiency of short-term memory is not wholly independent of the information content of the stimulus material. If a sequence is redundant because its parts are not independent, it is then easier to remember. For example, the memory span for a sequence of words forming a sentence is very much larger than for an equivalent sequence of words in random order. One reason why such redundancy increases the span may be that it makes the order of the items easier to remember. Indeed, the size of the span may be limited not so much by the difficulty of remembering the items of a sequence as by the difficulty of remembering their order.

A challenging finding in an early experiment on short-term memory was that as much could be recalled from a sequence of words with fifth-order redundancy as from a sequence of words taken straight from text. (In a sequence with fifth-order redundancy, the choice of each word depends on the previous four words so that the relative probabilities of successive groups of five words are the same as in text.) This suggested that it is not the meaningfulness as such of a meaningful sequence which makes it easy to remember but rather its statistical structure. Although this finding has not been wholly supported by subsequent work, it remains true that a meaningful sequence is easy to remember largely because of the redundancy due to its statistical structure.

Perception. Abstract visual shapes which are easy to perceive tend to be symmetrical and to involve straight lines or lines changing in a regular manner and tend to involve few corners. All these properties increase their internal predictability and therefore their redundancy as spatial sequences. It is relatively easy to guess missing parts of symmetrical shapes; it is also easy to guess the missing parts of regularly changing lines; similarly, predictability tends to be higher if there are few corners, since it is difficult to guess what is going to happen at a corner. Thus the ease of perceiving such shapes is probably due to their high redundancy. An interesting technique has been devised for exploring the information content of a shape. The shape has to be represented by empty and filled squares of a matrix. If the number of squares is large enough, quite a good representation of any shape can be achieved. Subjects are then presented with empty matrices and have to guess whether each square is filled or unfilled. At any point when the average number of incorrect guesses is high, the information content of that part of the shape can be presumed to be high. This technique can also be used to determine which of two shapes is the more redundant.

CONCLUSION

The system of measurement provided by Information Theory has been of considerable value in psychology. The case of choice reaction times provides a striking example. The statement, 'Choice time tends to be linearly related to the amount of stimulus information transmitted', goes a long way towards summing up the effects of: (1) the number of possible stimuli; (2) variation in the relative probabilities of the stimuli; (3) the number and nature of the erroneous responses made. Purists are apt to question the validity of applying information measures in psychology. Consider a reaction time experiment with two equally likely stimuli. According to the experimenter, the amount of information per stimulus is one 'bit'. However, from the subject's point of view, this may not be so. He may regard one stimulus as more likely than the other stimulus. Furthermore, he may not completely lose his sensitivity to outside stimuli. Most subjects waiting for the stimulus in a choice time experiment will respond to a cry of '*fire*' or, less dramatically, to their name. While it is important to recognize such complications, one should not assume in advance that they will prove serious in practice: they have not, for example, prevented the discovery of a lawful relation between choice reaction time and the experimenter's estimate of stimulus information transmitted. Excessive caution in applying new ideas is a vice.

Further reading. See Attneave, 1959; Cherry, 1957; Garner, 1962; Shannon and Weaver, 1949.

6. REASONING

P. C. WASON

One of the curious things about the earlier, introspective studies of thinking was that they demonstrated more than anything the inade-quacies of their own methods. The course of thinking is affected by factors which are not available to introspection. Modern experi-mental work has avoided some of the issues by restricting itself to studying what people do when they solve problems. This kind of study has been done with children, with psychotics, and to some extent with animals, as well as with normal adults. In thinking, we use concepts. Such concepts are formed mainly during childhood, and their formation has been studied especially by the Swiss psycholo-gist, Jean Piaget. With adults it is possible to investigate some-thing related – the way in which people discover a concept which the experimenter has thought of. By using what seem to be amusing guessing games, Dr Wason has investigated this kind of reasoning.

INTRODUCTION

WITHIN psychology relatively little is known about the so-called cognitive processes which include reasoning, thinking and problem-solving. Why is this? Firstly, cognitive phenomena are notoriously complex and often reflect the interaction of different sorts of behaviour. Consider a few different activities, all of which might count as reasoning: evaluating an argument, making a deduction, establishing a generalization, proving a theorem, resolving a dilemma, etc. In view of this diversity many psycho-logists believe that thinking and reasoning are not unitary topics which can be studied *sui generis*. Hence, until recently, research in this area has been much less prolific than research in more clearly defined areas such as learning and perception. Secondly, thinking seems to be essentially a 'private' process which is inaccessible to observation. A problem has a goal, and when it is reached the problem is solved. But the processes which lead to the solution are liable to elude the investigator unless he can devise techniques which 'externalize' them. This is not always feasible and, in any case, involves the risk of artificially distorting the processes to be observed.

However, in spite of these difficulties (or because of them) there are many experimentalists today to whom cognition exerts a challenge. What follows is a selective account of some recent empirical research devoted to different aspects of the reasoning process. In the limited space available many related issues must regrettably be neglected, e.g. the development of reasoning in children, the pathology of thinking, prejudiced thinking, etc. It seems preferable, in the space of one chapter, to concentrate on a few central issues, rather than attempt a more comprehensive survey which would be too discursive to be illuminating.

ABSTRACTION AND GENERALIZATION: THE BASIS OF REASONING

The concept formation, or concept attainment experiment is the traditional way of investigating abstraction and generalization in thinking. The subject is presented with a sequence of stimuli, e.g. pictures, geometrical designs, etc., which agree and differ in a variety of ways. At each presentation he is told that the stimulus either is, or is not, an instance of the 'concept' which the experimenter has in mind, the concept being a set of features or relations in the stimuli shared by all the positive instances, and not shared by any of the negative instances. The task is to discover this concept and demonstrate it by discriminating positive from negative instances, or by describing the concept in words. The concept attainment experiment provides a reasonably accurate model of certain types of reasoning which occur in everyday life. The subject learns only that particular instances either fit, or do not fit, an unknown rule. Hence, he has to abstract what is relevant and irrelevant in the stimuli, and then generalize this knowledge to instances which he may encounter in the future. Many interesting results have been obtained. For example, it is known that the ability to discriminate positive from negative instances frequently precedes the ability to formulate the concept in words, and that the information contained in positive instances can be assimilated and used much more readily than the information contained in negative instances.

In the traditional type of experiment the order in which the instances are presented is controlled by the experimenter, and the subject is not necessarily told what sort of thing would count as the concept, i.e. he does not know in advance the 'attributes' or 'dimensions' of the problem. In 1956 J. S. Bruner, J. J. Goodnow and G. A. Austin reported an experiment in which the subject knows all the possible concepts and is free to determine the order in which the instances are tested. The subject is presented with all the instances simultaneously in an array; the experimenter designates one as positive, and then the subject has to try to discover the concept by pointing to successive instances, the experimenter telling him each time whether they are positive or negative. The material consisted of eighty-one instances made up from all the combinations of four 'attributes', each exhibiting one of three 'values', i.e. shape (cross, square, circle), colour (green, red, black), number of figures (one, two, three) and number of borders (one, two, three). Thus every instance possesses one value of each of the attributes, e.g. 'two green squares with three borders', 'one black cross with two borders', etc. The concepts, on the other hand, consist of any sub-set of the attributes in particular values, e.g. 'square' (twenty-seven positive instances), 'green circles' (nine positive instances), 'two crosses with one border' (three positive instances), etc.

Using this task these investigators were able to 'externalize' the reasoning processes and to quantify the information transmitted by successive instances, neither of which can be done when the experimenter controls the order in which the instances are presented, and when the subject is unaware of the possible concepts. Several 'ideal strategies' were formulated which could be used in order to determine the concept. For example, the strategy of 'successive scanning' is to form a hypothesis about the concept, and then to try to confirm it by seeking further positive instances, e.g. if the subject thinks that 'two figures' is the concept, he will test instances exhibiting these features, and only revise his hypothesis when such an instance turns out to be negative. This strategy is easy to use, but wasteful of information. A more logical strategy, 'conservative focusing', is to use the initial instance as a focus, and then vary only one of its values at a time. If the outcome is a positive instance, then the attribute changed is irrelevant to the concept; if the outcome is a negative instance, then the value changed is at least part of the concept. The following example illustrates how rigorous adherence to this strategy ensures that any concept can be deduced in four successive tests.

Given: '3 green circles with 2 borders' (+): *

    1. '2 green circles with 2 borders' (+) (inference: '3 figures' is irrelevant)

    2. '3 green squares with 2 borders' (−) (inference: 'circles' is relevant)

    3. '3 green circles with 3 borders' (+) (inference: '2 borders' is irrelevant)

    4. '3 red circles with 2 borders' (−) (inference: 'green' is relevant)

Solution: The concept is 'green circles'.

This experiment marked an important advance in research on reasoning. Bruner and his associates were able to show how adherence to different strategies affected performance when different sorts of constraint were imposed, e.g. placing the instances in a random as opposed to an ordered array, making the subjects do the task 'in their head' instead of seeing the instances, etc.

The advantages of precision, however, which go with structured tasks of this type, also entail the disadvantage of a failure to match the characteristics of many real life problems. When we start to think about a problem we may disregard some of the crucial factors, and have an inadequate appreciation of what would constitute a solution. All the evidence is seldom displayed before us waiting for examination. On the contrary, we often have to make an important decision about how much evidence to acquire. Furthermore, tasks of this type do not strictly involve inductive reasoning, i.e. reasoning from particular instances to universal conclusions. It is a characteristic of such reasoning that conclu-

* The symbols (+) and (−) signify positive and negative instances respectively.

sions cannot be proved because the number of possible instances is infinite, and a future instance may always refute our generalizations. But in the type of task used by Bruner every concept can be proved since each is satisfied by only a finite number of instances. To overcome this constraint some investigators have tried to devise tasks in which the number of possible instances is, in principle, infinite. Two such experiments will be described.

CONFIRMATION VERSUS ELIMINATION IN REASONING

In 1959 the author carried out an experiment designed to investigate the extent to which people relax their hypotheses about an unknown rule in order to try out alternative possibilities.

The subjects (students) were told that the three numbers 2, 4, 6 conformed to a simple relational rule which the experimenter had in mind, and that their task was to discover it by generating sequences of three numbers, the experimenter telling them each time whether the rule held for their sequence. They were told they were allowed to 'announce' the rule only when they were *highly confident* that they had discovered it. At each trial the subjects wrote down their sequence on a record sheet, together with their hypothesis about the rule. If they announced a rule which was not the correct one, they were told it was wrong and instructed to continue with the task.

The rule was 'any increasing series of numbers' and the point of the experiment was not to see whether the subjects would discover it, but whether they would announce the more restricted hypotheses which entail it, e.g. 'intervals of two between successive numbers'. The very general rule was deliberately chosen in order to facilitate the entertainment of these merely 'sufficient hypotheses'.

This task differs in four ways from the type of concept attainment task discussed in the previous section: (1) the subject is free to generate his own instances; (2) the number of possible instances for any hypothesis is infinite; (3) the subject is not told the possible rules; (4) the correct rule cannot be proved, but any incorrect one can be decisively disproved, e.g. 'intervals of two between successive numbers' can be disproved by finding that an ascending sequence of numbers, without intervals of two, is a positive instance of the rule.

The results showed that more than three-quarters of the subjects (twenty-two out of twenty-nine) announced at least one incorrect rule and nearly half of these (nine out of twenty-two) announced a second such rule during the task. Twenty-one out of the twenty-nine subjects did eventually discover the correct rule, but the interest lies in the way in which they discovered it. The following protocol illustrates in a dramatic fashion the mode of reasoning adopted by the majority of subjects. (The hypotheses are presented after the sequences of numbers, and the announcement of rules is printed in italics.)

8 | 10 | 12 (two added each time), 14 | 16 | 18 (even numbers in order of magnitude), 20 | 22 | 24 (same reason), 1 | 3 | 5 (two added to preceding number). *The rule is that by starting with any number two is added each time to form the next number.* 2 | 6 | 10 (middle number is the arithmetic mean of the other two), 1 | 50 | 99 (same reason). *The rule is that the middle number is the arithmetic mean of the other two.* 3 | 10 | 17 (same number, seven, added each time), 0 | 3 | 6 (three added each time). *The rule is that the difference between two numbers next to each other is the same.* 12 | 8 | 4 (the same number is subtracted each time to form the next number). *The rule is adding a number, always the same one to form the next number.* 1 | 4 | 9 (any three numbers in order of magnitude). *The rule is any three numbers in order of magnitude* (correct: seventeen minutes).

It will be noted that this subject seeks only confirming evidence for her hypotheses ('successive scanning') and this, of course, compels her to announce them as rules in order to find out whether, or not, they are correct. For unlike the previous task, the instances which exemplify any rule can never be exhausted. The subject does finally discover the correct rule, but only after being *told* by the experimenter that each of her previous rules is wrong. There is a peculiar sort of helplessness about this kind of behaviour which was intensely interesting to watch but difficult to evaluate.

If a subject is to avoid making progress in this way, then the task virtually forces the use of an eliminative strategy similar to 'conservative focusing', except that it is not the properties of an initial instance which have to be varied but the properties of the hypothesis based on this instance. In other words, the subject must systematically generate instances which are inconsistent with different aspects of his hypothesis in order to see whether the rule holds for them. But subjects seldom do this. Indeed, in several cases they evidently prefer to reformulate the same rule in different words rather than change it. The following extract from a protocol is the most striking example. This subject had announced the following rule.

The rule is to start with a basic number, then double it and thirdly to multiply it by three. He then proceeded: 14 | 28 | 42 (the first number being half the second and a third of the third), 8 | 16 | 24 (same reason), 50 | 100 | 150 (same reason). *The rule is that the second number is double the first and two-thirds of the third.*

It seemed possible, however, that subjects knew how to use an eliminative strategy, but were simply reluctant to apply it. To investigate this possibility, one group of subjects in a subsequent study was given ten shillings and told they were allowed to keep it if they discovered the correct rule, but would forfeit half-a-crown for every incorrect rule which they announced. Another group had the same instructions without the money. There were no significant differences between the groups in the tendency to announce incorrect rules. The financial incentive only had the effect of increasing the number of instances generated before announcing a rule.

In another experiment, in which the author was assisted by M. Katzman, the subjects were told that they could announce only one rule during the task. If an incorrect rule was announced, they were not told it was wrong, but were asked: 'If you were wrong, how could you find out?' This question was asked in sixteen cases. Nine subjects replied that they would continue with instances of their rule and wait for one to be negative, two replied that they would try out other rules, two that they would generate instances inconsistent with their rule and three replied that no other rules were possible, e.g. 'I can't be wrong, since my rule is correct for those numbers'. (All cows eat grass, all cows are mammals, hence all mammals eat grass.)

In these experiments no differences were found in behaviour between the sexes, nor between psychology students with arts and science qualifications, but the samples are neither large enough nor representative enough to generalize about populations with much confidence. The results do suggest, however, that even intelligent adults do not readily adopt a scientific attitude to a novel problem. They adhere to their own explanations with remarkable tenacity when they can produce confirming evidence for them. And this evidence tends to block the notion that alternative explanations might be simpler, and hence more satisfactory.

THE 'GRAMMARAMA PROJECT': THE DISCOVERY AND USE OF RULES

In the previous task the entertainment and confirmation of incorrect hypotheses is encouraged. The subjects can readily generate positive instances of the rule which are also instances of their own hypotheses, and they come to grief because they conflate the information from these two sources. In the grammarama project, so-called because it uses artificial languages as problem material, no such misleading 'encouragement' is provided. The subject is not given an initial positive instance, and is more likely to generate negative instances at first. Hence, at the beginning of the task he will be confronted with hypotheses which will not work. The project, which was started only in the summer of 1963 at Harvard's Center for Cognitive Studies, is under the direction of G. A. Miller.

The subject's task is to discover the rules which will enable him to combine a set of symbols into 'admissible strings' (analogous to grammatical sentences), no limit being placed on the number of symbols which can occur in a string. The task is completely automated: a computer types out the symbols (consisting of either two, three or six letters), and then instructs the subject to type out any number of them, in any order, in order to discover the rules. The subject signifies when he has completed a string, and the computer types '*Right*', if it is admissible, and '*Wrong*', if it is not admissible. When the subject thinks he has discovered the rules the computer administers a test which requires him to identify strings as admissible and not admissible. If the test is failed, the subject is instructed to continue with the task.

Two types of artificial language have been used. In one type ('finite state grammar'), when six symbols are presented, an admissible string has the form either PJ^nL or OM^nK, where $n =$ any positive number, or zero. Thus P followed by L, and O followed by K would be admissible strings, in addition to any number of Js intervening between P and L, and any number of Ms intervening between O and K. In the other type ('mirror-image' language), every admissible string consists of any string immediately followed by the same string in the reverse order.

At the beginning of the task the subject faces considerable difficulties until he generates his first admissible string. The 'search strategies' which they do use seem to reflect a transfer of plausible assumptions derived from previous experience. Thus they use the symbols to spell out words, or generate strings which conform to some kind of cyclic or repeated pattern. Sometimes, however, the failure to find an admissible string seems to make the subjects abandon any kind of systematic procedure, and instead produce haphazard, random sequences of symbols in the hope of getting a chance 'hit'. The most systematic procedure ('tree strategy') involves the minimal assumptions about the material and it hardly ever occurred spontaneously. It consists in exploring *all* the possible strings of length two before exploring those of length three, length four, etc. Even when subjects were given a hint to use this strategy, which occurred if they had generated thirty strings without any admissible ones, they were apparently unable to utilize it efficiently. It generally had the effect of making subjects permute sub-sets of *different* symbols, rather than repeating the same symbol within a string.

When the first admissible string is generated, however, a different pattern of behaviour becomes evident. The majority of subjects behaved as if they were ignoring the possibility of alternatives to their current hypothesis. The typical subject would continue to generate strings according to his rule unless some negative instance invalidated it, at which point he would formulate another hypothesis and try again. In other words, these subjects were evidently adopting the same strategy ('successive scanning') which was predominant in the previous experiment. Instead of actively seeking to vary their own hypotheses, they passively generated instances consistent with them in order to see whether, or not, such strings were admissible. As a consequence the majority submitted themselves to the computer's test prematurely, just as they would 'announce' a rule in the previous experiment as the only way of finding out whether they were right or wrong. This tendency was particularly marked with subjects who were working with the 'mirror image' language, which, readily induces merely sufficient hypotheses, e.g. *an even number of occurrences of any single symbol*, or, *any triplet of the form ABA repeated an even number of times*, etc. With these mirrored artificial languages, twenty-four of the thirty-three subjects were satisfied with partial solutions of this kind, and so failed to pass the test. In Miller's words, 'once a subject finds a rule that seems to work, he is unlikely to suspect the existence of other positive instances that lie beyond the scope of his particular rule'.

In linguistic terminology, this is an experiment in the discovery of pure syntax, devoid of semantic support, and the artificial nature of the task may well contribute to the inadequacies of the observed behaviour. If, however, the strings of symbols were to refer to some universe of things or events, then the subjects' approach might become more intelligent.

To investigate this possibility a study is in progress in which each admissible string is associated with a graphical operation which the computer performs. If a subject types out an admissible 'paragraph' (any string of admissible strings), the computer will type out the picture corresponding to it. Each admissible string thus becomes an instruction to the computer, so the artificial languages acquire reference in the same sense that a computer programming language has reference. The task of learning the rules for generating admissible strings becomes incorporated into the more meaningful task of learning how to make the computer draw pictures.

The preliminary results of this study suggest that this semantic support for the artificial languages does indeed make a difference: the subjects do not tend to volunteer to be examined on the language before they are ready to pass the test. When the sentences have reference the subject has an operational definition of competence. He knows that he has learned the language when he can use it effectively.

Considerable work remains to be done, of course, before this more complicated learning situation can be understood. But the grammarama project illustrates in a particularly exciting way how the traditional concept attainment task can be generalized and extended to make contact with some of the more linguistic forms of our cognitive processes. The discovery of grammars counts as inductive reasoning just as much as discovering the explanation of a phenomenon.

ERRORS IN DEDUCTIVE REASONING

The experiments described previously have been concerned with inductive reasoning, i.e. reasoning from particular instances to general conclusions. The conclusions derived in this way cannot be proved unless the universe of instances is artificially restricted. In deductive reasoning, on the other hand, the conclusions follow necessarily from the premises, e.g. 'All men are mortal, Socrates is a man, therefore Socrates is mortal.' Such reasoning is less important in daily life, but the errors to which it is susceptible, the so-called 'logical fallacies', are of considerable psychological interest.

Given a statement like 'all x are y', a person is quite likely to say that 'all y are x' follows. Such mistakes have been attributed to an 'atmosphere effect' – the wording of the statement somehow conveys a global impression that the conclusion follows naturally from it. This interpretation was disputed in 1959 by two American investigators, L.J. and J. P. Chapman, who pointed out that the converse of concrete statements in this form is frequently true, and that subjects are simply transferring this fact to the abstract statement. The symbolic content of such statements does not indicate whether the relation of identity, equality or class inclusion is intended to hold. Hence, the errors are due to a very reasonable misapprehension about the logical form of the statement.

A small study by the author, which attempted to divide the process of inference into two stages, suggests that the issue is more complex. The subjects (students) were presented with an array of cards and told that every card had a letter on one side and a number on the other side, and that either would be face upwards. They were then instructed to decide which cards they would *need* to turn over in order to determine whether the experimenter was lying in uttering the following statement: *if a card has a vowel on one side then it has an even number on the other side.*

The task proved to be peculiarly difficult. The correct response is to choose cards displaying vowels and cards displaying numbers which are not even, i.e. odd numbers, since only this combination of letters and numbers on the same card would prove the statement false. The most frequent response, however, was to select cards displaying (a) vowels and (b) even numbers. No subjects selected cards displaying letters which are not vowels, i.e. consonants, and only a minority selected cards displaying odd numbers. However, when the subjects were instructed to turn all the cards and state which of them proved the statement was a lie, all the subjects said that vowels paired with odd numbers proved this, but hardly any claimed that consonants paired with even numbers did so. Thus even numbers were chosen as potentially informative, but were not thought to 'prove' the falsity of the statement. Moreover, this inconsistency between selection and classification persisted when the task was repeated for a further two trials. On the other hand, there was a significant tendency for subjects to learn that odd numbers should be selected as potentially informative.

As is usual in tasks of this kind, the subjects were unable to elucidate their reasoning, but the results are consistent with the following hypotheses. (1) Subjects assume implicitly that a conditional statement has, not two truth values, but three: true, false and 'irrelevant'. Vowels with even numbers verify, vowels with odd numbers falsify and consonants with any number are irrelevant. (2) In spite of explicit instructions to the contrary, they cannot inhibit a tendency to see whether the statement is 'true', in the restricted sense mentioned above. Thus even numbers are selected in order to see whether they are paired with vowels, making the statement 'true'.

The first hypothesis is plausible and in line with the explanation proposed by the Chapmans. A conditional statement with a false antecedent does not seem to be true. If someone says, 'If it rains I shall go to the cinema', we are disinclined to grant that the fact that it is fine inevitably makes his statement *true*. The question of truth does not seem to arise because the statement no longer seems relevant. It was because of this reasonable assumption that the subjects were instructed to find out whether the statement was a lie, i.e. false.

The second hypothesis, however, is more interesting. It implies that the need to establish the 'truth' of the statement predominates over the instruction. An even number with a vowel makes the statement 'true', and hence the subject forgets presumably that an even number with a consonant couldn't make it false. It is only when he *sees* even numbers paired with consonants that he realizes that this combination proves nothing about the statement. This apparent bias towards verification is analogous to the tendency to confirm, rather than eliminate hypotheses, which was noted in inductive reasoning. Similar results have been obtained in a different type of deductive task. More research is needed in order to investigate the 'depth' of this kind of mistake and the conditions which are most likely to correct it once it has occurred.

THE 'GENERAL PROBLEM SOLVER': A COMPUTER MODEL OF THINKING

The experiments which have been described so far were designed to illuminate one aspect or another of the processes of reasoning, rather than attempts to validate a particular theory. At the present time there are several theoretical approaches. For example, the Gestalt psychologists endeavour to explain problem-solving in terms of the way in which a problem situation is perceived. On the other hand, the so-called S–R (stimulus–response) theorists construct their theories in terms of the associations which are assumed to exist between overt and covert stimuli and responses.

Within the last decade attempts have been made to lay the foundations for a theory of thinking in terms of analogies between the way in which human subjects and digital computers process information. The strategy of 'computer simulation' research is to write a '*program*' for a computer based on a study of the methods used by human subjects to solve a problem. The program is then run off on a computer and the resulting performance is compared with that of the human subjects solving the same problem. Any discrepancies between the two are then resolved by varying the program in a systematic fashion and trying it out again. Thus, by a process of successive approximation, an attempt is made to attain an essential identity between the performance of the computer and that of the human subjects. When this is achieved the program which guided the computer is conceived to be a model of the mechanisms underlying human reasoning.

The 'General Problem Solver' (GPS for short), devised by A. Newell and H. A. Simon in 1957 is based on the notion of *heuristics* – general modes of procedure which subjects use when they are solving problems. The problems consisted in transforming a particular expression in symbolic logic into a different expression by means of a set of 'substitution rules', i.e. rules laying down which expressions can be substituted for other expressions. When the subjects were instructed to 'think aloud' while solving such problems, they generally proceeded by trying to relate what they had achieved at some stage in the task to some end which they were trying to reach. In the language of the GPS, 'operators' (substitution rules) were being applied to 'objects' (the symbols in the expressions) in order to reach goals. Within the program these heuristics are formulated in terms of different types of goal which the GPS is able to utilize by a continuous search process in order to solve the problem. Does the computer adequately simulate the behaviour of the human subjects in doing this?

This question cannot yet be answered with any finality. Many remarkable identities have been found between the 'trace' of the computer's performance and the protocols of subjects thinking aloud about the same problem. But there are also discrepancies which *seem* to be due to individual idiosyncrasies. In making these comparisons the most stringent test is known as 'Turing's test', named after the logician, A. M. Turing, who first proposed it in a brilliant paper published in 1950. It consists in asking suitably qualified people to try to tell whether different records of performance were produced by computers or human beings. If this discrimination cannot be made above the chance level, then it is claimed that the program which controlled the computer is a sufficient *explanation* of the human protocols. For the purposes of the test, of course, the protocols have to be 'edited', since the computer does not use language in the same way as a human subject.

The validity of Turing's test has been criticized. It has been argued that even if a program were to survive it, this would not imply that the processes of thinking are the same as the processes which controlled the computer's output. Similar end-products do not imply that they were achieved by similar processes. This criticism is doubtless true, but is not specific to computer simulation. The psychologist, unlike the neurophysiologist, generally has to be content with theorizing about the causes of behaviour by observing how an organism's output is related to its input. There is other evidence, however, which increases the plausibility of computer models of thinking. It now seems possible that theories based on chains of association between stimuli and responses are not adequate to account even for relatively simple motor skills. Hence the computer, which can simulate goal-seeking and goal-directed behaviour by means of mechanisms which can be rigorously specified, may eventually provide a better model for understanding complex information-processing behaviour.

CONCLUSION

In this chapter I have concentrated mainly on the mistakes, assumptions and stereotyped behaviour which occur when people have to reason about abstract material. But the reader may well object that in real life we seldom do reason about abstract material. We reason about the grounds given for refusing a pay rise, about the arguments which seek to justify the manufacture of bombs, about the sort of evidence which would be relevant to the abolition of capital punishment, etc. And in these spheres the claims of reason – the decisions about whether x follows from y – are frequently obscured by conflicts of interest, value judgements and sheer prejudice. The relation between cognitive and affective factors in thinking is, however, a problem for the future.

A deeper discrepancy lies between laboratory studies of thinking and the kind of thinking which occurs in scientific research. In the experiments which I have discussed the subjects know that a problem exists, and that it has an answer. But in research it is even more important and difficult to find good problems than to solve them. And there is no way of working which will ensure inspiration. Moreover, there is some evidence to suggest that people who are judged to be highly creative are not necessarily highly intelligent (see p. 179). The ability to see problems, or to ask good questions may be different from the ability to solve problems. The former is often a matter of intuitive rather than rational thinking, and we know very little about it.

The criterion of a good problem could be defined in terms of the merit of its solution, e.g. a striking reduction in uncertainty, or the re-ordering of a set of facts in a more economical manner. What has to be explained, however, is the ability to perceive that a problem exists, with only the vaguest idea of its possible solutions, and the persistence with which people try to clarify a problem without any immediate reward.

It may be difficult to investigate this aspect of thinking with artificial tasks because the criteria for good solutions are to some extent arbitrary. Certain intellectual activities which have been intensively studied, e.g. chess composition, may provide more suitable material. There are implicit criteria for judging the merits of chess problems and composed endings, in the sense that experts agree at least in differentiating the profound from the trivial. Hence, it should be possible to explore the cognitive processes involved in the construction of problems, as a function of different training procedures and familiarity with different themes and positions. Indeed, if such criteria could be formulated objectively, it would be possible, in principle, to write a program which might enable a computer to compose and evaluate problems, as well as solve them.

A project of this type is, of course, highly speculative at the moment, and it might turn out to be too limited in scope. Better ideas for experiments may be found. What is essential is that psychologists, who are concerned with cognition, should devote their energies to thinking about this little understood, but vitally important, area of human experience.

7. PSYCHOLINGUISTICS

E. DALRYMPLE-ALFORD

As time passes, there is a proliferation of subjects for scientific research. Psychology has been breeding in this way, and 'psycholinguistics' is one of the latest offspring. As one might expect, the parentage is mixed – Psychology and Linguistics, with Engineering as a rather unlikely godparent. Professor Dalrymple-Alford points out that language has been studied by psychologists for a long time, but the relation with linguistics is new, and deserves a name of its own. The chapter describes the sorts of topic which are covered.

LANGUAGE forms an integral part of our behaviour, whether as individuals or as members of a social group. It is not surprising, therefore, that language behaviour has always been one of the preoccupations of psychologists. However, interest has been centred largely around language as a key to the intellectual and cognitive processes of the individual. The development of linguistic skills in the child, for example, may give insights into the content of the child's mental life, while the study of language disorders may lead to greater understanding of mental pathologies. These interests continue, but recently a new trend has appeared. Under the new name 'psycholinguistics', which seems to have made its first appearance in the early 1950s, psychologists are studying language in its own right. The focus is on language behaviour and not child development, concept formation or mental disorders, though there is no question about the relevance of some of the work done in these and other areas.

One can identify at least three influences that have shaped this new trend and still continue to do so. These are: information theory (see also Chapter 5), the psychology of learning and retention, and contemporary linguistics.

INFORMATION THEORY

Information theory has provided a useful analytical framework for the psycholinguist, enabling him to characterize the communication process in terms of a communication channel with a 'source', where the message is generated and 'encoded', and a 'destination' where it is received and 'decoded'. When I speak, I am the 'source'. What I want to say has to be encoded as the message. The generation of this message involves using a linguistic code whose specification is one of the concerns of the linguist, who seeks to answer questions such as: what are the units? what are the rules for their combination? and so on. These questions also interest the psychologist, though he tends to consider them from the standpoint of the process of acquiring the code and the process of using it.

When I listen, I am the 'destination'. Message transmission will be perfect when I receive and decode the message correctly. This will depend largely on characteristics of the message (e.g. how well it was encoded) and on characteristics of my decoding 'apparatus' (how well I know and use the code employed by the source). The psychologist's interest in what happens at the destination concerns the decoding processes resulting in the perception and understanding of the message.

Chapter 5 of this book gives a general account of Information Theory. The reader who desires a fairly thorough coverage of its application to language is referred to Osgood and Sebeok (1954).

PSYCHOLOGY OF LEARNING

The second influence on psycholinguistics that we shall consider arises out of studies of the learning process. For some years now the majority of psychologists working in this field have attempted to reduce behaviour to simple associative connexions, such as stimulus–response bonds. One of the consequences of the belief that this is possible, is the view that we can study the fundamentals of human behaviour by investigating the behaviour of less complicated organisms, such as the laboratory rat. A difficulty that arises is that the human being differs from other animals in at least one important respect and that is in his possession of language. (Not withstanding the general wonder and amazement that is often displayed when accounts are given of the 'language' of bees and other creatures, communication between members of infra-human species is remarkably unlike human language.) Now while behaviourists (as psychologists having the orientation we have described are called) have shown little embarrassment when discarding concepts such as 'consciousness', they are forced to admit that linguistic behaviour does not fall readily into the same category as other behaviour and cannot be ignored if they wish to claim any great degree of generality for their theories, which, based mainly on animal experiments, are extended to humans largely by analogy. In recent years there have been three major elaborations of behaviouristic theories to account for language behaviour. These are associated with the names of Skinner, Mowrer and Osgood, all of the United States. Since any attempt at an account of these views within the present restrictions of space would be foolhardy, we shall pass over them, but not without a comment or two. In the first place, whatever their short-comings, they do suggest the sort of mechanisms that may be involved in the acquisition and maintenance of language habits and they certainly have played a part in the general revival of interest in verbal behaviour. However, they have had a rather limited influence on experimental studies in this area. It is true, of course, that Skinner's ideas (see Chapter 15) have led to many studies on verbal conditioning, but these fall into a very restricted class and leave large tracts of linguistic phenomena as yet unexplored. Osgood's theory has given rise to some work on semantic satiation (see p. 162). Osgood himself is associated with a large project on 'meaning', the principles of which were in fact developed independently of his 'mediation' theory of behaviour. On the whole, however, we have yet to see a large-scale attack, springing from these theories, on the many questions that linguistic phenomena give rise to.

The influence of the psychology of learning on psycholinguistics derives not only from work done within the strictly behaviourist framework. There is another tradition starting with the investigations of Ebbinghaus (1850–1909) who set the pattern for much of the work that is done in the area of human rote learning, or verbal learning as it is often called. One of his more doubtful contributions to experimental psychology is the nonsense syllable – a collection of three letters that do not make a word, e.g. H U L or QXM. The general idea at one time seemed to be that by using nonsense syllables as materials to be learned, it was possible to investigate learning and forgetting without having to cope with the troublesome variable 'meaning'. It did not take investigators long to realize that some nonsense syllables are more 'meaningful' than others and that they had by no means got rid of the problematical question of semantics. As the years have passed, increasing attention has been paid to this topic.

Studies in verbal learning have led to investigations of other aspects of language, such as its sequential structure. However, it is not so much the fact that psycholinguistic studies often have their antecedents in such studies that characterizes the influence of the one on the other, as the fact that the experimental procedures used in psycholinguistics are very often those of verbal learning. This is not surprising when we consider that the first generation of psycholinguists, with a few exceptions, were and still are workers in the field of human learning and memory.

CONTEMPORARY LINGUISTICS

That psycholinguistics should be influenced by linguistics would seem so obvious that the reader may wonder why it should be worthy of comment. After all, what would be more natural and fitting than for the psychologist studying language to acquaint himself with what other students of language have to say and to build on the basis of the work of others? However, the impact of contemporary linguistics can scarcely be accounted for solely in terms of common interests. Rather it derives from the increasing tendency of linguists to adopt what are basically behavioural approaches (see, for example, Fries, 1952), and the fact that the conclusions reached are often easily translated into psychological terms. One consequence of this is the increasing number of studies in psycholinguistics that are essentially tests of hypotheses derived from linguistics.

To say that the psycholinguistic movement is greatly influenced by contemporary linguistics, however, is not to imply that the psychologist and the linguist necessarily find that they can accept each other's conclusions. Further, it would be incorrect to assume that the linguist approves of much of what the psychologist is doing in this field – a sketch of which now follows.

THE SOUNDS OF SPEECH

Speech forms a very large part of our use of language. (There are still quite a few languages that do not have a written script and are by no means rudimentary.) It is to be expected therefore that much attention is paid to the building blocks of speech, the speech sounds. Most of the work to date has been done in acoustics laboratories and is concerned with the question of the intelligibility and, to a lesser extent, the perception of speech. The technicalities of this subject preclude consideration of this work in the present account. Instead we shall turn to a different problem.

The simplest elements of speech are the individual speech sounds, or *phones*. (Of course, a single phone by no means has a simple structure for it is the outcome of complex adjustments of the various parts of the vocal system.) All the phones that a human being is capable of emitting do not occur in any single language, and those that do occur in a particular language do not have the same importance. It is possible to substitute some sounds for others in a word without arriving at a change of meaning, i.e. without getting what is considered a new word or what is not accepted as a word. For instance, the sounds of *t* in '*sting*' and '*teem*' are in fact different (though most speakers of English who consistently maintain the difference in practice may have great difficulty in recognizing it). If we substitute one *t* sound for another in a particular English word, at most the word would sound peculiar but we would still identify it as the same word. As far as English is concerned, the different sounds of *t* are said to be *allophones* of the same *phoneme*, /t/. Another example is the long and short form of the vowel *o* in *mode* and *mote*. The puzzle is why these intra-phonemic differences are maintained. What function could they serve if they can be ignored without affecting the identity of the words concerned? The answer probably lies in the fact that while these differences appear to be of little significance linguistically, they may be psychologically relevant. (For one thing they serve to distinguish the 'foreigner' from the 'native'.)

The difficulty that the untrained person may have in identifying different allophones of the same phoneme has been mentioned. That it *is* possible to make and use the distinction has been shown in a study (quoted in Brown, 1958) using English-speaking and Navaho-speaking subjects. In the Navaho language differences in vowel length are phonemic. Thus, replacing a short vowel sound by a long one would result in a different word. When Navaho subjects were required to classify coloured chips which were named (orally) [ma], [ma:], [mo] and [mo:],* the chips were spontaneously classified into four groups corresponding to the four naming sounds. On the other hand, English-speaking subjects classified the chips into two groups, [ma] and [ma:] in one and [mo] and [mo:] in the other. That is, both the Navaho-speaking and the English-speaking subjects were using distinctions that were phonemic in their own languages as a principle of classification. When the English-speaking subjects' classification was rejected as being 'incorrect', they adopted the same scheme used by the other group. In other words, they were able to perceive and use a feature that was not distinctive in English, probably as easily as the Navaho, for whom it was.

On the whole the psychologist's interest in language at the phonemic level is somewhat restricted. One of the questions that is asked is whether this linguistic unit has any real relevance for the description and explanation of verbal behaviour. It was said earlier that sounds are the building blocks of speech – but are they the units used in the coding and decoding processes at the psychological level? We know that speakers untrained in linguistics spontaneously identify words as the fundamental units. This is made more obvious by the fact that when we write we put spaces between individual words. If these are removed or redistributed without regard to word boundaries decoding may become extremely difficult. Consider, for example, the following sequences:

leavingotherconsiderationsasideitispossiblenottobeableto
und erth espre adin gches tnutt reethe vil lagesmi thys tood

* The colon indicates the long vowel sound.

Further, when we are compelled to break up words into smaller parts, it is into syllables that the words are split. This is demonstrated when we try to speak very slowly. To accomplish this we invariably introduce longer pauses at syllabic and word boundaries. Phonemes as such are seldom isolated in language behaviour.

This question of what the psycholinguistic units are is an important though difficult one, and merits more attention than it has received up to now. Nevertheless, it seems fairly clear that the units are not likely to be identified with the ones that have been isolated by linguistic analysis. A more likely candidate is the 'word'. This being so, it is more worthwhile to study our behaviour with respect to these. It is to this topic that we now turn. Readers who wish to pursue the matter of the psychological unit of speech are referred to Osgood (1963).

WORDS

One of the most obvious characteristics of words is that some are used more often than others. Now the greater the frequency of usage of a word the more likely are we to be familiar with the word and to have stronger habits associated with it. One result that is generally found is that it is easier to identify more common words than less common ones when the words are flashed briefly on a screen. The manner in which word-frequency is related to word-perception is still, however, a matter of controversy. So, too, is the role of frequency as a determining factor in rote-learning studies in which words constitute the materials to be learned.

In contrast to the amount of work done on word-frequency, there have been relatively few investigations of the relevance of word-class (e.g. nouns, verbs, etc.) and word-formation (changes in the structure of a word according to its use) to the psychological study of language. There is, however, every sign that this will be remedied in the near future. Two examples of recent studies may give the reader some idea of the interests of psychologists in these features.

The first study concerns the grammatical class of a word.

Glanzer (1962) found that it was easier for subjects to learn 'content' words (nouns, verbs, adjectives, adverbs) as responses to nonsense syllables (and vice versa) than it was to learn similar associative connexions between nonsense syllables and 'function' words (pronouns, conjunctions, prepositions). For instance, *strange* as a response to *bip* was easier to learn than *of* as a response to *tah*. When, however, these words were sandwiched between two nonsense syllables and the triplets (e.g. *bip – strange – vec, tah – of – zum*) had to be learned, those triplets containing function words were found to be easier. Glanzer suggested that function words are less 'complete' as units and that they would function more efficiently in learning when they were surrounded by other elements. Stated differently, the function words are more readily 'bound' to nonsense syllables to which they seem to bear a more natural syntactic relationship than do the content words.

The second study concerns word formation ('morphology'), or, more particularly, the acquisition of morphological rules by children. These rules describe changes in the form of a word according to whether the word is used in the singular or plural number, or the present, past or future tense, etc. How do we learn the correct usage – to say, for instance, *cow* when we are referring to one of these animals, but *cows* when we are talking about more than one? Is it simply a question of learning by imitating others? Such a view would surely run into difficulties when we consider the relatively short time in which we acquire our native language. The behaviour of adults suggests that we learn 'rules' which we apply to individual words – we do not learn separately all the forms of all the words we use. Thus it is possible for the reader to supply the missing word in the statement:

one mel plus one mel equals two ——

even if he has not come across *mel** or its plural form, *mels* before.

Jean Berko (1958) obtained evidence that showed that children exposed to adult language usage learn rules and do not simply

* The unit of a psychological scale for pitch.

imitate word-forms that they have heard. The fact that they produce statements such as '*he bringed it*', '*there are two sheeps*', shows that simple imitation is not taking place. Indeed, there is a remarkable consistency in the way they form the past tense by the addition of *ed*, the plural with *s*. To get at the sort of rules used by children, Berko used nonsense '*words*', such as *bing*. Children were shown a picture of a man standing on the ceiling and were told:

This is a man who knows how to bing. He is binging.
He did the same thing yesterday. What did he do yesterday?
Yesterday he ——.

Berko reports that only one child out of eighty-six (aged from five to seven years) said *bang*, while the others said *binged*. Of the adults tested, fifty per cent said *bang* or *bung*. Further studies indicated that as children get older their use of irregular forms becomes more and more frequent.

MEANING AND MEANINGFULNESS

Fundamentally, many of the techniques used in investigations of meaning and meaningfulness derive from the association test whose first systematic use is credited to Francis Galton (1822–1911). Basically, the procedure involves stating other words that a particular word makes us think of. There is a remarkable degree to which individuals agree in the responses they give to common words. *Chair*, for example, was given as a response to *table* by more than eighty per cent of the individuals in one study. Does this imply that *table* means *chair*? Obviously not. On the other hand, if we are interested in the question: 'Does this word have more meaning for individual *X* than that word has?' we might find the association test useful – that is if we accept that the more meaningful a word is, the more associations it will evoke or the faster it will evoke them. Meaningfulness could thus be assessed by the number of associates produced in a fixed interval, or alternatively, by the speed with which a single association is given.

To date, the most ambitious attempt to 'measure' meaning is

that of Osgood, of the University of Illinois. The technique he devised, the *semantic differential*, is essentially a combination of the association method and a rating scale. The procedure requires a person to rate the word in question on a set of bipolar scales. An example is given in Figure 38. It shows one individual's ratings of the words *poison* and *laughter*. Eight bipolar scales (angular-rounded, weak-strong, etc.) were used. The individual

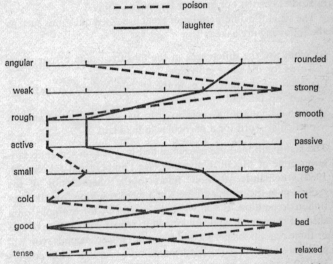

Figure 38. One person's ratings of the words *laughter* and *poison* on eight bipolar scales.

rated *poison* as being quite 'angular' and 'small' and extremely 'strong', 'rough', 'active', 'cold', 'bad' and 'tense'. *Laughter*, on the other hand, was rated as being slightly 'strong' and 'large', quite 'round', 'rough', 'active' and 'hot' and extremely 'good' and 'relaxed'. It should be rather obvious that the meaning we are concerned with here is of the affective variety. The 'profiles' of the two words give us a comparison of the sort of emotional responses the words evoked in the individual.

The polar adjectives used in the semantic differential (only a few are shown in our example) are chosen so that as wide a range as possible of affective meaning is covered. Osgood and his co-workers, using a technique known as factor analysis, isolated three main factors or dimensions of affective meaning for English-speaking Americans. These are 'evaluation' (good–bad, clean–dirty, tasteful–distasteful, etc.), 'potency' (large–small, strong–weak, heavy–light, etc.) and 'activity' (fast–slow, active–passive, hot–cold, etc.). Similar, if not identical, factors have been found in studies carried out in other language-cultures.

The semantic differential is of great use when questions such as the following are asked: *

(i) What are the differences in the affective value of particular words for the same individual?

(ii) What are the differences in the affective value of a particular word for different individuals?

(iii) What changes have occurred in the affective meaning of a particular word for a particular individual?

The last-mentioned use is exemplified in work on semantic satiation done at McGill University (see Lambert and Jakobovits, 1960). 'Semantic satiation' refers to the phenomenon of the reduction in the meaningfulness of a word resulting from its continuous repetition. If you write the word *car*, for example, on a sheet of paper and, while looking at it, repeat it at the rate of two or three repetitions per second for about fifteen seconds, you will probably find the word has become rather strange and 'colourless'. This loss in meaningfulness will be more apparent if you rate the word on the semantic differential before and after the repetition. The 'satiation' of meaning would then show up as a change in the semantic profile of the words – i.e. shifts in the ratings towards the neutral centres of the scales. It has been found that when words that have undergone this change are presented in a list to be learned, learning is retarded. Numbers subjected to this treatment tend to slow up the process of solving simple problems (such as $7 + 4 = ?$) in which they later occur.

Modification of the meanings of words through their repetition

* The use of the semantic differential has been extended to questions of quite a different sort.

can scarcely be considered characteristic of everyday language usage. Changes in meaning are normally accomplished by the use of other words as qualifiers. Thus, differences between the statements

this is rather pleasant

and

this is hardly pleasant

arise out of modifications of the sense of the word *pleasant* by the words *rather* and *hardly*. Unlike the case of semantic satiation, these modifications do not affect the meaning of *pleasant* when it is subsequently used without qualification, as in *this is pleasant*. A study of this sort of modification was published under the intriguing title 'Adverbs as Multipliers' (Cliff, 1959). It seems that the rating of a pair such as *somewhat charming* on, say, the pleasant–unpleasant scale, is predictable from the following relationship:

Rating of *somewhat charming* = (*c*) × (Rating of *charming* alone) + *k*

where *c* is the 'multiplying value' of the adverb *somewhat* and *k* is a constant number derived from characteristics of the scale. The multiplying value, which is empirically determined, is the same when *somewhat* is used to qualify other adjectives, such as *evil* and *ordinary*. The interesting thing about this result is not so much the implication that the action of the modifier is independent of the word it is modifying as the support it gives to the view that even seemingly intractable problems, such as that of meaning and its modification, may be amenable to mathematical analysis.

ASPECTS OF THE SERIAL NATURE OF LANGUAGE

Studies of words in isolation, however valuable, will not take us very far in our understanding of language behaviour. The strings of words that form speech utterances have properties that are not discernable if our analysis is entirely at the level of individual words. In fact, a little reflection will show that in order to study properties of individual words we must refer to their use in sentences. A psychology of language will therefore not be complete unless it offers a satisfactory account of how sentences are created and understood. A first step in this direction is the recognition of the significance of the sequential arrangement of words as they occur in normal discourse. Such arrangements are far from random. When I have uttered the sequence *he came*, the choice of words that can follow is narrowed down. Not only am I unlikely to want to continue with the word *elephant*, but I am also constrained by the conventions of English from doing so. That I still have a very wide range from which to choose should not be allowed to obscure the fact that my choice has been circumscribed.

This aspect of the organization of words in sentences has led psychologists to consider what is known as a 'finite-state grammar' as a model of the way human beings generate sentences. In this view, man is regarded as a sentence-producing machine that can be in any one of a limited number of states at a given moment. Each state corresponds to the selection of a particular word. The state the machine is in will determine those to which it can go next. Thus, if the initial state corresponds to *he*, it is possible to go to *went*, *rang*, etc., but not to *lovely*. Arriving at *rang* it is possible to go to *the*, but not to *she*. In this way it may be possible to produce a sequence that would be acceptable as a sentence. However, we soon run into difficulties. Recall that our finite-state machine is one in which transition from one state to the next depends only on the state of the machine at the time. This being the case, when the machine is in the state corresponding to *the*, a very wide choice would seem open to it and this choice would not be constrained by what occurred before the machine arrived at *the*. We know, however, that when *the* is preceded by *rang* the choice of the next word is more restricted than when it is preceded by *saw*. One way to remedy this defect is to make the transition dependent not only on the present but also on a certain number of previous states through which the machine has passed. Studies of the extent to which verbal context affects the identification of words deleted from a passage suggest that the number of antecedent states need not be much larger than five.

Refinements of the finite-state model still leave much to be desired. Noam Chomsky, a linguist working at the Massachusetts Institute of Technology, has shown that the model is essentially inadequate. He gives persuasive arguments for this view in a little book (Chomsky, 1957) that has had a great impact on both linguists and psychologists. He himself offers an alternative approach. According to this the generation of a particular

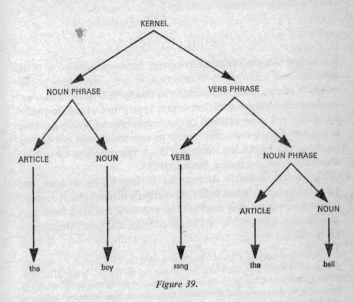

Figure 39.

utterance begins with one of several forms of what are called *kernel sentences* (e.g. noun phrase + verb phrase). We then use rules for expanding each part of the kernel. An example of the process is shown graphically in Figure 39. If we add to this *phrase-structure* model the rules of *transformational grammar*, which enable us to transform the kernel sentence into the passive (the bell was rung by the boy) or the negative (the boy did not ring the bell) and other forms, we arrive at a mechanism that could possibly generate all sentences that are grammatical and none that are not. Note that unlike the finite-state model, there is no suggestion that the final utterance is generated word by word in strict order from left to right – i.e. in the order in which the words are uttered. Indeed, the suggestion is that the production of an utterance begins with a plan of the sentence and finally emerges in the form of strings of words. The psychological implications of these views* have already received much attention and the reader is referred to Miller (1962) for an interesting account of some of them.

CONCLUSION

It is hoped that the sketch I have given, however incomplete in its coverage and arbitrary in its selection, conveys some idea of the interests of psychologists working in this field. I have, of course, made no mention of some important topics that would normally be considered in an account of the psychology of language. This is because I have restricted myself to new trends and not just to recent work. To readers interested in a wider coverage we recommend the book by Roger Brown (1958).

The psycholinguistic movement is still in its infancy. Its achievements may seem paltry, its methods inadequate. However, its record over the first decade of its existence reveals a fresh and imaginative approach to the study of linguistic behaviour that is promising.

* Strictly speaking, I have sketched a version of Chomsky's position that until recently has been current among psychologists. Note, also, that though little space has been devoted to it, the 'transformational' school is beginning to dominate the psycholinguistic scene. The interested reader is referred to the important book by Fodor, Jenkins and Saporta.

8. CREATIVITY

MOYA TYSON

Economic and political factors affect psychology, as they do all sciences. The current interest in creativity is one result. Manufacturers need creative ideas and so do nations. The interest has also arisen because of the suspicion that standard intelligence tests might have been failing to pick out children with creative talent, since most tests are designed to measure abilities in conventional thinking. However, the subject of creativity is of paramount interest in its own right, and Dr Tyson describes the beginnings of research which is likely to go on for some years.

WHEN psychologists talk about 'creativity' research, they frequently intend a more specific meaning of 'creativity' than would be found in everyday usage. Much current research stresses 'discovery' and 'innovation'. This is partly because it is the Space Race that has focused attention on creativity, especially in the U.S.A., for it is considered that the future of a whole society rests on the creative discoveries and innovations of its scientists and technologists. For this reason scientific creativity has been highlighted: it is asked in what ways, if any, creative scientists are different from others. More intelligent? Harder working? Different personality? Different environment, upbringing or education?

However, there is also a generalized and growing interest in the act of creation itself, the processes underlying it, the characteristics of all creative people and in how to elicit and nurture creativity, more so because it has been suggested that there may be a common basis to creativity in both science and the arts. This implies that there are criteria which can be used to grade people – or products – as more, or less, creative, and this presupposes a working definition of creativity. But there is as yet no unanimity about definition. Creativity can be defined in terms of the product of the process and in terms of the process itself (Anderson, 1959; Brogden and Sprecher, 1964). For research purposes, creativity is usually identified by the product, but unfortunately this still raises problems. Who is to judge which products are creative? The history of science has many examples of creative work which was unrecognized at the time. For instance, the French mathematician Evariste Galois (killed by a political enemy in a duel in 1831, at the age of twenty) was so in advance of his time that his work on higher algebra was rejected as unintelligible by the Academy of Science. Galois spent the night before his death feverishly pouring out his ideas, communicating in a letter to a friend a theorem of which the implications could only begin to be understood a quarter of a century later, when mathematical thinking was sufficiently further advanced to be able to use his ideas (Hadamard, 1954).

Irving Taylor, a social psychologist, has analysed over a hundred definitions of creativity and found evidence for five levels of creativity (1959). He suggests that it 'varies in depth and scope rather than type. It is misleading to distinguish between scientific and artistic creativity since creativity involves an *approach* to problems, more basic than the accident of professional training.' The first level is *expressive* creativity, exemplified in the spontaneous drawings of children as in Plate 8. It is the most fundamental form, and probably necessary for the emergence of more advanced levels later. It involves 'independent expression where skills, originality and the quality of the product are unimportant'. At the next level of *productive* creativity (also Plate 8) there is a tendency to restrict and control free play and improve technique; products may not be very different from those of other people. 'The realistic representation of a person by an older child displaces the earlier spontaneous and free expressive conception.' Plate 9 exemplifies *inventive* creativity. The idealized, heroic figure represents a new, exciting way of conceiving man. Invention and discovery are the important characteristics of this level, which involves flexibility in perceiving 'new and unusual relationships between previously separated parts'. *Innovative* creativity is a fourth level demonstrated by few people. It involves significantly modifying the basic foundations or principles underlying a whole field of art or science. This is exemplified in Plate 10, where a 'somewhat Cubist representation of the human form' is produced. The highest form of creative power is *emergentive* creativity (also Plate 10), where 'an entirely new principle or assumption . . . emerges at a most fundamental and abstract level'. The human form emerges in a new, abstract form, 'still capturing human qualities, but departing radically from representational art'.

Apart from problems of level, there is also the question of the areas of human behaviour to which a definition of creativity can apply. How valid is it to talk of creativity in human relationships, for example? A housewife and mother, providing a happy, supportive background for her family, may be being creative, although it may not be possible to assess what appears to be an intangible product.

Despite these problems of definition, research is continuing into several aspects of the creative process and product. Some work is concerned with the study of creative people as identified on the basis of their products, by authorities in pertinent fields, peer groups, supervisors or teachers. The central problem in these studies is that of the *criterion* – the evaluation of the product or process by the amount of creativity revealed; in terms of the criterion some people will be selected as being more creative, or producing more creative products, than others. Writers, architects, chemists, physicists, engineers and research scientists among others have been studied in this way, and some of those studies are described below.

Another type of criterion employed has been that of scores on 'creativity' tests. In this case, the product measured has been the score on various 'open-ended' tests (to be discussed later in this chapter). The inference is that some of the characteristics of successful performance on these tests, such as originality, flexibility and fluency, are also characteristics of creative people; hence the possibly misleading description: 'creativity' tests. The main problem arising when tests are used is not so much that of a suitable criterion, for provided the test results can be scored satisfactorily the criterion may be simply a matter of deciding where the cut-off point or points will be for purposes of comparison (for example, the top ten per cent, or high scorers, compared with the bottom ten per cent, or low scorers). The problem rather is one of *validity* – can inferences be made about the creative potential of high scorers? Are people who show originality within the limits of the tests likely to be creative in other fields also, or at a later point in time? In other words, is it possible to use the tests as *predictors* of creativity? This is a matter of particular relevance to the considerable amount of work that is taking place with school children. This is yet another aspect of creativity research which will be discussed later.

There are various ways in which 'creativity' tests could be validated. For prediction, obviously the best way would be to follow up all the subjects tested, and find out whether the results really did predict creative performance, that is, that the high scorers turned out to be more creative people than the low scorers. Unfortunately, this will involve waiting many years until long after the children now being tested have grown up, and although records will obviously be kept, it would hardly be sensible to abandon the tests until such time as they can be proved right or wrong. An effort is being made to provide *concurrent validity* in various ways, discriminating people on the basis of scores on certain tests and then checking whether the test scores are related to other characteristics which may have value as indicators of creativeness – which brings us back full circle to the criterion problem!

Other research has attempted to study the creative process itself, in individuals, and in groups. It is often considered that the highest type of creative performance (Irving Taylor's 'emergentive' creativity) will come only from outstanding *individuals*. But how far can groups be creative, and will the creative process be the same in a group as it is in an individual? And even if the group cannot attain the highest pinnacles of individual creativity, can it do better collectively than the individuals who compose it? And can study of the creative process in individuals help other individuals and groups to be creative?

Finally, all people live in an environment of some kind all the time: home, school, work, play, other people. There are many differences between kinds of environments and within the same kinds of environment. Some may inhibit creativity, others facilitate it. The final question asked in this chapter – and by no means the last that could be asked – is whether research in the field of creativity has as yet suggested any possible answers.

Creativity

THE CREATIVE PROCESS

Although the upsurge of widespread psychological research into creativity is a comparatively recent phenomenon, general interest in creativity is not new. The process by which discovery and innovation takes place, particularly in individuals, has fascinated and awed man down the centuries. An early explanation of the insight that led to a reinterpreting of human experience and knowledge was that this was a divine madness, a seizure of the individual by the gods. The Greeks – as usual – had a word for it: *enthousiasmos* (from which they derived their word for inspiring creators *enthusiasts*) means *God, within*. Perhaps vestiges of this view remain, and explain the reluctance of some creative people to permit inquiry into the springs of their creativeness, from a feeling almost of sacrilege, and a fear that in so doing the 'God, within' may depart. Yet others have reported on their own creative experiences, and speculated as to the ways in which these came about in themselves and in other people ... there is a 'star-studded' literature on the subject, from Homer and Socrates onwards, and much of what is known about the creative process today comes from this personal documentation. Graham Wallas (1926), enlarging Helmholtz's analysis of what generally appears to take place during the creative process, suggested that there are four stages: preparation, incubation, illumination and verification. Preparation includes an awareness that a problem exists, and possibly the gathering of information about it; incubation involves a waiting period, when the problem is allowed to 'lie fallow' until illumination, the apparently sudden arrival of an insight into its solution, is achieved, after which verification, a filling-in, revising process, follows.

Experimental work such as that of Catherine Patrick (1935, 1937) studying poets and non-poets, painters and non-painters, and J. Eindhoven and W. E. Vinacke (1952), studying painters, has attempted to examine whether these stages occur generally and at all levels. Patrick was able to differentiate the four stages, but showed that they were, in fact, interwoven. Vinacke and Eindhoven also found evidence for the stages, and further illuminated their interplay. They suggested that the stages were not

171

really stages at all, but continuing dynamic processes which occurred during creation. This work suggests that the process is the same both in people in professions generally regarded as requiring creativeness, and in non-professionals, although there will be differences in technique, speed and attack.

'BRAINSTORMING' AND 'SYNECTICS'

Study of how the creative process takes place has led to attempts to make use of this knowledge to help individuals and groups to be more creative, especially in problem-solving (possibly Taylor's 'inventive' level). It is generally considered that the unconscious mind plays an important role in the incubation process prior to the achievement of a creative insight, and some methods deliberately try to facilitate unconscious processes. The intention is to free a person from inhibitions to thinking, and to stop him making premature critical judgements. Alex Osborn (1957) (a member of an American advertising firm) in a book called *Applied Imagination* suggested many techniques for increasing problem-solving ability and developed the approach known as 'brainstorming'. These techniques have been widely used. By calling for a free and uncritical flow of associations and ideas, a large number can be accumulated before any evaluation takes place, and in the meantime the free flow of ideas may have released unconscious associations which have relevance to insightful solutions. The value of brainstorming as an aid to the creative process is still the subject of research. A study by Donald Taylor and colleagues at Yale University (1957) suggested that, in fact, brainstorming inhibited creative problem-solving. They used ninety-six subjects, forty-eight of whom were put into twelve 'real' groups of four people. The other forty-eight were put into twelve 'nominal' groups of four people after the completion of the experiment, when their individual contributions, also using the principle of deferred judgement, were pooled and scored as though each group of four had really worked together. The performance of the twelve 'nominal' groups was found to be superior to that of the twelve 'real' groups in all three problems used.

Various criticisms have been made by Parnes and Meadow at the University of Buffalo. They report (1963) that forty individuals working under conventional thinking procedures (instructed to produce good ideas) produced significantly fewer good ideas than ten groups of four people using the principle of deferred judgement in a leaderless discussion. They further report that forty other subjects instructed to use the principle of deferred judgement were also matched in 'nominal' groups with the original ten groups, and results indicated no significant differences between the 'real' groups and the 'nominal' groups on the two problems involved. The principle of deferred judgement appeared to be valuable, whether used by individuals or by a group (although, in fact, there was a tendency for the 'real' group to do better). Differences in problems used may be partly responsible for the discrepancy between Taylor's and Parnes's findings. Perhaps this type of experimental study produces, in any case, a qualitatively different performance from regular brainstorming groups where more frequently the group is larger, members know each other better and the background of the problem is usually given in advance.

Another possibly better, more structured approach to training in creative problem-solving is that developed in 'Synectics' by W. J. J. Gordon (1961). Synectics method is intended for both individual and group use (see also p. 393). The word *synectics*, from the Greek, literally means the joining together of diverse elements. It is considered that this is what the unconscious mind utilizes in apparently random thought processes, so producing new relations and associations. Therefore, Synectics theory takes as its point of departure the setting up of conscious mechanisms which help the individual or group to utilize both rational and other-than-rational elements of thought. An analysis has been made of the psychological mechanisms employed by highly creative people working at their best ('detachment–involvement', 'deferment', 'speculation', 'autonomy of the subject'). Over the past twenty years Synectics theory has been developed in an attempt to provide a way of reproducing these mechanisms at will, in technology and in the arts. The Synectics process uses two basic operations: 'Making-the-strange-familiar', and 'Making-the-familiar-strange'. The former involves understanding the problem: it is essentially an analytical phase. The latter involves a radically new departure, in that three mechanisms, analogical in character (Personal, Direct and Symbolic Analogy) are used in order to view the problem in a new way, to 'achieve a new look at the same old world, people, ideas, feelings and things'. In so doing, new insights may be obtained which will suggest a more 'elegant solution' exhibiting 'a high degree of utility and simplicity in proportion to the variables involved'. Personal analogy is imagining one's own feelings if one were, say, the tin-can or the lever under discussion. Likening a pipe organ to a typewriter is an example of Direct analogy – biological analogies especially are considered the richest source of direct analogies. Symbolic analogy strives to state the implications of a key word, such as 'focused desire' for 'target', or 'dependable intermittency' for 'ratchet'. Fantasy is encouraged; the ability of the mind to play is considered important, and attempts at hasty evaluation or criticisms of irrelevancies are discouraged. Although 'Synectics' is not as widely known as 'brainstorming', it would appear to have greater potentiality for innovative problem-solving in that there is a more disciplined, specific attempt to utilize the psychological states and emotional aspects which are considered by Synectics theorists to characterize the creative process.

'CREATIVITY' TESTS

In 1950, J. P. Guilford of the University of Southern California, gave his Presidential address to the American Psychological Association on the subject of 'Creativity' (1950). He has remarked (1959) that he was subsequently amazed at the evidence of widespread interest in the subject, particularly from outside the field of psychology. In fact, although there have been in the past some attempts by psychologists to study creative thinking, imagination and the characteristics of gifted people, it is really only with the changing *Zeitgeist* that American psychologists in the past decade have shown an intense and widespread interest in the subject. Sir Francis Galton is perhaps the father of creativity research with his study (1869) of hereditary linkages among people of eminence in nine fields: judges, statesmen, commanders, literary men, men of science, poets, musicians, painters and divines. In the following eighty years a few names were linked with reported psychological research and tests of originality and creativeness, but, in general, interest was not very great. Guilford suggests (1959) that one reason for this was the general adoption, particularly by American psychologists, of the stimulus–response model of behaviour. Although useful, it has had obvious limitations in the study of higher thought processes, especially creative thinking. Guilford's own work has been partly a continuation of war-time research, and has been concerned essentially with exploring the full scope of human intellect, using factor analysis (a statistical technique which identifies the underlying factors responsible for the correlations between tests). Guilford's theory of the structure of intellect has influenced much creativity research. He has suggested (1956) that there are two major groups – thinking and memory – into which the intellectual factors fall and most are thinking factors. These are of three kinds, cognition (in the sense of discovery), production and evaluation factors. The production factors are again significantly subdivided into *convergent* and *divergent* thinking abilities. Convergent (reductive) thinking implies the narrowing down of possibilities in the production of the one possible answer to a problem: i.e. tall is to short as high is to ——? Divergent thinking requires the production of as many answers as possible, as in 'How many uses can you think of for a brick?' Guilford suggested that divergent production was an important factor in creative thinking, and has used and produced many tasks which measure this ability at various levels and with different contents. He also considers that some factors of memory, cognition, evaluation and convergent production are related to creative work. In particular, he believes that creative talent can be measured by tests involving factors of originality, fluency and flexibility of various kinds, and factors of redefinition, elaboration and evaluation. In order to identify these intellectual characteristics, many 'open-ended' (no limit placed on the number of possible answers) tests are being used of which one example is shown in Figure 40. So far the

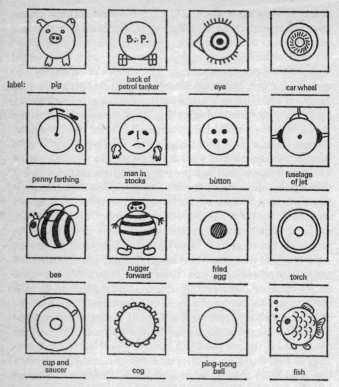

label: pig | back of petrol tanker | eye | car wheel

penny farthing | man in stocks | button | fuselage of jet

bee | rugger forward | fried egg | torch

cup and saucer | cog | ping-pong ball | fish

Figure 40. Open-ended test. The subject is required to invent different drawings all based on the same circle.

results of these tests with groups of people chosen as highly creative have been equivocal.

Other intellectual characteristics of creative people have been postulated on the basis of research; such as intellectual thoroughness, 'curiosity in action', 'openness to relevant experience' and being observant. Attempts are being made to devise tests related to many such distinct intellectual components. But the individual's intellectual performance is influenced by his emotions, his ways of seeing himself and the world and his expectations and beliefs of the world's reaction to him. Therefore, personality and motivation of the creative person have been studied too.

THE CREATIVE PERSONALITY IN VARIOUS FIELDS

Several studies have now been made of creative people in different fields. One institution, in particular, has made many contributions to this aspect of research. This is the Institute of Personality Assessment and Research (IPAR) at the University of California, where present work, like Guilford's, grew out of Second World War research interests. War-time requirements of the Office of Strategic Services involved devising methods of assessing and selecting possible secret service agents and saboteurs. Independence and goodness of judgement were essential. The method of selection used was lengthy, a kind of 'country-house party' extending over several days, while tests of many kinds, interviews and observations took place. On the basis of these a composite picture could be attempted of the individual as a person and predictions made as to how he might behave in emergencies. One surprising thing that emerged was that many individuals with traumatic early life histories were highly effective as people, when it might have been expected that they would be psychologically crippled in later life. Out of the need to know more about human personality, particularly the highly effective personality, the IPAR was established in 1949, and has continued the 'country-house party' method. Groups of people considered highly creative in a particular field are invited for a week-end stay, to be tested, interviewed and observed. The people considered creative are chosen carefully, usually on a basis of ranked nominations by their own professional peers. Attempts are made to compare them with other, less creative people in the same professional field. In this way creative writers, architects, mathematicians, scientific researchers and engineers have been studied.

Researchers at IPAR were impressed by the tremendous quantity of work produced by these individuals. They were characterized by 'diligence, discipline and total commitment' as well as having considerable scope for flexibility. There were possible differences between groups depending on the type of creativity involved – it may be that a writer, poet or other artist displays a different type of creativity from a mathematician or a scientist, in that the former is concerned more with reflecting inner states, the latter with theoretical explanations of natural phenomena. Architecture may involve a different type of creativity again, in that the architect has to be both artist and scientist and more besides.

Although there were differences between the people and groups studied, some interesting facts emerged. All the people studied were intelligent, but it has been suggested that beyond an I.Q. of about 120, measured intelligence is a negligible factor in creativity. It would appear that intelligence is necessary for creativity, but that personality and motivational aspects are more important beyond a certain level, which may be very high. Barron (1963), for instance, reports that the highly creative, prolific writers he studied had I.Q.s of 140 or higher, and it has been suggested that some highly creative scientists have I.Q.s in the 160–200 region. Other characteristics of creative persons included independence, originality, 'openness', intuitiveness, playfulness and a sense of destiny.

Studies by other researchers on various professional groups including physicists and chemists have corroborated some of these personality findings, but produced many others too. When E. P. Torrance recently reviewed a large number of these studies (1962), he compiled a list of eighty-four personality characteristics mentioned in one or more of them!

MOTIVATION FOR CREATIVITY

It is frequently considered that the urge or wish to create is a vital component of creativity. Some research work suggests that deep involvement in and commitment to the field of work is important. Curiosity, an inner need for recognition and a need for self-actualization have also been hypothesized as reasons for creativeness. There are several psycho-analytical theories, too, of how creativity comes about.

Creativity

CREATIVITY AND INTELLIGENCE

The research studies described so far have been on adults considered creative, using various criteria. But the study which really publicized creativity research was that with adolescents reported in 1962 by J. W. Getzels and P. W. Jackson in a book entitled *Creativity and Intelligence* (1962). Most of the adolescents came from middle-class families in Chicago, and were above average in intelligence: the *mean* I.Q. of the sample studied was 132 (the mean I.Q. for the whole population, based on a normal distribution of test scores, is placed at 100 and approximately ninety-five per cent will come within the I.Q. range 70–130). Getzels and Jackson administered a battery of 'creativity' tests to their subjects, including measures such as 'Uses for Things' (give as many uses as you can think of for a brick, etc.). 'Word-Association' (as many definitions as possible to common words such as *bolt*, *bark*, *arm*), 'Fables' (making up three endings, 'moralistic', 'humorous' and 'sad' to four incomplete fables), and 'Make-up Problems' (making up as many problems as possible, given four complex paragraphs containing numerical statements; it was not required to solve, or know how to solve them). On the basis of test results, Getzels and Jackson selected two groups, one of adolescents in the top twenty per cent on I.Q., but not in the top twenty per cent on 'creativity', and vice versa. They then compared these groups on school achievement, aspects of their behaviour and attitudes, and how teachers and parents regarded them. Both groups turned out to be equally good at school achievement, suggesting that 'creativity' is as important a factor in academic success as 'intelligence'. It had been hypothesized that the structure of intellect included 'divergent' as well as 'convergent' thinking abilities, but many conventional intelligence tests appeared to use mainly 'convergent thinking' items. Now it appeared that 'divergent thinking' tests were just as important in academic achievement. Since many selection methods in education are related to measures of I.Q., did this mean that potentially high achievers were being rejected? And if 'creativity' tests were also predictors of future creativeness, what loss did this imply for society?

The controversy has continued. Some studies reported by Torrance have supported the findings of Getzels and Jackson, others have negated them. When groups with an I.Q. range more like that of the general population have been studied, as by Carson McGuire and colleagues (Liberty, Jones and McGuire, 1963) and by Irwin Flescher (1963) there has been much less relationship between 'creativity' alone and academic achievement than 'intelligence' and academic achievement.

Getzels and Jackson did not study those children high on both 'creativity' and 'intelligence', or low on both. Studies by Torrance, McGuire and Flescher suggest that it is particularly the individuals high on both who are the 'stars' of the classroom. Paul Liberty Jr has commented (1962), that Getzels's and Jackson's subjects, and some of Torrance's, were in laboratory schools and possibly already highly selected as far as intelligence was concerned. Therefore, they may in fact be more like the 'high Intelligence and Creativity' groups of the general population. It may be that above a certain level of 'intelligence', there is little differentiation in performance on achievement tests – or the achievement tests may not 'stretch' the highly 'intelligent' sufficiently. Flescher found also (1963) that there was little relationship *between* the various 'creativity' measures he used, which could imply that 'creativity' as measured on tests is not a unitary ability, and that, apparently 'certain divergent-thinking tasks were also widely divergent from each other'. This makes for further difficulties in creativity research, for a large battery of tests may be needed to identify several 'divergent' thinking abilities. What may be in the long run a more important finding of Getzels's and Jackson's study, was that there were also other characteristics which differentiated the 'high I.Q.' and 'high creative' groups. The 'high creatives' were significantly more stimulus-free, fanciful, humorous and tended to express more aggression and violence. Although their academic achievement was equal to that of the 'high I.Q.' group, their teachers preferred the latter; perhaps the pronounced sense of humour was rather trying in class! Although both 'high I.Q.' and 'high creative' groups agreed on what qualities made for success in adult life, and what qualities teachers preferred in students, there were marked differences between the groups on the qualities they valued for themselves, and their career aspirations. There were differences again in the characteristics of the families of the two groups, the 'high I.Q.' family being one in which 'individual divergence is limited and risks minimized', and the 'high creative' family one in which 'individual divergence is permitted and risks are accepted'.

Torrance (1962, 1963) has reported a great deal of research using 'divergent thinking' tests with children of all ages, and also on the characteristics of 'high creative' children (chosen on the basis of his battery of tests) and the attitudes of other children to them. It would appear that the pressures to conformity are strong, and that the 'high creative' child has either to become acceptable to his peers, perhaps thereby sacrificing originality, or become alienated from the group; Torrance suggested that evidence was available for both results. According to Liberty (1962), the children high on both 'intelligence and creativity' appear to be 'the effective blend of individuality and social acceptability'.

CREATIVITY AND THE ENVIRONMENT

This finding that there are pressures to conformity on children selected as original thinkers leads to consideration of factors in the environment which may inhibit or facilitate 'divergent' thinking. From Torrance's work it would appear that pressures to conformity begin at an early age, and if educational values are related to 'convergent' thinking, then the school is a powerful agent for discouraging 'divergent' thinkers. It may be that certain academic disciplines, or methods of teaching them, encourage 'convergent' thinking more than others. In Great Britain, Liam Hudson of the Cambridge Psychological Laboratory, has found (1962, 1963) that there is a tendency for 'convergent' thinkers to specialize in physical sciences and 'divergent' thinkers in history and literature. On the other hand, it may be that a particular discipline attracts a 'convergent' thinker rather than a 'divergent' one, and that this is related to personality.

It will be recalled that Getzels and Jackson found differences in the family attitudes of their 'high I.Q.' and 'high creative' groups. In studying adults considered highly creative, biographical information has been obtained, and this has been considered of such proven value that it is being used in predictive studies. Finally, it is depressing to note that there is as yet 'little scientific knowledge concerning the effect of environment and training on creativity' (Taylor, 1964). Some training methods in use particularly with adults have been described earlier, and Torrance has attempted to use some of Osborn's methods with children. But about the 'creative climate' very little is yet known, although much has been hypothesized; for example, in Carl Rogers's view (1959) it provides 'psychological safety' in which the individual is accepted as having unconditional worth, external evaluation is absent, and there is empathic understanding, and 'psychological freedom', which involves complete freedom of *symbolic* expression. Carl Rogers has suggested ways in which these hypotheses may be tested. Perhaps this will be done in the near future, in which case it may be possible to find answers to some at least of the many challenging questions the study of creativity poses.

ORIGINS OF BEHAVIOUR

Behaviour has origins in several senses. If all people were exactly alike, there would be no such thing as a concept of personality, and there would probably not be a science of psychology. One way of looking at the differences between people is in terms of historical explanations – what happened originally which might have resulted in the differences? Two of the more important answers come from the study of genetics, and of the different experiences which people have early in life. But there is another useful way of thinking of the origins of behaviour, and that is in terms of evolution. The assumption is that human behaviour has developed from the simpler forms found in animals, so that by studying these the psychologist hopes to arrive at basic principles which, with appropriate elaboration, will make sense of human behaviour.

9. THE GENETICS OF BEHAVIOUR

KEVIN CONNOLLY

For behaviour to occur at all there must be an underlying 'structure' – sensory organs, nervous system, muscles, hormonal system and so on. These structures vary between different species of animals, with the result that they show different kinds of behaviour. They also vary between individuals in the same species, so that one can say that behaviour is partly determined by genetic factors. It is a commonplace that heredity should affect intelligence and personality. Recently geneticists, zoologists and psychologists have been experimenting to discover the way heredity controls some of the simpler, instinctive patterns of behaviour. Mr Connolly describes some of his own experiments of this kind as well as surveying the topic as a whole. The study of genetics uses some unusual terms, and a glossary is given at the beginning of the chapter.

GLOSSARY

Allele – One of two or more alternative forms of a gene occupying a particular locus.

Autosome – Any chromosome other than sex chromosomes.

Diploid – Having two sets of chromosomes.

Enzyme – Substance which promotes chemical changes in living material. There are many of these highly specific catalysts.

Gamete – A mature sex cell, ovum or sperm.

Genotype – The whole genetic complement of an individual.

Geotaxis – Orienting response to gravity.

Haploid – Having one set of chromosomes.

Heterozygous – When members of a pair of genes are in different allelic forms.

Homozygous – When members of a gene pair are in same allelic form.

Hormones – Chemical substances secreted by endocrine glands directly into the blood stream; often have profound effects on bodily function and behaviour.

Locus – Position on a chromosome occupied by a given gene.

Meiosis – Process involving two successive cell divisions in which chromosome number is reduced from diploid to haploid.

Metabolism – The chemical processes occurring within an organism. This involves the breakdown of complex compounds (catabolism) and the building up of complex substances (anabolism).

Mutation – Alteration in hereditary material.

Phenotype – Observable or measurable characteristic.

Phototaxis – Orienting response to light.

Pleiotropy – Situation in which single gene has measurable effects on different phenotypes.

Polygene – Factor with multiple action.

Segregation – Separation of a pair of genes during meiosis and random combination with other genes at fertilization.

Sex Chromosomes – Chromosomes involved in sex determination, in humans, females have two homologous X-chromosomes, males have one X and a different Y-chromosome.

Zygote – Cell produced by the fertilization of an ovum by a sperm.

BOTH genetics and psychology are comparatively new branches of experimental science and they have recently joined in the study of the inheritance of behavioural characters. Though it is obvious from animal husbandry that man has known about the inheritance of behaviour for a very long time, it is only in recent years that the science of behaviour genetics has developed beyond a few people in fewer laboratories. The behaviourist influence of J. B. Watson (1924) has been so strong in modern psychology that his assertion that there was no real evidence for the inheritance of traits has dominated psychological thinking for the better part of thirty years. True, there were early experiments on the inheritance of behaviour, but the genetic framework has been totally neglected in theorizing (Hirsch, 1962). Technical difficulties have, of course, played their part along with the environmentalist bias. In the past ten years, however, the research output on the genetics of behaviour has increased enormously (Connolly, 1964).

What has behaviour genetics to offer psychology? This is a very pertinent question and what follows is an attempt to answer it. Not only are we concerned with the transmission of behaviour from generation to generation, in a strictly biological sense, but in addition we may well gain information about the physiological mechanisms controlling behaviour and about the evolution of behaviour. This chapter gives a brief introduction to some basic ideas about genetics and then examines the methods and some of the important findings in this field of research.

SOME GENETIC PRINCIPLES

The basic units of heredity are genes. They are located on the chromosomes, which in turn are found in the nucleus of each cell. Genes are thought to be large and elaborate molecules of deoxyribonucleic acid (DNA), which is known to be associated with the way in which information is genetically coded. The effects which genes exert on an organism are through the control of various biochemical reactions involved in the development and functioning of the animal. Chromosomes, the threadlike structures on which genes are located, are present in pairs in the nucleus of each cell. In the zygote, which is formed by the fusion of the sex cells (ovum and sperm), one member of each chromosome pair is contributed by each of the parents. The various gene *loci* on each chromosome are the same for each member of a pair, though the genes present at these *loci* may be of different forms. These alternative forms of a gene are called alleles, and there may be many alleles for each *locus*. If the genes at a particular *locus* are identical on each member of the chromosome pair they are said to be homozygous, but if contrasting alleles are found at the same *locus* of a chromosome pair they are called heterozygous.

An organism's genotype, that is its genetic constitution, interacts with its environment to produce the resulting phenotype, for example, emotionality, intelligence or height. The number of genes is large; in man, for example, each cell is thought to contain 40,000–80,000 and each gene may produce effects both individually and in interaction with others. From what has been said it should be clear that genes and not phenotypes are inherited; a gene can, of course, only act within an environmental framework. This is an important point, and failure to appreciate it has often led to faulty reasoning.

Dominant, Recessive and Intermediate Genes

In man about thirty per cent of the population is unable to taste an organic compound called phenylthiocarbamide (PTC) in concentrations of 50 p.p.m. (parts per million). The ability to taste PTC is due to the action of a pair of genes which we can designate *TT*. However, they may exist in another form, or allele, which we can call *tt* when the person is unable to taste PTC. These genes are

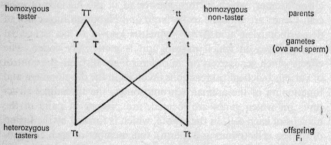

Figure 41. Production of heterozygotes from homozygous types for taster gene (PTC).

carried respectively on a pair of homologous chromosomes. During the reduction division involved in producing gametes (ova and sperm) one member of a chromosome pair passes into each gamete. This process of reduction division which is called meiosis brings about the formation of sex cells which have half the usual number of chromosomes, so that when two sex cells fuse in the process of fertilization the original number of chromosomes, with half from each parent, is restored. Thus people who can taste PTC in great dilution produce gametes *T*, while those who cannot produce gametes *t*. Figure 41 shows the production of heterozygotes from homozygous types.

When the taste test is applied to children from marriages of homozygous tasters and homozygous non-tasters, that is parents who have the genes *TT* and *tt* respectively, it is found that they are able to taste PTC in very dilute solutions. In this case, the effect of the *T* gene is dominant over that of the *t* gene, which is said to be recessive.

If we consider a marriage between two heterozygotes we find that from this sort of cross three distinct genotypes arise, though only two phenotypes, tasters or non-tasters. Figure 42 shows how this comes about. Where an effect can be shown to be one of degree rather than an all or none phenomenon, then intermediate genes are found, neither being dominant or recessive. Quantita-

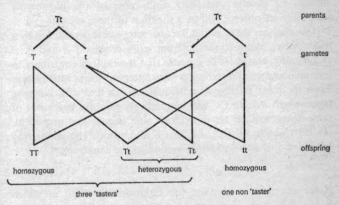

Figure 42. Results of a cross between two heterozygous tasters for PTC.

tive inheritance, as this is called, is almost the rule in dealing with behavioural characters, particularly when these are not rare pathological conditions.

Polygenic Inheritance

Genes such as *T* and *t* which produce conspicuous phenotypic differences are called major genes. The effects of these major genes do not, however, end there; they will have other effects either directly or indirectly. For example, one gene in the fruit fly *Drosophila* causes an abnormal or vestigial wing. The effects, however, are also found in other characteristics such as reduced fecundity and life span. Human albinos not only have an absence of pigment but also are on the whole of smaller stature, less fertile and less intelligent. These other effects of single genes are called pleiotropic effects.

Most of the characteristics which are of interest to the psychologist are of the quantitatively variable kind; that is to say not the all-or-none variety, but those producing 'more' or 'less' effects. These polygenes as they are called have individually minute effects, but cumulatively produce differences in stature, emotionality, intelligence and many other important traits. Because of these polygenes an organism will possess an enormous amount of genetic variability, and most of the phenotypic variability we observe will be a function of these systems.

If we suppose that a particular characteristic is determined by a triple heterozygote (three different pairs of genes) A and a, B and b and C and c, let us suppose that the capitals contribute to high intelligence and the lower-case letters to lower intelligence. Then the most intelligent individual we can find with the gene constitution $AA\ BB\ CC$ will be relatively rare, for every one of these there will be six individuals one degree less intelligent, $Aa\ BB\ CC$, $aA\ BB\ CC$, $AA\ Bb\ CC$ and so on. The population graded in this way will be a function of the expansion:*

$$(\tfrac{1}{2} + \tfrac{1}{2})^6 = (1 + 6 + 15 + 20 + 15 + 6 + 1)\,(\tfrac{1}{2})^6$$

If we generalize and write the expansion $(p + q)^n$ in which $p + q = 1$, then as n gets bigger we get a closer and closer approximation to the normal curve (Figure 43) with the majority of the population being of average intelligence and comparatively few high and low.

It is a characteristic of polygenes that their phenotypic expression, i.e. measured intelligence, is subject to environmental modification. We know that certain conditions such as very severe traumatic shock or near complete sensory deprivation can produce conditions of idiocy in all genotypes. On the other hand, we know little of environmental factors which produce superior behavioural adaptability. An environment which may stimulate one genotype may have a depressing effect on another. Eye size

* For an explanation of the binomial expansion, see Chapter 7 of H. J. Moroney, *Facts from Figures*, Penguin, 1951.

in two fruit fly mutants offers an example, in one case raising the temperature during development produced an increase in eye size, while in another it reduced it, and vice versa. Much controversy and interest has centred around the nature/nurture issue and statements have been made regarding the extent to which genetic variability governs intelligence. At best these findings can only be applied to the population from which the particular

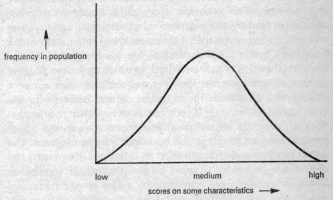

Figure 43. The normal distribution.

sample providing the data came. At this stage in our knowledge it is not possible to say which is the most important environment or genotype, and even knowing this may not be of great help.

METHODS OF INVESTIGATION AND SOME FINDINGS

As with most areas of research, the amount published in the field of behaviour genetics is already large and increases annually by leaps and bounds; consequently, all that can be done in a short article is to consider a few studies which demonstrate the ways in which the problem can be approached. Broadly speaking the approaches to behaviour genetics may be divided into the phenotypic and the genotypic ones. Most behaviour genetics is phenotypically oriented. The investigators start with behavioural characteristics, which are easy to observe or of adaptive value to the animal, and attempt to find a correlation between behavioural and genetic variation. Research of this kind often leads to estimates of heritability being made.

In the genotypic approach the experimenter starts with a standard genotype and studies the effects upon behaviour of substituting various components of the genotype. These substitutions may be single genes, chromosomes or whole sets of chromosomes. This genotypic approach is analogous to other techniques used by the experimental psychologist such as drug administration (see Chapter 14) and electrical stimulation of the brain (see Chapter 12). A particularly interesting aspect of this approach is the study of gene substitutions which are known to affect certain enzyme systems. Enzymes are complex chemical substances which facilitate the metabolic changes necessary to the body's efficient working. If such genes can be shown to affect behaviour, then the physiological and chemical pathways which mediate between genotype and behaviour may be explored. The genotype of an organism can affect its behaviour in two ways: by determining structure (it may control the neural connexions which are made in the brain); or by acting on the functional aspects, for example, the chemical regulation of central nervous system processes.

Selective Breeding

Long before Mendel, man had captured wild animals and bred them in captivity for a variety of characteristics, many of which were behavioural, tameness being a fairly obvious one. The technique is quite simple. One chooses a characteristic pattern of behaviour which can be measured and in which individual differences occur. High scorers and low scorers on the measure which is being used are then separated and males and females at each end bred together. That is to say, high-scoring males are mated with high-scoring females, and similarly at the opposite end of the distribution. The intention of this experiment, of course, is to produce strains which are quite distinct from each other in terms of one particular variable. Obviously this technique can only be used with animals, and only certain species at that. The practical difficulties, let alone the social impediments, make it impossible to use humans.

Anyone who has kept pets will know that there are marked differences in the activity level of different animals. Some are hyperactive, while others are singularly lazy. It would seem after a little consideration that spontaneous activity is probably an important characteristic since it is a precursor to other more complex behaviour patterns. Once a measure of this character has been devised it is possible to apply this to a population and examine the distribution of scores within it. Some experiments of

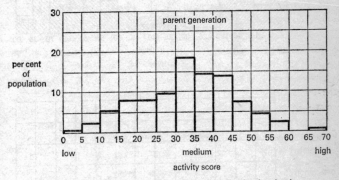

Figure 44. Initial base population from which selection begins.

the writer's have been directed to selecting for high and low spontaneous activity in the fruit fly (*Drosophila*). Activity was measured by assessing the amount of movement the animal made in a standard environment within a certain period of time (see Plate 11). Figure 44 shows the distribution of spontaneous activity in the base population, that is to say, the flies which had not undergone any selection, the parent stocks. Now, if males and females from the low end are bred together, and the same is done for the high end of the distribution, we are selecting for these particular characteristics. Figure 45(*a*) shows the distribution of the high and low lines after fourteen generations of selective breeding; Figure 45(*b*) shows the unselected control population which has been randomly mated for fourteen generations.

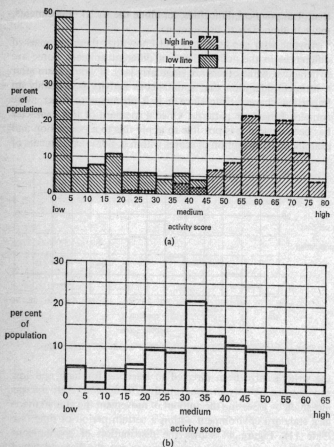

Figure 45. (*a*) After selection for fourteen generations, the emergence of two distinct populations is discernible.

(*b*) Distribution of scores in unselected control population at F14.

Comparing Figure 44 with Figure 45(*a*) we can see that selection has brought about a very marked change in the population. We now have two quite distinct populations, one being composed of very active animals, the other of very inactive animals. That this is almost certainly a function of our selective breeding can be seen by comparing Figure 44 with Figure 45(*b*). They are substantially the same, though these animals have suffered the same vicissitudes, apart from selection, that the other lines have. Genetically, what is happening is this: as a result of the selection process the genes which control activity are being segregated, and so, with the concentration of 'high' and 'low' genes respectively, we are developing two phenotypically different strains of animals. It is, of course, necessary to maintain an unselected population in exactly the same way, so as to control for the possibility of the effect being a function of some other variable.

This technique has been used extensively to investigate a wide variety of behavioural characters, concerned with sensory, receptor and cognitive processes as well as temperament. One famous experiment in the literature of behaviour genetics was performed by an American psychologist, R. C. Tryon, over a period of years and published in 1940. Tryon selectively bred 'bright' and 'dull' rats, whether the rat was 'bright' or 'dull' being determined by the number of errors they made in learning a maze. After selectively breeding the animals for a number of generations, Tryon produced quite distinct strains (which separated similarly to the *Drosophila* in Figure 45(*a*)). A great deal of work has been done on these strains, though the original experiments have come in for a good deal of criticism. Searle (1949) investigated Tryon's selected strains using psychological methods and came to the conclusion that the difference between the 'bright' and the 'dull' rats could be better described as 'timidity', the inferior learning ability of the dull strain being a function of the fact that they are more upset by the experimental conditions, their distress resulting in an increasing number of mistakes.

There is a good deal of evidence to show that some of the psychological processes related to emotion and temperament are to some extent under the control of hereditary factors. Genetic differences affecting emotional traits have frequently been demonstrated; aggressiveness and timidity vary not only between individuals but also between breeds of dogs. P. L. Broadhurst (1960) has repeated and extended some earlier experiments of an American psychologist, Hall (1938), in which he bred strains

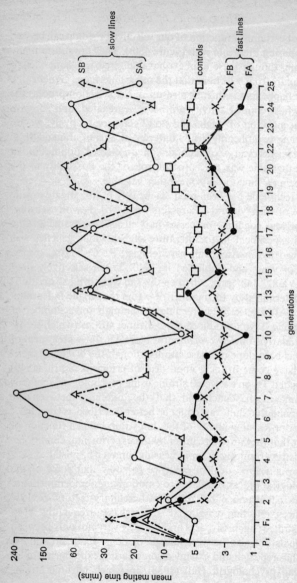

Figure 46. Selection for fast and slow mating speed in *Drosophila*. Selection was relaxed in generations 11, 14 and 21. (From Manning, A. (1961). *Anim. Behav.*, 9, 82–92.)

of rats for 'high' and 'low' emotionality, the measures of emotionality he used being defecation and ambulation score in a standard environment. These strains of rats have now been investigated in many different ways, and several other factors on which they differ significantly have been demonstrated, both behavioural and physical characters.

Other selective breeding experiments have been instrumental in providing us with information about the evolution of behaviour and the importance of behaviour in the evolutionary process.

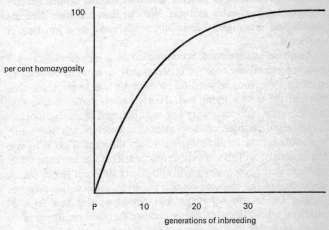

Figure 47. Genetic variability as a function of degree of inbreeding.

Dr Aubrey Manning (1961), of the University of Edinburgh, carried out an experiment in which he selected fruit flies for fast- and slow-mating behaviour. The course of this selection is shown in Figure 46. Starting from the same point Manning bred the two extremes of his base population until, after the twenty-fifth generation of selective breeding, the average time for courtship and mating in the slow line was about forty minutes, while the fast line took on the average only three minutes. Mating speed is likely to be an important aspect of behaviour for the survival of a population and an experiment indicates how particular behavioural traits may have evolved. It also shows how important behaviour can be in on-going evolution; the slow-mating line are likely to be much less well adapted for survival.

Comparison of Inbred Strains

Long-continued inbreeding (brother and sister matings or first cousin matings) leads to the production of very homozygous stocks. That is to say, the amount of genetic variability is reduced, the animals comprising the population, as a result of inbreeding, tend to have genotypes which resemble each other. Figure 47 shows the reduction of genetic variability plotted against generation for brother–sister matings. We can thus compare different strains and investigate behavioural differences as a function of genotype.

As a rule inbreeding is accompanied by a reduction in vigour and reproductive capacity, consequently it is often difficult to stick to a rigorous inbreeding programme and at the same time prevent the strains dying out. There is some evidence also that homozygous individuals are less well buffered against minor environmental changes, and so although genotypically the same, the animals may be phenotypically very different. That is to say, the animals will be much more sensitive to environmental changes and consequently will show very different responses. A great deal of the research carried out to investigate the effects of genetic factors on behaviour has employed this technique of studying inbred lines, probably because this method allows more direct investigations of the genetic factors involved and their properties.

Mahut (1958) investigated emotional behaviour in breeds of dogs. Several dimensions of emotionality were observed, including the dogs' response to teasing, their curiosity and the avoidance of a specific situation. Significant differences between breeds were found in some of the categories, and in addition, the study showed how genetic differences may be obliterated by experimental factors. Rearing in a restricted environment, for example, tended to increase fearfulness irrespective of genetic constitution. Behavioural differences between breeds of dogs is common knowledge; we all know that bloodhounds have something special about their sense of smell, that collies can be used to herd sheep, that alsatians are used as guard dogs; we know, too, that these differences are not merely a result of training but also of breeding. No amount of training given to a fox terrier will produce an animal which is of much use to a shepherd.

A very different type of study, but one of great theoretical and practical importance is the investigation of alcohol preference by different inbred strains of mice. Two psychologists working at the University of California, Rodgers and McClearn (1962) have carried out a series of investigations designed to determine genetic factors in the alcohol preference of mice. They used strains of mice which had been rigorously inbred (brother and sister matings from 17–100 generations) for various research purposes, though not for psychological investigations at the outset. These studies showed significant differences between the strains in terms of alcohol preference. One strain, C57BL mice, showed such a preference for the ten per cent alcohol that about ninety-eight per cent of their fluid intake was alcohol solution. Other strains such as C3H/2 consumed almost no alcohol whatever, and these exhibited a marked preference for water. Various crossing experiments were carried out, such as measuring the preference of the offspring of high and low preference lines (the F_1 generation), which tended to be intermediate between the two. Crosses between two low strains produced offspring whose alcohol preference was low, indicating that heterozygosity alone does not always produce intermediate alcohol preference. In order to demonstrate that the preference for alcohol is not a result of dietary deficiency in the mother's milk, nor a function of imitation, offspring from high preference strains were fostered on mothers from low preference strains. The results showed that the preference of these fostered pups did not differ significantly from young reared by their natural, high preference, mothers. The conclusion drawn from these is that the strain differences already demonstrated were not due to the differences in maternal behaviour, or in nutrition during the period from birth to weaning. All the evidence so far gained from these experiments suggests that there is a genetic basis for these differences. Little information is available about heritability, additivity or dominance, but a polygenic model is favoured by the researchers to account for the

findings. Although the genetic mechanism remains to be discovered, the evidence for the genetic basis of alcohol preference is
strong; accordingly, we are interested in the physiological pathways which mediate between genes controlling this and the
behavioural phenotype. Various physiological factors have been
shown to affect alcohol consumption in rats and mice; the amino-
acid glutamine decreases alcohol preference, whereas vitamin
deficiencies can increase the intake, though decrease in alcohol
preference is not necessarily produced by increasing the intake of
any one vitamin. These and other differences which have been
reported suggest that the differences in alcohol preference of the
various strains is a function of differences in the way in which
alcohol is metabolized by them.

Another example of attempts to unravel the relationship between genes and the behaviour involved is seen in the work of
Grunt and Young (1953) on the sex drive of male guinea pigs. In
an experiment the animals were classified as being of 'low',
'medium' or 'high' sex drive according to their performance on a
series of standard tests. Castration of these animals reduced their
sexual activity to a uniformly low level. When the sex hormone
androgen was implanted into their bodies the level was raised
again. In each case, however, the recovery of sexual activity only
went as far as the pre-castration level, no matter how much
hormone was given. Low drive animals presumably remained
low because of limits imposed by the animals' genetic constitution. We can see also that the genetic control on the amount of
hormone released is not the only factor.

Single-gene Mutants

Another approach to the study of genetic effects on behaviour has
been the comparing of organisms which are different in respect to
a single known gene, mutations at a single *locus* in fact. This
approach is most easily carried out using animals where techniques of genetic control are highly developed, the fruit fly
Drosophila being excellent for the purpose. Margret Bastock
(1956), a zoologist working in Oxford University, studied the
mating behaviour of mutant flies, the particular mutant under
investigation being called *y* or *yellow*, because it resulted in the

flies having a yellow body colour. Bastock discovered that the mating success of yellow mutant males when competing with normal males for normal females was reduced. Yellow males take longer to mate, the average time taken from the beginning of courtship to copulation being 10·5 minutes, whereas the normal (wild type as they are called) males take on the average only six minutes. After a very careful analysis of behavioural differences between the wild type flies and the mutants she found that one element in the courtship pattern was different in the mutant flies. The wing vibration of the male in courtship has been shown to provide important stimuli which are perceived by the female's antenna, the bouts of vibration in the mutant being shorter and the intervals between them longer. Accordingly, the mutant males do not provide the female with as much stimulation. One could, in fact, infer that the sex drive in respect of the vibration element of courtship is reduced. The possibility that this change in behaviour might be indirect, for example, a result of the yellow colour, was carefully checked and discarded as an explanation. Bastock concluded that the mutation changed the behaviour pattern by affecting the level of sexual motivation. How this is brought about is not yet known, though in all probability it is associated in some way with the functioning of the central nervous system.

Many coat colour mutations are known in mice, some of them quite exotic as can be inferred from their names; black, yellow, pink eye, maltese dilute, *café-au-lait*, black and tan. These mutants have recently been the subject of an investigation by a Dutch scientist Hans von Abeelen (1963). Von Abeelen has shown that there are differences between the mutants in respect of certain aspects of their exploratory behaviour and their mating competitiveness. So changes at single *loci* may well have several effects, even behaviourally.

A rare human mutation which results in behavioural changes is a condition known as phenylketonuria (PKU). Less than one per cent of mental defectives suffer from this, which is described as an inborn defect of metabolism. Individuals who carry two abnormal PKU genes are entirely unable to metabolize the amino-acid phenylalanine. These homozygotes for the mutant gene are always of low intelligence and seldom above the imbecile level. The precise cause of the mental defect associated with P K U is not known, though one theory is that it results from the toxic properties of one of the chemicals which is not broken down. Research is going on in an attempt to determine the exact cause of the mental defect, and also into attempts to alleviate the condition.

Family Pedigree Studies

The most direct method of determining the mode of inheritance of a trait is to examine the pedigree of a family, which has the relevant trait, and to attempt to fit to it a hypothesis of dominant, recessive or sex-linked inheritance. An example of the sort of characteristic which may be studied in this way is that of colour blindness. In a series of cases it appeared only in the male members, though the females were apparently carriers; hence it is possible to infer that the character is sex linked, that is, carried on the sex chromosomes. By tracing the incidence through a family we can show that it is a sex-linked recessive gene which determines colour blindness. There are difficulties and dangers involved in this method; inevitably tracing back a family tree it becomes impossible to apply scientific tests to long dead ancestors and one can rely only on anecdotal information which has often been shown to be quite inadequate and misleading.

Sir Francis Galton (1883) was the first person who attempted to trace family pedigrees scientifically. He was particularly interested in eminent men or people of unusually high intellectual endowment. On the basis of reputations and records he constructed pedigrees of distinguished statesmen, literary men, scientists, poets, musicians and so forth. Galton found from his data that the chance of eminent men having eminent relatives was high, from which he inferred that intellectual ability was clearly inherited. To what extent this is a result of the environment, however, poses a great problem, and the results must remain questionable. Pedigrees of royal families and other similarly distinguishable classes of people cannot be described in precise terms, but they are worth an examination. The Bach family, which was studied by Galton, is an interesting case in point. Although the problem of separating nature from nurture is an insuperable one in this case, the amount of musical ability that consistently appears in the Bach family for a number of generations is strongly suggestive of hereditary components. But the value of pedigree studies is limited by the complications of environmental factors. Intelligent parents supply their children not only with genes for high intelligence but also with a type of environment which is stimulating to mental development.

Twin Studies

Twins may be monozygotic (*MZ*), when they are derived from the splitting of a single fertilized ovum, or dizygotic (*DZ*), derived from the fertilization and development of independently formed ova. Monozygotic co-twins share identical sets of genes. They have, in fact, a common genotype, and are normally called 'identical twins'. Actually this description is not strictly accurate, since few traits are determined solely by heredity and the differences between identical twins may become considerable as they grow up. Dizygotic twins are no more alike genetically than ordinary siblings (brothers and sisters), and are commonly called 'fraternal twins'. Since *DZ* twins share a common prenatal environment and usually grow up together, one might expect them to be more alike than siblings born at different times. These greater similarities, however, are a function of environmental and not genetic factors.

There are many important points which must be taken into account when carrying out twin studies, and too often these factors have not been adequately controlled. Determining whether a set of twins is identical or fraternal is not, in fact, as easy as one might expect and usually requires a very careful analysis of their blood groupings. It is of great importance that all pairs should be taken from the same population as defined by age, culture and geographical location, so as to reduce the complications that differences in these factors would add.

It follows from what has been said above that the differences between members of an *MZ* pair arise from an environmental origin, while differences between members of a *DZ* pair arise from environmental and genetic sources. In its simplest form the reasoning involved in any comparison of the two twin types is as follows. If *DZ* pairs are more unlike than *MZ* pairs the excess is a result of hereditary factors. Fuller and Thompson (1960) have expressed it symbolically in the following way:

$$D_{dz} = E + H$$
$$D_{mz} = E$$
$$D_{dz} - D_{mz} = H$$

where E and H are differences in environment and heredity respectively, D_{dz} differences in scores between dizygotic co-twins and D_{mz} differences in scores between monozygotic co-twins. The way in which the relationships are stated above gives the impression that this sort of investigation is really rather straightforward. There are, however, a number of complications which may lead to somewhat distorted results. A number of sources of error have been assumed to diminish D_{mz} as compared with D_{dz} and lead to an over-emphasis of the importance of heredity. *MZ* pairs tend to be together more, to select similar surroundings and friends to a greater extent than *DZ* pairs. *MZ* twins are treated more alike, and are even confused by parents and members of the family, and in addition, *MZ* co-twins model their behaviour on each other to a much greater extent than do *DZ* co-twins. Other possible sources of error might enlarge D_{mz} relative to D_{dz} and result in an underestimation of the importance of heredity. The uterine conditions of twins having only one set of membranes (monochorionic), particularly because they have a common circulation, may be unfavourable for one of the twins and result in environmental variation which is unique for *MZ* pairs. Older identical twins have been known to adopt complementary roles in their outside contacts; sometimes a rebellion against identification with the co-twin may lead to the adoption of a different role. To some extent these two sources of error balance themselves out, and little control can be exerted over natal and pre-natal biases which are essentially part of being a twin. Similarly, it is impossible to keep in step developmentally, genetically different *DZ* pairs, as is possible to a much greater extent in *MZ* twins. The different genotypes of the *DZ* pair must act differently on the environment and their responses lead to yet further differentiation on the genotypic case.

Basically, two types of approach are used in twin studies. The first is concerned with determining the intra-pair variability for both mono- and dizygotic twins which may enable one to calculate the extent to which hereditary factors control specific aspects of behaviour within any given sample. McNemar (1933) studied twin resemblances on five tests of motor skill. He found that the correlations in monozygotic pairs was much higher than within dizygotic pairs. This, he concluded, was strong evidence for hereditary factors being at work. After practice, the differences still existed to the same extent, though the level at which the skills were manifested had increased. Galton (1883), using data he obtained from questionnaires given to a large number of twins, found a close similarity between members of a pair for a variety of different characters. His conclusions, though based on rather meagre information, have since been largely substantiated. Since Galton's early work there have been many studies comparing the intelligence and intellectual abilities of *MZ* and *DZ* twins. Between pairs in a population we see quite clearly that there is a greater degree of relationship between *MZ* pairs on the same tests. From these findings it has been inferred that part at least of intelligence is inherited. Blewett (1954) published the results of an investigation in which he compared *MZ* and *DZ* twins on a series of tests which enabled him to study some of the components of intelligence. The Thurstone test of Primary Mental Abilities was one that he used. This test can be broken down into such factors as verbal ability, spatial ability, number ability, reasoning and so on. From the results obtained, tests of verbal ability, verbal comprehension and reasoning showed determination by heredity to a much greater extent than number and spatial ability. Of these findings Blewett said, 'One might speculate on this basis that good General Arts students, relying as they do on facility with verbal material, are born; whereas the mathematicians, statisticians, engineers and so forth must toil to earn their skills.' If this conclusion is correct, then it is obviously of great importance.

All these studies show much greater similarities between members of an identical pair (*MZ*) when compared with members of a fraternal pair (*DZ*). However, to what extent this is a function of their having more similar environments is unknown, and the method of co-twin control does not tell us much about this. Observations on twins reared apart attempt to overcome this difficulty (and also to assess the plasticity of psychological expression of a single genotype). Differences between twins reared apart and reared together represent the differentiating effects of the environment. Cases of twins reared apart are rare, and when they are found may well be a very unrepresentative sample of twins. In other words, there may be many special complicating factors, and certainly one needs to ask why they were separated. In 1937 Newman, Freeman and Holzinger investigated nineteen pairs of *MZ* twins reared apart. They compared identical twins reared together, fraternal twins reared together and the nineteen pairs of identicals reared apart. There were several important variables which proved difficult to control. The age ranges of the sample, for instance, varied from eleven to fifty-three; moreover, equally large differences were found in the educational background of the twins. Despite these factors, however, the correlations between members of any *MZ* pair reared apart in respect of intelligence test scores was higher than the *DZ* group reared together, though less than the *MZ* control group reared together. These results are perhaps what one might expect. The evidence supports the heredity hypothesis, though there is little doubt that large differences in environment can affect the similarity between separated *MZ* twins.

Since this early work there have been a few more studies on identicals reared apart, one of the most recent being that carried out by James Sheilds (1962) at the Maudsley Hospital, London. Sheilds, whose primary interest lay in discovering the part played by genetic factors in determining personality, obtained his sample of twins, reared apart, by a television appeal. His results were in agreement with the earlier workers and he emphasized that family environments could vary considerably without obscuring the basic similarity in a pair of *MZ* twins, and at the same time, that *MZ* twins brought up together can differ quite widely. No doubt the importance of genotype will vary for different psychological characteristics, and one task of future research will be to discover these variations.

The Genetics of Behaviour

LOOKING TO THE FUTURE

To predict significant developments in an area of scientific research as wide as this one is difficult and in consequence any selection is inevitably arbitrary. The work of Hirsch (op. cit.) on geotaxis and phototaxis provides an excellent example of the level of experimental sophistication which can be reached in tackling some problems. In many ways we may expect developments in this field to throw new light on old problems, for example, the experiments of Moray and Connolly (1963) on the inheritance of acquired behavioural characteristics may lead to new views on the origin of instinctive responses. Broadhurst and Jinks (1963) have shown that the powerful tools provided by biometrical methods of analysis can be applied to extract information from experimental data. In the field of human behaviour increasing research in biochemical genetics may well provide new methods of treating some behaviour disorders, and developmental studies on infant twins should also provide a great deal of information and insight into the factors which determine behaviour.

Since this chapter was written an important new book has been published by Scott and Fuller (1965). It gives an account of some thirteen years' work at the Jackson Memorial Laboratory in Bar Harbor on genetics and the development of behaviour in the dog.

Scott and Fuller have devised a variety of situations for studying the development of behaviour in puppies. Using these techniques they have investigated behavioural development in several pure-bred strains. By means of crossing experiments and measuring the resultant hybrids they have also attempted genetic analyses for these characters. Various stages of development were examined: neonatal, transition, socialisation and juvenile, in the development of sensory and motor capacities for both individual and social behaviour patterns. About 5000 'pure' bred and hybrid puppies were observed throughout their first year of life in some thirty-five different test situations. They found breed differences in emotionality, problem solving and learning, and they have produced a most comprehensive study on the behaviour of puppies from an ethological standpoint.

Behaviour is not biologically inherited as such. The first

activity of the organism as a whole occurs during the foetal period when developing muscles begin to twitch. As a consequence it follows that behaviour must be *developed* and developed under the combined influence of hereditary and numerous environmental factors. The work of Scott and Fuller takes this developmental approach and in so doing adopts the position which Thoday (1965) has recently made explicit. 'Genotype determines the potentialities of an organism. Environment determines which or how much of these potentialities shall be realised during *development*.'* That the interaction of genotype and environment is responsible for the resultant phenotype is widely acknowledged but research of this kind reinforces the view in a practical manner.

Acknowledgements. I would like to thank the Kittay Foundation for a research grant which facilitated my experiments reported in this paper.

* Italics mine. K.C.

10. THE BEHAVIOUR OF INVERTEBRATES

J. D. CARTHY

The rat is still the favourite animal for psychological study, and for many investigations it is the best animal to use, if for no other reason than that so much is already known about it. However, for many purposes, it is too complicated an animal, and psychologists have recently been turning their attention to simpler organisms. The intention is to study instinctive and learned behaviour in its simplest forms, partly to get a clearer idea of the origins of behaviour, evolutionarily speaking, but also in the hope that the physiological correlates of behaviour will be easier to identify. Dr Carthy summarizes some of the more important features of invertebrate behaviour. He does this from a zoologist's viewpoint, with no attempt to extrapolate to 'higher animals'. This is the subject matter of what has been called 'protopsychology'.

To look at the invertebrates is to look at a very diverse collection of animals built on widely differing plans. Their behaviour is as varied as their looks, ranging from the restricted reactions of a sea anemone towards its food, to the adaptable learning ability, coupled with a well-organized visual perception, shown by insects and cephalopods. Just as the body plans differ, so do the patterns of the nervous systems. The nerve nets of the anemones and jellyfish can, as their name implies, conduct in any direction through the 'strings' of the net the 'knots' of which are formed by nerve cells. With the development of a head which generally leads in locomotion and upon which are concentrated sense organs, the nervous system enlarges at that end to form a protobrain. Along the body stretches a chain of nerves consisting of two strands with interconnexions which are themselves ganglia. The brain serves to collect the incoming information from the sense organs and to control the activities of the ganglia in the light of this sensory inflow. Each ganglion often has its own ability to function at some particular rhythmic rate which is modified by the brain and, in arthropods, by hormonal influences as well (Highnam, 1964).

However simple their effector or receptor equipment may seem, it is characteristic of animals that they behave, for they react to stimuli from their environment. Lack of sophisticated sense organs reduces the detail of the information which enters the nervous system. Thus, the eyes of a planarian worm are stimulated by light and can distinguish the direction from which it comes, but they cannot receive the complex images which a honey-bee can see. Hearing in many invertebrates is often no more than a general alarm reaction to vibration, though the songs of grass-hoppers are organized, specific sound signals which attract members of the same species to the singer.

In very general terms, if in the nervous system there are few possible interconnexions between the incoming sensory information and the outgoing motor instructions the repertoire of behaviour is restricted. The greater the quantity of the inter-nuncial nerve cells forming the interconnecting links, the greater the variety of the behaviour which the animal shows. The more plasticity there is in making these interconnexions, the more adaptable is the animal's behaviour. From this plasticity comes the ability of the animal to learn.

THE EFFECTIVENESS OF UNDIRECTED RESPONSES

But even the simple behaviour of these organisms serves to pro-duce efficient behaviour. (Efficiency here is measured by the fact that the animal survives and reproduces in what is essentially a hostile environment.) Such behaviour is exemplified by aimless wandering or by movement directed towards or away from the source of stimuli. Thus woodlice will wander about more quickly in a dry place than they will in a wet one. Though their pathways lead this way and that being, in fact, random, they will spend more time in the moist air than in the dry simply because they move more slowly when they encounter damp conditions. Move-ments of this sort are known as *orthokinesis* (Fraenkel and Gunn, 1961). Animals showing this sort of behaviour usually move faster in areas in which the conditions are unfavourable to them than in those more favourable.

Much the same result comes from a change in the rate of turning, termed *klinokinesis* (Fraenkel and Gunn, 1961), though the direction of the path remains random. On passing from favourable to unfavourable conditions an animal may begin to turn more frequently; this may have the effect of leading it back into the more favourable place. Thus a dark-loving animal which crosses the edge of shadow into the light may turn violently, re-entering the dark. But the very opposite also will be effective, that is, when the animal turns more frequently in favourable conditions. As it turns frequently in small circles it will tend to keep in the area. A small crab which lives in the tubes of a tube-dwelling worm will react to chemicals from the worm in water. It moves up the gradient of chemical to the area of highest concentration, where its turning is more frequent than in other parts having a lower concentration of worm chemical (Davenport, Camougis and Hickok, 1960).

To show how this sort of behaviour is effective, it is worth considering Evans's (1951) analysis of the behaviour of a small mollusc, one of the coat-of-mail shells. This animal lives on the surface of stones between the tide-marks on the shore. It is therefore exposed twice a day to the drying effect of sun and wind. It has to feed while the tide covers the stones. Laboratory experiments showed that the animals responded to gravity by moving downwards across the surface of a vertical sheet of glass so long as they were in air, but if the sheet was immersed in water the animals went in all directions across it. In other words, when the stones are exposed the molluscs will tend to move downwards, round and underneath the stone into the shaded and moist part beneath it. In addition, measurements of rate of movement showed that the stronger the illumination the faster they moved (orthokinesis). Their speed therefore diminishes as they pass from the strongly illuminated upper part of a stone into the shadow below. When the stones are first covered by the tide the animals move out from underneath the stones. At this time the illumination of the stone is fairly uniform, the light being diffused through the water, so they will not tend to collect on the lower parts of the stones as they will when in the air.

This example also illustrates the need there is for variability even in such apparently fixed behaviour. Too rigid a behaviour pattern would have kept the coat-of-mail shells permanently under the stones. But the changes that occur when the animal is immersed or exposed enable the simple pattern to be selectively successful. Indeed, modification of most of the simple responses which fall into this group of undirected behaviours can be shown. The reactions to light of an animal which has been kept in the dark will be different from those of an animal which has been kept in the light (Carthy, 1958). To take an even more obvious example, the state of hunger of an animal will influence its reactions to the stimuli from food whether it is an amoeba or a rat. Activity may bring changes; the reactions of aphids to light are altered by a period of flight. At first they are attracted by light from the sky, but later the wavelengths which are reflected from plants on the ground attract them more and they settle (reviewed in Carthy, 1965).

DIRECTIVENESS OF RESPONSE

But simple directed responses can occur as they do when a beetle runs towards the light in a dark room or a fly larva crawls away down a light beam. These are the reactions called taxes; they may, of course, occur to other stimuli as well as light. In addition, some animals will move at a constant angle to the light. Dragon-flies in flight, and many water insects while swimming, keep their backs towards the light, showing the *dorsal light response*. This serves to keep them the right way up. Others use taxes to find their way about. An ant will run out from its nest, find food and return to it again. If it is trapped in a dark box during its return journey it may head in a different direction when released from the box. The angle between its new direction and the old will often be found to be equal to the angle through which the sun has moved while the ant was imprisoned. The ant is performing a *light compass response*, for it holds the sun at a certain position in its eye, thus using the sun as a landmark (for other examples see Carthy, 1958).

Though the ant's compound eye is an ideal instrument for this type of behaviour, composed as it is of many ommatidia each of which can function almost independently, this sort of orientation is possible by other animals. Winkles, for example, begin to feed when the retreating tide uncovers them. The tracks which they leave show that the great majority move towards the sun at first. After a lapse of time they reverse their direction and crawl back roughly in the direction in which they came (Newell, 1958). They are positively phototactic at first, but later become negatively phototactic for some reason. This behaviour has the advantage that it keeps the animals in the part of the beach where the conditions are most favourable. Without the reversal of their direction they would become distributed all over the beach, at the same time entering many places where the conditions would not be so advantageous.

Sun orientation, however, cannot be accurate unless allowance is made for the movement of the sun. Winkles do not need to return to the exact place from which they came. But other animals can allow for the change of the sun's position during the day, permitting them to orientate more precisely. One of these is a sand hopper which remains buried in the moist sand of the shore. When left by the retreating tide the animals bury themselves below the surface where the sand does not dry out. If they are disturbed and placed on the dry sand they will hop off in the direction of the sea. By shading them from the sun and projecting its image on to them from a direction opposite to the actual position of the sun the animals can be made to turn round and head in the reverse direction. This demonstrates that the sun's position determines their direction of movement. Since they head in the same direction at all times of the day they must be correcting for the movement of the sun, and experiments support this.

'CLOCKS' IN CONTROL

Such observations are evidence for a clock mechanism within the animal which is consulted regularly and times the change of angular orientation to the sun which the animal performs (various papers in the Cold Spring Harbour Symposium for 1960 demonstrate this). That this clock is synchronized by the environment is shown by experiments in which animals are placed under conditions of changed time of light and dark. Thus hoppers, which were kept in the laboratory with the lights coming on at six at night instead of six in the morning and being switched off at six A.M., headed in a direction at roughly 180° to the one taken up by animals which had normally timed lighting. The clock had apparently been put wrong by half the cycle of 360° by a time change of twelve hours – half the whole twenty-four-hour cycle.

This example of a clock is typical of many that have been demonstrated in invertebrates as well as in vertebrates. A similar clock controls the onset of activity in the daily rhythm of cockroaches as Harker (1956) has shown. A cockroach will become active a little in advance of darkness when under a régime of twelve hours light/twelve hours dark. Activity increases until about two hours after dark, when it begins to decline to the daytime level which is maintained throughout the rest of the twenty-four hours. Insects which have been hatched from eggs kept in continuous darkness do not have a rhythm of this sort; their activity shows no daily peak. But if they are exposed to a short flash of light they begin to show a daily peak, though they continue to be kept in the dark. The flash apparently serves to synchronize a number of clocks in the animal's body, each of which has an approximately twenty-four-hour rhythm.

The blood of a rhythmic cockroach when transferred to a rhythmless roach causes the second insect to show rhythmic activity. The hormone which causes this is produced in neurosecretory cells in the lower part of the 'brain' (Harker, 1960). These cells are rhythmically active. Cooling to 3°C holds up the secretion and also delays the onset of activity, thus proving the relationship of the cells to the control of activity.

There is a great deal of evidence in other animals that these clocks which control activity rhythms are not under complete control of factors in the environment, though, as we have seen, they may be set by the change from light to dark. However, if the rhythmic cockroaches are kept in constant darkness or light their rhythm persists, though after a week or so it begins to be less marked and slowly to disappear. The cycle does not remain fixed to the twenty-four-hour period but takes up its own periodicity, which in some animals is less than twenty-four hours;

in others more. The adjective circadian is therefore used in place of diurnal for such rhythms.

The clocks are, then, motivated from within the animal, though the precise nature of the clock is unknown. The cyclically secreting cells of the cockroach's brain are not the only clock but a manifestation of others with over-riding control. Indeed, since cyclic activity of various sorts is observed in protozoa and in cells in tissue culture it would seem that the clock is some mechanism which resides in every living cell. The behaviours which we see are the outward signs of a deeply seated universal process.

SPECIES-CHARACTERISTIC BEHAVIOUR

Patterns of behaviour are often species-specific because it is as important for them to be characteristic as it is for the species structure to be typical of those animals alone. In particular, this is true of behaviour which is involved in courtship. The patterns displayed by one sex must attract the other sex of the same species only thus ensuring that interspecific breeding does not take place. The separation of two species on grounds of different behaviour is a powerful source of species isolation though not, in all probability, the prime cause of their initial separation. The patterns of courtship behaviour are no less elaborate among invertebrates such as insects than they are in vertebrates, say, among birds (Carthy, 1965).

Most of these courtship patterns are inherited and are classified as instinctive behaviour. It has been possible to use models with some animals to analyse the stimuli responsible for the evocation of the courtship behaviour. These stimuli are called releasers and are considered to be the external cause for the production of the instinctive acts which go to make up the particular courtship pattern. Crane (1949) has described the mating of some salticid spiders from South America. These are not web builders but spiders which hunt their prey by sight, stalking it and finally leaping upon it. Needless to say, they have well-developed vision.

The spiders are about six or seven millimetres across. A male courts a female by standing in front of her with the fore-part of his body slightly raised. His abdomen is lowered and the palps beneath his eyes hang motionless. He then begins to rock from side to side. After a time he extends his front legs forward at about 45° to the horizontal. This serves to attract the female and he then moves up to her to pose in front of her.

If a male's eyes are covered he does not react to a female; thus vision is of over-riding importance. But in addition, chemical stimuli play a part, for a male would not court a female which had been dead for a long time. One supposes that such a body would have lost any scent that it had.

Even a freshly killed female must be moved about to evoke courtship behaviour from the male, so clearly movement is important. Chloroformed females are not effective until they begin to move, when the male will court them. It is the two white stripes across the female's abdomen which are noticed by the male, for with these painted out the female loses her attraction. Thus vision is the most important sense used by the male to recognize not only the striped pattern on the female but also her movement. This is supported by the scent clues which come from her.

In most courtship patterns there is an element of aggression and it is difficult to disentangle the threat behaviour of a male towards another male from the courtship pattern. For one thing, the male is usually in a particularly aggressive mood when he is in reproductive condition. In spiders the male will threaten another one or a model. In Figure 48 are shown the models which will release threatening in the left-hand column and those which are ineffective in the right-hand column. The yellow band of the male across his face and palps is important, for models without a simulation of this pattern do not produce threat. In addition, 'legs' must be visible. During its threat display the male raises its legs successively backwards so that the fore pair are on the ground, the next slightly raised, the next higher and the hindmost the highest. The effective models all have stripes which represent the legs. Thus the stimuli which are releasers for threat in these salticids are the male's facial pattern and his raised legs.

But courtship is not always a visual affair; some insects use well-differentiated sound patterns to bring about mating (Haskell,

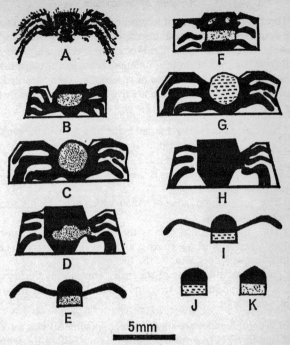

5mm

Figure 48. Models used in tests to determine the stimuli responsible for evoking threat from male jumping spiders. Those in the left-hand column were successful, those on the right unsuccessful. Yellow areas, stippled; white areas, dashed; backgrounds of all, light green. Some of the successful patterns differ from the unsuccessful ones only in colour (Crane, 1949).

1961). This is particularly true of grasshoppers and crickets, cicadas and some flies. Sounds are made by insects in a variety of ways. The tone of the wing-beat of a female is the stimulus which attracts a male mosquito, but often there is a special mechanism for sound-production on the insect's body. Grasshoppers chirp by rubbing their hind legs across their forewings, which lie folded along their backs; the bowing action of the legs sets the wings into vibration to produce the sound. Crickets, however, rub the fore wing of one side against that of the other; cicadas trill by 'clicking' a tymbal which is under tension.

217

Though the wing note of a mosquito is not a patterned sound the sounds made by other insects have formal patterns which distinguish the calls from those of other species, and also each call from another made in a different behavioural context. The song vocabulary of a number of species has been recorded and analysed behaviourally. There are five main types of song which are commonly found. They are:

(i) 'Normal' song. This is the call made by a male in the presence of males or when it is alone. It serves to aggregate the males into a singing band; it is often sung as a duet in a group.

(ii) The courtship song. This is the male's reaction to his recognition of a female.

(iii) The 'jumping-on' song of a male which precedes his attempt to copulate.

(iv) The 'rivalry' song. This is the threat sung by a courting male when another approaches and is likely to interrupt. Often this, too, is a duet sung by the two males.

(v) The 'copulation' song of the male. This is sung during pairing, and appears to pacify the female preventing her from moving about.

In general females are silent, though in some species a female will sing in reply to a male's courtship song. Often the female's song indicates that she is in reproductive readiness, for she will not sing unless she has ripe eggs in her ovary.

SOCIAL LIFE

Though courting animals are interacting behaviourally with each other they are not considered as being social. This term is reserved for those animals whose young remain with their parents. Such societies are highly evolved among the insects where they are maintained largely by behavioural specializations.

The work of maintaining a honeybee's colony involves work in construction and cleaning of the comb, of feeding the young, of guarding the hive and of collecting food. A worker bee on emergence goes through a series of jobs as she ages. At first, for some three days, she acts as a cleaner. Then her labial glands enlarge so that she is able to feed the young larvae with their secretion, and she takes on the duties of a nurse. She continues to do this until about the tenth day of her life, when the glands which produce wax have developed on her abdomen. With the plates of wax secreted by them she builds new comb and repairs old. At about her sixteenth day she begins to receive the food brought into the hive by foragers and to store it in the comb. Later she becomes a guard standing at the hive entrance, but a few days after she begins to leave the hive to forage, a function she fulfils for the rest of her life.

Though many bees follow this sequence of work, it is not immutable. A hive can be divided in two, so that one contains all the older workers and the other the younger ones. Despite the fact that the younger bees are not of an age to forage they soon do so and in the reverse way the older bees revert to the work they did as youngsters. Lindauer (1961) has done what amount to 'time and motion' studies on individual honeybees who were watched round-the-clock. They spent a great deal of time idling, but also much time 'patrolling'. This is apparently unorientated exploratory activity which brings the bee into contact with the work to be done. When the stimuli are adequate to release any of these essential social activities – and provided the glandular secretions are available in the body of the bee – the bee performs the work required. Foraging involves an elaborate communication system as we shall see, but there seems to be no similar system for communicating information about the work to be done. Lindauer believes that patrolling obviates the need for such a system.

In a colony of social insects there is continual food exchange (trophallaxis) not only between larvae and adults but also between adults. This 'food current' serves to carry round the colony a substance, 9-oxodec-2-enoic acid, which is produced by the queen from her mandibular glands (Butler, 1964). This is a signal of her presence, and so long as it is circulating the workers do not produce queen cells, the specially large cells in which larvae destined to be queens are raised. But if the supply of acid is stopped building soon commences. Butler has, in addition, shown that the acid serves as a sex attractant for the drones. It is an example of a biologically active substance produced by another animal which causes behaviour; substances such as this are called pheromones, and can be likened to hormones which act outside the body on an inter-individual basis. Their importance as determinants of behaviour in many animals, both vertebrate and invertebrate, is only beginning to be appreciated.

A good example of the organization which has evolved with the social habit in insects is the behaviour connected with foraging (Carthy, 1964). It is clearly essential that a steady flow of food should enter the colony for the nourishment of the larvae whose rearing is, as it were, the *raison d'être* of the group. Therefore, efficiency in foraging with the least possible waste of effort may be expected to be of selective value.

Many ant species lay a trail of chemical for foraging. This line of spots of chemical substance is only laid by foragers which have been successful in obtaining food. Since the spots themselves are evanescent, lasting a matter of minutes, the trail erases itself if it is not reinforced by foragers. Thus the trail will not attract attention after the food source has been exhausted. The trail substance of the fire ant is a secretion from Dufour's gland on the ant's abdomen. The amounts in which the material is laid on a trail are minute, but at higher concentrations the same chemical acts as a general excitant. Crushed Dufour's gland placed outside a nest of fire ants brings them out in large numbers, running in quick staccato manner. It acts therefore as a pheromone.

The trails do not seem to be orientated. An ant reaching one midway is as likely to turn in the direction of the nest as it is towards the food. Since a trail is normally encountered at one of its ends this is of no disadvantage. The classic experiments of the reversal of segments of trail and the disturbance of the ants when they arrive at the reversed section should rather be interpreted as being due to interruption of the trail's continuity than that any polarization of the trail is reversed.

COMMUNICATION

The chemical trail of an ant acts to inform the forager emerging from the nest of the direction of the food. This information as well as an indication of the distance of the food is passed more explicitly by a successful foraging honeybee on her return to the hive (von Frisch, 1954). She dances on the surface of the comb which hangs vertically in the hive. If the food is at less than 100 metres she performs a 'round dance' which gives no specific information about the position of the food other than that it is within 100 metres of the hive. However, for food farther away the forager performs a figure-of-eight dance which specifies the direction and distance of the place. As the bee dances along the central part of the pattern she waggles her abdomen; the direction of this part of the dance with respect to gravity represents the direction of the food with regard to the sun. Up the comb – contrary to the direction of gravity – indicates the direction of the sun. Distance is conveyed by the time spent in waggling, the longer the proportion of the total time passed in this manner the farther away is the food. During this part of the dance the bee, in addition, makes a sound at about 250 c.p.s. in pulses of about thirty-two per second. Both the length of the train of pulses and the number of pulses within the train seem to be correlated with the distance of the food. This may be the important distance indicator in the dance.

The bee obtains its direction by using the pattern of polarized light from the sky and has to learn this direction each time it leaves the hive. The memory may remain with her as long as seven days when the hive is shut up during the intervening time because of bad weather.

Wilson has applied information theory to an analysis of the errors of fire ants following an odour trail and of honeybees reacting to the information from a dance. The information conveyed in the two systems seems very alike; that is, four 'bits' of information with regard to direction and two with regard to distance.

LEARNING

It is by the nature of things necessary for honeybees, and other insects, to have to learn landmarks. Those surrounding a food place are learned by the bee as she approaches the source; symbols exposed while she is drinking or as she leaves are ignored when offered in a choice test. The more distant landmarks are, however, learned when she leaves. Rather a similar organization of the perceptual field has been shown to exist in a solitary wasp,

Philanthus triangulum, by Tinbergen (reviewed in Carthy, 1958). This wasp digs a small hole which she stocks with bees upon whose bodies she places an egg before finally closing the nest. Each bee is brought in separately, so while she is provisioning the nest the wasp makes sorties to hunt for the next victim. She recognizes the objects in the immediate neighbourhood of the nest after viewing them in an orientation flight lasting some ten to thirty seconds which she makes by circling above the nest. Experiments by van Beusekom showed that the wasp recognizes the Gestalt of these patterns. Thus, if, while the wasp is away, fir cones, which have been put in a ring round the nest entrance, are placed in a heap to one side and black blocks of wood placed in a circle on the other side of the real position of the nest, the wasp searches within the circle on her return. The spatial relationships of the landmarks one with another are also of great importance.

The ability to learn is not the prerogative of the insects among the invertebrates. Many other arthropods, as well as worms, molluscs and so forth also display learning. Thorpe (1963) has summarized the evidence for this. (See also A.S.A.B. Symposium, 1965.) But probably the most interesting investigations have been those into the learning ability of octopus carried out by Young and Boycott, and Wells (reviewed in Wells, 1963 and Young, 1964).

The octopus are kept in a tank where they spend much of their time among stones. They can be drawn out from their home by the offer of a crab. At the same time an object such as a white square can be displayed. After a few trials an octopus will come out and attack the white square alone. Discrimination between two shapes, one accompanying the food reward and the other with no reward, is slow, but can be enhanced by giving a mild electric shock with the negative stimulus. A variety of shapes can then be distinguished (Figure 49). Shapes which are alike in area or outline can nevertheless be distinguished if they differ in shape. The

Figure 49. Pairs of shapes that octopuses can and cannot learn to distinguish. Percentage figures show the proportion of correct responses made by groups of octopuses in the first sixty trials (pairs 1–4) or 240 trials (pair 5) of training. The projections show the theoretical effect of these shapes if their images fell on to a field composed of horizontal and vertical rows of receptors (Wells, 1962, after Sutherland).

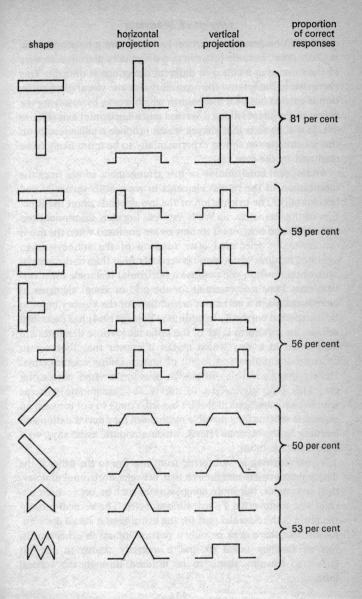

shape	horizontal projection	vertical projection	proportion of correct responses

discrimination between a vertical rectangle and a horizontal one is easily done, but one between two diagonally placed rectangles of the same area inclined in different directions is difficult. This suggested to Sutherland the possibility that the visual discrimination is carried out by a mechanism which works by resolving the extent of the shapes along a vertical and a horizontal axis (Figure 49). It will be seen that shapes which produce similar results on this scheme can be shown experimentally to be more likely to be confused by the eye.

Anatomical confirmation of this arrangement comes from the distribution of the retinal elements in rows both vertically and horizontally. The orientation of the eye depends upon the function of the statocysts, as Wells showed. Further, discriminations of vertical and horizontal rectangles are confused when the eye is not normally orientated after removal of the statocysts. An operated octopus whose pupil is vertical rather than in the normal horizontal position will confuse a horizontal rectangle for a vertical one. Thus it is essential for the grid of visual elements to be maintained in a particular orientation for the sensory input to be interpreted correctly. In addition, Young (1964) has described cells in the plexiform layer of the optic lobe whose dendrites are distributed in a way which makes it appear that they act to measure orientation and length of images falling on the retina. He has drawn parallels with similar cells in the visual cortex of a cat. This type of analysis of ability to discriminate patterns coupled with anatomical studies has led Young to put forward an elaborate scheme for a possible mechanism for discrimination and learning in the octopus (1964), which amounts, as he says, to a model for the brain.

Visual learning is transferred from one eye to the other if the discriminations are simple like that between horizontal and vertical rectangles, but more complex ones such as between an upright and an inverted T show little transfer. The vertical lobe of the brain is the essential part for the learning of a visual discrimination, but there need be only a portion intact; in other words, just as Lashley failed to find a memory centre in the rat cortex so learning seems to be diffused through the vertical lobe.

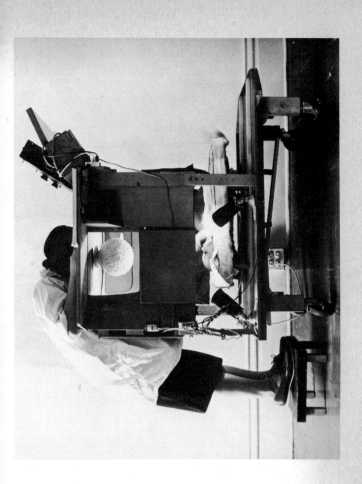

Plate 1. Observing a baby's direction of gaze (Fantz, 1961).

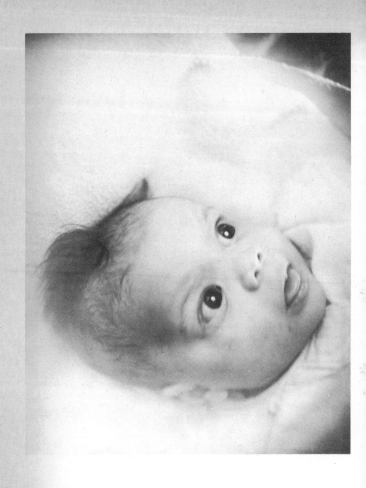

Plate 2. View of infant as seen in apparatus shown in plate 1.

Plate 3. The visual cliff (Gibson and Walk, *Scientific American*, April 1960).

Plate 4. MacKay's ray figure. This shimmers in an odd way, and after looking at it for a few seconds, if the gaze is directed to a blank wall, a curious streaming of 'grains of rice' is seen in directions at right angles to the rays. Is this due to upset brain mechanisms, or to stimulation of retinal 'on' and 'off' receptors by small tremors of the eyes giving after-effects of movement? We do not know for certain.

Plate 5. Photograph of Ames's Room. The room is an odd shape but seen as rectangular, and so the 'trading' of distance for size is upset. This is not, however, a distortion illusion. (Ittelson, 1952).

Plate 6. An inside corner of a room. This is the same as the Muller-Lyer arrow giving expansion.

Plate 7. An outside corner—the same as the illusion figure giving shrinking.

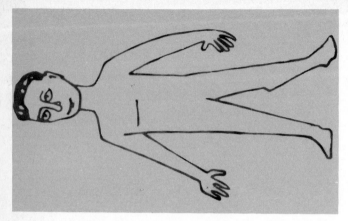

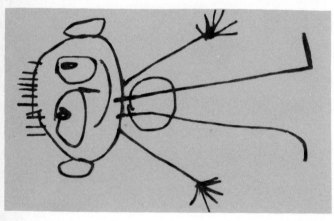

Plate 8. Expressive and Productive creativity.

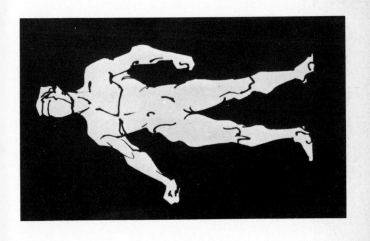

Plate 9. Inventive creativity.

Plate 10. Innovative and Emergentive creativity (All five figures from *Creativity*, (ed. Paul Smith), Hastings House).

Plate 11. Fruit flies being placed in an apparatus for measuring their activity.

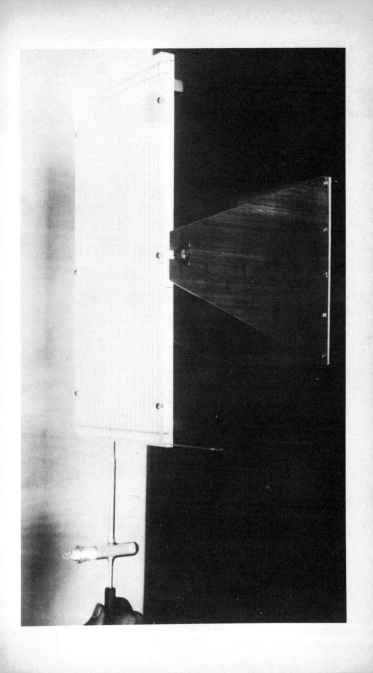

Plate 12. Chick following moving box in alley.

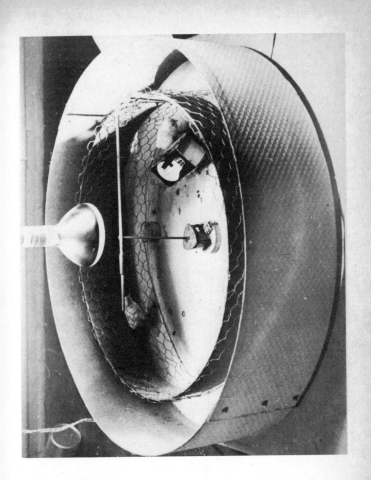

Plate 13. Chick in circular alley.

Plate 14. Professors Lumsdaine (seated) and Glaser with three machines. On the left is the 'Atomic' machine, a Pressey-type device in which the student answers a multiple-choice question by pressing one of four keys. The next question appears only after the correct answer has been chosen. In the middle is the Foringer machine, a Skinner-type device. The frame is exposed on the left and the student writes his answer on the right. The black shutter in the middle reveals the correct answer when the lever (left) is pulled. Professor Glaser (standing) holds a linear programmed textbook.

Plate 15. Auto Tutor Mark 11.

Plate 16. Army apprentices working with Auto Tutor machines.

Tactile discriminations can also be carried out. These depend upon the integrity of the sub-frontal lobe.

Planarian worms have brains whose plans are far simpler than those of the cephalopods, but they are capable of showing what may be conditioning when touch (the unconditioned stimulus) is paired with electric shock or light (the conditioned stimulus). The power of regeneration of these worms is very great. Such learning and other simple discriminations in a Y-maze appear to be passed on to each of the parts when the worm's body is cut in two. The regenerate from the head end shows unaffected scores, while those from tails, in which a 'brain' has been reconstituted, show only slightly diminished abilities. The search for the mechanism by which the memory pattern is impressed upon the new nervous tissue has led McConnell and others to propose that the intermediary is RNA (ribose nucleic acid) for regeneration in a solution of an enzyme which attacks this substance causes the regenerates from tails to show much reduced transfer. Whether or not this substance will finally prove to represent coded memory remains to be seen.

The lower animals are proving of great interest to psychologists because they present the possibility of connecting psychological characteristics with physiological parameters. Particularly among the arthropods the knowledge of sense organ function and of the organization of the central nervous system is growing fast. It is known, for example, that the central nervous system of an insect is in constant activity even when isolated from the body. This activity is affected by hormones which occur in the insect body. Thus one has a possible explanation for mood and drive in insects. Dethier (1964) has argued persuasively that insects are not mere 'push-button machines' whose behaviour can be explained entirely in terms of stimulus–response. Certainly individuality is a characteristic of insect behaviour. Possibly, as Dethier has suggested, it is a desire to eschew anthropomorphism which has prevented us in the past from seeing vertebrate-like behaviour in the patterns of behaviour of lower animals.

11. EARLY EXPERIENCE

W. SLUCKIN

Freud thought that the first five years of life were potent in deter-mining a personality. Experimental psychologists agree that what happens early in life is important not only for personality but also for many other aspects of later behaviour, in animals as well. Some of the work on early experience has been concerned with the effects of living in an impoverished environment. Here Professor Sluckin looks mainly at the opposite effect – the results of specific kinds of stimulation early in life. He has himself experimented on one of these effects – imprinting.

THE nascent individual, mammal or bird, emerges from the embryo's stable environment into a world which offers a great variety of new experience. The change in the individual's cir-cumstances is a radical one. Independent existence begins with an impact of a range of stimuli previously absent. This early ex-perience of life cannot but leave some mark. What are the effects of such early experience? Are they slight or profound? Are they momentary or lasting? In what way does early exposure to one or another kind of environmental stimulation influence the indi-vidual?

Any attempt to answer these questions must depend on the results of continued and methodical observations of growing animals and human beings. Investigations of this type may be concerned with the character of the immediate responses of the young to different kinds of environmental stimulation; or they may set out to study the more lasting effects of various sorts of early experience. Such studies are experimental in that the condi-tions under which the observations are conducted are controlled and systematically varied. This is necessary if clear conclusions are to be drawn from any findings. Let us, then, see what has been firmly established about the role of early experience in the de-velopment of animals and men.

Early Experience

EARLY STIMULATION AND RESPONSIVENESS

Such sense organs as are functional very early in life enable the infant individual to respond to external stimulation in a variety of ways. These responses may consist of no more than movements of limbs or head towards or away from the stimulus. However, in the so-called precocial species, i.e. in which the neonates are so well developed as to be capable of locomotion, stimuli of certain kinds may evoke quite complex patterns of behaviour. Thus domestic chicks, ducklings and goslings, and the young of many related wild species, readily approach and keep close to a variety of visual and auditory stimuli; the mother bird which is normally followed about is only one of a range of sources of stimulation that can evoke such behaviour in the young. In a similar manner newborn hoofed animals – lambs, kids, calves, colts, etc. – stay with and follow their mothers and, in suitable circumstances, follow other animals, or human beings, or vehicles – indeed, almost any sizable thing that moves.

The young of altricial species, that is those in which the neonate is entirely helpless, are seemingly less alert. Neither their sense organs nor their ability to move are as yet properly developed. Nevertheless, before long, these infant animals, too, show characteristic responsiveness. The human infant, for instance, turns its head, opens its mouth and makes grasping movements with its lips in response to appropriate tactile stimulation, all such actions together constituting the so-called rooting response. Babies also follow movement with their eyes, extend their arms, and – at the age of some months – smile at certain objects including human faces. Some types of research have been primarily directed towards finding out which stimuli release in different species which patterns of response. Other studies have set out to investigate the effects of overall deficiency of stimulation. This latter approach has clearly indicated that both young animals and babies behave as if they actively sought stimulation, becoming seemingly more alert as stimulation is relatively lacking. Of course, the less the young organism experiences, the less it learns; and this has short- and long-term consequences.

THE CONSEQUENCES OF EARLY STIMULATION

A number of investigators have compared the behaviour of animals reared in a stimulating environment, and in a sheltered environment. Rats that grow up under conditions which offer little opportunity for exercise and visual experience are subsequently both inferior at problem-solving and more 'emotional' than rats reared in comparatively stimulating surroundings. Dogs restricted in their early experience later turn out to behave in a strange manner; while being more active, they are much slower at different types of learning than normal dogs (see, for instance, Thompson and Melzack, 1956).

Other investigations have set out to study the lasting effects of certain brief but intense experiences occurring early in the life of animals. It has been found, for instance, that young mice given occasional electric shocks are later more readily conditioned than mice without such early experience. Rats that have been handled in order to be shocked develop into better learners than rats not so treated; and it appears that the handling rather than the shocking is responsible for this enhancement in docility. All in all, it has been clearly established that the experience of being momentarily handled in infancy no more than once a day is sufficient to improve the rats' later ability to be trained by reward and punishment to perform simple tasks (Levine, 1962).

It is a far cry from lowly mammals to human beings. Yet it may be asked whether a deficiency of early stimulation affects babies somewhat as it affects young animals. Restricted experience early in life does not appear to blunt curiosity. But there is ample evidence that young children brought up in stimulating surroundings develop intellectually faster and more fully than children growing up in a restricted, impoverished environment, which at one time was rather typical of such institutions as orphanages. The beneficial effects of variety and richness of early experience have been demonstrated in studies of genetically identical twins brought up in different homes from an early age. Furthermore, the disadvantages of certain kinds of institutional upbringing appear to be both intellectual and emotional. However, in considering emotional development, and in particular the effects of the absence of stable emotional attachments early in life, it seems appropriate to begin lower down the evolutionary scale.

IMPRINTED ATTACHMENTS

The most definitive studies of affective attachments have been conducted with very young precocial birds and with infant monkeys. Such studies of bird behaviour come under the heading of imprinting; this field of research has been pioneered by the leading German ethologist, Konrad Lorenz, although interest in related phenomena has a longer history. Studies of the development of affectional responses in monkeys stem mainly from the work of the American comparative psychologist, H. F. Harlow.

Imprinting often develops from approach and following responses which may be readily observed in newly hatched precocial birds. These young animals tend to attach or imprint themselves to their own parents, or to parent-substitutes – animals, people, moving objects, even flickering lights. The time when these attachments are formed is not strictly critical; but imprinting occurs most frequently very early in life, before the animal has been exposed to much sensory stimulation. Imprinting is not instantaneous, as originally suggested, although it may be quite rapid; the longer the fledgeling is exposed to a given figure, the more firmly it becomes attached to it.

In a very early experiment in which the writer took part, some 500 chicks were exposed individually the day after hatching to a small box suspended a few inches above the floor inside an enclosed alley ten feet long. Some of the chicks were confronted with a stationary box for one minute, some saw ten jerks of the box moving up and down the alley over about $2\frac{1}{2}$ minutes, and some experienced fifty jerky movements of the box over about nine minutes. Chicks in each of the three groups were all later individually tested with a moving box; however, some were tried one day, some two days, some three, some four, some five and some six days after the initial experience. It was found that chicks which had seen the box move during the first confrontation later approached and followed the moving box more readily than chicks without such experience (see Plates 12 and 13). This tended to be so on whichever day the second confrontation occurred, except the sixth day; at that age hardly any chicks would follow the moving box. Further, birds with the nine-minute experience of the box appeared to respond on test some-what better than those which initially had only $2\frac{1}{2}$ minutes with it.

The findings suggested that chicks with experience of a moving box were apt to become attached to it. However, imprinting attachments are more often considered to have occurred if exposure to a given moving figure later results in a preference by the animal for this particular figure over any others. As a matter of fact, by saying that an animal has become imprinted we mean that when some time later the animal is re-confronted with the original figure, it will approach and follow the figure again, and that when confronted with the familiar figure together with a strange one, the animal will choose the one it had experienced before and flee from the other; the firmness of imprinting may readily be assessed in terms of these criteria. Imprinting is not wholly irreversible, as earlier thought, in that any attachment may become gradually forgotten with time, and the young animal may be attached to more than one figure at once. The numerous field and laboratory studies of imprinting conducted in recent years have been summarized and discussed by Sluckin (1964); see also an earlier short survey by Sluckin and Salzen (1961).

It has been established that any intermittent stimulation of moderate intensity attracts newly hatched, precocial birds; when the animal has been exposed long enough to a figure which provides such stimulation, it forms an attachment to the figure. Now stationary objects in the environment do not provide intermittent visual stimulation and are not initially approached. But young animals exposed to such objects for a relatively long time tend to become attached to them; young precocial birds have been found to discriminate in favour of familiar stationary objects and against strange ones, showing signs of fear of *anything* unfamiliar. There is also some evidence that the choice of nesting sites in at least one altricial species is influenced by the fledgelings' early experience of 'home'.

Again, the character of the song of another altricial bird, the chaffinch, is influenced by early imprinting-like learning. It has been found with the aid of an electronic instrument, the acoustic spectrograph, that only some features of chaffinch's song are innately based; the full refinements of the song of any specimen are acquired early in life, and not later than the bird's first spring. The temporal pattern of the song is learned from other chaffinches in the locality and, once learned, it remains invariant for the rest of the bird's life (see Thorpe 1956, 1963, and Thorpe's earlier research reports).

Birds often behave as if they did not recognize their own kind instinctively. On the contrary, 'birds of a feather flock together' frequently as a result of early experience of one another. In one experiment in which this writer participated, newly hatched domestic chicks kept individually for a day with a moving box later greatly preferred it to the company of other chicks, just as chicks reared communally later preferred their own kind to the moving box. Social behaviour of mammals also appears to be moulded by their early exposure to other members of the species. Rhesus monkeys reared without the company of their peers have been found to be socially 'maladjusted' later in life (Harlow and Harlow, 1962). The tameness of dogs has been shown to be contingent upon their early experience of people; and it is the exposure to people that has been found to matter, rather than reward training by them (Scott, 1958).

Early imprinting may also affect later sexual behaviour of animals. Sexual responses of birds, especially in altricial species, do sometimes become misdirected to species other than their own. Many such cases have been reported, and there is little doubt that exposure early in life may 'fixate' the objects of courtship. No such fixation occurs in lower mammals; but monkeys and apes need early heterosexual contacts if they are later to develop normal mating responses.

Probably the most famous of Harlow's studies have been those of affectional responses of young rhesus monkeys to cloth-covered objects, known as 'cloth mothers'. A cloth provides the kind of tactile stimulation which normally elicits clinging responses from these infant animals. In the so-called open-field test a baby monkey with some experience of a 'cloth mother' is simply placed in a strange room; in the absence of its 'mother' the young animal shows signs of fright, including crouching and clutching its own body. When, however, the 'cloth mother' is present during the open-field test, the infant rushes to her, rubs its body against her and shows a range of signs of recognition and attachment. As in a test of imprinting, the young animal reared with a suitable object returns eagerly to this object when allowed to do so after a spell of separation from it.

An object of about the same size as the 'cloth mother', but one made of wire, and from which milk is actually obtained, is known as the 'wire mother'; the 'wire mother' evokes no clinging and no 'love' responses in baby monkeys. In the so-called home-cage fear test and the open-field fear test the young monkey is confronted with strange objects or 'monsters'. In these circumstances the infant animal rushes to the shelter of the 'cloth mother' and not the 'wire mother'. It runs back to the familiar cloth-covered object and away from anything unfamiliar in a manner reminiscent of the behaviour of a chick or duckling in a discrimination test of imprinting. A monkey – it should be noted – will initially flee from all strange objects, even of the kind it would have 'loved' had they been encountered early enough in life. The tendency to explore anything strange appears to be inhibited by fear. In the presence of mother or mother-surrogate this fear is soon overcome, and exploratory activity begins. Infant monkeys have been found to be poorer explorers when without 'mother' than when 'mother' is around (see, for instance, accounts of experiments by Harlow, 1959b, and Harlow and Zimmermann, 1959).

EARLY EXPERIENCE AND PERSONALITY DEVELOPMENT

It is widely believed that the experience of an affectionate and stable relationship with his parents, and especially mother, is conducive to the human infant's normal, and psychologically sound, development. It has even been said that the early months of life are crucial in the development of human personality. How justified is the view that early experience irretrievably moulds the character of man?

It has been observed repeatedly that a prolonged separation of the infant from its mother tends to result in some form of 'disorganization' of the child's behaviour. Up to the age of six months or so, such disorganization bears the marks of sensory impoverishment or deprivation. A baby which is not given much mothering, is not cuddled, and not much talked to, is understimulated. Whether this leads to any adverse long-term effects is not entirely certain; but the surmise is that it might.

There is no evidence that an infant under the age of about six months can clearly distinguish between its mother and other people. Consequently, it is unlikely that such an infant will have formed an attachment to one particular person. The tie between a child and its mother develops gradually. The child's attachment appears to be built upon his initial unconditional responses, such as sucking, clinging or smiling, to stimulation emanating from the mother-figure. When the child knows its mother and is attached specifically to her, then the experience of being separated from her for some appreciable time can have pronounced immediate effects and, possibly, also long-lasting effects.

The adverse effects of deprivation of motherly affection have been repeatedly reported in psychological literature for well over twenty years. It has been said that the 'institutionalized child' is handicapped intellectually and emotionally, and that such an 'affectionless character' is later prone to delinquency (see, for instance, Bowlby, 1951). Further meticulously conducted studies by Bowlby and his colleagues have indicated that mother-separated children, though later tending to be more maladjusted than normally reared ones, do not necessarily or commonly develop psychopathic traits. In fact, in the light of the available evidence it has been necessary in recent years to reassess somewhat the role of maternal deprivation in personality development (Ainsworth *et al.*, 1962).

Nevertheless, early experience is clearly important in the life of the individual. Early learning is the foundation for later learning. It is said that the young are impressionable; and experimental studies of imprinting and the development of affectional responses in animals suggest that the very young are possibly even more impressionable than might have been suspected. Whether any imprinting-like, infantile learning occurs in human beings is still not altogether clear. Whether traumatic experiences in children's lives leave truly indelible marks upon their characters is not certain. And it is a matter of some doubt as to whether reward and punishment conditioning is at all effective at the very beginning of the infant's life.

Despite the many studies concerning the effects of deprivation of maternal care, our knowledge of the role of early experience in the development of human personality is still very slight. It is important that the extent of this ignorance be fully appreciated. A clear recognition of what is uncertain in this sphere should be the basis of all future systematic observations and experimental investigations. Recent research has already shed a great deal of light upon the influence of early experience on the behavioural development of animals. There is no reason why persistent study, conducted with scientific humility, should not eventually tell us as much about ourselves.

PHYSIOLOGICAL
AND PSYCHOLOGICAL STATES

It is not surprising that we spend so much time inquiring about each other's health and talking about our states of mind and body. Everything we do is dependent on such states. Even an amoeba's behaviour depends on whether or not it has recently fed. Psychologists have for many years studied a variety of states – emotional and motivational, states generated by particular beliefs and attitudes, or by something which has just happened; and they have looked at them from both physiological and psychological points of view. All behaviour depends on being in a motivated condition, and all textbooks of psychology devote a considerable amount of space to the topic. Sleeping and dreaming have more recently become respectable for scientific study. And one of the most recent experimental methods of all involves the use of drugs to modify a person's state. These topics are dealt with in the next three chapters.

12. THE ROLE OF THE BRAIN IN MOTIVATION

P. M. MILNER

Many people express an interest in psychology because they want to know 'what makes people tick'. Roughly speaking, that is what motivation is about; but in the way psychologists use the word it covers a wide range – from a man's aims in life all the way down to having an irresistible need to scratch himself. Other words are often used instead of motivation. A basic, physiological 'need', such as a need for more sugar in the blood, gives rise to a hunger 'drive'. (Both words are needed, because some needs do not have corresponding drives, and vice versa.) *In the past, physiologists and psychologists have explained needs and drives in terms of the chemical changes occurring in the body, but in the last decade attention has shifted to the part played by the central nervous system. Professor Milner took part in one of the most germinal experiments in 1954.*

THE writings of Freud and the exploits of the advertising industry have ensured that almost everybody has some knowledge of the complexities of human motivation, and how a fundamental motive like sex can spread its influence to energize a wide range of unsuspected activities. It may never have occurred to most people, however, that we know very little about the way in which even these fundamental motives actually operate.

When an animal hunts for food and eats it, for example, we suppose that things must be going on in its brain. But what? Hunger makes an animal more responsive to signs of food; motivational states can apparently modify the way an animal's motor system reacts to sensory input, acting as a sort of filter to determine which stimuli shall exert control. Thus the hungry animal approaches and consumes food, as it would not have done if it had just eaten its fill, or if it had been under the influence of a stronger motive such as fear. The experiments to be described in this chapter were directed to finding out which parts of the nervous system are involved in these motivational mechanisms, and, as far as possible, how they work.

There have been intimations, in clinical reports dating back well over a hundred years, of relationships between parts of the brain and the expression of motivations. For example, physicians have noted from time to time that a tumour located at the base of the brain sometimes appears to cause the patient to eat compul-

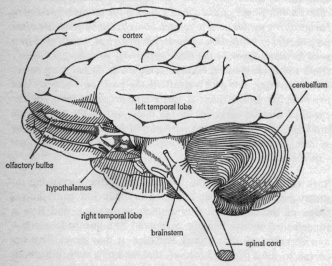

Figure 50. Human brain viewed from slightly below.

sively. Although they were useful in providing leads for further research, these early clinical findings left a good deal to be desired from a scientific standpoint, and progress was speeded up by the development of suitable experimental techniques using animals as subjects.

Before this century, experimental surgery on the brains of animals was very primitive and tended to be restricted to the outer mantle, or cortex, which is most accessible. One nineteenth-century experimentalist, Goltz, removed the whole of the cortex of a dog and found that the animal became very bad-tempered and flew into a rage at the slightest touch. At about the same time Brown and Schaefer removed parts of the temporal lobes of several monkeys and noticed that one of them began to eat more heavily, and to accept food that it usually spurned. The temporal lobes are large folds of brain lying along the side just beneath the temples (see Figure 50), and consist of a layer of cortex over a core of subcortical tissue. Thus the operations of Brown and Schaefer removed more than just the cortex.

Since this pioneering work, there have been innumerable experiments involving cortical removals; they have contributed greatly to our understanding of the processes underlying perception and learning, but little to motivation. It now seems unlikely that the cortex has much to do with the basic mechanisms of motivation.

EATING AND DRINKING

Studies of subcortical structures, especially those near the base of the brain, had to await the development, by Horsley and Clarke, of an instrument for placing a needle accurately into any part of the brain without significant damage to overlying tissue. With the aid of this stereotaxic instrument, as it is called, an experimenter can conveniently destroy, anaesthetize or stimulate predetermined subcortical structures. Although Horsley and Clarke first used it in 1908, the instrument did not come into wide use until the late 1930s, and one of the first problems to which it was applied was the question of what part of the base of the brain was involved in the compulsive eating behaviour seen in the tumour patients mentioned above. Some speculated that the symptoms resulted from damage to the pituitary, which is not part of the brain at all but a gland lying just below it which acts as an intermediary between the brain and the many other glands throughout the body that secrete hormones. Others thought that the hypothalamus was the culprit and the experiments proved them to be right.

The hypothalamus is a small but vital part of the brain located roughly in the middle of the undersurface and lying close to the pathways that connect the spinal cord to the higher centres of the brain. It is just above the pituitary and joined to it by a stalk. Although it is only about half an inch across, it can be subdivided into a number of nuclei, or aggregations of nerve cells, arranged in symmetrical pairs on either side of the midline. It is possible, though not easy, to knock out a single pair of nuclei using the stereotaxic instrument, and, as a result of experiments in the laboratory of Professor Ranson in Chicago (Hetherington and Ranson, 1940), it was found that the compulsive eating syndrome could be reproduced in a variety of animals by damage to one pair of hypothalamic nuclei called the ventromedial (or VM) nuclei. Damage to other parts of the hypothalamus does not produce the effect.

The VM lesions often have the additional effect of giving the animals an exceedingly evil disposition; previously tame cats and rats become impossible to handle. Possibly this is an extreme example of the relationship that is often noticed between hunger and irritability; such a coupling would, after all, have some survival value in animals that have to compete for food.

Psychologists did not immediately recognize the significance of these experiments for theories of motivation, and it was only some years later that Professor Neal Miller (1957) and his colleagues at Yale began to do more critical tests of animals with lesions in the VM nuclei. To everyone's surprise, they found that, although the animals ate almost continuously as long as they were provided with palatable food, they showed little interest in working for it. Moreover, if their food was diluted with cellulose, they would eat less, though normal animals ate more to compensate for the lower nutritional value. Apparently the effect of the lesion is to make the animals' feeding more dependent on the taste of the food and less on the bodily need for it.

One hypothesis advanced to account for these findings is that the VM nucleus is provided with cells that are sensitive to the sugar in the blood stream (the hypothalamus is richly provided with blood vessels) and that when they fire they suppress the activity of an eating system. When the readily available stores of sugar in the liver are nearly depleted, the VM nucleus cells stop firing and release the system responsible for eating behaviour.

This hypothesis assumes that there is a feeding system, and, though the American workers may not have been aware of the fact, such a system had been discovered some years earlier by Professor W. R. Hess of Zürich (1954) in the course of an extraordinary series of experiments for which he was later awarded a Nobel Prize. Professor Hess developed a technique for implanting electrode wires into the brains of cats, so that the animals could be stimulated as they walked freely around after recovery from the operation. Although he could not direct his electrodes to a precise point, he was able to tell afterwards where each electrode had been by examining the brains of the animals.

This work continued for many years and provided an enormous fund of data concerning the functions of subcortical structures. Hess's stimulation techniques have been adapted for use with chickens by von Holst (1962). Birds have a large repertoire of instinctive responses to motivational situations, many of which can be elicited by hypothalamic stimulation. One of Hess's findings was that stimulation in the region of the lateral hypothalamus (a nucleus which is just lateral to the VM nucleus) would make cats eat voraciously, even chew on inedible objects although they had just finished eating. Recently, workers in Professor Konorski's laboratory at the Nencki Institute in Warsaw (Wyrwicka Dobrzecka and Tarnecki, 1959), have taught a goat to raise its foot to beg for food and then shown that the goat will make this learned response when stimulated in the lateral hypothalamic feeding centre. This demonstrates that the stimulation does not just force the animal to make motor responses, like chewing and swallowing, but makes it give voluntary responses as if it were naturally hungry.

It was not until about ten years after the discovery of the satiety centre in the VM nucleus that animals were stopped from eating by hypothalamic lesions. Professor Anand of New Delhi (Anand and Brobeck, 1951) found that after bilateral destruction of the lateral nuclei an animal would refuse food until it starved to death if it were not forcibly fed. This nucleus thus seems to be a crucial part of the feeding mechanism, and it is probably the part that is inhibited by the VM nucleus. The lateral nucleus also seems to be a link in the drinking mechanism; after its bilateral destruction rats are even more resistant to drinking water than they are to eating.

Stimulation in this lateral hypothalamic region will also sometimes elicit drinking instead of eating, and some animals have been forced to consume a considerable fraction of their weight of water over a period of an hour or so by repeated stimulation. It is known that there are cells in the hypothalamus that are sensitive to the concentration of the blood, and if the concentration rises they cause the pituitary to release a hormone into the bloodstream which stimulates the kidneys to recover more water from the excreted urine. At the same time the animal begins to search for water and drink, so that it seems reasonable to suppose that the same sensitive cells control both the internal and the behavioural components of the water regulation mechanism.

Although the drinking and eating systems seem to occupy the same hypothalamic nucleus, they clearly act independently most of the time, and Grossman has recently shown that the cells of the two systems respond to different chemical agents. Traces of one chemical introduced into the hypothalamus on the tip of a needle will initiate drinking and no eating. Traces of another in the same place will initiate eating but no drinking. Probably there are many functional systems whose cells are similarly intertwined within an area. If the functions are related and require a common input or output, there may be considerable advantage in this arrangement.

In addition to the concentration of the blood, it is now fairly well established that temperature also affects the drinking system. If the body temperature rises above normal, drinking increases. Eating is affected in the opposite manner. The contents of the stomach also influence eating and drinking, so it seems likely that there are receptors in the stomach which send information to the appropriate centres in the hypothalamus.

The hypothalamus is not the only part of the brain that regulates eating. It was mentioned earlier that Brown and Schaefer found that removal of the temporal lobes made monkeys eat more. It is not necessary to remove the whole lobe to produce this effect; there is a group of nuclei called the amygdala located below the cortex near the tip of the temporal lobe and destruction of this alone will suffice to change the animal's eating behaviour. The amygdalae are part of a group of structures known as the limbic system which has many connexions with the hypo-thalamus.

In general, it is more difficult to do precise work on the nuclei of the amygdala than it is on those of the hypothalamus, so that it is not yet known with any certainty which of its nuclei are responsible for the various effects seen after ablations of the structure. Usually, after large lesions there, the animal becomes less finicky about what it eats, differing in this respect from those having VM hypothalamic lesions. Electrical stimulation of part of the amygdala has been shown to halt eating in a hungry cat; on the other hand, eating and drinking have been induced by chemical stimulation. Apparently some amygdaloid cells inhibit the eating system whereas others excite it.

The amygdalae receive input from the receptors for smell, and lie close to the sensory cortex for taste and the motor cortex for chewing and swallowing, and are thus in a good position to monitor eating and drinking. Some cells in the amygdalae have the peculiarity that, if they are stimulated for a time, they become more and more sensitive and finally continue to fire spontane-ously for long periods with no further input. One theory as to the role of the amygdaloid nuclei in eating is that they 'clock up' the amount of chewing and taste stimulation of the mouth and throat, and, when it reaches a critical total, they fire and thus shut off the feeding system. They continue to fire until after the food has been digested and has produced an increase in the sugar content of the blood.

It is also possible that the amygdala are especially sensitive to the input from inedible or bad-tasting substances in the mouth, causing the feeding system to shut off immediately. These are sheer speculations, but they would explain most of the experi-mental findings, and they are consistent with experiments that suggest that the amygdalae act as a satiation mechanism for other forms of motivation.

TEMPERATURE-REGULATION MECHANISMS

Most motivation can be considered as an extension into the be-havioural sphere of regulatory mechanisms designed to maintain an animal in its most efficient state. For example, sugar is stored in the liver after eating, and released between meals to maintain its concentration in the blood as nearly constant as possible. Eating takes place again when signals to the liver calling for the release of more sugar are ineffective. Similarly, there are elaborate systems of temperature regulation in warm-blooded animals, employing sweating as a means of cooling and such things as raising the hairs on the body to keep warm (though our hairs are not much use as insulation, we still try to fluff them out and the result is what we call goose pimples). Shivering, which generates heat in the muscles, is another reflexive response to cold.

When these measures approach the limit of their effectiveness, the animal begins to look for a cooler, or a warmer place. In insects and reptiles, which have little internal control of temperature, behavioural methods (moving in and out of the sun, for example) assume more importance, but they are also very important in man in spite of his efficient internal thermostat. The building, heating, and air-conditioning of dwellings, and the production of clothing (not to mention deciding what to wear) are major undertakings, and force us to recognize that the effort to achieve a comfortable temperature is one of our most important motives.

Physiologists have known for a long time that the hypothalamus is essential for reflexive temperature regulation. If it is heated by a probe, sweating and panting are evoked and the body temperature will fall. If the hypothalamus is cooled, the animal will shiver and its temperature will rise above normal. We have already noted the interaction between the temperature-sensitive cells and the eating and drinking systems. Presumably, the cold animal eats to provide the extra energy and, as a long-term measure, to lay down an insulating layer of fat. An overheated animal drinks to provide the fluid needed for sweating. Evelyn Satinoff has shown that rats, in which the anterior hypothalamus is cooled, will learn to press a bar to turn on a heat lamp.

* *Amer. J. Physiol.*, 1964, *206*, 1389-94.

In rats, the building of nests is correlated with temperature. Pregnant females also build nests just before the young are born and it has been suggested that the hormones present at that time act on the temperature-sensitive cells to make the rat feel cold. It would be possible to test this theory by seeing if any of the reflex responses to cold are present. It is, however, more likely that the hormone acts directly on another part of the hypothalamus, and the system that controls nest-building receives input independently from both the temperature-sensitive cells and the hormone-sensitive cells.

SEXUAL AND MATERNAL BEHAVIOUR

The hypothalamus is also important for sexual motivation, as may be inferred from the fact that animals or humans with damage to the anterior hypothalamus lose interest in sex. In animals with seasonal mating habits, the hypothalamus, in conjunction with the pituitary gland, first plays a role in bringing the sexual organs to maturity. This is usually in response to some outside influence, such as an increase in temperature or in the length of the day.

When the gonads are fully developed, they produce sex hormones which find their way back to the hypothalamus in the bloodstream and establish a state of sexual motivation. This finds its outlet in a variety of activities, apart from copulation, depending on the species. Frequently, the animal is first motivated to select a suitable breeding territory, and this may involve migrations of thousands of miles. Quite often, especially in males, it involves fighting, either to defend their territory or to drive other males away from their mates or harems. Courtship rituals and nest-building are other features of sexual behaviour in many species.

The relationship between the hypothalamus and sexual behaviour has been demonstrated experimentally by introducing hormones into certain hypothalamic nuclei through implanted needles. Dr A. Fisher (1964) has shown that it is possible to provoke abnormally intense male sexual behaviour in rats by injecting minute quantities of hormone into the lateral part of the anterior hypothalamus. By this means, even female rats can be induced to mount other rats vigorously and repeatedly, a clear indication that, in this species at least, the necessary neural organization for male sexual behaviour is present in both sexes and only needs the proper priming to become effective.

Dr Michael (1960) has demonstrated a similar phenomenon in female cats. These animals will only tolerate the advances of the male during a short part of their oestrous cycle, thus, if their ovaries are removed they reject the male at all times. In one experiment, needles with a small quantity of hormone fused to their tips were implanted into different parts of the brains of a number of such ovariectomized cats. The hormone dissolved very slowly, diffusing in minute quantities into the region around the needle-tips. It was found that more than half the cats with needle-tips in the hypothalamus were continuously receptive to males for a period of several months, until the hormone was exhausted. Practically none of the cats with needle-tips in the other parts of the brain would mate. It is thus clear that the sexual receptivity of females is also dependent on the action of sex hormone on the hypothalamus; the behaviour is not dependent on the presence of the hormone in the rest of the body, including the sex organs. Components of the courtship behaviour of hens and cocks have been produced by electrical stimulation of the hypothalamus in the experiments of von Holst.

The amygdalae have also been found to influence sexual behaviour. In 1937 Klüver and Bucy (1939) repeated the experiments of Brown and Schaefer and noticed that their monkeys without temporal lobes not only ate more but that they were also hypersexual, particularly the males, who indulged in almost continuous sexual activity.

It is possible that the role of the amygdala in sexual behaviour is similar to its role in eating; i.e. some of its cells are fired by sexual stimulation, or by orgasm, and continue to fire for some time thereafter, partly depressing the hypothalamic sex centres. When a critical amount of sexual activity has taken place the amygdaloid firing completely inhibits sexual motivation, even though there is still a great deal of sex hormone in circulation. The animal will then be incapable of further sexual activity for several hours or days until the amygdaloid after-discharge tapers off.

It is not known whether electrical stimulation of the amygdala will stop sexual activity (as it should if the above hypothesis is correct), but it appears that patients with temporal-lobe epilepsy, which leads to intense firing of the amygdala each time they have a seizure, are often either impotent or take a subnormal interest in sex.

Parental behaviour is closely related to sexual behaviour, and in many animals it is also dependent on hormones generated by the sex organs. In lower animals both parents (or sometimes just the male) may look after the young, but in mammals the job falls primarily to the female because she provides the milk. The hormone which stimulates the mammary glands to secrete milk seems also to act on the hypothalamus to stimulate the behaviour necessary for the survival of the young, though other sex hormones can also arouse maternal behaviour if present in sufficient quantity.

The mother rat builds a nest, and when the young are born she collects them into it and tucks them under her (with an action, incidentally, that is almost the same as that used to construct the nest). If the pups crawl away or are scattered, she retrieves them in her mouth and puts them back in the nest. Males do not normally build nests unless they are cold, and they are more likely to eat the young than to retrieve them, but if a small quantity of hormone is injected into the part of the anterior hypothalamus just medial to the region from which male sex behaviour is elicited, all rats, including males, will build nests and retrieve pups during the hour or so that the hormone remains in effect.

SLEEP

Although it may seem paradoxical, one can advance a good argument for considering sleep as a form of motivation, or rather as a goal. The urge to sleep leads to the search for a suitable place, and to relatively stereotyped behaviours like the circling of dogs, or the habit chimpanzees have of building a tree 'bed' every night.

The problems of sleep are considered more fully in Chapter 13, but it might be mentioned here that sleep, like other motivated behaviours, can be elicited by stimulation of the brain. This was one of the more startling results of Hess's early experiments; those of his cats that were stimulated in certain nuclei of the thalamus (a larger structure lying just above the hypothalamus) would go through all the rituals of finding a place to sleep, curling up in the characteristic posture, closing the eyes and within a few minutes going to sleep.

These and other observations suggest that sleep is not just a running down of the body or nervous system but the result of a neural activity in one part of the brain which inhibits activity elsewhere. They may also arouse speculation as to whether the brain really needs sleep to recuperate from the day's activity, as is usually assumed, or whether instead the sleep mechanism evolved, like those for sex and eating, because the behaviour was of survival value, perhaps by keeping our remote ancestors quiet and out of trouble during the night when they were at a disadvantage in the dark.

FEAR AND ANGER

Fear and anger are subjective states; in this section we shall really be discussing 'freezing', running away, fighting and so on, behaviours that we assume to be correlated with fear and anger. These motives are different from those we have met so far; food does not produce eating in an animal that is not food deprived, but fear can be elicited by certain stimuli with no preparatory change in the internal state (though it is true that the presence of hormones may determine the intensity of the response, or whether the animal responds with fear or with anger).

Primitive avoidance of painful stimuli is seen in animals after complete removal of the brain. Spinal-cord reflexes exist which withdraw an injured limb from the source of damage. If the lower part of the brainstem also remains intact, the animal will show a more integrated response to a noxious stimulus, with general struggling, crying out, etc., and if the hypothalamus is also left undamaged, not only is the animal capable of a full pattern of rage responses but these now also occur to quite trivial stimuli, as they did in Goltz's decorticated dog. It seems that the hypothalamus is organized to call out attack at the slightest input from touch receptors, but that the higher parts of the brain are capable of restraining this reaction.

In view of these findings it is not surprising that stimulation in parts of the hypothalamus can give rise to fearful or aggressive behaviour. These responses were among those seen by Hess in cats, and by von Holst in chickens. Stimulation of parts of the amygdala will also produce fear. At low voltages the stimulated animal looks around apprehensively, and, as the voltage is increased, may flee towards the nearest shelter and hide. Possibly the amygdala is a relay station for fear-evoking visual stimuli, as the lower part of the temporal lobe is an important visual centre. Patients who have their amygdala stimulated during the course of brain operations may experience anxiety, or even cry out in terror, and a feeling of fear is a common prelude to a seizure in epileptics whose focus is in the temporal lobe.

Destruction of some of the pathways leading from the fore-brain to the anterior hypothalamus makes an animal very nervous and aggressive, presumably by cutting off the restraining impulses from the cortex and other higher centres. Rather surprisingly, amygdala lesions will tame wild animals like the monkey or the lynx; after the operation such an animal will even approach a human to be petted. One might expect amygdalectomized animals to be less frightened, especially of visual stimuli, but hardly that they would seek tactual stimulation. Perhaps the change has something to do with a release of sexual motivation, which would undoubtedly have an antagonistic effect on the hypothalamic mechanism for escaping tactual stimulation.

CURIOSITY AND EXPLORATORY BEHAVIOUR

Curiosity resembles fear in that animals do not need internal priming before they will explore. Often, too, the same object will elicit alternating fear and curiosity, as in Darwin's monkeys, who would repeatedly approach to peep at a snake and then run away again. It seems that, if there is no strong motivation from some compelling internal need, the animal will treat almost any stimulus as a goal, with a preference for the less familiar stimuli.

About the only aspect of this behaviour that has been studied physiologically is its satiation. Eventually, an animal will tire of a particular toy, just as it will adapt to being touched, and the pathways involved in the two processes seem to be similar. Lesions of the hippocampus, another limbic system structure that feeds into the hypothalamus, greatly extend the period during which rats will continue to explore a new place. Monkeys with amygdala lesions spend much longer manipulating a few objects than do normal monkeys. Probably activity in these parts of the limbic system suppresses the hypothalamic mechanism by which objects attract the animal, and this activity is only transmitted after a stimulus has been present for some time, or is familiar so that learned circuits are available. The satiation of curiosity may thus fit into the same model as that suggested to explain the amygdaloid component of the satiation for food and sex.

THE MECHANISMS OF MOTIVATION

It must be recognized that in this brief chapter many motives, and many aspects of motivation, have not been mentioned. For example, nothing has been said about the influence of learning; nor has it been made clear that only one motive can be effective at a time. Even though an animal is thoroughly food-deprived, it is not considered to be food-motivated if, for example, it is seen to be pursuing a female, or avoiding a shock. We assume that the various motivational systems suppress one another so that only the strongest, or perhaps the one with the most accessible goal, is effective. If we could be simultaneously attracted by two goals, we would be lucky to achieve either.

What we would really like to know is how these mechanisms work. How, for example, the animal whose lateral hypothalamic nucleus is being stimulated becomes a food-seeking organism for the time being. One possibility is that the nucleus acts as a switch through which, when it is active, input from food stimuli can pass to the motor system. The input then acts on the motor system in such a way that when the animal makes a response which brings it nearer to the food, and the input increases, then that response is maintained; but, when a response is made that weakens the input, that response is quickly shut off. Thus, as the animal tries one response after another, those responses that bring it nearer to the food are carried out more vigorously and for a longer time than those which do not, and by this process of trial and error the food will be reached. When the animal is near enough to touch the food with its nose and mouth, the different stimuli thus produced will elicit reflexive eating. Naturally the higher animals soon learn short-cuts, but they must have some automatic goal-seeking mechanism, using feedback, for use before they have had the opportunity to learn, and on which to base their learning. One can imagine a single goal-seeking mechanism common to many forms of motivation, with hormones, or changes of internal state, determining in some way what sort of stimuli (food, water, sex-partners, etc.) are allowed to gain control of the mechanism.

The mechanism suggested finds some support in a series of experiments stemming from the discovery by Olds and Milner (1954) that rats will learn to make any response that leads to their being stimulated electrically in certain parts of the brain. The stimulation points which give rise to the effect include the lateral hypothalamic nucleus, and many of the pathways leading into the hypothalamus, as well as some of those leading from it towards the motor system.

It may seem paradoxical that a rat will press a lever to stimulate itself in the lateral hypothalamic nucleus and thus make itself hungry. It is certainly not in keeping with the idea that we work in order to assuage our appetites. But if we consider what happens when we are preparing to eat, it may appear less strange. When we see and smell food our hunger is sharpened, but we do not therefore turn away to reduce the stimuli, quite the reverse. Similarly, if the suggested model of motivation is correct, as long as the rat is doing something that increases activity anywhere along the path from the input to the motor system, it will keep on doing it. At points near the sensory end of the path the animal might be expected to respond only if one of the 'switches' to the motor system is closed, i.e. if the animal is motivated. To some extent this is the case; rats respond less vigorously if they are castrated and well fed than if they are starved and injected with sex hormone. But if the stimulation is in the hypothalamus, or its output, the rat responds very vigorously whether its bodily needs have been met or not.

In conclusion, then, it appears likely that there is a motivational mechanism, closely associated with the motor system, which causes an animal to approach any stimulus that is switched through to it. Only one stimulus can control the mechanism at a time; it is selected by a network of competing systems centred on the hypothalamus. These systems receive information about the needs of the body, and the recency of satisfaction or experience with a particular goal; between them they determine an order of priority based mainly on what needs are greatest and what goals are most available.

Acknowledgement. I would like to acknowledge the assistance of research grant APT 66 from the National Research Council of Canada during the writing of this chapter.

13. SLEEP AND DREAMS

ROBERT WILKINSON

Sleep is one of the most puzzling conditions of an organism, partly because it has proved very difficult to discover its functions. Some people sleep very little and yet show little or no impairment as a result. To most people dreaming is even more puzzling and has been the basis of all kinds of superstitions. The analysis of dreams has been one of the main techniques used by psycho-analysts, with some experimental basis. However, new techniques have led to something of a breakthrough in investigating both dreams and sleep, and Dr Wilkinson, who has published many important experiments on sleep, describes the discoveries which have been made.

IN this chapter no attempt will be made to cover all aspects of sleeping and dreaming. We shall be concerned mainly with some of the more important advances over the last forty years to which *behavioural* studies have made a contribution. The field is one in which, perhaps more than most, effective research relies upon an interdisciplinary approach. In particular it will be seen in the pages which follow how rewarding has been the cooperation of the psychologist and the physiologist in trying to achieve some measure of the depth of sleep, in the search for ways of knowing when dreaming is taking place, in charting patterns of sleep and their flexibility, in seeing the extent to which learning can take place during sleep, and, finally, with the aid of the biochemist, in observing the disintegration of behavioural and bodily function when sleep is lost.

NATURE OF SLEEP

There is no need to enlarge upon the aspects of sleep with which we are all familiar. What we are concerned with are those facts which are not obvious to everyone, or which seem obvious but have been shown to be false by objective studies.

An excellent example of the latter concerns the duration of sleep, a measure which one might think would be relatively easy to take. Since 1930 the Children's Bureau of the U.S. Department of Health, Education and Welfare has been issuing a publication on Infant Care which suggests that a one- to two-week-old child should sleep for twenty-two out of the twenty-four hours and that children up to six months in age can be expected to sleep fifteen to seventeen hours. Recent years have seen studies of the actual sleep taken by large numbers of children in these age groups; much lower figures have been indicated, about sixteen to seventeen hours in the first two weeks of life falling to thirteen to fifteen hours over the first six months.

With increasing age fewer hours seem to be spent asleep, although existing data for age groups over thirty are rather inadequate. Here are the full figures representing a composite impression from most of the empirically derived data:

	Hours of sleep
First 3 days of life	16·5
3rd week	15·0
26th week	14·0
2nd year	13·5
6th year	12·0
13th year	9·5
21 years	7·8
Adulthood generally	7·5

It will be noted that the figure for adulthood generally is $7\frac{1}{2}$ hours and not eight, which is the common impression. It is, in fact, possible to find medical views on the amount of sleep people *should* take which range from under seven hours per night to as long as nine hours. This very lack of agreement underlines the inadequacy of medical opinion on this point. Nor, for that matter, can the scientist presume to say how much sleep a given individual should take. What *is* clear, however, from the study of the number of hours actually slept is that individuals vary widely about the averages shown above. This suggests that it is as unrealistic to insist, for example, that all adults should sleep eight hours a night as it would be to expect them all to be 5 ft 5·3 in. high. People vary.

One factor which may influence the duration of the sleep of

different people is its quality. Forty years ago this was another dimension of sleep which the scientist could not assess; now perhaps he can.

The most valid criterion of the quality or depth of sleep may well be its restorative powers as measured by, say, the feeling of well-being the following day, or, perhaps more objectively, by the level of mental and physical performance. Unfortunately, this yardstick has been largely ignored experimentally, possibly because it can only refer to the night's sleep as a whole and also because extremely (though not impossibly) precise and sensitive measures of performance would be needed.

There is another behavioural measure, however, which suffers from neither of these disadvantages, and which has been used experimentally since at least the mid nineteenth century. This is the test we all make to see whether a person is asleep or not – we apply an external stimulus – we say quietly, 'Are you asleep?' If there is a reply, even if it be 'Yes!', we are inclined to judge the person awake. A more scientific version of this procedure is to sound tones of gradually increasing intensity in the ear of the sleeper. The depth of sleep is judged by the intensity required to produce behavioural signs of arousal. Unfortunately, this form of measurement has its limitations too. There is at least one combination of circumstances, as we shall see later, in which it may fail to reflect the depth of sleep. But, considering for the moment only the practical disadvantages, the first is that one cannot go on waking a person throughout the night without seriously disturbing the natural course of sleep, quite apart from the risk of losing one's subject altogether. Secondly, if a sound is repeated frequently throughout the night it may become less arousing through habituation, quite independently of the depth of sleep. For these reasons investigators using this method had to limit their awakenings to three or four per night, which in turn meant that they had to test many subjects over many nights to obtain enough points to draw a single composite curve of the depth of sleep. Such curves were determined, notwithstanding. They showed an increase in the depth of sleep to a low point about one hour after onset, followed by a gradual ascent from this level through the rest of the night.

It was recognized, of course, that this curve was probably a drastic over-simplification of the true one, but the question was how to obtain a valid moment-to-moment record? The solution came with the arrival of the electroencephalograph (EEG for short), a technical development of the utmost importance in recent research upon sleep, as well as in other fields. This machine records the patterns of varying electrical potentials on the scalp due to the activity of the brain beneath. These changes are picked up by electrodes and amplified to activate pens, which then write out a continuous record of the varying brain potentials on slowly moving paper. Four patterns which are relatively easy to distinguish are shown in Figure 51. The first trace is one of desynchronized waves of low amplitude and varying untidily at frequencies of between 20–50 c.p.s. The second trace is of the well-known 'alpha' activity which is a more tidy fluctuation of higher amplitude and of a frequency around 10 c.p.s. The fourth pattern has been given the name of 'spindles' because of its distinctive shape; it is one of short bursts of frequencies at about 14 c.p.s., forming an envelope of first rising and then falling amplitude. The last trace shows the highly distinctive 'delta' waves of very large amplitude and low frequency, usually 1–3 c.p.s.

As soon as these patterns were noticed, as long ago as the 1930s, it was seen also that they appeared to be related to the level of arousal of the body. A person in an active waking state typically showed the fast, low amplitude desynchronized activity. As he closed his eyes and became drowsy the 10 c.p.s., alpha pattern would predominate. With the apparent onset of sleep these alpha patterns would become sporadic, the record flattening to take on an appearance not unlike that of the waking state. This came to be regarded as Stage 1 of sleep. Stage 2 was reached when spindles began to appear in the record, all clear signs of alpha rhythms having vanished. In Stage 3 spindles were still present, but now superimposed upon sporadic large slow waves. In Stage 4 the spindles had vanished, leaving these large delta waves to dominate the record.

To those who first observed these patterns it seemed reasonably obvious that they corresponded with increasing stages in the depth of sleep. But something more objective than this was

required. The obvious course was to see if the standard behavioural measure – the intensity of sound required to waken the
sleeper – varied in the expected way with the stage of sleep as
indicated by the EEG. The experiment was first carried out in
1936 by Blake and Gerard of Chicago University and has been
repeated in various forms since. Occasionally, subjects would be
surprisingly difficult to waken in Stage 1, the lightest state of

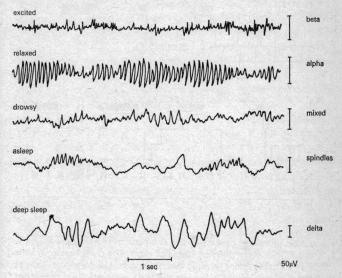

Figure 51. Typical EEG patterns in sleep and wakefulness. (From Jasper
H. H. *Epilepsy and Cerebral Localization* (eds W. Penfield & T. C. Erikson)
1941. Courtesy of Charles C. Thomas, Springfield.)

sleep, but at other times Stage 1 would correspond with the lowest
threshold for behavioural arousal. Then, as the sleeper passed
through Stages 2, 3 and to 4, it was found that progressively
louder sounds were required to awaken him. In short, the EEG
stage of sleep was found to correspond well with the behavioural
assessment of the depths of sleep. The way was now open to examine in more detail the variations in the quality of sleep during
the course of a single night, and without disturbing the sleeper.

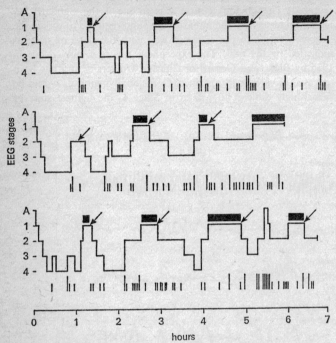

Figure 52. Continuous plotting of five EEG patterns (Awake, and Stages 1, 2, 3 and 4) over three different nights of sleep. The thick bars above the EEG lines indicate periods of rapid eye movements. Longer vertical lines at the bottom of each record indicate major body movements, i.e. changes of position. The shorter ones indicate minor movements. The arrows mark the successive cycles of EEG pattern. (From Dement, W.C., and Kleitman, N. (1957). *EEG clin. Neurophysiol.*, *9*, 673.)

One of the best illustrations of this work is an experiment by Dement and Kleitman (1957) working at Chicago University. As well as the continuous EEG record these investigators took measurements of body and eye movements throughout the night. Figure 52 shows the picture of sleep which emerges. The depth of sleep by the EEG criterion waxes and wanes through the night in a series of cycles of about 1½ to two hours duration. As people fall asleep they descend quite rapidly through the stages of deepening sleep to reach Stage 4 with its large slow waves after about forty-five minutes. Perhaps twenty minutes may be spent in this state, probably the deepest sleep of the night. It will probably be disturbed by a gross body movement accompanied by an ascent, perhaps through the stages or perhaps directly, to the lighter sleep of Stage 1 or possibly Stage 2. After about five minutes or so of this the next cycle will commence with a second descent to deep sleep. There may be three, four or even five of these cycles during the course of the night, all, in general, similar except that successive ones will include less time spent in the deep and more in the light stages of sleep. This reflects the gradual lightening of sleep after the first hour which previous behavioural measures had discerned. What has been described is, of course, the general pattern of sleep about which the records of individual nights may fluctuate considerably, as is apparent in the three examples shown in Figure 52.

This measure of recent success in recording the depth or quality of sleep is encouraging and may open the way to many fresh discoveries, practical as well as theoretical. But it must be evaluated with some restraint. It is true that the EEG and associated measures portray a picture of the fluctuating level of sleep through the night which is highly credible, but it is disconcerting that different measures are not always in agreement, particularly in the Stage 1 state of sleep. Also the EEG itself is not an ideal form of measurement. It often requires skilled interpretation to distinguish patterns corresponding to the various stages of sleep, which are not always as clear as they appear in sample traces provided to illustrate them. Scoring the EEG is therefore time-consuming and not wholly objective. It is true the record can be scored automatically for, say, the frequency and amplitude of the variations, but these correlate only modestly with the threshold behavioural measure of the depth of sleep. More progress will have to be made, if this is possible, in developing objective and automatic methods of quantifying more meaningful aspects of the EEG record. Meanwhile we must rest content that what goes on during a night of sleep is much less of a mystery than it was forty years ago. We turn now to a further illustration of this – the study of the state of dreaming.

DREAMS

In the last ten years or so there have been interesting developments in the study of dreams, again made possible mainly by the availability of electronic methods of recording electrical-brain potentials and eye movements. The story again has been one of basically physiological measures being first validated with reference to behavioural ones and then permitting a more penetrating study of the behavioural aspects of the problem. From time to time investigators had noticed that, if sleepers were woken up at the time when their eyes could be seen moving under the lids, there was a good chance that a dream would be reported. In 1953 Aserinsky, another associate of Kleitman, made use of a more refined technique for recording eye movements. This is similar in some respects to the EEG. Electrical potentials due to the movement of the eyeballs are picked up by electrodes placed at each side of the eye. From this a continuous paper record is obtained of any movements the eye may make throughout the night. At the same time Aserinsky and Kleitman recorded brain potentials from the scalp on the EEG itself. They noticed, as indeed you may have done in Figure 52, that eye movements occurred mainly when the Stage 1 pattern was present in the EEG trace. Could this be the dreaming pattern of sleep? The possibility was investigated by waking the sleepers five minutes after the occurrence of a Stage 1 EEG pattern accompanied by eye movements, and, for comparison, at times when no such combination was present. As was suspected, it was found that the vast majority of recalled dreams followed the Stage 1 eye-movement state.

Armed with this method of detection, a series of experiments was initiated to discover more about the incidence and possible significance of dreaming. The first finding to emerge was that probably everyone dreams. Out of many subjects tested not one failed to report at least one dream when awakened repeatedly out of the Stage 1 eye-movement state of sleep, and this included a number of people chosen particularly because they 'never dreamt'. A bonus for the clinician was that much fuller and clearer descriptions of dreams appeared to be available now that patients could be asked to relate them soon after they had occurred.

Another old idea to be discounted was that dreams, however long they may appear to last subjectively, are over in a flash; on the whole the subjective duration of dreams appears to correspond with the duration of the Stage 1 eye-movement periods which immediately precede their recall. It has even been claimed that the patterns of eye movements sometimes correspond to the nature of the dream, for example, that ascending stairs in a dream may be accompanied by up and down eye movements, and that active dreams yield a greater number of eye movements than passive ones.

During the course of these studies it was noticed that people who were woken frequently during the Stage 1 eye-movement state of sleep for the purpose of recalling dreams seemed subsequently to spend more time in this state when allowed to fall asleep again. This suggested that they were perhaps being deprived of the activity of dreaming and that therefore their dreams were fulfilling some useful purpose. To test this more rigorously an experiment was mounted by Dement (1960) in which subjects were woken as soon as the EEG and eye movements suggested that a dream had started. After a few minutes awake they were allowed to go to sleep again, but were again wakened throughout the night whenever any sign of a dreaming pattern occurred. For comparison, another group of subjects were awakened the same number of times but during periods of sleep when no dreams were indicated on the EEG, that is Stages 2, 3 and 4 with no eye movements. These procedures were continued for a number of nights and then both groups were allowed to sleep normally. It was found that the 'dream-deprived' group spent much more time dreaming than those who had been allowed to dream normally. Dement (1960) concluded that dreams may indeed have some useful function, possibly one of resolving the conflict and frustrations which have built up during the day. In line with this conclusion is the rather surprising fact that people appear to dream more than usual during the sleep which follows a prolonged period without sleep. This is reasonable if we assume that this, too, deprives people of the opportunity to dream.

So far the story is an admirably clear, simple and logical one. Unfortunately, as often happens when original research is followed up by further investigation, things now turn out to be less straightforward. The first qualification concerns the exclusive rights of the Stage 1 state of sleep to the dream process. Recent workers have claimed to have recorded numerous instances of dream recall from awakenings in all stages of sleep. Much may turn on what is regarded as a dream and how soon after the termination of an eye-movement period the recall is asked for. Perhaps the best general statement is that mental activity of some sort can be present at any stage of sleep, and indeed may be present all the time. Its nature may vary, however, from 'thinking' to processes which possess that quality of experience which we normally attribute to fully fledged dreams. For the recall of the latter experiences in their most vivid form a sleeper should be awakened from the Stage 1 eye-movement state of sleep, which to this degree may still be regarded as that corresponding most typically to a dreaming pattern of sleep.

As soon, however, as we admit the possibility of some form of dream activity taking place outside the Stage 1 eye-movement state we have to question whether Dement was, in fact, preventing his subjects from dreaming when he woke them repeatedly out of this stage of sleep. Perhaps all he was depriving them of was this 'kind' of sleep, which they hastened to make up when given the chance. This immediately suggests that one kind of sleep (that of Stages 2, 3 and 4) is no substitute for that of Stage 1 with eye movements. In short, it is just possible that there may be two kinds of sleep, fulfilling, perhaps, different needs and giving different patterns of ill-effect when not taken. We must await further research to settle what Dement was really depriving his subjects of.

LEARNING DURING SLEEP

Subjective though the impression must be, few of us would deny recalling quite complex mental processes having taken place during our dreams. If this can happen, may not other forms of relatively complex intellectual activity occur during sleep, for example, learning? This possibility has attracted much popular attention and has also been exploited commercially, in the form of sleep-teaching machines. Typically, if you invested in such a course you might become the possessor of a tape-recorder which repeated throughout the night, for example, combinations of English and French words and phrases so that you might learn to speak French while you slept. Scientific evidence is often quoted to support the efficacy of these methods and, indeed, there have been a number of experiments carried out since 1916, which appear to show that learning of this kind can take place during sleep. In a typical study, sets of questions and their answers were played to one group of subjects while they slept and not to another group of sleepers. When tested, subsequently, on their ability to answer the questions the group who had the training during sleep were found to answer the questions more accurately.

In 1955 two investigators, Simon and Emmons, embarked upon a critical review of the experimental evidence. Their conclusion was that all of it was unacceptable on one or both of two counts. Their first criticism, which we will not enlarge upon here, was that the experimental techniques employed were unsatisfactory in a number of ways. Their second point was that in none of the experiments had it been possible to be sure that there were not occasions when the subjects had been awake for short periods during the presentation of the material. Simon and Emmons (1956) followed up their review by an experiment which incorporated, for the first time in this area, the EEG as a guide to presenting material only when the subject was asleep. Their criterion of sleep was that none of the 10 c.p.s. alpha rhythm should be present and that it should have been absent for at least thirty seconds. Subsequent tests showed virtually no learning of material presented when the depth of sleep corresponded to Stages 2, 3 or 4 on the EEG record and only moderate retention of the material presented during Stage 1 of sleep. Thus only in the lightest state of sleep, by EEG criteria, when it is often difficult to tell whether a person is awake or asleep, does it seem possible to learn externally presented material. This does not, however, invalidate earlier, less rigorous claims that if material is presented to a sleeper throughout the night some of it will be retained the following day. Although they may not be aware of it in the morning people may often become fully awake for short periods during the night and at such times any material which has been continuously presented will 'get through' and may be learned. It may even be learned better than if it had been presented for similar periods during the day. There is evidence that learning which is followed shortly by sleep is retained much better than that followed by normal waking activity. This would apply with particular force to scraps of learning achieved during short waking periods of the night.

THE PERIODICITY OF SLEEP

We all know that the normal human daily cycle of activity is of some 7–8 hours' sleep alternating with some 16–17 hours' wakefulness and that, broadly speaking, the sleep normally coincides with the hours of darkness. Our present concern is with how easily and to what extent this cycle can be modified.

The question is no mere academic one. The ease, for example, with which people can change from working in the day to working at night is a question of growing importance in industry where automation calls insistently for round-the-clock working of machines. It normally takes from five days to one week for a person to adapt to a reversed routine of sleep and wakefulness, sleeping during the day and working at night. Unfortunately, it is often the case in industry that shifts are changed every week; a person may work from 12 midnight to 8 a.m. one week, 8 a.m. to 4 p.m. the next, and 4 p.m. to 12 midnight the third and so on. This means that no sooner has he got used to one routine than he has to change to another, so that much of his time is spent neither working nor sleeping very efficiently.

One answer would seem to be longer periods on each shift, a month, or even three months. Recent research by Bonjer (1960) of the Netherlands, however, has shown that people on such systems will revert to their normal habits of sleep and wakefulness during the week-end and that this is quite enough to destroy any adaptation to night work built up during the week.

The only real solution appears to be to hand over the night shift to a corps of permanent night workers whose nocturnal wakefulness may persist through all week-ends and holidays. An interesting study of the domestic life and health of night-shift workers was carried out by Brown in 1957. She found a high incidence of disturbed sleep, digestive disorder and domestic disruption among those on alternating day and night shifts, but no abnormal occurrence of these symptoms among those on permanent night work.

This latter system then appears to be the best long-term policy, but meanwhile something may be done to relieve the strains of alternate day and night work by selecting those people who can adapt most quickly to the changes of routine. One way of knowing when a person has adapted is by measuring his performance, but this can be laborious. Fortunately, we again have a physiological measure which correlates reasonably well with the behavioural one, in this case performance at various times of the day or night, and which is easier to take. This is the level of body temperature, as taken by an ordinary clinical thermometer. People engaged in normal daytime work will have a high temperature during the hours of wakefulness and a low one at night; when they change to night work the pattern will only gradually reverse to match the new routine and the speed with which it does so parallels, broadly speaking, the adaptation of the body as a whole, particularly in terms of performance and general alertness. Therefore by taking body temperature at intervals of two hours throughout the period of wakefulness it can be seen how quickly a person can adapt to a reversed routine, and this could be used as a basis for selection. So far, however, such a form of selection does not seem to have been applied in practice.

Another way of modifying the sleep-wakefulness cycle is to change its length, that is to establish a 'day' which is either longer or shorter than the normal twenty-four-hour one. An instance in which there may be a case for a shorter 'day' is the manning of small sea- or space-craft. Suppose the full complement of such a craft were three men and its operational duties required that two men should be on duty all the time. What would be the best system of on- and off-duty periods? One based on the normal twenty-four-hour day might be that shown in Figure 53(*a*). In a staggered system each man enjoys a continuous eight-hour period for sleep, but at the cost of having to spend sixteen hours continuously on duty, a stint which in many working situations could give rise to boredom and inefficiency. An alternative is shown in

Figure 53(*b*). Here the system is based on a six-hour 'day', which requires no more than four hours of continuous work at one time. The penalty, of course, is that only two hours sleep can be taken at one time, a normal day's sleep having to be taken in four

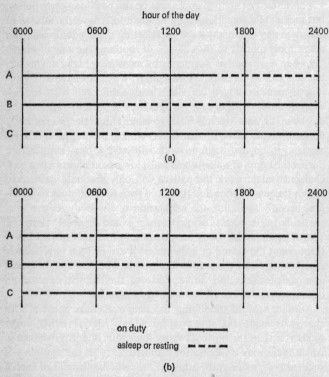

Figure 53. Two ways in which the work and rest periods of three men, A, B and C, can be arranged so that two are always on duty: (*a*) with a twenty-four-hour 'day' of sleep and wakefulness; (*b*) with a six-hour 'day'.

separate instalments. For normal people this would be highly unsatisfactory, and inefficiency might now result from loss of adequate sleep. The question, however, is whether men can be trained to take their sleep effectively in such instalments. By no means enough research has been carried out for us to be able to answer this question with confidence, but a very cautious affirmative is suggested by two investigations. In one of these a group of highly selected and well-motivated servicemen followed for fifteen days a pattern of work and rest similar to the six-hour 'day'. There appeared to be no marked fall in their working efficiency towards the end of this period. The second study sought to establish whether man could adapt to a 'day' of twenty-eight hours comprising continuous periods of nine hours sleep and nineteen hours of wakefulness. Two scientists (Kleitman, 1963, p. 178) retired as subjects to the permanent darkness and constant temperature of the Mammoth Cave in Kentucky, there to live such a twenty-eight-hour 'day' for five weeks. One of them adapted successfully. His sleep–wakefulness cycle and that of his body temperature showed a regular twenty-eight-hour fluctuation by the end of the period. The other, significantly the elder of the two, failed to adapt.

LOSS OF SLEEP

So far the topics considered have not borne very closely on the question of why we need sleep. One approach to this problem is to see what happens to the body behaviourally, physiologically and biochemically when it is deprived of sleep. Experiments of this type have been going on since 1896, but only recently has any real progress been made.

What is the effect the following day of foregoing sleep the whole of the previous night? Physiologically and biochemically it must be admitted that research so far has failed to find any deviation from normal in response to this moderate sleep deprivation. Up to the turn of this century the same verdict would have had to be passed on in attempts to find behavioural changes, but in the last fifteen years improved methods of measurement have demonstrated conclusively that there are certain kinds of task in which performance is seriously impaired. This finding must mean that the body is changed in some way by the loss of one night's sleep and it constitutes a challenge to the physiologists and biochemists to discover how.

Meanwhile psychologists have attempted to provide a clue by

studying in some detail the nature of the behavioural and performance changes which ensue (Wilkinson, 1965). The first point to
note is that any short-lasting task is extremely unlikely to be im
paired by one night's loss of sleep. Only when concentration has to
be maintained for half an hour or more is a decrement to be
observed. Secondly, a crucial factor is the type of work or activity
a person is engaged upon. Comparatively simple, repetitive tasks
will be affected most. Examples are watching almost changeless
displays for the occurrence of occasional faint signals (similar to
the job of look-out on board ship) or repetitive simple decision-
making (similar to sorting letters). Tasks involving calculation
or learning will be less susceptible to loss of sleep and, right at the
other end of the scale, essays of complex decision-taking and problem-solving requiring great intellectual effort may remain completely unimpaired even if prolonged for one hour or more and
even when two or three days have passed without sleep. What is
surprising about sleeplessness, then, is not how much it impairs
performance but the degree to which its impact can be overcome
if the work, notwithstanding its complexity, is interesting or
stimulating enough.

Does this mean that the sleep-deprived man is no different from
normal in such a situation? Experiments in which physiological
and performance measures have been taken have shown this not
to be so. In one such study (Wilkinson, 1962) measures of muscle
tension were taken upon sleepless men as they carried out a series
of calculations. The level of muscle tension remained normal in
those whose performance deteriorated, but rose in those who
maintained normal performance in spite of their loss of sleep.
This suggested that the normal performance of the latter was only
achieved at the cost of some extra effort physiologically. Thus in
one way or another, behaviourally or physiologically, efficiency
appears always to be reduced by loss of sleep.

Further evidence for this proposition has emerged from biochemical studies of much longer periods of sleep deprivation
carried out at the Lafayette Clinic in Detroit (Luby *et al.*, 1960).
It is possible, by analysis of the blood, to determine the activity
of the energy transfer systems of the body – the mechanisms
primarily responsible for providing the fuel to maintain muscular

and neural activity. As the subjects strove to maintain wakefulness for over 100 hours the activity of these systems increased steeply. Beyond the 100-hour point it appeared that emergency methods not normally utilized were brought into play – clear evidence, it was thought, of some degree of exhaustion of the normal sources of bodily energy.

Thus, as a person goes without sleep he appears to resemble in some respects an automobile engine which is becoming inefficient through over-use. Its performance may be impaired, but it may still be possible, within limits, to achieve satisfactory levels at the cost of increased fuel consumption.

What then happens to the human when he is either no longer willing or no longer able to provide the resources necessary to counteract the effects of sleeplessness upon behaviour? Recently there have been a number of experiments in which individual subjects have remained awake for 200 hours or more. Almost invariably it has been found that after some 100 hours without sleep (the point at which the energy transfer systems were found to break down, it may be noted) there ensues a progressive disintegration of personality and rational behaviour. Paranoid symptoms emerge in which the subject may, for example, accuse the experimenters of trying to ruin his attempt to remain awake for the prescribed period. In two cases experimenters have been attacked. At the same time powers of rational perception appear to be disturbed. Imaginary objects may be seen, imaginary persons addressed. Surfaces may appear filmy or covered by cobwebs. A familiar tactual illusion is one of having a tight band around the head. These symptoms, and the sleepiness which accompanies them, appear to come in waves, so that at one time the subject may seem reasonably normal and at another be in a severe delusional state. The effects are more marked during the hours of night than in the daytime.

Thus with sustained and total loss of sleep a person gradually becomes a psychopathological case, although it should be stressed that four to five days with no sleep at all are usually needed for such symptoms to become clear. It has even been suggested that sleep deprivation should be used as a method of producing experimental psychoses in humans. This might seem a highly dangerous and reprehensible idea. Its justification relies upon the lack of any evidence of permanent defect in men who have remained awake for over 200 hours. After a terminal sleep of only twelve hours or so they appeared quite restored to normal.

CONCLUSION

In this chapter I have been looking almost exclusively at the more important psychophysiological aspects of recent research into sleep and dreaming. Much has had to be omitted as falling outside the scope of the present book, in particular some neurological and biochemical research over the past fifteen years which has made an important contribution to a better understanding of the internal mechanisms of sleep. An excellent entry for anyone wishing to pursue these aspects of the subject, as well as for those wishing to go more deeply into the topics of the present chapter, is provided by the revised edition (1963) of Kleitman's classic, *Sleep and Wakefulness*. No one reading this, or perhaps even the present brief review, is likely to deny the measure of achievement during the last forty years. And yet, despite all that has been learned, there are many practical problems connected with sleep about which the scientist, if his advice is sought, can only answer with that most deceptive of ploys, an educated guess. Perhaps the outstanding example is that growing affliction of modern society, insomnia. Impressive though the theoretical advances of recent years have been, society may be entitled now to ask when this knowledge is to be applied to the solution of some of its everyday problems of sleep.

14. DRUGS AND PERSONALITY

C. R. B. JOYCE

It is in the nature of experiment that one or more factors should be manipulated and the results observed. Sometimes such manipulations are done in an exploratory fashion, just to see what will happen, but as a subject advances it becomes possible to test hypotheses by such methods. One of the most interesting advances in psychology is concerned with altering man's 'internal environment' by means of drugs. There is a great deal of work of this kind, which has now become a separate subject – psychopharmacology. Dr Joyce, who is a psychopharmacologist, shows how much of this experimentation has passed beyond the exploratory stage, and how it has provided new ideas about personality.

PERSONALITY

EVERYBODY thinks he knows what personality is, and for once everyday speech and technical language are in reasonable agreement. Personality is the psychological 'style' of an individual, the rather consistent foundations on which reactions to life situations are based. Personality is what gives our friends and close acquaintances a chance of predicting our responses in given circumstances. Of course, in some cases (or sexes, or ages) unpredictability is itself a feature of an individual's personality; and, anyway, it is fortunate that at the best of times inspired guessing is seldom completely accurate. Even the simplest individual possesses a rich response repertoire, and his final choice between alternative courses of action depends upon the relative weights he attaches to features arising from his experience or from the environment itself. One can thus only speak of tendencies to behave in a certain way, not of standard patterns of behaviour. Nevertheless, people can be compared with each other in respect to the strength of these tendencies; or the same individual can be compared with himself on different occasions and under different influences.

Physiological and Psychological States

DRUGS

Most people, too, would probably reckon to be able to define a drug, although perhaps not to the satisfaction of a pharmacologist. For him, a drug is any chemical which is introduced into a living organism and which leads to physiological effects – such as a rise in body temperature, or a change in the blood sugar - which can be detected by objective means. These involve some kind of measuring device which is not itself under the direct control of the subject. Two aspects of this definition require comment.

First, drugs are not only substances used for therapeutic reasons: many kinds of alcohol, opium, 'purple hearts', cocaine and the fantasticants beloved of Aldous Huxley, are all drugs for none of which, in my view, are there any *therapeutic* indications whatsoever. But the careful *experimental* administration of such chemicals has produced evidence about some of the ways in which the central nervous system works, including that part of it which is concerned with personality. In addition, the uncontrolled taking of the same group of drugs, by naïve sophisticates in search of kicks, or the frank addicts that they all too frequently become, is a major *social* problem and an important aspect of the personality of our sick society.

Second, the definition tries to keep the word 'drug' for those substances that produce their effect by means that are known to be purely physiological. However, everything in the environment – smell, sight or sound, wife, dog or doctor – in fact gains a conscious or unconscious significance for the organism that on later occasions can cause changes in blood pressure, in the appearance of the skin or, indeed, in any index of physiological response at all. These relationships are of great importance in psychological and psychosomatic medicine, as well as in the laboratory (and it will be necessary to return to them below), but the pure pharmacologist tries to exclude them from consideration in order to avoid arrogantly incorporating much of psychology, physics and medicine into his territory as well. To the pure all things are said to be pure, but in fact no scientist is as pure as all that – even the physicist depends upon his own perception to an extent that might frighten him if he knew. But the use of objective methods to detect changes (that is, methods that are not under the direct physical control of the subject) does not guarantee that the changes themselves are not initiated by psychological means: it is well known that a gelatine capsule filled with table salt, and given with the assurance that it will bring sleep, very frequently does so (about once in three times over the population at large – Beecher, 1955). Such sleep is accompanied, or even preceded, by all the physiological changes that go with normal or drug-induced sleep (deeper, slower, respiration; changes in the EEG; slowing of the heart): yet so small an amount of salt, if presented to the subject as salt, may have as its only detectable effect – if that – an appropriate and transient increase in the amount of salt that he excretes.

THE PLACEBO EFFECT

This kind of phenomenon has been known at least since Chaucer's day (Kissel *et al.*, 1964), when, indeed, most so-called medicines were of such a class (as some practitioners realized even then). In medieval fashion substances that produced such reactions were given a Latin name. '*Placebo*' means '*I will please*'. The best medical opinion has always considered that there is nothing un-ethical about the use of placebos in proper circumstances – where no specific treatment is known, for example, or where reassurance and a firm indication of sympathetic understanding of the problem are all that is required. (The occasions, incidentally, when this *is* all that is needed are far less numerous than many medical practitioners, or laymen, suppose.)

But since the Second World War a more scientific attitude to-wards medical treatment, and the application of controlled experi-mental methods to the investigation of the hundreds of new pharmaceuticals that assail the profession each year, has shown not only that many of these substances are placebos (that is, they have no specific physiological activity at all) but that every trans-action involving an active drug, even of an antibiotic or a local anaesthetic, contains a 'placebo' element. That is to say, any offer of a remedy in the customary way contains an implication that it will benefit the patient. Were this not so, the offer would not normally be made. The recognition that this is the case has given rise to a certain amount of experimental work intended to separate the specific, pharmacological action of the drug, from the non-specific, psychological factors inherent in the transaction and – as it turns out – in the whole situation in which it is given (Joyce, 1961). This includes the physician, the nurse, other patients, the patient's family and friends and, of course, the patient himself, not to speak of the setting in which he finds himself at the time: hospital, out-patient clinic, general practitioner surgery or home.

NON-SPECIFIC FACTORS

Experiments of this kind are in principle no more complicated than others: they are only as meaningful as is allowed by proper framing of the questions to be asked, correctly identifying the things that matter, and adequately controlling experimental conditions. There has as yet not been a great deal of work in this field that reaches the necessary standards, but from such as there is some interesting points emerge. For example, we can briefly show how important is the interaction between drug, patient and his surroundings by the observation that, whereas the dose of sleeping draught to help a child to rest at home is on the average larger than that required in hospital, the reverse is true of the dose for an adult. Similarly, the amount of medication a depressed patient requires seems to vary inversely with the number of family or social contacts to which he is exposed. Even the blood-pressure, taken when the subjects are at rest, is different in home and hospital – it seldom falls quite so low, no matter how long the rest period, in the out-patient clinic as it does in the surgery and still less so than in the parlour; but once the patient is admitted into hospital, his blood-pressure is more likely to fall further than if he stays in bed at home. It will already be clear that personality must have something to do with all this, and, indeed, interactions between drug, personality and medicine are the invariable rule: only their importance may differ from one example to another.

Such examples suggest some of the reasons why new drugs that have been thoroughly tested in the laboratory and in the wards of the great research and teaching hospitals not infrequently disappoint when they are tried in the world at large – their actions, genuine though they may be, may in fact be insufficiently strong to overcome the effects of even stronger stimuli to the patient's central nervous system, such as a child who will not sleep or a husband who will.

NON-COOPERATION

But studies of this kind have also suggested other reasons for our too frequent failures to pick out useful drugs. They may be due to premature rejection of the useful no less than to wrong acceptance of the useless – it is just as mistaken to keep the bath water as to throw away the baby.

A surprisingly frequent reason why treatment fails is that the patient does not cooperate (Joyce, 1962a). He or she simply fails to obey instructions, perhaps (often) because he has not understood them, even more often because he has felt better before completing the course prescribed, perhaps most often because he has little belief in their efficacy to start with whether or not this is undermined by a friend or fellow-patient, or because he has initially, or comes to have, little faith in his doctor. Not surprisingly, it makes an enormous difference to the apparent value of a new remedy if this is determined on people who have actually taken it, rather than on those who are only supposed to have done so. This kind of information is very seldom available, but in several studies the average number of pills taken by patients as a proportion of those they were prescribed has fallen as low as fifty per cent. It seldom seems to be greater than eighty per cent. This is not to deny that there are patients who do exactly as they are told, though they may not be very numerous: but whether or not such paragons exist, there are certainly those who take no treatment at all, although they do not make this plain to their doctors. This discovery seems to come as no surprise to a lay audience, but it usually amazes the medical profession, whose members have been inclined to assume complete obedience in those who come to them for advice.

PERSONALITY DIFFERENCES IN PATIENTS

However, such differences in behaviour become really interesting when we try to relate them to differences in the personality of cooperators and non-cooperators. Men are as likely as women to default, but it is the younger women and older men who are the worst offenders: female backsliders are prone to dose themselves (especially with purgatives), to a greater extent than cooperators. They also pay rather more attention to their own bodily processes, but are not noticeably more neurotic or introverted. However, it is a striking fact (though we must guard against irrelevant conclusions) that they are less likely to be or to have been married than their more cooperative colleagues.

Many of these facts differentiate them from another interesting sub-group, the so-called 'placebo-reactors'. These are patients, or experimental subjects, who are especially likely to respond to the administration of an inactive substance, the placebo or dummy already mentioned, by the reporting and, indeed, the objective presence of changes in their bodily state: or they may react to truly active drugs in accordance with their – sometimes quite mistaken – belief about its action, perhaps one that is incubated in them at the suggestion of the experimenter, rather than in the way to be predicted from its normal pharmacological action. In the case of patients, changes like these may be either beneficial or undesirable, and it even appears likely that there are sub-divisions of placebo-reactors who differ from each other in personality – so-called 'positive' (i.e. therapeutic) and 'negative' (toxic) reactors. The former appear to be more extraverted and in general to take a more active part in social activities (Lasagna *et al.*, 1954). They are also more suggestible and incline (in the case of Americans at least) to stronger religious beliefs; but they do not differ from the others either in intelligence or in the length of schooling they have received. Laboratory and clinical studies have made it clear that the reactions of such people to medication are predictable. Of course, they are not perfectly so, but they are very far from totally dependent upon environmental vagaries.

Drugs and Personality

PERSONALITY DIFFERENCES IN THE DOCTOR

One factor in the environment is of supreme importance in this respect: the doctor. Patients have different degrees of faith in individual doctors, apart from their attitude to the profession as a whole. Although (for various but obvious reasons) it is almost impossible for us to ask patients to estimate their faith in their doctor, and to relate this to the outcome of therapy, we can ask different doctors to compare the same two or three drug treatments on similar patients. This they do under what are called 'double-blind' conditions – that is, when neither the doctor nor the patient knows the identity of the drug until the period of treatment is over (Joyce, 1962b). It has been found in psychiatric as well as other kinds of practice, that whereas in the hands of doctor A treatment X will prove most effective, doctor B gets his best results with treatment Y. Doctor C, however, may be unable to show any differences at all between X and Y and an inactive control treatment. This sort of result is very surprising and not easy to explain. It presumably means that whereas some features relevant to the improvement that his patients experience and report are in some way permitted or even encouraged by one doctor, these are minimized or rejected by the other.

Little is known as yet about the reasons for these differences in attitude, and in the personality to be inferred from them; but it is probable that they are related to differences in the seniority of the doctor (this may reflect his experience, or merely his age) and to his capacity to participate in the interests of the patient. But it is clear, experimentally, that some combinations of drug and doctor are more beneficial to the patient than are others, and that it is not just a question of the right disease encountering the right physician or the right treatment: one must have the quack and the drug and the sick one all together.

DRUGS AND PERSONALITY

If there are differences in the ways that people of different personality react to inactive substances, and in the effects that doctors of different personality can produce with drugs, it seems very

277

probable that different personalities will react differently to drugs as well. That is quite true, and is indeed within the everyday (or at least once every year) experience of most of us. There is a great deal of folk-lore about alcohol, among which is a commonly held belief that whereas some people get raving mad on the smell of the barmaid's apron, others grow only more gentlemanly as they down pint after civilizing pint. McDougall (1924) suggested that such differences were related to measurable differences in a personality dimension now called extraversion–introversion, and that these in turn were related to differences in concentration of 'E' and 'I' substances in the central nervous system. These have so far escaped chemical detection. In fact, this kind of relationship has been known (in the sense of put to empirical medical use) for nearly two thousand years at least. Dioscorides, the Greek who was Chief Pharmacist to the Emperor Nero, noted that 'white hellebore should not be taken by old men, youths, such as are weaklings, nice or effeminate or fear strangling'. Much later, but even so, more than a century ago, Kidd, an early experimenter with anaesthetic ether, knew that hysterical or nervous women required larger quantities to make them unconscious; and fifty years ago Hanzlik, observing the extraordinary variation in the individual dose of aspirin required to lessen pain, decided that this was because people are different from each other. A not very revolutionary concept, one would have thought, but evidently one that is news to those members of the medical profession who are to be overheard in the columns of their learned journals, some time after a new drug appears on the market, solemnly warning each other that, 'It may be necessary to vary the dose according to the needs of the individual patient.'

Eysenck and his collaborators at the Maudsley Hospital have developed an indirect method of investigating relationships between personality and the hypothetical neural functions of McDougall, which they prefer to think of in terms of excitatory and inhibitory states of the central nervous system resembling those suggested by Sherrington. This approach involves a combined attack by personality testing to establish the categories into which the subjects fall (this has, in fact, been one: the introversion–extraversion continuum, and to clinical analogies to this: see

Chapter 18); drugs; and performance tests to define the changes produced (reaction times, perceptual tests and so on). The inter-relationships found and Eysenck's interpretations cannot be fully described here; but in very general terms his two main findings can be summarized as follows. Subjects with high extraversion scores (or patients classified clinically as hysteric) are characterized by rapid development of central inhibition: 'stimulant' drugs have little effect upon them, but they respond to small doses of 'depressants' by marked changes in behaviour. Introverted subjects (or dysthymic patients) show the reverse behaviour. They are centrally inhibited and more susceptible to stimulants, but can take large quantities of depressants with little overt change. The volume of experimental work is large, and covers even aspects of pure learning theory with which we are not concerned (Eysenck, 1963).

It is always impressive to see an attempt to comprehend different disciplines, or even different areas of the same discipline, within the same framework of theory. But the results in the present case are not overwhelmingly impressive. Of course, a failure to support a prediction that involves a relationship between a human being, a drug and test may be due to a misclassification of any or all of the factors involved; especially since the prediction is based upon inferences about physiological substrates for psychological phenomena, sites of actions of drugs and centres and pathways concerned with different kinds of performance. Only the middle one of these, the sites at and ways in which drugs act is at all accessible to anything like direct observation, and the evidence we have is that it means little to speak of a drug as a 'stimulant', or 'depressant' in neurological terms, although this may be useful in speaking of gross behaviour. If units of behaviour – for example, the number of decisions made or of words uttered in unit time – are definable, then it can be seen whether a given drug increases or decreases the output. But the same drug may increase the output of one kind of unit and decrease another ostensibly similar one: for example, some tranquillizers reduce certain agitated movements but initiate other, involuntary ones. Again drugs commonly classed as similar may have quite different effects – for instance, in a study of the effects of alcohol and phenobarbitone

(Luminal) upon typewriting skills alcohol increased typing speed and the number of mistakes made, whereas the barbiturate slowed speed, reduced errors and increased the likelihood of the errors being detected and set right. Even more indigestible in simple terms of depression and stimulation, however, was the observation that when both drugs were taken together, the effects of one did not neutralize those of the other: instead, the subjects behaved as if they had taken a particularly large dose of alcohol (Joyce *et al.*, 1959).

As Sherrington and Hughlings Jackson, great experimental and clinical neurologists respectively, pointed out a long time ago, excited behaviour can arise from a change in the opposing function of another level, as can the converse. If a single dose of any drug is sufficiently large, it will produce an effect that is characteristic of the group to which it belongs – any 'depressant' will produce unconsciousness, and any 'stimulant' will cause convulsions. At still higher concentrations, any drug of either group will kill – even water (although under such special circumstances that this is not to be taken as scientific evidence for a belief fairly widely held in some communities). But after single low or moderate doses, the effects on different people may be rather variable, owing to the operation of those factors, among others, that have already been mentioned above. The effects, too, are usually rather transient, and wear off after a few hours as the drugs are changed to inactive substances by the metabolic processes of the body, or excreted; and the final state of the individual is not fundamentally changed, as a rule, by his use of them: except, for example, that he may feel refreshed by the sleep that would otherwise have eluded him.

Thus, although the personality of the patient may modify the action of the drug, it looks as if the drug can do little to modify the personality of the patient. In a certain sense, this is because the problem is one in semantics and not pharmacology: the difficulty arises from the definition of personality as that aspect of the individual's behaviour that is relatively unchanging. Hence, it is not surprising that a casual encounter with a drug makes as little permanent impression upon his inmost self as a breakfast of toast and marmalade. Why then, is it claimed more and more frequently nowadays that drugs *can* change the personality, that the mentally sick can be helped by the products of the pharmaceutical revolution?

DRUGS AND MENTAL ILLNESS

The two ways of putting the point are not equivalent. The first, as we have seen, begs the question, but in the second there is some truth. Drugs, if they are properly chosen with him in mind and given in the correct dosage, at the right time and for a sufficient period, can help the individual to re-establish contact with his environment; especially with some kind of therapist (perhaps a friend or member of his family – not necessarily, although most frequently it may be, a psychiatrist). His disturbed behaviour may first have to be quietened (a compulsion or reiterated pattern broken, or an habitually aggressive attitude to other people diminished) or he may need to be driven out of his lethargy (the volume control turned up, as it were) before this relationship can be established. Unless the drug or some other kind of physical spanner is thrown into the works, this may not occur at all; but if some other human being does not seize the opportunity when it occurs, the drug is quite certain to be useless. If this intervention is successful, the personality that emerges from the therapist's care is likely to bear a close relationship to the personality that was visible before the illness. The drug doesn't change this; nor, apparently, does the therapist, who simply helps the patient to accept the personality in which his genes, his maturation and his early experience have conspired to dress him. Doctors who insist that drugs alone can work cures are either modest, overworked or incompetent. A maniac quietened by a depressant but otherwise untreated represents an advantage to the society of the mental hospital; but it does not necessarily follow that the patient shares in this.

FUTURE DEVELOPMENTS

Thus I am extremely sceptical when it is predicted that, among other things, we shall have drugs with specific effects, either upon aspects of behaviour, or even upon localized groups of nervous cells, or 'centres'. Any nerve circuit is involved in too many integrations of behavioural units, and any single item of behaviour can be initiated by too many circumstances for this to be a practical possibility: for example, you may kiss one woman for pleasure and another from a sense of duty, and each of them may perfectly understand your motives; yet both may slap your face.

Such claims for specificity have been made by the drug companies – one substance has already been advertised for obsessive–compulsive symptoms, another (may God preserve us) for 'mild anxiety'. Like many, but not all, drug company claims the first of these was not justified; if the second ever is, it will be a rather sorry day.

It might be claimed that we already have one group of drugs with a specific action – the hallucinogens, or psychotomimetics already referred to on p. 272 (Blum, 1964). Popular interest in these drugs was stimulated by the late Aldous Huxley (1954), whose writings on such subjects constituted one of the few arguments in favour of retaining an Iron Curtain between the Two Cultures. Huxley made the mistake – as have almost all writers and many scientists who have experimented with these substances – of thinking that his own experiences were typical and would be general. As an artist with a vivid imagination, based on wide reading and acquaintance, he attributed the action of the drugs to alterations in perception, although he was himself almost blind at this time. Other writers have made similar claims for the euphoriants (the morphine-like substances) and have sought Nirvana, the suspension of the emotions, with their aid. But Nirvana is not to be unlocked with a chemical key, whatever chemical changes in the central nervous system accompany its attainment. Hallucinogens do not affect all people the same way (some they drive mad) nor are they devoid of actions on other systems of the body; nor do the euphoriants depress only the emotions. They constipate; they also depress the respiration, and so they kill. The effects of both groups depend upon prior experience, present mood – in fact, as usual, all the things discussed above.

However, these drugs have a peculiar place in the study of interactions between drugs and personality. The euphoriants, as well as other substances not discussed here, are addictive: that is to say, a certain number of individuals who have once experienced them – for medical or non-medical (and so, in the first instance, illegal) reasons continue to seek out supplies. In America, where there are conservatively estimated to be 50,000 addicts or one in 4,000 of the population, this continued use is regarded as illegal; in Britain, where there may be four or five times as many addicts as the official estimate of one in 80,000, addiction is taken to be an illness in itself (Editorial, *Lancet*, 1964). Although the figures are small, the frightening thing is that they are *rising* faster each year. But whether the problem is considered by society to be one for the police or for the doctor, it is a tragedy for the sufferers, because this is an illness that at the moment is exceptionally hard to treat. Such evidence as we possess about its natural history is in sociological and psychological terms; but these are not all the same for the two countries. In the United States, it is the economically deprived who suffer – the Negroes, the Puerto Ricans; but in Britain, addicts are usually young, white and often self-sufficient. At the moment it is hard to say more than that 'users' are clearly different from 'non-users', but they are known to be so only after they have started to use the drug. So it is impossible to know which is the cart and which the horse. But personality studies now in progress are intended to *predict* who will become a user.

Hallucinogens are not, apparently, strongly addictive; but there is some evidence not very clear as yet (and here again chickens and eggs are scrambled together) that they interfere with participation in life in the real world by substituting phantasies for action. This would be a matter of little concern to anyone except the user, the Ministry of Pensions and National Insurance, and eventually the taxpayer, were it not that these drugs appear to have an especial fascination for some members of the community who, except for their obsession, would appear among the most useful and productive. As his sight failed, Huxley himself tried by means of special exercises to avoid the use of spectacles, which he referred to as 'crutches'. As he believed that no cripple would prefer to go on using crutches, if he could have the broken leg properly set, it is hard to see why he did not consider such pharmaceutical props to the broken soul as mescaline and morphine to be crutches of another kind: crutches of a particularly vicious kind, for once used they may lock themselves in place and the key may too often be mislaid. Crutches, too, that can be and are deliberately offered by the unscrupulous to the susceptible, perhaps to affect the security of a whole society no less than that of an individual mind.

This naturally leads us to wonder about the future part to be played by drugs in the 'control' of human behaviour. Recent newspaper stories have made it clear that some western nations are experimenting with other chemical means to control crowd behaviour than tear gas and stink bombs. Psychiatrists and other experts have known for a long time about the – so far rather unsuccessful – use of 'truth drugs' (usually hypnotics in steady, submaximal concentration) to treat neurosis, encourage confessions and wash brains. But too many psychologists seem to be speaking these days of the control of human behaviour as though this were something as simple and as necessary as house-training a puppy, and eventually no less a matter for satisfaction to the subject, although more far-reaching in its consequences. They speak like Skinner (1948b), in his mood of *Walden Two*, but though they are as intolerant of error as he, they are more intolerable: for their judgement of what is good and bad is often based on a less universal ethic. The greatest contribution to human happiness that could be made by the pharmaceutical industry, I believe, is the discovery of a drug to make the individual resistant to the effects of all kinds of technological suggestion, particularly when under the influence of any other drug. This in itself would help in the attainment of another highly desirable objective: an overall decline in the use and abuse of drugs of all kinds. After the thalidomide tragedy, the medical and pharmaceutical professions rightly took part of the blame upon themselves because they had been content with inadequate safeguards and information. In my view the responsibility of the general public was as great: for just as a country gets the government it deserves, society gets the poisons it asks for.

Further reading. See Joyce, 1964 and Lindemann *et al.*, 1961.

LEARNING AND TRAINING

People are often mystified by the way that psychologists use the word 'learning'. To a psychologist, the concept has enormous scope. He uses it to describe any change in behaviour which is the result of experience, which is more than transitory, and which cannot be ascribed to maturation or senility or illness. In looking for the historical *explanation of behaviour he will more often than not find a situation where behaviour was modified as a result of learning. Learning in this sense includes what somebody does when they are being educated, trained or teaching themselves. But it also includes the way a child may learn to be afraid of school, or learn tricks for avoiding doing homework. It even includes the modification of behaviour to be seen in a worm when it is given an electric shock if it takes the wrong turning in an experimental maze. There need be no intention to learn, nor need there be any intention to train.*

Because the concept is so wide, theories of learning have come to have all the appearances of theories of behaviour as a whole, all the more so because learning theorists often minimize the influence of heredity and of instinct.

15. OPERANT CONDITIONING IN THE STUDY OF ANIMAL BEHAVIOUR

ROGER STRETCH

Professor B. F. Skinner of Harvard University has developed one of the most influential systems for studying learning. He is interested in contingency explanations – 'what leads to what' (see page 9) – and is therefore concerned with the prediction *of behaviour, rather than the understanding of it; so that his system is not strictly a theory. During the course of his work, Skinner has devised potent methods of* controlling *behaviour, and to some extent he is therefore concerned with training methods. His ideas are of general interest to educationalists, but have also led to specific training methods, such as teaching machines and programmed learning (next chapter). However, the validity of his method, known as operant conditioning, is clearest in experiments done with animals, and Dr Stretch, who has done many such experiments himself, gives a survey of this branch of psychology.*

To understand behaviour, whether we are concerned with the acquisition of a new response or the performance of a well-established skill, we must be able to define the conditions under which it occurs. However, human learning is a highly complicated process and it is hardly surprising to find that throughout the history of the experimental analysis of behaviour, a strong emphasis has been given to the comparative method. Interest in animal learning has not necessarily taken the form of a pre-occupation with the behaviour of individual species. Rather, it has been directed towards the discovery of general principles governing the learning process as a whole.

In the lower vertebrates, many activities concerned with the primary biological functions of nutrition, reproduction and defence are subserved by relatively inflexible and stereotyped patterns of behaviour and we sometimes use the term *instinct* to describe them. In mammals, on the other hand, biological needs are satisfied by means of complex, variable patterns of activity that reflect predominantly the influence of learning and experience. Indeed, in many, it is difficult to define any pattern of behaviour as wholly innate (Zangwill, 1950). Although a rigid distinction between instinctive and acquired behaviour cannot easily be made, it seems clear that evolution has resulted in the development of animals of progressively greater capacities for learning. If we can assume some degree of continuity in the processes of evolutionary development, we may be able to understand complex instances of behaviour by recourse to the study of simpler organisms. Basic mechanisms that in man are obscured by the complexity of his behaviour may often be clearly discernible in less highly evolved forms (Nissen, 1951).

Psychologists usually draw a distinction between two types of laboratory situations in which learning processes may be studied. One is called *respondent* conditioning which was developed by the distinguished Russian physiologist, Pavlov, and his associates. The second situation, with which this chapter is mainly concerned, is that of *instrumental* or *operant* conditioning. This form of conditioning stemmed from the early work of Thorndike, but, in the hands of Professor Skinner of Harvard University, operant conditioning has recently emerged as an independent technology of appreciable significance in the experimental analysis of behaviour.

THE CONDITIONED REFLEX

Most people have heard of Pavlov's famous dogs and of the way in which they were trained to salivate at the sound of a bell. Briefly, Pavlov found that if a neutral or 'indifferent' stimulus, such as the sound of a bell is presented a few seconds before a natural stimulus that evokes salivation, e.g. powdered meat, and the combination of the two is presented twenty or thirty times, the sound alone comes to evoke a measurable flow of saliva. In other words, a reflex normally produced by food can now be elicited by a sound. Pavlov also found that if he continued to present the sound by itself, the conditioned salivary reflex gradually diminished. This procedure, whereby an acquired response may be weakened, is known as *experimental extinction*.

Operant Conditioning in the Study of Animal Behaviour

It is seldom appreciated that these experiments call for elaborate experimental controls. First of all, the dog must be isolated from all extraneous stimuli, including the experimenter! Some means of measuring successive secretions of saliva must be found, and a device is needed whereby food can be delivered automatically. Finally, the acquisition of the conditioned reflex depends intimately upon the time intervals that are allowed to elapse between the conditioned and unconditioned stimuli. These arrangements were provided for in the following way: the dog was placed inside a sound-insulated chamber and held in a loose harness to prevent undue movement. Salivary secretions were collected in a tube attached to the animal via a cheek fistula, and food was delivered by a dispensing mechanism situated on the outside of the chamber.

The important feature of Pavlov's method is that the experimenter retains complete control of the stimuli that are presented. Pavlov found that if the conditional stimulus (the sound of the bell) was presented two or three seconds before the unconditioned stimulus (food), the conditioned reflex could be established quite quickly. In fact, conditioning may be said to have taken place when the sound of the bell elicits a salivary secretion in the interval just *preceding* the presentation of food. However, during the acquisition of the conditioned reflex, it is not important *as far as the experimental procedure is concerned* whether zero, five or fifty drops of saliva are secreted during the interval between the two stimuli! The experimenter continues to present food in association with the sound until the conditioned reflex begins to appear. In other words, the appearance of the conditioned salivary reflex (as distinct from the secretion of saliva that is produced by food) is not a prerequisite for the presentation of the reinforcing stimulus, food.

Although Pavlov's experiments have had a profound influence upon the development of modern psychology and were the first in which a part of an animal's activity was controlled by manipulating the environment in a systematic way (Ferster, 1963), there is a sense in which this procedure merely brings an already existing reflex under the control of a new stimulus. To many psychologists the conditioned reflex does not reflect the sensitive interaction between an animal and its environment that they have come to regard as an essential characteristic of behaviour.

OPERANT CONDITIONING

The significance of operant conditioning is that it demonstrates a second way of handling the reinforcement procedure. In these experiments, an animal must *emit* an appropriate response in order to produce the reinforcing stimulus, food. Imagine a rat in a small box which includes a lever projecting from one of the walls. Unlike the classical procedure, the hungry rat must press the lever and unless he does so, food is not forthcoming. The animal explores freely and, in the course of this activity, emits a response that changes the environment in such a way that his own subsequent behaviour is affected. These changes in the environment could be called rewards, but the term 'reinforcing stimulus' is usually preferred. When such stimuli follow a response, they increase the likelihood that the animal will behave in the same way again. Thus, the animal learns and his behaviour is shaped so that it becomes more effective in dealing with the environment.

Perhaps a crucial distinction between respondent and operant conditioning procedures can now be seen. In the situation devised by Pavlov, reinforcement is not contingent upon performance of the conditioned response whereas, in operant conditioning, the response alone defines the necessary condition for reinforcement.

AN ILLUSTRATIVE EXPERIMENT

The experiments chosen to illustrate operant conditioning deal with the behaviour of pigeons, rats and monkeys. Pigeons are usually required to peck a small disc mounted on the wall of the experimental space, but, with rats and monkeys as subjects, the response consists of pressing a small lever. The choice of these responses is not entirely arbitrary. These experiments deal with a selected segment of the behaviour of a freely moving animal and it is essential that the response chosen for study should be one that can be repeated frequently and over long periods without fatigue.

Figure 54 shows the kind of situation in which the experiment may be carried out. A hungry pigeon is placed within a sound-proof box which is divided into two compartments. The box is well-ventilated since the bird will spend several hours inside it each day. On one of the walls, above the food aperture, a trans-

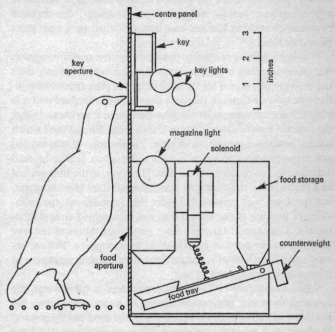

Figure 54. Experimental arrangements for the pigeon. (From Ferster and Skinner, 1957, p. 15.)

lucent disc is mounted and the box is equipped with an automatic food-dispenser. Pecking at the disc activates the feeding mechanism and a small quantity of grain is made available to the bird.

The experiment can now begin. First, the pigeon is trained to obtain grain from the food aperture beneath the disc. Since a pronounced click accompanies the presentation of the food magazine, the bird quickly learns to approach the aperture whenever this noise occurs and tends not to look for food in its absence. We may then increase the frequency of some part of the bird's behaviour by operating the feeding mechanism as soon as the bird emits a bit of behaviour we wish to encourage. Thus, to increase the frequency of head movements, one waits until the response occurs before operating the magazine. By a process of successive approximation, usually referred to as 'shaping', the required response of pecking the key can be established in a very short period of time.

It is important to recognize that the effective reinforcement in our demonstration is not food but the click which accompanies the delivery of grain. This stimulus acquires the capacity to reinforce behaviour through frequent association with food and it is a significant component of the situation since it serves to bridge the interval between the response and the ingestion of food which occurs perhaps a second or so later. Zimmerman (1963) carried out an experiment recently in which a pigeon was reinforced periodically for pecking at one disc. However, if the bird pecked at a second disc, the click that accompanied food reinforcement, but not food, was produced. Under these conditions, the behaviour of pecking at the second disc was maintained almost indefinitely. The experiment provides a good illustration of the way in which behaviour can be sustained by secondary, 'token' rewards. And, incidentally, the analogy with monetary rewards in everyday life is not hard to see!

When an operant conditioning experiment is carried out, the investigator is not necessarily interested in food-procuring behaviour and eating as such. He makes use of food-reinforcement, however, as a practical technique to generate a sample of the animal's behaviour so that he can study it (Sidman, 1960). The measure of behaviour he records is the *rate* at which the response occurs over time. This measure may be obtained in several ways, but, frequently, a cumulative graph of responses plotted against time is used.* These records provide a continuous description of

* The record is obtained with a *cumulative recorder* which consists basically of a kymograph moving the paper horizontally at a constant speed (30 cm/hr) and a pen which moves vertically across the paper by a small increment (0·125 mm) each time a response is made. The pen resets to zero

behaviour and have one important advantage: they permit immediate inspection of the rate at which the animal is responding.

'SUPERSTITIOUS' BEHAVIOUR

Sometimes, an 'irrelevant' bit of behaviour occurs just before the response that secures reward. For example, a monkey may be scratching his head at the time he presses the lever. When food is delivered, the chances are that both bits of behaviour will be reinforced. Within minutes, especially if the monkey is hungry and has not been rewarded very frequently, we can observe him busily scratching his head each time he presses the lever as if this activity formed an essential part of the business of securing a reward. Skinner (1948a) refers to this as 'superstitious' behaviour, since the monkey behaves as if he is obliged to make this response to obtain reward, although no such contingency has explicitly been arranged. Ferster (1963) suggests that we may find many instances of accidental reinforcement operating in human behaviour. For example, the course of treatment a doctor prescribes might be fortuitously reinforced. Many diseases run a natural course of development, regardless of treatment, and any therapeutic procedure put into effect at the turning point of an illness may be reinforced by the prompt recovery of the patient. In other words, it is not inconceivable that a form of treatment may continue to be used simply because a patient recovered, even though it is ineffective in dealing with the disorder.

Although one can think of many possible instances of accidental reinforcement, we do not yet know enough about the specific conditions favouring the development of these responses. It has been suggested, however, that when we do, we may be able to understand some of the deviant forms of behaviour, e.g.

---

whenever a complete excursion of several hundred responses has been made. The slope of the curve is a sensitive index of the response rate and small oblique 'pips' are used to show which responses have been reinforced. When these graphs are presented (see Figures 55, 56 and 57), they usually appear in a 'telescoped' form and a scale is included in the diagram to illustrate some representative rates of responding.

phobias, that characterize certain types of emotional maladjustment or neurosis.

SCHEDULES OF REINFORCEMENT

Once a response has been shaped, a reinforcement may be delivered on each occasion it is made. Although continuous reinforcement generates high rates of responding initially, the response is emitted more spasmodically as the animal's need for food diminishes. Nor can continuous reinforcement be regarded as a particularly representative feature of life outside the laboratory. Most of our activities are reinforced only intermittently. In fact, subtle refinements of behaviour we call skills could hardly occur if reinforcement resulted from every performance of the response. The skill of a trout fisherman must surely depend upon the fact that he does not succeed every time he casts a fly!

These considerations imply that the effects on behaviour of intermittent reward are likely to be important and of greater interest than continuous reinforcement. Many schedules of reinforcement have been studied in the laboratory and it is quite clear that intermittent reinforcement produces stable rates of responding which are maintained for as long as the schedule is continued. But even slight changes in the schedule may produce dramatic differences in behaviour (Ferster and Skinner, 1957).

The main dimension of a reinforcement schedule is the manner in which behaviour can produce reinforcements: on the basis of elapsed time (*interval* reinforcement) or on the basis of the number of responses required (*ratio* reinforcement).*

* An alternative conceptual framework for the classification of reinforcement schedules has been proposed by Schoenfeld, Cumming and Hearst (1956). The system defines two basic variables: t^D and t^A, time periods during which a reinforcement may be obtained or is never obtained, respectively. During operation of the schedule, the respective durations of t^D and t^A are held constant, they are alternated, and only the *first* response to occur in t^D is reinforced. When, for example, t^D is decreased from thirty seconds to 0·5 second, a transition from 'interval-like' to 'ratio-like' behaviour is observed. Thus, the system enables an investigator to generate in an animal response rates characteristic of interval and ratio schedules within a single time-correlated contingency by manipulation of the duration of t^D. It

Operant Conditioning in the Study of Animal Behaviour

Interval Schedules

These may be either fixed or variable. A *fixed-interval* schedule (FI) is one in which the first response to occur after a specified interval, measured from the preceding reward, is reinforced. Thus, in FI 4, the first response to occur after an interval of four minutes since the last reinforcement is reinforced. A *variable-interval* schedule (VI) is similar except that reinforcements are varied around a specified average interval. Thus, in VI 4, reinforcements occur, on average, once every four minutes although some are delivered within seconds of a preceding reinforcement while others are delivered only after five or six minutes have elapsed.

Ratio Schedules

Ratio schedules may also be either fixed or variable in character. A *fixed-ratio* schedule (FR) is one in which a specified number of responses have to be made for each reinforcement. Thus, in FR 20, the animal must make twenty responses to obtain each reinforcement. *Variable-ratio* schedules (VR) have an *average* ratio of responses to reinforcements. In VR 10, a response will be reinforced on average after ten responses have been made, but sometimes two or three responses will produce a reinforcement, while on other occasions more than ten must be made before a reinforcement is given.

As the number of responses required for each reinforcement is increased on fixed-ratio schedules, longer periods of inactivity are seen in the cumulative record and, at extreme values, behaviour shows appreciable 'strain'. In Figure 55, record *A* shows the performance of a pigeon on FR 185. A pause in responding after each reinforcement is a noticeable feature of the graph. When the ratio requirement is reduced to sixty-five (record *B*), the pauses are of much shorter duration and although they do not disappear

---

should also be noted that this system has been extended recently into the area of *negative* reinforcement. Hurwitz and Millensen (1961), using rats as subjects, have described avoidance behaviour (which can occur in the absence of a warning signal) in terms of a temporally-defined contingency derived from the system proposed by Schoenfeld *et al.* for schedules of positive reinforcement.

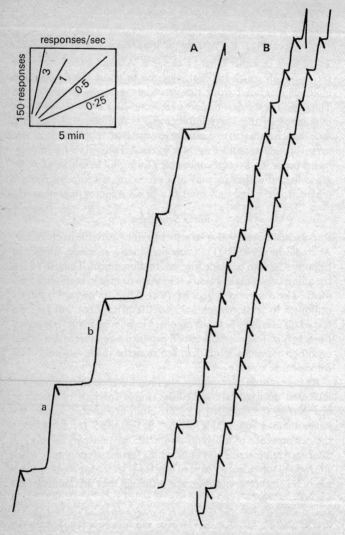

Figure 55. Cumulative records representing FR 185 (*A*) and the transition to FR 65 (*B*) in a pigeon. Oblique 'pips' denote reinforcements. (From Ferster and Skinner, 1957, p. 56.)

immediately, eventually the bird reached a stable performance in which periods of inactivity were largely absent from the record. It is interesting to note, in the case of FR 185, that whenever the pigeon responds, it does so at a high rate, even though the ratio requirement is inducing 'strain'.

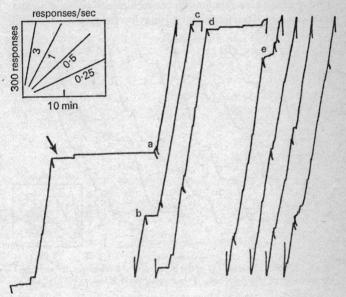

Figure 56. Cumulative records showing the transition from FR 360 to VR 360 (marked by an arrow) in a pigeon. (From Ferster and Skinner, 1957, p. 409.)

However, if a variable-ratio schedule is introduced in which the same number of responses per reinforcement on average is required, stable rates of responding may be generated, although the corresponding fixed-ratio requirement would produce long periods of inactivity. Figure 56 shows the transition (marked by an arrow) from FR 360 to VR 360. A long pause occurs because of the recent FR schedule and the first reinforcement on the VR schedule occurs at *a*. A second reinforcement occurs immediately after a few responses. The reinforcement at *b* occurs after 750 responses and is followed by a pause. However, by the reinforcement at *e*, the transition to the VR performance is almost complete, with consistently high rates of responding immediately after reinforcement.

By contrast with fixed-ratio schedules, interval schedules reflect a more continuous relationship between rate of responding and the frequency of reinforcement. Even at low frequencies an animal

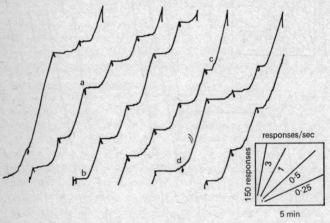

Figure 57. Cyclical variability in the behaviour of a pigeon on a fixed interval schedule of reinforcement. (From Ferster and Skinner, 1957, p. 159.)

will continue to respond fairly continuously, although at a relatively low overall rate.

The question of *why* a given schedule generates a particular pattern of behaviour is an important one and calls for a good deal of interpretative skill. Consider, for example, the cumulative records in Figure 57. At first sight, these data seem to reflect a degree of behavioural variability that is hard to explain, but a closer appraisal of the graphs reveals that this need not be so. The record describes a pigeon's behaviour on a fixed-interval (FI 4) schedule. The flat part of the curve immediately following reinforcement varies in duration: sometimes it is brief and the bird begins to respond again quite quickly, whereas, at other points, inactivity occupies nearly the whole segment of the curve between two reinforcements. However, these data represent a self-regulatory process.

When the flat portion of the curve is brief, the terminal rate is reached quickly and a relatively large number of responses occurs before reinforcement is forthcoming. The pay-off, in terms of reinforcements per response, is low. One or more such low pay-off cycles weakens the behaviour, and the pause after reinforcement becomes longer, perhaps extending throughout the whole four minutes. Such long pauses make reinforcement available after a relatively small number of responses, thus increasing the pay-off in terms of reinforcements per response. The behaviour is strengthened and the pause after reinforcement becomes short again. (Sidman, 1960, p. 175.)

These data provide a beautiful illustration of a continuous process of adjustment between behaviour and the reinforcement contingency whereby it is maintained.

POSITIVE AND NEGATIVE REINFORCERS

We have seen that a reinforcing stimulus may be defined in terms of its effects upon behaviour and, if one employs an empirical definition of this kind, *any* stimulus can be regarded as a reinforcer if it increases the frequency of a response. Such stimuli fall broadly into two classes: a *positive* reinforcer is a stimulus which, when added to a situation, increases the probability of a response. Thus, food is a reinforcing stimulus to a hungry animal, whereas a response that enables an animal to remove a source of painful stimulation will be strengthened and provides an example of *negative* reinforcement.

But how can we measure the relative effectiveness of different stimuli that reinforce behaviour? Hodos (1961) has used a *progressive* ratio schedule of reinforcement to determine the 'attractiveness' of various rewards. He trained rats to press a lever on a ratio schedule in which the number of responses required for each consecutive reinforcement increased, i.e. the rats had to make two responses for the first reward, four for the second, six for the third and so on. If at any time an animal failed to press the lever for a period of fifteen minutes, the experimental session was terminated. The effectiveness of various rewards can now be assessed in terms of the number of responses the animal is prepared to make before giving up. The results showed that when a rat was not particularly hungry, he pressed the lever about thirty times on the final ratio 'run' to obtain a small quantity of sweetened milk (0·05 ml), but if he could obtain a larger quantity (0·20 ml) he pressed the lever over forty times. When the rat was hungry, he made about ninety responses for the small reward and almost 120 for the larger one. Since performance correlates well with variations in the amount of reward and the level of hunger, this technique is a useful one to assess the relative 'attractiveness' of rewards used to maintain behaviour.

The question of *how* reinforcing stimuli produce their effects is not an easy one to answer. One possibility is that such stimuli reduce recurrent bodily needs. However, since learning sometimes occurs in the absence of any easily identified form of need reduction, the question remains a challenge to physiological psychology and behaviour theory alike.

SOME APPLICATIONS

Earlier in this chapter it was said that operant conditioning procedures have emerged as a new behavioural technology in their own right, and some evidence is needed to support this assertion.

Dr Annett's chapter on Programmed Instruction describes the application of operant conditioning principles to human learning, and Skinner's work in this context undoubtedly represents a major extension of his achievements in the animal laboratory. But, even if we remain in the domain of animal behaviour studies, it is clear that the experimental analysis of reinforcement contingencies enables an experimenter to achieve a degree of control which is of an entirely new order. It is hardly surprising, therefore, to find that these techniques are being applied to a variety of complex problems including, for example, the determination of sensory thresholds (psychophysics), the evaluation of drug effects on behaviour (psychopharmacology) and direct manipulation of the central nervous system by means of implanted electrodes or ablation procedures (neuro-psychology). Let us consider briefly the first of these applications.

A Method of Determining Psycho-physical Thresholds

A good deal of work in psychology has been devoted to the determination of sensory thresholds. For example, if a faint patch of light is presented to a human observer, he may state that he cannot detect this signal. However, if the intensity of the light

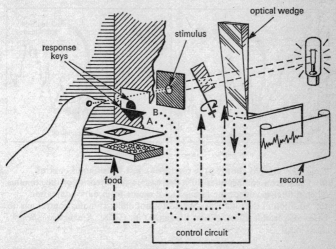

Figure 58. A schematic diagram of the apparatus used to determine visual thresholds in the pigeon. (From Blough, D. S. (1958). *J. exp. anal. Behav.*, *1*, 31–43.)

is increased gradually, it eventually exceeds the visual threshold and the response, 'Yes, now I can see it', is given. Of course, most readers will have experienced the phenomenon of dark-adaptation: once we 'get used to' a rather dimly illuminated room we can see objects more distinctly than at first. But suppose we wish to measure visual thresholds and plot the course of dark-adaptation in an animal. We can no longer rely on verbal reports and we must arrange an experiment in which a response will be made when the stimulus is visible and an alternative response will be made when it is not.

Blough (1958) has described a particularly ingenious technique which solves the problem. The experimental arrangements are shown in Figure 58. The hungry pigeon stands in a completely darkened chamber and views a variable patch of light. The bird is trained to peck at the two response keys, *A* and *B*. It would take too long to describe all the details of the training procedure, but, briefly, the bird is trained to peck at key *A* when it can see the patch of light and to peck key *B* when the stimulus is no longer

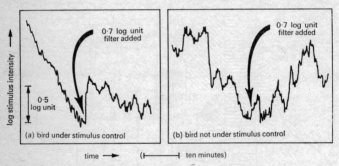

Figure 59. Graphs showing the results of a test for stimulus control.
(*a*) The pigeon compensates for a decrease in the intensity of the stimulus when a filter is added; the falling curve results from dark adaptation.
(*b*) Addition of the filter when the bird is not under stimulus control has no easily discernible effect. (From Blough, D. S. (1958). *J. exp. anal. Behav.*, *1*, 31–43.)

visible. Once the bird has acquired this discrimination, the apparatus is adjusted in such a way that responses on key *A* move the optical wedge down, decreasing the intensity of the stimulus, while pecks on key *B* produce the opposite effect. Reinforcement is available intermittently and is dependent on key *B*. The threshold measurement is obtained as follows: the bird pecks key *A* until the stimulus becomes so dim that it falls below the bird's absolute threshold. Since the patch appears dark, the pigeon pecks at key *B* to obtain food. Pecking at key *B* increases the intensity of the stimulus and it soon becomes visible again. When this happens, the bird switches to key *A* and the stimulus disappears. Thus, by switching from one key to the other the bird plots a graph representing its own visual threshold!

Operant Conditioning in the Study of Animal Behaviour

Figure 59 illustrates the precise degree of stimulus control that may be gained. The graph on the left represents the performance of a bird under stimulus control and the record reveals two important points. First, the falling curve results from dark-adaptation: the absolute threshold diminishes as the bird 'gets used to' the darkness. And, second, the bird compensates rapidly for a decrease in the intensity of the stimulus when a filter is added. However, if the reinforcement contingency fails to secure a satisfactory degree of stimulus control, behaviour remains highly variable and a change of stimulus intensity has no easily discernible effect (graph *b*).

As a final illustration, it is interesting to examine some recent work in psycho-pharmacology.

A Technique to Evaluate the Effects of Drugs on Behaviour

Recent developments in the treatment of mental disorders by means of drugs have increased the need to find laboratory testing methods whereby new drugs may be evaluated, and it has become increasingly apparent that stable behavioural baselines of the kind generated in an operant conditioning experiment may serve this purpose (Cook, 1964).

The approach is particularly well-exemplified in a series of experiments by Brady (1959). In this work, hungry rats and monkeys were trained to press levers to obtain food reinforcement which was available aperiodically (a variable-interval schedule was used). When rates of responding showed little fluctuation from day to day, a conditioned emotional response (CER) of the fear or 'anxiety' type was established. A clicking noise was presented at various times during the daily session and this stimulus was terminated by a brief electric shock which was delivered to an animal's feet after two or three minutes. With repeated presentation of the noise together with the shock, a pronounced pattern of behavioural suppression emerged. Although the animal continued to respond freely and to obtain food reinforcements in the absence of the noise, responding ceased altogether during the periods in which this stimulus was presented. In other words, 'anxiety' generated by the noise had the effect of suppressing ongoing appetitive behaviour, even though the animal was well-motivated to secure food.

However, if the animal was injected with a drug called reserpine (which is sometimes used in psychiatry to treat chronic anxiety), the drug had the effect of reducing the overall rate of responding; but, during presentation of the clicking noise, the animal responded *quite freely*. These results require careful interpretation; even so, they appear to suggest that one effect of the drug is to reduce the disruptive effects on behaviour of 'anxiety-provoking' or aversive stimulation. They certainly demonstrate the feasibility of employing operant procedures to evaluate the effects of drugs upon behaviour.

CONCLUSION

Although this chapter presents a rather sketchy outline of operant conditioning procedures and is incomplete in many respects, perhaps enough has been said to whet the appetite of the reader. One thing is plain: the experimental analysis of animal behaviour has reached a point whereby complex processes can be studied in lower organisms at a new level of scientific rigour. The ways in which behaviour may be sustained by means of reinforcement schedules are of interest in their own right. However, they possess an additional advantage. Specific levels of activity may be sustained, with little variation, for long periods of time. These 'steady states' enable an investigator to make a detailed study of the behaviour of individual subjects and, because of their stability, he can more readily interpret the effects of any variable he introduces.

16. PROGRAMMED LEARNING

JOHN ANNETT

One of the applications of Skinnerian psychology (last chapter)
*to humans has been in the training methods known as Programmed
Learning. Skinner invented one of the first 'teaching machines', and
his techniques have provided one of the main streams in this kind
of applied psychology. Dr Annett has worked and written extensively on the topic. He describes Skinner's methods and others being
currently developed.*

INTRODUCTION

PROGRAMMED learning has been one of the most striking and
significant developments in applied psychology in the last decade.
In 1954 B. F. Skinner of Harvard in an article entitled 'The
Science of Learning and the Art of Teaching' (1954) proposed
ways in which principles derived from learning experiments on
rats and pigeons could be applied to the education of children
and adults. He went even further by suggesting that these principles could be applied more effectively by an automatic 'teaching
machine' than by a human teacher. Coming at a time when
education was becoming increasingly a matter of public concern
these radical proposals caused something of a stir. Parents and
teachers, prompted perhaps by magazine articles, began to ask
'Can children be taught like pigeons?' and 'Can a robot replace
the human teacher?' Skinner soon backed up his claims with
evidence that a properly programmed teaching machine *can* teach
effectively, often more effectively than normal class instruction
conducted by a human teacher. Ten years later programmed
learning, the term now used to cover various kinds of automatic
teaching, is being used successfully throughout the world and a
preliminary assessment of this new development can be made.
The rather emotional talk of pigeons and robots has been replaced
by more serious consideration of the translation of laboratory
results on learning into rules for practical teaching and attempts
to analyse the possible role of automation in educational systems.

The two central ideas are the 'teaching machine' and the 'program'.* In its currently most popular form the teaching machine is a box which holds a program of instruction. The program is a text in question and answer form, usually printed on sheets or rolls of paper. Instructional items or 'frames' can be seen, one at a time, through a small window in the box and answers are written, through another window, on a paper tape. The machine is designed so that the student sees and answers items in a prescribed order, is shown the correct answer immediately after completing each question and is prevented from changing what he has written, should it have been wrong. The student is active since the questions are frequent and require him to do something, and he works at his own pace, only going on to the next step when he has mastered preceding steps. Each correct response he makes is immediately and automatically confirmed and he is made aware of any error at once. The learning situation is very close to individual tuition in most respects.

Information is presented to students individually, the pace is determined by the rate at which the student can 'take in' the material and he is actively involved. The major difference, apart from the fact that the student is involved with a machine rather than another human being, is that the sequence of instruction is prearranged. The interplay between a student and a real tutor can often be more flexible. Because a single sequence is followed this type of programmed learning is called 'linear'.

In this form the machine is primarily a piece of ancillary equipment designed to facilitate the use of the programmed text and, indeed, a cooperative student can work with the text alone quite as effectively. In other systems the teaching machine may have more elaborate functions and, as an intermediary between the student and the task to be learned, may either wholly or in part determine the course of the lesson. In these systems, which can take a variety of physical forms, the sequence of instruction is determined as we shall see by the design of the machine and the program is therefore said to be 'intrinsic'. The linear programmed

* The spellings '*program*' and '*programme*' are given as alternatives in the *O.E.D.* The former is preferred to distinguish its use as a technical term in the present context.

text and 'intrinsic' techniques are the most common current examples of programmed learning. As well as sharing some, but not all aspects of the tutorial situation they have in common the essential feature that the instructional items have been carefully selected and ordered into a sequence or program. In the 'linear' type the sequence is prearranged; in the 'intrinsic' type the student's actual behaviour partly determines the sequence, thus if an error is made the machine interposes some extra remedial material – a 'branch' – before allowing the student to proceed on the main stream of the lesson.

Since, by historical accident, the term 'teaching machine' is better known than the term 'program' we shall first take a look at several types of educational hardware so that we can see how these two concepts are related.

VISUAL AND AUDITORY AIDS

Slide projectors, tape-recorders, closed-circuit television and working models take advantage of machinery of one kind or another to enrich the presentation of information. They imply the presence of a teacher who uses them as an extension of his own voice and hands. The teacher retains responsibility for the organization of lessons, assessment of students and so on. These are teacher *amplifiers* rather than teacher *substitutes* and are not generally classed as teaching machines.

LANGUAGE LABORATORIES AND SIMULATORS

In these superficially dissimilar cases the dimension of direct student participation is added. In the language laboratory the student not only hears a canned lesson but also attempts to reproduce words and phrases, and his efforts are recorded so that both he and the teacher can compare these with some standard and assessments of progress are possible.

Simulators are now widely used in flight training. A more or less accurate mock-up of, say, an aircraft cockpit provides not only the relevant display (sometimes even including such features as 'stiffness' of the joystick) but also the opportunity to practise a variety of manoeuvres in safety and without using expensive operational equipment. Again practice can be monitored and evaluated by both student and teacher.

In both these cases the lessons may be carefully arranged and sequenced by the teacher, but this is not intrinsic to the machinery used.

AUTOMATIC SELF-SCORING AND TESTING DEVICES

A whole class of devices which does not necessarily simulate inputs to the student provides for automatic and immediate evaluation of performance and thus relieves the teacher of a fairly considerable burden of testing and marking. The devices designed by S. Pressey (1950) during the 1920s are both typical of this group and are historically important in the development of teaching machines. The 'Tester–Rater' is an effective if unglamorous example. The student has a printed sheet of test questions in multiple-choice form. In a matrix of holes on the face of the 'punch-board' rows represent question numbers and columns answer choices. The student tries to push a metal stylus through the hole representing his chosen answer to a given question. If he is right a template allows the stylus to pass through making a hole in a piece of paper and if he is wrong the stylus stops halfway, in each case leaving a distinctive mark which cannot be altered and later can be scored either by hand or by a special machine (modern versions often use standard punched cards for this purpose). The student is encouraged to go on trying if his first answer was wrong, and in this way the student not only receives confirmation of his correct answers but is also able to discover or rediscover the right answers to all items on the test, and in this way the device not only tests but teaches.

Test items can, of course, be in random or sequential order, and there may or may not be an accompanying text. When there *is* the system approaches a complete self-instructional device, although again, apart from the provision of knowledge of results, the teaching function is not intrinsic to the device but depends on the lesson plan or program.

Programmed Learning

PRE-PROGRAMMED TEACHING MACHINES

The important advance which Skinner made on the pioneering work of Pressey was to concentrate on the form of the lesson presented on an automatic self-scoring device. As will be seen later in this chapter and in the chapter by Stretch (Chapter 15), Skinner had in his studies of animal learning paid considerable attention to the scheduling of training trials. Learning takes place when an act (technically an 'operant') is followed immediately by some reward which is said to reinforce the learned behaviour. To build up complex behaviour it is necessary to arrange a schedule in which individual components are reinforced singly and in proper sequence. Typically in the early stages approximately correct responses are reinforced and later only more and more precise versions of the desired response are rewarded.

By analogy, therefore, a typical Skinnerian teaching machine presents a carefully arranged sequence of items each providing the stimulus for an appropriate response and providing reinforcement for correct responses. The pigeon or rat is rewarded with food or water, but the human student is rewarded by the knowledge that he is right. A typical Skinner teaching machine, the Foringer, is shown in Plate 14. The stimulus (information and question) appears in the left-hand window and the student makes his response by writing the answer in the window on the right. He pulls the lever which moves his answer under a perspex cover, reveals the correct answer and the next item. An example of the linear type of program used in these machines is illustrated in Figure 60. On such a machine the lesson is self-administered so that the teacher is not required and the student can work at his own pace in his own time and never misses a point due to inattention.

An important modification of this type of device is to get rid of the hardware altogether. The function of the box is simply to guide the student's attention to the relevant stimuli in a prescribed sequence and to get him to make an active response before being able to see the correct answer. A moderately cooperative student can follow these instructions, especially when he finds it does not help to skip ahead or to cheat and that it is easy to follow the

THE CONDUCTION OF
THE NERVOUS IMPULSE

FRONT OF CARD	BACK
1. The basic unit of which the nervous system is composed is the NERVE CELL or NEURONE. Hence we say that the brain and nervous system are made up of large numbers of ___.	nerve cells *or* neurones
2. Now make a copy of *Picture 1*, and put it on one side where you can see it.	
3. 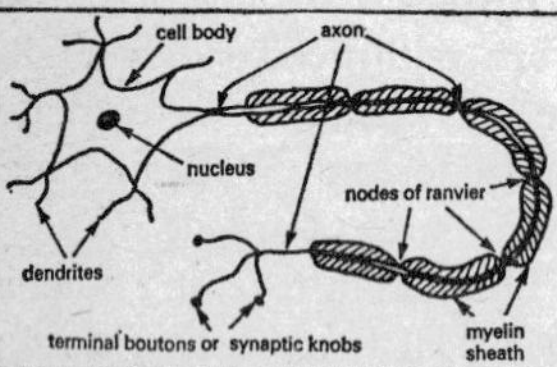	
4. The body of the cell contains the _____ .	nucleus
5. From the body of the cell several processes stick out. 1. The single long one is called an _____. 2. The short ones are called _____.	axon dendrites
6. The axon, which is the _____-est of the processes which leave the cell body, is covered by the _____ sheath.	longest myelin
7. The myelin _____ is made of fatty material, and is interrupted every few millimetres by the _____ of _____.	sheath Nodes of Ranvier
8. The axon finished by dividing into fine fibres which end in _____ _____ or synaptic knobs.	terminal boutons

Figure 60. Sample of a linear program used experimentally at the University of Sheffield. Frames are typed on cards with the correct answers on the reverse side.

prescribed program. Without the box the system simply becomes a *programmed textbook* and this is, in most cases, as effective as the machine plus text and, of course, rather cheaper.

A different kind of pre-programmed device is due to N. A. Crowder (in Lumsdaine and Glaser, 1960) and also exists in both machine and textbook form. Crowder, uncommitted to Skinner's views on learning, was struck by the fact that an important function of the teacher is to diagnose the student's strengths and weaknesses and to take appropriate steps to remedy incipient fallacies, to provide missing items of information and, when appropriate, to send the student on to more advanced material. Crowder devised a system in which this interplay between student and teacher was intrinsic to the design of the machine. In the Auto-Tutor Mark II a filmed program is shown on a rear-projection screen as illustrated in Plate 15. Each frame gives a paragraph or two of information (rather more than appears on one frame of a Skinner program) and asks a question in multiple-choice form. The student answers by pressing the appropriately labelled button and the film is rapidly moved on to another frame, the next step in the lesson, if the answer was correct, or a remedial 'branch' if the student made a mistake (see Plate 16). The questions are intended to be diagnostic so that by answering the student automatically presents himself with an appropriate 'cure' for his error. The lesson goes on somewhat like a game of snakes and ladders, but with learning rather than chance as the criterion of progress. As in the Skinner devices learning is individual and self-paced.

In its 'software' form the program is presented as a 'scrambled' book (see Figure 61). Instead of reading the pages in order the student starts on page 1 and has to answer a multiple-choice question in order to find out which page to go to next. The difference between this and the AutoTutor is simply that the student turns the pages himself rather than having the machine do it for him. The scrambled book, like the programmed text, is a little more clumsy and more open to abuse by uncooperative students than the machine counterpart, but considerably less expensive.

It could be said that the Crowderian 'intrinsic' programming adds a further dimension to the Pressey–Skinner concept of a

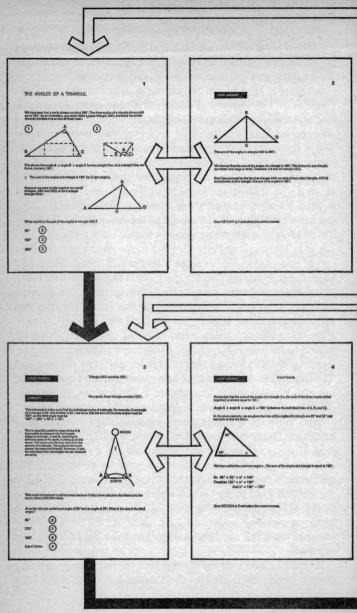

Figure 61. A typical branching sequence

5

YOUR ANSWER

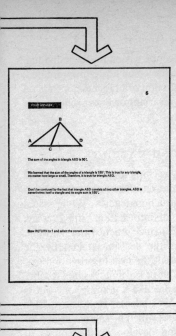

The sum of the angles in triangle ABD is 90°.

We learned that the sum of the angles of a triangle is 180°. This is true for any triangle, no matter how large or small. Therefore, it is true for triangle ABD.

Don't be confused by the fact that triangle ABD consists of two other triangles. ABD is nevertheless itself a triangle and its angle sum is 180°.

Now RETURN to 1 and select the correct answer.

6

YOUR ANSWER   The size of the third angle is 180°.

The sum of the angles of a triangle is 180°. Obviously, if three angles added together make 180°, and two of those angles are 85° and 35°, then the third can't be 180°.

Let's draw a figure:

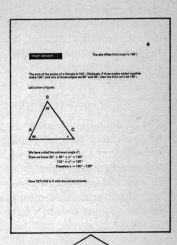

We have called the unknown angle x°.
Then we know 35° + 85° + x° = 180°
$$120° + x° = 180°$$
$$\text{Therefore } x = 180° - 120°$$

Now RETURN to 3 with the correct answer.

7

YOUR ANSWER   The size of the third angle is 120°.

It looks as if you added together 85° and 35°, but that is not the value of the third angle.

Remember that the angle-sum of a triangle is equal to 180°. And, of course, every triangle has three angles. So, in this case:

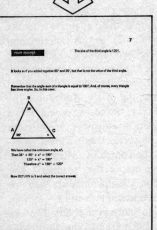

We have called the unknown angle, x°.
Then 35° + 85° + x° = 180°
$$120° + x° = 180°$$
$$\text{Therefore } x° = 180° - 120°$$

Now RETURN to 3 and select the correct answer.

8

YOUR ANSWER   The size of the third angle is 60°.

CORRECT

We know that one angle is 85°, another was 35°, so the third was the difference between their sum (120°) and 180° (the sum of the three angles of any triangle).
$$180° - (85° + 35°) = 60°.$$

RIGHT-ANGLED TRIANGLES

A right-angled triangle is any triangle that contains one *right* angle. To draw a right-angled triangle we draw two lines, of any length, meeting at right angles, then join up the free ends with a third line.

AC and BC are the two lines meeting at right angles. Angle C = 90°.
Join A and B, and we have a right-angled triangle.

AB, the side opposite the right angle, is always the longest side in such a triangle. It is called the *hypotenuse*, from the Greek word meaning 'line stretched under' (under the right angle).

Now, just what do we mean by a right-angled triangle?

A triangle whose angles add up to 90°.

A triangle whose angles are all right angles.

A triangle containing one right angle.

---

from an AutoTutor program.

teaching machine in so far as it makes provision for the individual characteristics of the learner. While the lesson is pre-programmed, even the remedial branches, the selection of branches depends on the individual students unlike the invariant or linear sequence of a Skinner program.

ADAPTIVE TEACHING MACHINES

The final stage in the hierarchy of teaching machinery is reached with machines designed to play an even more important role in the selection and ordering of instructional items. While visual aids mechanize the presentation of information, the Pressey, Skinner and Crowder machines mechanize practice and marking, the adaptive machine mechanizes the decisions taken by the teacher. It takes over to a large extent the task of programming, and to do this it must itself be capable of learning. A good teacher does not simply reproduce his lessons like a gramophone but is sensitive to the varying needs of his students. He has available to him a variety of teaching strategies which he can use as appropriate, and which he can test and develop in the course of practising the art of teaching.

One of the most sophisticated examples of an adaptive teaching machine is described by Smallwood (1962). In this experimental system lessons are controlled by a digital computer which can be programmed to function in much the same way as a tutor, that is, presenting information, testing and providing new or remedial items. Unlike the prearranged branching of the AutoTutor the computer could vary its tactics so that in the course of teaching a number of students it could learn which sequences typically led to error, and which sequences were most effective in a given situation. The built-in decisions about the course of instruction are modifiable according to the experience of the 'teacher'. The details of this system, although of considerable interest, need not concern us here since computer-based teaching is still a long way from being a practical proposition for normal use. Smallwood's system and others like it (Coulson, 1962) are of value in providing a first approximation to a fully automated teaching system which simulates most of the distinctive features of the teaching process. We should not be deceived by the lack of resemblance to a human teacher. The limitations – and there are many – are principally in the varieties of student behaviour and subtleties of mood which the system can detect and the range of pedagogical gambits from which it can select to meet the demands of a teaching situation. The fully adaptive system provides a heuristic model for research rather than an immediately practical tool for teaching.

SUMMARY

This brief outline of the main types of teaching mechanization illustrates the central concept of programming. Only those systems which pay special attention to the lesson plan and in particular make use of measures of student performance to modify the lesson plan can strictly be termed *programmed learning*. This may or may not involve the use of machinery, although Skinner saw clearly that the human teacher is limited in the extent to which he can perform important teaching functions when faced with a large class. In particular, a teacher cannot score and reward students with the desirable speed under classroom conditions. Even though he is capable of detecting a wider range of student behaviour than any existing machine he is not in a position to do so often enough nor can he always take the appropriate action.

At the present time the devices I have termed 'pre-programmed' are most popular. They are cheaper and easier to maintain than highly automatic systems, and the printed text is more familiar and therefore more acceptable than a complex device. The rest of this chapter will therefore be devoted to showing how these methods came to be developed.

THE PSYCHOLOGICAL BASIS OF SKINNER'S PROGRAMMING TECHNIQUES

The typical Skinner machine with its printed program in question and answer form proceeding in a carefully programmed sequence of small steps has already been described.

From his animal studies Skinner has concluded that the process of reinforcement in which an act is followed immediately by a reward, is crucial to all learning. He starts from the point of view that learning must be discussed only in terms of behaviour and changes in behaviour. We teach people and animals in order that they should be able to do things in appropriate circumstances and their behaviour is at once the goal of instruction and the measure of its effectiveness. The Skinnerian programming technique therefore emphasizes a constructed response (rather than simply button-pressing) and the response must be immediately reinforced. But behaviour cannot be reinforced until it occurs, so that instructional items must be written such that a correct (reinforceable) response is likely to occur. This means that items must be carefully graded in difficulty, according to the actual abilities of students, that increments of new knowledge must be small and that hints and prompts of various kinds should be used, at least initially, to make correct responses highly probable.

Developing from this notion of eliciting and rewarding correct behaviour is Skinner's concept of *shaping*. If the aim is to teach complex forms of behaviour one does not have to wait until it occurs spontaneously. The simple technique is to begin by reinforcing gross approximations to the behaviour desired. For example, a pigeon can be quickly taught to walk in a figure-of-eight if we begin by rewarding it for any turning movement. By gradual stages the reward is provided only for better and better approximations to the correct sequence of right and left turns. In a similar way an animal can be taught to make a given response only in the presence of more and more precisely defined stimulus patterns. A pigeon can be rewarded first for pecking at a disc, then only when it is illuminated from behind, and finally, only when it is illuminated by light of a particular colour. So precise is this method that it has become possible to carry out quite precise experiments on the biochemistry of colour vision in these birds.

Despite the impressive results in animal-training most experimental psychologists are inclined to be more cautious in extending these principles to all aspects of human learning. The points at issue are complex and involve primarily matters of research strategy and technique rather than matters of fact. However, the analogy between 'reinforcement' in the pigeon experiments and 'knowledge of results' in programming is a central theme and is worth examination.

Skinner has always stressed the necessity for frequent responses followed immediately by confirmation – reinforcement – and he has consistently criticized Pressey and Crowder for their use of the more convenient multiple-choice technique on the grounds that choosing an answer is not the same as producing the response to be learned and that inevitably students are often wrong and are therefore not reinforced. As it turns out, research has not confirmed that multiple choice is inferior nor has it been shown decisively that it is necessary for the student to overtly construct his response. Indeed, reading the program with the answers already supplied is usually no less effective than having the student provide the answers. But linear programs are written in a heavily redundant style and frequently revised until correct responses are highly probable. So it should not surprise us that the student who reads conscientiously has little more to learn by writing down the obvious right answers and being told that they are right. Pigeons, reinforced with food, will stop working after a while if the food is withheld, but the human student does not always need frequent reinforcement by an external agent.

It has been suggested that the student is covertly reinforcing himself when reinforcement is not provided by an external agent. To say this, however, is not very helpful because it puts reinforcement into the category of internal variables which cannot be controlled by the experimenter and (even more important in this case) by the teacher. There have been many demonstrations of operant conditioning in humans. Sometimes social reinforcement (a smile from the experimenter) can be used to condition certain responses, for example, some gesture or use of words which can be made to appear more and more frequently. The technique is not, however, infallible and subjects who catch on to what is happening tend to withdraw abruptly. Small children can be reinforced by sweets or trinkets, but they, too, are much less prone to control than a hungry pigeon.

Both human and animal subjects clearly do learn from the consequences of their actions – by knowledge of results – and this fact is often used to support the assertion that knowledge of results or reinforcement is necessary to learning. However, there would seem to be a difference between an expected and an unexpected result following a response. When an unexpected result occurs as, for instance, when a chosen answer turns out to be wrong, new information is gained. When, however, the result is as expected, confirmation provides little, if any, new information – the result is redundant. In the former case knowledge of results is essential to learning and in the latter case it is not, and this supposition is confirmed by the experimental results. In the linear program knowledge of results is made highly redundant by making each answer dependent on a very small increment of knowledge, heavily supported by cues and hints and it is not surprising that knowledge of results is largely unnecessary. To postulate a process of reinforcement occurring covertly or occurring as the result of an unspecified reinforcing agent (social approval, the desire to do well, etc.) is to infringe the law of parsimony, but Skinner has been led into this position by his attempt to preserve a weak analogy between different types of learning situations. To account for all learning by the same process would seem to be parsimonious indeed, but, unfortunately, it conflicts with the facts.

The theoretical debate on the nature and role of reinforcement will continue, but the practical outcome is that it always pays to provide a learner with knowledge of results as an insurance against the perpetuation of mistakes, but the preparation of the program in a logical order and an intelligible form would seem to be the key to effective programming in view of the present state of our knowledge about the mechanisms of human learning. In this sense Skinner's concept of shaping has been extremely helpful and the overt constructed response has been of even greater value to the program writer than to the student. Shaping implies a gradual progression of learning with the student managing to 'get the hang of it' virtually all the time. The requirement to produce an overt response or answer at frequent intervals is the means by which the program writer can discover, by trying the material out on students, if he is writing at this level. If the students fail to answer correctly the programmer has failed in his task of communicating.

Programmed Learning

We turn now from theoretical debate to the programming techniques which have been developed, originally on the Skinnerian model, during recent years.

HOW PROGRAMS ARE WRITTEN

The program writer begins, not at the beginning but at the end by attempting to define the object of the course of instruction. In many traditional educational systems the goals of teaching are often ill-defined and it is not unknown for practices to continue so long after the original goal has changed that new reasons for doing the same things have to be found. Thus Latin was once taught with the modest object of enabling students to read the language in which most important documents were then written. When this was patently no longer true objectives such as 'training the mind' were produced to justify the continuation of the syllabus. While this is an extreme case it is true that precise educational objectives have received less attention than they deserve. The value of a clear statement of the objective is simply that it enables one to measure the efficiency of teaching, the discrepancy between the achievement and the desired result. Such discrepancies enable the programmer to evaluate and revise his program.

Skinner's behaviouristic viewpoint is highly consistent with this requirement that educational objectives are best stated in terms of the kinds of behaviour we want to teach. A modest goal might be to teach students to be able to read the colour code of a resistor, or to be able to manipulate trigonometric ratios, or to be able to detect and discriminate between a variety of faults in samples of paper and so on.

Programmers are inclined to fight shy of some of the grander objectives of education, such as 'character building', but investigators are looking seriously at such important questions as defining 'creativity' and 'problem-solving capacity'. While it is, as yet, not possible to provide anything approaching complete behavioural definition of creativity this is the first and necessary step towards tackling the problem of being able to teach the special kinds of skills which lead to the development of new attitudes and concepts. But this is a field which we must for the present pass over to return to the programming of more mundane objectives.

Given that one or more objectives have been defined in measurable behavioural terms a formal analysis of the subject-matter must be undertaken. It is necessary to specify in some meaningful way the components of the knowledge or skill to detect any logical hierarchy among these components and to trace out relationships between sub-skills.

A useful technique known as the Ruleg System, has been devised by Evans, Glaser and Homme (1960). It is supposed that instructional material can be classified into rules and examples, the rules being general statements and examples being specific instances of one or more rules. Instruction often begins with a general statement followed by the presentation of a number of more specific exemplars, but it is also quite common to begin with examples and later to present or ask the student to deduce the rule. Tests of achievement typically require the person tested to produce or to complete general statements or to categorize specific examples under the appropriate rules or to construct or complete specific examples given a general rule. At an early stage in programming it is useful to list all the relevant rules and to assemble as large as possible a selection of specific examples. These will be the basic materials from which the text is constructed.

The next stage is to reach some decision about the ordering of these rules and examples. An expert on the subject matter is, almost by definition, one who can recognize the internal constraints which determine the logical order or presentation, but it can be that there is more than one possible order and that the traditional order is not necessarily the best. The wind of change currently blowing through traditional mathematics curricula is evidence of such a possibility even in a highly organized subject matter.

To help in the process of deciding on the ordering of subject-matter Evans *et al.* suggested that rules should be arranged in the margins of a series of matrices, the cells being used to trace any relationship between a given rule and any other. One can then compare rules, systematically, according to any chosen type of relationship, logical inclusion/exclusion, priority and so on. A similar system is worked out thoroughly in a book by Thomas *et al.* (1963). At this stage rigorous systems for subject-matter analysis do not exist and the programmer may well decide to devise his own system, but the point is to have a system, however crude, as an explicit basis for program development.

When some means of ordering the lesson content has been devised the writing of individual items can begin using the lists of rules and examples as the basic material. Although it was shown earlier in this chapter that overt responses add little to learning efficiency it is necessary at this stage to get student responses in some detail in order to test the effectiveness of the items. Often the choice of examples will depend on which of these are found, empirically, to be helpful to the student. Whether he needs more or fewer examples before the rule is introduced is also an empirical matter to be decided on the basis of actual use of the program.

Skinner has made some fairly precise recommendations about the form of individual frames. For example, in introducing new material the correct response should be supported by prompts and cues which in later items are gradually withdrawn. To give a simple example in teaching the spelling of a word the first response may simply be to copy it out. Later one or more letters are withdrawn, and finally, the student is required to construct the entire word without any support or prompting. There are several variations on this basic technique. Context frequently is used to provide support as are analogies and sometimes even rhymes. On the whole it is best for the programmer not to copy the kinds of cueing methods he sees in other programs until he is convinced that they are appropriate. Rhyming prompts may appeal to nine-year-olds in some contexts, but cause hilarity or disgust if used with management trainees.

Programmers have found it convenient to try out the draft program on a few students before it has reached too advanced a stage. The programmer sitting with a student can quickly see where his exposition is lacking in clarity or interest. Failure of a program can show up in several ways. Although a student who has made a wrong response, perhaps through insufficient care in reading, can learn by being shown the correct response, one cannot, with a linear program guarantee this. A student error is often symptomatic of some confusion in the presentation of the material and a simple statement of the correct answer is not adequate. The programmer must trace the source of the error and may often have to include additional frames in his revised version to eliminate the error.

This process of eliminating errors during the writing of a program is known as *internal evaluation*. However, a further stage of *external evaluation* in which the efficiency of the program in teaching students up to an agreed criterion of performance is highly desirable.

The claims, some perhaps extravagant, which have been made for programmed learning do require some substantiation, but more than this a principle is involved. An automatic teaching system, either a machine or programmed text, is designed to exert a high degree of control over the student's behaviour in the learning situation. Whereas an ordinary textbook can be used quite successfully, in a variety of ways a program not only provides information but also prescribes the manner in which the student should work. The prescription is often very precise and neither demands nor permits attempts on the part of the student to teach himself. In this way the programmer shoulders a heavier responsibility than the author of an ordinary textbook. To fully discharge this responsibility the programmer should show that the detailed study procedures are actually justified in terms of results.

External evaluation. Three things are especially to be borne in mind: the target or criterion behaviour, the target population and the anticipated conditions of use. Any criterion that should adequately sample the behaviour specified in the original objectives. For limited objectives this is relatively easy. A student can either remember the values of a resistor colour code or he cannot. With more extended subject-matters the question becomes more complex for criterion tests can only sample the desired behaviour. Further complexity is introduced by asking when, or for how long it is desired that the student be capable of criterion performance, and sometimes we are interested in how much the learning of one subject or skill can facilitate the learning of some other subject-matter or skill. Such criteria are as difficult to satisfy as they are to specify and even in the modern educational setting there is considerable resistance to 'reducing' the outcome of teaching to test score results.

The problems of sampling the student population are, compared with those of sampling behaviour, much simpler. A random sample of students is desirable for the evaluation trials, but it seems that linear programs at least are capable of being used effectively by a fairly wide range of students although there may be some loss of time (and perhaps temper) among the brighter ones. Sampling the conditions of use is quite another matter. For the time being at least many programs will be used in a classroom situation with various kinds of interventions on the part of the teacher. For complete self-tuition (say, for example, on correspondence courses) very comprehensive programs are desirable. Clearly there is a danger that programs developed in one context may turn out to be inadequate in another.

Both the American Psychological Association and the British Psychological Society have sub-committees working on the possibility of setting some minimal standards of program evaluation. Whatever these turn out to be it does seem desirable that publishers should present data on the effectiveness of their programs. Such data are normally collected in the proper development of a program.

The points which have been made about the linear program apply in general to the construction of a branching program. The definition of objectives must be made and a subject-matter analysis carried out. Crowder's rules of frame construction are, however, simpler to state. Straightforward and unambiguous prose is recommended, but the programmer has to master the art of setting multiple-choice questions in such a way that guessing is to a large degree eliminated and the choices, especially the wrong ones, represent fully the range of possible ways of misunderstanding the material.

RESEARCH IN PROGRAMMED LEARNING

A useful bonus from the development of programmed learning has been the stimulus to research. Some, at least, of the psychologists engaged in laboratory research on learning have turned to programmed learning and teaching machines as a way of bringing rigorous controlled conditions into the classroom where real students learn real subjects. Many of the early studies were concerned with the apparently simple question of whether programmed learning works and teaching machines teach. The general procedure has been to compare learning gains of students taught by traditional or 'normal' methods and students using machines or programs. In some cases retention at a later date has also been compared and most studies compare the amount of student time required to reach a given criterion under the two methods. The results of an unselected group of such experiments are summarized in Table 1.

TABLE 1. *From Hartley*, Some Guides for Evaluating Programs, *published by the Association for Programmed Learning, 1963*

Measure taken	Number of Studies	Program Group		
		Better	Equal	Worse
Immediate retention	54	35	17	2
Long-term retention	10	5	4	1
Learning time	26	24	1	1

The table refers to fifty-six studies, not all of which used all three measures, involving over 5,000 students of all kinds.

In general, programmed learning gives better results, often with a considerable saving in time and subsequent retention is as good or better. This is encouraging, but there are some difficulties. 'Normal' teaching is not a standard procedure but can be anything which is not programmed learning, and the 'normal' teacher may vary from a highly experienced person with a small class to an inexperienced teacher with a large class. In fact, most of the comparisons have been fair, the best teacher available has been put up against the machine, but in several cases where the programmer himself has been the control teacher it has been found that he did as well as or even better than his own program.

324

Programmed Learning

A more sophisticated approach is to ask under what circumstances is programmed learning more efficient and/or cheaper than the existing techniques. For example, a sophisticated and very expensive simulator is more efficient, cheaper and safer than using a real aircraft, but a computerized typewriter trainer may not compare so favourably in terms of cost and efficiency with much simpler methods. A programmed textbook on mathematics may be the only feasible way of bringing reasonable maths teaching to an understaffed girls' grammar school while still being less effective than class teaching carried out by a dedicated expert at another school.

On the general question of comparisons the argument should not be overlooked that programming is essentially a self-adjusting process which, by the use of feedback, 'homes' on to the desired target. The question that then remains is to find the most effective means of writing successful programs.

A great deal of research has recently been carried out to compare different aspects of programmed learning: such as the comparison of multiple-choice and constructed response modes, the optimal size of step, the usefulness of branching, machines versus programmed texts, various ways of providing or not providing knowledge of results and so on.

Most of these comparisons, recently surveyed by Schramm (1964), have failed to show significant differences between these variables, and studies which do find differences on one direction are not infrequently contradicted by other studies showing a significant result in the opposite direction. It is an axiom of statistical inference that failure to reject the null (no difference) hypothesis is not proof that no difference exists. Sampling error and lack of discrimination in measuring the dependent variable can obscure differences which really do exist. Once again one might criticize the over-general nature of the questions which have been asked. A series of multiple-choice questions may be an appropriate technique for establishing a fine discrimination, but in learning to play golf a complete response would, at some stage, appear to be necessary. Some variables, such as how much information per step, are difficult to define or rather admit of a whole series of definitions ranging from the number of words to a frame to the frequency of questions. Here again a more detailed analysis of specific teaching and learning problems seems, with the aid of hindsight, to be more appropriate.

The most generally valid conclusion which can be drawn from the first ten years of research into programmed learning is that careful analysis linked with empirical evaluation can be relied on to reap its reward.

There remain many important questions not simply to do with possible underlying learning processes. Should programmed learning come to be generally adopted, as indeed it may, some fundamental features of our educational system will have to be thought out afresh. A large number of students proceeding at their own pace alone could require a fresh outlook on school time-tables, streaming, examinations and even the physical arrangement of classrooms. The question of setting up the appropriate machinery for the production and evaluation of programs has barely been considered. It is clearly not a task for the individual teacher working in his spare time. Above all, programmed learning has raised a wealth of new possibilities and problems which, in a world still starved of education and training can hardly be ignored. Some of the theories and some of the superficial characteristics of programmed learning are, no doubt, ephemeral, but a scientific approach to the analysis and synthesis of the teaching process can be regarded as a genuine and lasting development in recent psychology.

17. BACKWARDNESS AND SEVERE SUBNORMALITY

N. O'CONNOR

People differ in their learning abilities and in their capacity to be trained. Backwardness is of great interest to the psychologist trying to explain the nature of intelligence, in much the same way that the study of all extreme types is likely to increase one's understanding of the average. But backwardness is also a social problem, and one of the important motives behind recent work has been the desire to find remedial methods of teaching. There are many kinds of backwardness, some of them general and some of them more specific. For instance, it is possible to find a child of reasonable intelligence who is nevertheless unable to read. Dr O'Connor is a psychologist who has specialized in studying backwardness and subnormality, and in this chapter he presents the research and theories, and considers future possibilities.

INTRODUCTION

BACKWARDNESS and severe subnormality do not have the same meaning. Backwardness has been traditionally defined by Burt (1951) and others as two to three years' retardation in school. Severe subnormality is the new name assumed in the 1959 Mental Health Act to cover cases of arrested or incomplete development of mind which includes subnormality of intelligence. It must be severe enough to make such a person incapable of living an independent life. Thus, backwardness is a general term covering mild or severe scholastic retardation. It makes no assumption about causes of backwardness and may find them in non-attendance or irregular attendance at school as well as in low intelligence. Subnormality and especially severe subnormality, however, involves intellectual deficit which is held to account for the educational incapacity, i.e. ineducability, or social disability of the children concerned.

This division is a characteristic one which in some ways makes a very clear and useful distinction and in others is confusing. By contrasting environmental and constitutional sources of mental retardation the division has been scientifically valuable. In relation to what has been known as the nature–nurture dispute, however, a great deal of futile discussion has been generated by the division of causes into genetic and environmental. As in so much of psychology, problems which are difficult, perhaps impossible of solution by presently available methods, seem easy. So with this problem, early investigators moved boldly forward to establish one of these hypotheses or the other. Too often they found themselves obliged to retreat, while admitting the inadequacy of their methods, or worse still to suffer defeat without awareness.

THE KEY PROBLEMS

Something can be said of the heredity environment problem in a later section, but in this introduction other topics must be outlined so that the scope of the subject and its main problems can be clearly grasped.

Let us, therefore, ask some simple questions and give them brief answers, keeping in mind the backwardness: subnormality division.

What is the purpose and subject-matter of the psychology of backwardness and severe subnormality?

It is an academic tradition to ask questions, but traditionally to avoid answering them by pointing out, correctly enough, that many of them are unanswerable. Despite this tradition, to give an answer, premature or not, and so invite contradiction is also the clearest way to convey one's meaning. I will do just this. The purpose of the psychology of backwardness and severe subnormality is to describe the mental abilities and qualities to be found in backward and subnormal children and to show the relationship of these abilities and qualities to each other and to neurological and medical signs. Its subject-matter is, therefore, the performance of the subnormal on mental tasks, and the attempt to account for this kind of (poor) performance. What tasks these are will be mentioned below.

To say what are the key problems of the psychology of backwardness is to invite contradiction even more openly, but to attempt an answer will settle the subject-matter of this chapter and is, therefore, worth while.

What are its key problems?

The key problems of the psychology of severe subnormality and backwardness can be judged by looking at the chapter heads of two recent general texts, one English and one American. In the English text, edited by Clarke and Clarke (1958), which aims to present some medical as well as psychological knowledge, titles include classification of types of subnormality, the measurement of intelligence, genetic and environmental studies, aetiology, individual differences, learning, brain damage, cerebral palsy, psychological measurement, educational problems, trainability and rehabilitation, psychotherapy, speech disorders, follow-up studies, fostering and adoption, and of course, prevalence. Broadly speaking, psychology is seen as being concerned with counting heads (prevalence), measuring (assessment of intelligence, etc.), aiding diagnosis (aetiology, classification, etc.) and suggesting treatment or educational techniques. Theoretical considerations arise from this set of studies such as issues connected with learning and with the genetics versus environment problem. The American text edited by Ellis (1963) was compiled with less attention to the medical aspects of mental deficiency. Its chapter headings are, therefore, more obviously psychological. Some of these are field theory, social learning, Hullian learning theory, stimulus trace theories of memory, attention, intelligence and brain damage, intelligence and genetics, problem solving and conceptual behaviour, psycho-physiology, motor skill, perception, sensory processes and academic skills. In other words, this text comprises studies of perception, memory and all aspects of learning, as well as some discussion of a number of theoretical issues such as Gestalt field theory in relation to mental deficiency.

These two leading textbooks indicate the kind of problems basic to the psychology of mental deficiency. In other words, the measurement of intelligence, the study of learning and concept formation and the growth of language are the key empirical fields of study. Key theoretical problems of psychology, arising from these studies are those concerned with environment and inheritance, the nature of the learning process and the study of the dynamic interaction of learning processes and types of stimuli.

What is new in the psychology of backwardness?

If we now try to answer the question, 'What is new in the psychology of mental deficiency?', the answer is very easy. Nearly everything to do with learning is new. In fact, most of it has appeared since the end of the Second World War and a lot of it between 1950 and 1960. Quite a lot of the study of intelligence, however, is earlier. In fact, the whole concept of intelligence began in the study of mental deficiency and backwardness. The idea of a measure of backwardness began with Binet in Paris at the turn of the century. At this time, and between Binet in Paris and Burt in London, the psychology of backwardness and severe subnormality in modern times, was founded through the development of the notion of intelligence. In the next quarter of a century the notion of intelligence developed by Binet, Spearman (1926) and Burt, and later by Thurstone (1935), in the U.S.A., took over not only backwardness but also a great deal of psychology and education as well. The day of the primacy of the I.Q. is now past, but the notion of general ability as a measure of scholastic skill has had a great and widespread effect in France, England and the U.S.A., but especially in England. It began in Binet's attempts to measure backwardness in schools in Paris.

Leaving aside the historical development of intelligence, it is worth emphasizing once again the importance of the growth of the study of learning among defectives. However, this subject has not always interested psychologists. It has been a process which sprang out of a newer attitude to care, and the process has been confined largely to children at one time classified as severely subnormal. The history of studies of learning in the field of the education of the backward has been somewhat different. In this field the emphasis has always been on reading and backwardness in reading, writing or arithmetic. The post-war years have seen a revival in this field also, but the outcome is not so clear. Summaries of recent studies of backwardness in reading, such as those of Vernon (1962) and Harris (1964), show that reading disability, like other cognitive disabilities, can have a variety of causes. But the revival of interest in learning in the subnormal and reading in the backward is a recent product of the new social status of such groups.

How does psychology aid medicine and education in the study of mental retardation?

This question concerns the aid which psychology may give to medicine or to education in the field of backwardness and severe subnormality. Obviously, the position of the psychologist in one situation is different from his position in the other. In relation to medicine, the psychologist can aid the doctor to determine a doubtful diagnosis with the intelligence test. He can check the results of difficult births and early brain damage with appropriate measures. He can make predictions concerning levels of development in particular cases, and he can suggest appropriate educational techniques which may aid in partially rehabilitating subnormal patients. He cannot in the nature of most of these cases effect a cure and it is not particularly his role to suggest modes of prevention in diagnostic sub-categories such as mongolism, phenylpyrivic amentia, brain damage and so on. This latter activity is the special function of the geneticist, biochemist or gynaecologist. In other words, in this field the psychologist's role is to some extent an auxiliary one as it frequently is in relation to medicine. In this respect he is in a different position from the biochemist who may suggest a technique capable of controlling a particular form of behaviour. In relation to education and backwardness, however, the psychologist's role may conceivably be more positive. For example, some psychiatrists such as Goldfarb (1943) and Bowlby (1951) claim that early maternal deprivation gives rise to permanent serious mental retardation. If this were in fact so, psychologists would be in a position to recommend regimens which would help to avoid such contingencies. A number of authors, including O'Connor (1956, 1964), have drawn attention to the inadequacy of the evidence for the phenomenon. They have, however, all tended to agree that backwardness can be caused by severe sensory, or social plus sensory isolation over a long period, even though they may not think that such damage is permanent. Thus the psychologist and the psychiatrist have been able to suggest the importance of at least one factor in child-care, the need for an optimal level of stimulation during development. In addition, psychologists can suggest early treatment for embarrassing and distracting emotional developmental disturbances which may impede learning. Such conditions as enuresis and disturbances resulting from anxiety and maladjustment can be treated. The manner in which psychology can help education and educators can also be seen in the work of such investigators as Vigotsky (1962) and Piaget (1959) and Luria (1961), who have attempted to define the difficulties which arise in relation to learning and to suggest means of surmounting them.

Is it likely that there will be any break-throughs in this field of psychology?

To answer this question honestly is to assume a knowledge of the meaning of the question. What, in fact, is a break-through? Do we mean something like the recent developments in nuclear physics or something like the recognition of the germ theory in medicine, or the realization of the connexion between smoking and air pollution on the one hand and cancer of the lung on the other? If any of these is meant, then it is unlikely that similarly important advances will appear in the next decade. Psychology is at a brick-building stage and its structural outlines are sufficiently incomplete to make the possibility of identifying a major contributory trend unlikely. However, there is no question that rough lines of thought have already emerged, and although these may correspond only very roughly with factors which will be later identified, there is no doubt that marginal gains are already accruing. For example, more rapid and certain treatment for enuresis has resulted from behaviour therapy, and its principles may be applicable to some sorts of obsessional behaviour. In the field of backwardness, localization of speech difficulties is proceeding and the mechanics of input or perception, and immediate memory are beginning to be understood. Such investigations must multiply considerably before the full complexity of the underlying picture can emerge. None the less there is good reason to be hopeful in the light of recent work, that such investigations will aid teachers not only at the level of severe subnormality but also with normal pupils.

In view of what has been said above concerning subject-matter and key questions, the remainder of this chapter will be given over to describing some of the major psychological research which has contributed to answering such questions. A policy of describing the work of a few leading investigators will be followed. This is unjust in so far as it neglects many contributors whose work inspires and produces research and raises important questions. However, this kind of injustice is inevitable in the interests of clarity.

LEARNING AND INTELLIGENCE

There can be no question that the major concern of a psychologist involved in the study of backwardness must be learning processes and the data attendant to their deficiencies. Binet (1906) in two studies in Paris showed that backwardness was related to social deprivation. He also showed that much educational effort applied to educating the backward was misapplied and unproductive. Burt (1951) brilliantly followed this lead and left us an inheritance of information about the relationship between living conditions and educational backwardness which has never been surpassed in England, or possibly anywhere else. Recent surveys in the L.C.C. area where Burt did his work have always tended to repeat his findings. These were essentially the same as Binet's, but in more elaborate detail. They demonstrated unequivocably that poverty, ill-health and educational backwardness were found together. Burt does not draw from this association any conclusion concerning any one social factor as the cause of backwardness. If anything he represents the association as accidental and presents intelligence level as the basic source of backwardness. Intelligence is defined by Burt as (p. 11) 'innate, all-round, intellectual efficiency'. He makes backwardness a function of intelligence and says (p. 447), 'Intelligence . . . is almost synonymous with . . . "Educable capacity". Capacity must obviously limit content . . . it is . . . impossible for a child's educational attainments to rise higher than his educable capacity permits.' This seems to be a clear enough statement to the effect that backwardness is a function of poor intelligence or poor innate capacity. Thus Burt seems to indicate that the poor health, perceptual deficiencies, such as short sight and deafness, and social disabilities, such as ill-health and poverty, are not so basic to backwardness as such an innate condition as intelligence. In his summary chapter Burt once again emphasizes this and points out that lower correlations are found between backwardness and poverty than between backwardness and general intelligence (pp. 571, 572). Of course, Burt cannot be held rigidly to this view and there are, compared with some of the statements summarized above, some passages in which he distinguishes the educationally retarded from the mentally defective, allowing that, in the case of the former, the disability may be temporary and social in origin. However, in general, the emphasis is on the relative performance of early determined levels of ability.

AN EARLY APPROACH TO LEARNING STUDIES

While Binet and Burt form the spearhead of the modern scientific psychology of backwardness their conclusions in terms of the newly developed concept of intelligence are pessimistic. This has not always been the case; in nineteenth-century France, Itard (1819) and Seguin (1846) had developed educational techniques which were thought to be applicable to very backward children. Binet's (1906) statements and Burt's seemed to have the effect of putting an end to this optimistic approach to education, at least among psychologists. Thus, even though Seguin's ideas were perpetuated in the work of Montessori and Froebel, they tended to benefit normal more than backward children. This situation continued with spasmodic interruptions until about 1945.

At this time many things happened which led to a revolution in the psychology of backwardness and mental deficiency and it cannot be said that this revolution is yet over. To attempt a history of this period is not my task. My opinion is that in England at least two forces were present at the same time, an unusual state of full employment following the depressed pre-war years and at the same time a new state of general economic welfare extending to all aspects of life including family life. These conditions immediately affected the possibilities of the care of the mentally defective. For the first time, their best interests were served not so much by offering them asylum, i.e. in their case warmth, food and shelter, but some greater degree of independence. They could now be supervised in the community. This situation and the psychological problems it gave rise to have been discussed by O'Connor and Tizard (1956). The main problem was one of training the feeble-minded (subnormal) in visuo-motor skills. Work leading to a partial solution to this problem raised another general question, that of the educability of the subnormal. As a result a number of researches began in England. But at the same time, for other reasons, studies of scholastic skill were beginning in the U.S.A. The period of this work was from the late 1940s or early 1950s to the present. It will be of interest to give some of the major results of this work and refer to the leading authors responsible.

Before looking at this work, however, it is necessary to refer to the situation in schools. The special educational provision in terms of special classes, remedial classes and special schools has improved and is improving, but is as yet far from adequate. Part of the reason for this situation was the idea of innate intelligence prevailing in pre-war years. At present, although this idea is not interpreted in such a negative fashion, special schools, classes, and especially the number of specially trained teachers, are by no means adequate. A full assessment of the situation is currently proceeding. Educational writing is voluminous and much of it is concerned with reading skills. It is reasonable, therefore, to assess this work in terms of its contribution to our knowledge of reading skills. For this reason I will deal briefly with the subject of mild backwardness by considering research on reading in a later section.

RECENT LEARNING STUDIES

Learning among defectives is a process which can be prevented by many kinds of deficiencies. The operations involved in learning, as O'Connor and Hermelin (1963) have made clear, are such as perception, in all senses of the term, input in the sense of immediate memory, recall, transfer, coding into speech, signs and symbols and such operations on symbols or signs or concepts as inclusion and induction, comprehension, classification and deduction, reversal and the recognition of identity or difference. These, and perhaps other operations, are essential to learning.

Which is most handicapped in subnormality and backwardness and which is least affected?

I have suggested elsewhere that there is a pattern of deficiency in these operations in which attention or input deficiencies are most prominent, coding difficulties exist but may be overcome, and difficulties of recall scarcely exist. A number of other workers consider that this pattern is a possibility. Notable among these are Ellis (1963) and Spitz (1963) who have supposed deficiencies in the input organization of data. From somewhat different points of view, therefore, O'Connor and Hermelin (1963), Ellis (1963) and Spitz (1963), all agree that one of the greatest learning problems for the severely subnormal is the primary acquisition of data. There is a sense in which House and Zeaman (1963) also agree with this statement. As this group of investigators is responsible for a major part of the contributions in this field, it seems likely that from a psychological point of view, the problem of input or acquisition is a key one for investigation.

Each of the authors mentioned has approached it in a somewhat different way. Ellis is concerned with decay of a stimulus trace, assuming that this happens rapidly in defectives as compared with normals. House and Zeaman are concerned with the problem of attention as affecting discrimination learning. Their view is that discrimination learning in retarded children requires the acquisition of a chain of two responses: (1) attending to the relevant stimulus dimension, and (2) approaching the correct cue of that dimension. The difficulty that retardates have in discrimination learning is related to limitations in the first, or attention, phase of this dual process rather than the second.

House and Zeaman develop an attentional model which suggests that defectives have to learn to attend. They apply many interesting aspects of learning theory to discrimination tasks like telling the difference between a triangle and a circle, and show that learning can be rather rapid once the patient realizes what it is he has to learn. Their work is typical of some of the best experimental psychology in the United States. Despite the fact that they are not interested in the pathology of their subjects, or of the effect of central nervous damage on learning, they are bound to influence many new developments in research in this field. If, in fact, learning by defectives is quite rapid once the intent of the instructor is known, then new efforts can be concentrated on the display of the data rather than on teaching method. The technique of House and Zeaman draws something from Harlow's (1959a) animal experiments, but is based on theories of perception and learning expounded by Wyckoff (1952), Burke and Estes (1957), and Bush and Mosteller (1951).

Ellis (1963) has put forward a somewhat different point of view based on a psychological assumption about the lack of adequate reverberating circuits in the damaged brains of the severely subnormal. Like Hermelin and O'Connor (1963) he is interested in short-term memory. A stimulus trace theory is used to account for immediate memory and deficiencies in the central nervous system are used to account for deficiencies in immediate memory. The notion advanced here is an important one with which I would agree. It is very simple. If an event does not impress itself on the mind of the beholder for long enough to leave a permanent mark, then it cannot become part of that person's stock of knowledge. This, in simple language is the hypothesis which Ellis hopes to establish and which already he has gone some way to verify. Theories of this kind, like similar theories in England depend on the assumption of two kinds of memory, short- and long-term. It is often supposed that long-term memory involves a structural change in the nervous system whereas short-term memory depends on a temporary reverberatory state of the unchanged nervous system like the ripples in a pond following the throwing of a stone. The latter phenomenon, on this analogy, could only be compared with the former by imagining a very sudden cold snap in which the ripples froze solid. In long-term memory we have a relatively permanent state of the mind which can be readily drawn on in future thought processes.

Herman Spitz is another American who is concerned with the same problem of learning in the backward. He is inclined to regard input as the basic problem in the learning of the severely subnormal. His approach draws upon Gestalt psychology. He has invoked the theory of cortical satiation of Köhler and Wallach (1944) to help explain certain facts of the perception and learning of defectives. This theory belongs to the group of psychological theories which, like those of Ellis, associate physiological and psychological events. Spitz (1963) says, 'A corner stone of this approach is the conception of a structural and functional identity between the organism's experiences and the physiological process underlying these experiences.' As Köhler (1947) states it: 'When the visual field exhibits a thing as a detached entity, the corresponding process in the brain is relatively segregated from surrounding processes.' Psychologists are familiar with this Gestaltist view. However, in Spitz's opinion, this cortical electrotonic system corresponding to a seen figure produces an electrotonus, impedance or satiation in the area concerned. In defectives it would be reasonable to expect these effects to be greater than in normals. In a number of ingenious experiments, Spitz and his colleagues demonstrate that the apparent reversal of a Necker cube (Figure 23) takes place at a rate which increases more slowly than with normals and is less affected by a rest pause. The repetition of this finding in other sense modalities leads Spitz to conclude that reduced satiability probably arises from reduced cellular functioning in the brain of the severely subnormal person. Such a notion is, of course, not the only possible interpretation, but Spitz thinks, for example, that attentional and motivational factors, such as those put forward by House and Zeaman, cannot be the whole explanation of psychological deficits. In this he is obviously right so far as cases of severe subnormality are concerned. For the less severely handicapped his reasons may not be so forceful.

Each of the points of view put forward above, express some aspects of the truth concerning the deficient learning of the backward. Backwardness is complex, however, and no one single approach can explain it. For example, as the term was defined at the beginning of this chapter and as it is used in educational parlance, it means backwardness in reading and writing and perhaps arithmetic.

BACKWARDNESS IN READING

Reading gives rise to much research among educational psychologists, and an organization exists to promote the study of reading problems, the International Reading Association. However, although a good deal of hard data has emerged from many investigations, there is still a good deal of unclarity concerning the dynamics of backwardness in reading. Vernon (1962) has provided one of the clearest summaries in recent years. She has divided bad readers into three groups: culturally deprived and badly educated; emotionally disturbed; and specifically disabled. Of the first two it can be said that the approach to treatment is likely to be effective to the degree that the condition is recognized and corrected early. The reading backwardness here is not specific to the task but might conceivably apply to other tasks which were being learned at the time. Specific dyslexia has recently attracted the attention of more psychologists, however, because it is a specifically cognitive problem. In such problems psychologists are able to draw on a more soundly based theory than in other aspects of mental processes. The analysis of specific reading disability or specific dyslexia has given rise to a number of sub-classifications of the mental operations involved. For example, the perception and recall and recognition of shapes might be one problem for poor readers. Another problem might be the analysis of word outlines into letter outlines. A third might be the association of sounds and shapes, and a fourth the combining of letter sounds into the sounds of words. The sound of a word is by no means the same as the sound of its letters combined. It is on the synthesizing of sounds that Vernon lays most emphasis and in this she sees at least two possible difficulties. First, there is the difficulty of putting together a complex process involving immediate memory and some memory span. Secondly, there is the problem of arranging letters or sounds in the correct order. Ingram (1960) draws a useful distinction between language and speech difficulties on the one hand, and spatial or directional difficulties on the other. Such different difficulties might be related to damages in different parts of the cortex. Whatever pathological and neurological studies may ultimately reveal as their techniques improve, it is clear that certain behavioural symptoms are commonly found associated with specific reading disability. For example, slow speech, speech disorders, hyperactivity and motor incoordination are common. Zangwill (1960) has shown that the poor development of handedness has a complex relationship to specific dyslexia and directional confusion and finger agnosia, i.e. not knowing when blindfold, which finger is being touched, is common. Many of these symptoms can be shown to be associated with childhood illness and brain damage.

The problems of reading disabilities in this sense are, therefore, partly well analysed, but in need of considerable further exploration. Their exact association with central nervous damage and its location in the brain apart from some broad generalizations, is unknown.

CONCLUSIONS

In this chapter I have tried to present some broad issues in the study of the psychology of backwardness and severe subnormality. In such a short space I have had to exclude such areas of research as the personality, the rehabilitation and the social problems of mental defectives. These subjects have been described elsewhere by O'Connor and Tizard (1956) and in recent years social services have become a prime concern of services for the backward. It is a remarkable comment on the dissociation between research and society's awareness of research findings that obvious measures of social welfare can be so long neglected. Although Burt long ago showed an association between backwardness and social and economic deprivation, nearly a quarter of a century elapsed before any attempt was made to profit from his observations. Prophylaxis in social medicine has scarcely begun. Properly organized, however, social hygiene could be as effective as was physical hygiene when introduced through public health services many years ago.

Perhaps one of the reasons why this has not happened has been the commonly held belief that mental backwardness is due to innate lack of ability. Unfortunately, as I have tried to suggest in previous remarks, the heredity–environment controversy has been conducted with more enthusiasm and partisanship than objectivity. There is little doubt that environmentalists and geneticists have both made ridiculous claims and the truth is still obscure. Backwardness is frequently social in origin, but such social deprivation does not affect all types of ability. Where circumstances can be ameliorated conditions of backwardness often prove to be only temporary. However, if such conditions continue for more than say twenty years, their cumulative effects stifle all initiative and actually destroy innate ability.

There is despite the presence of some mild backwardness caused by socio-economic pressure, a great deal of subnormality and severe subnormality which is caused by damage to the central nervous system and which exists from an early age. This kind of situation can often be shown to be genetic in the sense that it is not uncommon to find relatives suffering from similar syndromes. There is, however, always the possibility that constitutional factors pre-dispose the individual to certain weaknesses which will only appear if certain conditions prevail. Mongolism is, for example, genetically determined, but it is clear that most mothers of mongols are well beyond the optimal child-bearing age. Why, therefore, should we not consider the effect of environment on genetics and vice versa? The psychology of subnormality is primarily a study of learning processes, but, ultimately, every psychologist hopes that backwardness as we now know it, will disappear. When that happens, the results of learning experiments may be applicable to normal children. Any psychologist working in this field, likes to consider that his investigations could at any time be considered to form part of the wider body of knowledge of experimental psychology.

18. PERSONALITY THEORIES AND BEHAVIOUR THERAPY

H. R. BEECH

Since personality is partly modelled by experience, one would ex-pect that theories of learning should have something to say about the 'historical' explanation of personality. Several learning theorists have met this challenge, and in doing so have provided an alternative approach to therapy. Methods of treatment are based not on the ideas of 'dynamic psychology' (Freud, etc.), but on the notion that personality is a collection of learned habits. Therapy amounts to habit-changing. Dr Beech assesses the validity of behaviour therapy and compares it with other methods.

UNTIL fairly recent years psycho-analytic theories and treat-ments based upon those theories were virtually unchallenged in the field of neurotic illness. They stemmed mainly from the work of Sigmund Freud, whose teachings gave impetus to a number of break-away movements which still preserved many of the basic notions elaborated by him. The emphasis in all these varied branches of the psycho-analytic tree was, however, clinical and philosophical rather than experimental and scientific, and the evidence on which complex theories about the nature of psycho-logical illness was based was gathered without any precise control and experimentation. The evidence was, in fact, the clinical observations and impressions made during the course of treating patients. This has led Eysenck to argue that psychotherapy, with its unscientific nature and development, actually reverses the usual procedure of science by attempting to deduce facts and laws from the process of treatment itself. Ordinarily we would expect the laws and facts to stem from careful, painstaking experiment.

In addition, a further fundamental difficulty of the psycho-analytic theories has been that of setting up testable deductions. The acceptability of any theory depends upon its power not only to account for all the observations which can be made but also its susceptibility to testing, and only by making testable deductions from our theories can we gain confidence in our ideas or reject them if they are disproved. Certain psycho-analytic notions are not formulated in a way which can lead to testing their validity so that we may never really know if they are palpably false or consistent with the evidence gained from experiment.

Against this background a movement was developing which, at first, had relatively non-specific aims but which had as its main objective the investigation of the conditions under which learning takes place. In the forefront of this movement was I. P. Pavlov, the Russian physiologist. His basic experiment was to demonstrate that while a dog will salivate (respond) to the food with which it is presented, it will *not* do so if one simply rings a bell. However, if the food (the unconditioned stimulus) is presented at the same time as a bell (the conditioned stimulus) is rung, then the food and the bell will, after a number of 'pairings' acquire the same significance for the animal. In fact, the dog will eventually salivate when the bell alone is rung, and this salivation to the bell alone was called by Pavlov the conditioned or conditional response. Pavlov had further shown that if the *bell alone* was presented a large number of times following the conditioning process, then the response of salivation gradually diminished and eventually became absent altogether.

Watson, an American psychologist, was quick to perceive in Pavlov's experiments that this process might very well account for the development of abnormal or irrational fears and carried out a critical experiment to test this possibility. He took as his experimental subject a one-year-old boy named Albert, who happened to be fond of a white rabbit, and attempted to induce a fear or phobia for this animal. Watson achieved this by making a loud noise, which frightened Albert, whenever the child reached out for the rabbit. We could express this in Pavlovian terminology by saying that the loud noise was the unconditioned stimulus which evoked the response of fear; after the loud noise and the rabbit had been 'paired' together on a number of occasions Albert now showed fear (conditioned response) to the rabbit alone. He had acquired or learned, by a process of classical conditioning, to fear an object of which previously he had been very fond. Watson then carried out the second part of his experiment, that of *unlearning* the conditioned fear of rabbits in Albert. He did so by placing the animal some distance away from the child while at the same time feeding him chocolates. Gradually the rabbit was moved nearer and nearer to Albert until a point was reached where the boy could once again tolerate close contact with the animal.

Now while Watson had derived his experiment from the simplest of Pavlovian considerations it had really become necessary to integrate all the work carried out on learning processes and weld them together in fairly complex theoretical terms. Clark Hull, a distinguished American psychologist, was able to get close to this objective of integrating all the findings and elaborating a comprehensive learning theory, and the psychologists who have examined the practical applications of learning theory considerations probably owe most to him. The specific application of learning theory to the explanation and treatment of neurotic disorders had very small beginnings, however, and Watson's insightful grasp of the application of the conditioning paradigm did not have the impact one might have expected. Nevertheless, slowly but surely learning theorists began to elaborate the principles laid down by Pavlov and Hull and to apply them to explaining the development of neurotic disturbances and also to therapeutic considerations. Foremost among these have been Mowrer, Dollard and Miller, Sears, Spence, Eysenck and Wolpe. Let us consider three of these theories in some detail.

THE THEORY OF J. DOLLARD AND N. E. MILLER

The basic aim of these psychologists was to see how far Hull's theory could be applied to the fields of social and abnormal psychology (Dollard and Miller, 1950). *Drive* was a basic concept for them, and by this they meant some kind of stimulus to action, some kind of pressure (internal or environmental) which prompted the individual to embark on a course of action. Such activity was thought of as persisting until the 'drive state' was reduced, and learning was seen as being mainly concerned with the development of effective ways of reducing drives. Some of these drives were called 'primary' or instinctual, such as the hunger, thirst and sex drives, while others were 'secondary', i.e. acquired or learned. In modern, complex, societies primary drives are rarely operative in their basic form and for the most part we are dealing with the elaboration of basic drives into 'secondary' drives such as 'status seeking'.

Apart from drive, three other concepts were central to Dollard and Miller, *cue*, *response* and *reward*. Drive impelled the individual to activity, cues (usually from the situation with which the individual is faced) served to direct and determine what the individual did (i.e. his response), and successful responding led to rewards or satisfactions. The more often a particular action or response had been rewarded the more likely it was to occur again, but as reward is identified with the 'reduction of drives', then there is a limit to the value of repetition. There would, obviously, come a point in time when the drive had been reduced to zero so that no matter how long the individual went on repeating the response this behaviour would not produce any additional satisfaction, and under these conditions the response or habit would cease to occur. A weak habit would very quickly decay if rewards were absent, while a strong, well-developed habit might continue to manifest itself for quite a long time in the absence of rewards for its production.

Two other principles were important in Dollard's and Miller's analysis, these being the *gradient of generalization* and the *gradient of reinforcement*. The first of these referred to the fact that, while no two situations are exactly alike, the same response seems to occur in many of them. It is argued that the likelihood of the same response occurring in two situations depends upon their similarity, and Pavlov had demonstrated this in a very simple experiment. First he trained an animal to salivate to a bell of a particular pitch (say, 1,000 c.p.s.), and measured the amount of saliva produced. He then measured the strength of the habit or conditioned response to tones of higher or lower pitch and discovered that the closer the similarity of the tone to the original one of 1,000 c.p.s., the more the response resembled the original in terms of the amount of saliva produced. In this way we learn to generalize our experience and apply it to situations which are similar in some respects.

The second of these principles, that of the gradient of reinforcement, simply refers to the point in time at which the reward is given. Generally speaking, the closer in time the reward follows the response the better will be the learning. With older children and adults some token of reward (say a promise of reward the next day) will often suffice, but for very young children unable adequately to conceptualize time intervals, immediate and tangible rewards are necessary, as with animals.

Perhaps the most central and relevant issue here, however, is the analysis of how fears are acquired. Fear, according to Dollard and Miller, is a drive because it *impels action,* and the reduction of fear can be considered to be rewarding. They believed that the validity of this analysis could be demonstrated in a critical experiment. In this experiment they taught rats to 'fear' a box (*A*) in which they were placed, by giving them strong electric shocks inside this container, and then allowing them to escape from the shocks by operating a lever opening a door to a second box (*B*). After some practice trials, consisting of being shocked in box (*A*) and escaping to box (*B*), the current was switched off. In spite of no longer receiving electric shocks in box (*A*) the rats continued to show fear when placed there, and their desperate escape attempts might appear, to the uninformed observer, as irrational and unnecessary. The acquired fear of box (*A*) with the consequent behaviour might be likened to the panic attacks and phobias of the neurotic, which may appear strange or contrived until one understands how the fear has developed.

How strong the acquired fear (habit) becomes depends mainly upon the amount of drive reduced in the original learning situation and the number of times the habit has been evoked. If a child has been badly bitten by a dog only once, it may develop a strong aversion to this and other animals (gradient of generalization), but if the bite was hardly painful at all the fear may not be very intense. Again, if the child has been unfortunately bitten on several occasions there is a much greater probability that he will develop a strong fear than if he has been bitten only once.

Dollard and Miller, like psycho-analysts, place great emphasis on early childhood experiences as probably contributing to emotional difficulties in adulthood. They believe that part of the trouble here is the young child's inabilities to conceptualize situations in verbal terms, e.g. often we require the child to be competitive in one situation and cooperative in another where both circumstances may appear to be identical to the child. The differences between these two situations may only be apparent in terms of refined verbal descriptions which are incomprehensible to the young child, and he may be constantly exposed to the *conflict* of not knowing whether he should be either cooperative or competitive, or, putting it in his terms, whether he will be punished or praised.

Because of their desire to link psycho-analytic theory with learning theory it is natural that Dollard and Miller should try to formulate certain psycho-analytic concepts in learning theory terms. An example of this is seen in the way they account for the phenomenon of repression, i.e. the process of 'forgetting' unpleasant and hurtful thoughts. According to psycho-analytic theory thoughts which have been relegated to the 'unconscious' mind cannot easily be brought back to our awareness, but these *repressions* continue to cause us discomfort and influence our behaviour. Dollard and Miller argue that, at first, the thought of some action may cause us to experience fear, and so we may practice *deliberately* putting it out of our minds. By so doing we can temporarily reduce the drive (fear) so that the habit of 'putting-it-out-of-mind' is strengthened by being rewarded. After a time the response of 'not-thinking-about-it' is firmly entrenched and the thought now never enters our awareness or conscious mind.

THE THEORY OF O. H. MOWRER

Mowrer (1950) shared the interest of Dollard and Miller in forging links between psycho-analytic concepts and learning theory. His most important contribution within this framework was his suggestion that the reduction not only of primary or instinctual drives but also of secondary or acquired drives (such as anxiety) may act as rewards. His analysis of neurotic behaviour is an interesting one in that he argues that much of the apparent irrationality of this kind of behaviour is related to the point in time at which rewards occur. For example, if the individual engages in 'neurotic' behaviour leading to a small immediate reward and large but later punishment, the small reward may be sufficient to preserve the neurotic response, i.e. the behaviour *closest in time* to the reward is learned best. Alternatively, a small immediate punishment may lead to abandonment of a particular piece of behaviour even though a sizeable reward has followed at some later stage. In other words, the *gradient of reinforcement* may explain the drastic unconcern for the long-term consequences of his behaviour in the neurotic patient.

However, Mowrer is generally dissatisfied with the simple view that rewards strengthen habits and punishments weaken them. He argues that, as humans, we do not learn fixed habits at all – behaviour is always constantly varying – and, while we do acquire motives and rewards by a conditioning process, what we really learn are ways of thinking about situations. In this view man is not just a creature of multiple blind 'habits' but one with inherited and acquired drives who is capable of selecting and shaping his behaviour by *thinking* processes. He claims that the simple 'habit' theorists have not explained complex neurotic behaviour, nor have they found a satisfactory treatment. In his view there are two basic ingredients of neurosis, conflict and defective feedback. While the first is perhaps readily appreciated the second ingredient does require amplification. We all, says Mowrer, have a kind of corrective force, negative feedback or *conscience* which provides self-regulation. This kind of 'psychic thermostat' is acquired through training and experience and, among stable persons, preserves the balance between what is possible in our society and our selfish uninhibited impulses. The Freudian view seems to hold that in the struggle between our lusts and greed on the one hand, and conscience on the other, the latter assumes too tight a control and this results in anxiety and depression. Mowrer's argument reverses this view and assumes that a neurosis arises when *our appetitive nature has won the battle against conscience*. The result of giving free reign to the satisfaction of impulses and desires leads to some kind of intensified 're-bound' of conscience. In this situation only two courses of action are open to the individual, either to confess and make amends for allowing conscience to be thus overridden, or to sever diplomatic relations with conscience. According to this theory neurotics have opted for the latter course, but can never be completely successful in doing so as conscience continues to haunt them in the guise of anxiety, panic, depression and inferiority feelings. In other words, neurotic patients do not have 'guilt complexes' but experience *real* guilt for which the remedy is confession and atonement.

THE THEORY OF H. J. EYSENCK

Eysenck should properly be regarded not as a formal learning theorist but as a personality theorist who has sought to show that relationships exist between certain aspects of personality and learning (Eysenck, 1953, 1960).

His starting-point in considering neurotic behaviour and treatment is to point out that there is little if any acceptable evidence for the effectiveness of psychotherapy in dealing with this kind of illness. He believes that neurotic symptoms are learned patterns of behaviour which are unadaptive or inappropriate, and which have been created through a process of conditioning. If, indeed, we are dealing with maladaptive habits then we should inquire into the means available for breaking down these conditioned links and thus disconnect the maladaptive association.

Why do neurotic symptoms persist? Eysenck's answer is that in many cases maladaptive behaviour *is* 'lost' and that even neurotics show spontaneous recovery, with or without treatment. However, while simple *classical conditioning*, by association, may account for the growth of 'symptoms' (as in Watson's experimental subject) the *persistence* of neurotic behaviour is really attributable to a process of *instrumental* conditioning. What this means is that, because we are, relatively speaking, free agents we can easily reduce our anxiety drive by avoiding the feared object or situation, e.g. by never going out of the house, or always running away whenever there is the smallest possibility of our fear being evoked. It is this *avoidance* of the acquired fear which may make it impossible for us to deal with and overcome our irrational behaviour. Therefore, having learned to fear something, perhaps by simple association, we stamp-in this habit by continually reducing our fear (e.g. running away) and thus reward our irrational and maladaptive habits.

Sometimes we recognize the importance of the part played by instrumental conditioning, e.g. in inducing a pilot who has just had a crash to take up another plane immediately and thus avoid learning that 'running-away-leads-to-anxiety-reduction'.

Eysenck's personal contribution to behaviour therapy rests, however, on his contention that certain personality characteristics are directly related to conditioning. He argues that individuals differ in the speed with which conditioned responses are acquired, the strength of these responses or habits, and their resistance to being broken down. His investigations have led him to conclude that introverted persons are characterized by fast acquisition of habits, and strongly established habits which are resistant to modification. Extroverts, on the other hand, are alleged to be poor conditioners and are more prone to 'lose' a conditioned response under conditions where the habit is no longer rewarded. It follows that individuals who are constitutionally neurotic and who are highly introverted will very quickly acquire maladaptive habits (symptoms) which tend to persist in time.

Eysenck, unlike Dollard and Miller and Mowrer, emphasizes the contrast between psycho-analytic theory and learning theory rather than the similarity. However, it is of some interest that he too attempts to show how psycho-analytic concepts can be expressed in the simpler language of learning theory. For example, he attempts to deal with the phenomenon of transference, a central concept for the psychotherapist, and which refers to the development of emotional relationships between the patient and therapist. The account he gives involves the argument that at some time, perhaps fortuitously, the patient feels somewhat better. Now if we consider the therapist to be the conditioned stimulus (like the bell in Pavlov's experiment), and the unknown cause of the improvement to be the unconditioned stimulus (like the food in Pavlov's experiment), then the response (feeling better) may clearly come to be associated with the therapist and the feelings thus aroused will be centred upon him. In support of this line of argument he quotes the case of Connie, a five-year-old enuretic, treated by the bell and blanket method.* When the treatment began to succeed, Connie spontaneously hugged and kissed the apparatus used in the treatment, saying, 'Ting-a-ling is my best friend.'

Having briefly discussed three theories concerning the nature and treatment of neurotic disorders it is pertinent to discuss the techniques which have evolved from theories like these and the evidence concerning their usefulness in practice.

THE TECHNIQUES OF BEHAVIOUR THERAPY

The term 'behaviour therapy' is a useful description implying that the kind of treatments offered derive from a 'behaviourist' approach with the emphasis on direct attack upon observable abnormalities. The potential scope of the application of modern learning theory to the treatment of neurotic symptoms is very great indeed, but so far only a few formal procedures have been worked out and put to practical testing. Perhaps the most familiar of these is *aversive conditioning*.

Because of its similarity to straight-forward punishment it is sometimes difficult to see what contribution learning theory and experiment have made to developing this procedure as a treatment. Basically, the therapy involves subjecting the individual to some noxious stimulus (such as a loud noise or an electric shock) whenever the maladaptive response occurs. It would, however, be a mistake to regard this as purely and simply a punishment for producing 'bad' behaviour; rather, as Estes has shown, punishment alone simply serves to interrupt any behaviour going on at that moment and of itself does not change or modify habits. The critical condition is that of providing an opportunity to *escape punishment* by producing the 'correct' response. Let us take, as an example, the treatment of writer's cramp by aversion therapy. One can use strong electric shocks which immediately

---

* The enuretic patient sleeps on a blanket which, when wet, completes a circuit triggering-off an alarm bell. In time the patient learns to wake up before the bell rings (i.e. before urine is passed) by associating *feelings of bladder tension* with the response of 'waking up'.

Learning and Training

follow the appearance of a symptom (say, a spasm in the index finger), and which are only terminated when the cramp has been spontaneously corrected by the patient. In other words, the patient is being trained to *escape shock by producing the specified correct response* (i.e. not having cramp spasms) and this is achieved by rewarding the adaptive behaviour through drive reduction. The electric shock is seen as inducing a strong drive state which is reduced when the shock is terminated, the latter being dependent upon correcting the spasm.

Perhaps a more familiar example of aversion therapy is that sometimes offered to alcoholics. Typically, the patient is given some drug which produces very intense feelings of nausea and vomiting, and it is hoped to associate these feelings or 'responses' with the presence of or drinking alcohol. Theoretically, by this means a strong connexion should be built up between the sight, smell and taste of alcohol and feelings of great physical discomfort.

The second category of technique in behaviour therapy is often referred to as *negative practice*. The process here has, in certain respects, some similarity to an everyday experience. If we lift a heavy weight repeatedly we sooner or later reach a point in time where fatigue necessitates a rest before we can raise the weight again. Yates has shown that the same outcome results if we over-exercise a simple motor abnormality such as a tic. If we have the patient practise his tic *voluntarily* and repeatedly, then we reach a point when the patient finds it very difficult to produce a tic at all. After a rest his *involuntary* tic reappears, but we notice that it is now less frequent than before the 'massed-practice' session, so that some part of the tic-ing habit has been permanently lost. Repeated sessions of this kind produce further inroads on the habit until, according to theory, one should reach the point where the habit no longer shows any recovery after the treatment. How has this occurred? In learning theory terms what has happened is that the over-practice produces a fatigue state which operates as a drive, in this case the drive is to stop the tic-ing activity. When the individual has practised to the point where no further tics are produced, and he stops trying to produce more of them, then *this drive state is reduced*. The response occurring closest in time to this reward or reduction of drive is 'not tic-ing', so that it is this response (the 'not-ticing' habit) which is being learned.

One might ask whether ideas or thoughts are susceptible to the same influence, as it is often these rather than motor responses which cause distress among neurotic patients. So far there is little evidence for or against this, but the writer has used the technique in dealing with a pathological fear of cancer in a woman patient. Deliberate 'massed-practice' of the ideas which were abhorrent to her (but continually obtruding into her consciousness) led to a progressive reduction in the spontaneous and involuntary appearance of these ideas.

Perhaps the most important technique derived from learning theory for the treatment of neurotic symptoms is that of *reciprocal inhibition*, the development of which is largely due to Wolpe (1958). In essence this form of therapy has two basic aspects. The first requirement is that the feared stimulus or situation needs to be broken up into constituent parts in some kind of hierarchical order from 'most feared' to 'least feared'. The second requirement is to discover a response which can be evoked in the patient and which is *incompatible with the presence of anxiety*. The following case might serve to illustrate these two points.

A patient with a pathological fear of spiders was asked, before treatment commenced, to describe those characteristics of spiders which produced greatest anxiety in her. These turned out to be size (the larger the spider the more afraid she would be), colour (the 'blacker' the spider the greater the fear) and hairiness (the more hairy in appearance the more the anxiety). To these could be added movement (the more active the spider the greater the anxiety), and proximity (the closer the spider the more fear would be generated). Clearly, the least frightening spider in this patient's *generalization gradient* would be a small, light-coloured, non-hairy, dead spider exhibited at some distance! Gradually, as one works up through the hierarchy, each of these elements is changed until, at the last stage, the patient is dealing with a large, black, hairy spider which is very active and close at hand.

However, the patient must learn to associate this stimulus complex (spiders) with feelings other than those of anxiety, and these alternative feelings must be made sufficiently strong to overcome whatever anxiety is present at each stage of the treatment. There are many ways of inducing such feelings, but none of them would be effective enough in counteracting the overwhelming anxiety experienced if one began treatment with the last stage in the fear hierarchy instead of the first. Supposing we argue that pleasant feelings and anxiety cannot be experienced at the same moment in time and that one or the other must 'win-out', then we must always ensure that it is the former which are always predominant. In practice this means reducing the anxiety to a level where pleasant feelings are the stronger, even though by only a small margin, and this is the real purpose of forming the hierarchy respecting the feared situation.

In the case of the spider phobia it was apparent that the patient experienced pleasant feelings which were incompatible with the presence of anxiety whenever a particular piece of music was heard. At each stage in the treatment, therefore, the recorded music was played on the assumption that feelings other than anxiety would become associated with the presence of spiders. At the end of treatment this patient could handle very large specimens of house spiders, embodying all the feared characteristics, with complete ease and tranquillity.

We are now in a position to say that modern learning theories give a consistent account of the origins of neurotic symptoms, and also that therapeutic practices based upon these theories can be derived and applied. But can we say that the case for behaviour therapy is in no doubt? Is the evidence forthcoming from the practical application of such treatments conclusive? Are there any objections which can be raised to the explanation of neurotic symptoms and their responsiveness to the techniques employed?

There are really two basic questions involved. The first is whether behaviour therapy (i.e. techniques derived from learning theory principles and used for the relief of neurotic symptoms) produces favourable results in terms of clear-cut experimental demonstration. Secondly, whether the successes which have been attributed to behaviour therapy really are explicable in terms of learning theory principles.

Personality Theories and Behaviour Therapy

Looking at the first of these two major problems one is immediately struck by the dearth of critical evidence concerning the efficacy of behaviour therapy. In one study by Cooper it was found that the results were not better than those accruing to psychotherapy, a finding which might seem strange if the two therapies differed so much in terms of their experimental and scientific origins. However, Cooper's evidence did suggest that the special group of patients with phobias might benefit to a greater extent from behaviour therapy than from any alternative treatment. In addition, it was obvious that Cooper's sample included a number of 'hard-core' cases who had been unsuccessfully treated by a number of different therapies and it would seem unreasonable to expect behaviour therapy to succeed with the kind of patients who would not be helped by any alternative treatment, although this sometimes appeared to happen.

A second study, carried out by Lazarus, compared the effects on common fears of behaviour therapy and conventional psychotherapy. The sample of people chosen for this experiment was, unfortunately, *volunteers who had no psychiatric history*, and it could be argued that perhaps these individuals were not comparable to those who have actively sought psychiatric assistance for their disorders. While the results of the inquiry showed a markedly greater success rate for behaviour therapy than for psychotherapy, it does not follow that this differential outcome would be found among neurotic patients as it is just possible that we are dealing here with the difference between 'bad habits' and 'symptoms'.

These and other studies so far conducted to examine the outcome of applying behaviour therapy techniques have been characterized by some defects, and no firm conclusions are possible at this stage. However, the evidence does seem to be pointing in favour of behaviour therapy, especially in the treatment of phobic conditions, and even if the outcome of using such techniques turned out to be no better than that obtained using psychotherapy it is certainly true that the former procedures produce much quicker results than the latter and, consequently, have a great deal to recommend them from the point of view of both therapist and patient.

Learning and Training

The second major problem, that of deciding whether successes attributed to behaviour therapy are in accord with learning theory principles, raises a number of crucial issues. One of these concerns the relationship between the therapist and the patient, and some evidence that this might be important stems from the observation that behaviour therapists differ in the proportion of cures obtained. In theory, treatments based on the principles of learning could be carried out without the presence of a therapist at all, but in practice behaviour therapists tend to cultivate strong relationships with their patients which, it is suggested, serve to reduce the anxieties of the patient and thus facilitate treatment. It is difficult to know whether it is the 'relearning' aspect or the close emotional ties with the therapist (or perhaps both) which is producing the favourable result. However, if it could be shown that behaviour therapy produces better results than psychotherapy, in spite of both involving an emotional relationship, then it would follow that the cures obtained are not wholly dependent on deep personal involvements.

Another relevant issue is concerned with the view taken of the symptoms exhibited by the patient. The psychotherapist often takes the view that a symptom is only the outward expression of the 'real' underlying difficulty, while the behaviour therapist will tend to regard the symptom as evidence of faulty or inappropriate learning. If the latter view is the correct one, then two things would be likely to follow: that removal of the symptom should be sufficient to achieve a cure, and that symptoms should exist in 'isolation' as 'habits' without being prompted by a complex network of ideas.

According to the psychotherapeutic view removal of a symptom would not remove the 'cause' which lies in the relatively inaccessible reaches of the patient's mind. Consequently, removal of one symptom would lead to the appearance of another and this process of *symptom substitution* would continue until we finally remove the basic cause. The evidence for the occurrence of symptom substitution is not very well documented but probably does occur in some cases. Such evidence does not deal a fatal blow to behaviour therapy as the phenomenon of symptom substitution seems to occur relatively infrequently, but it certainly

356

does complicate the issue. The writer has suggested, and demonstrated in one case, that to some extent the behaviour therapist can overcome this difficulty by asking the question, 'What symptom requires attention?' The case in point concerned a patient with both writer's cramp and a stammer who, on investigation, showed evidence of a relation between the production of his symptoms and his fears of dealing with people in authority. Instead of treating the two 'symptoms' directly, it was decided to treat the patient's attitudes towards authority figures *by behaviour therapy techniques*. This case was successfully concluded and suggests that sometimes a naïve view of symptomatology might be misleading and result in inappropriate treatment, and that careful inquiry into the nature of the obvious symptoms might unearth a more basic and meaningful 'symptom' which can still be effectively dealt with by relearning procedures.

Among the numerous additional criticisms which may be levelled against behaviour therapy one might single out for special attention the relative failure to deal with the 'thinking' aspects of neurotic illness. To some extent this neglect may be responsible for the relatively poor success rate of aversion therapy in the treatment of alcoholics.* Getting rid of the 'habit component' of homosexuality, for example, might not be successful if treated by aversion therapy unless the individual is given some opportunity to learn to redirect his sexual impulses.

The dubious outcome of the 'simple' approach to such disturbances is perhaps best pointed out by considering what might happen if we applied aversive learning procedures to an individual's *heterosexual behaviour*; would he, then, become a well-adjusted homosexual? Probably not.

There are also examples of the misapplication of learning theory principles by behaviour therapists which have resulted in a cure for the patient. To the extent to which treatment which is inappropriate on theoretical grounds turns out to be successful in practice, doubts must be raised about the theory rather than the practice. Such doubts are also raised by Wolpe's description of the method of reciprocal inhibition. He argues that if a

* Quite often this treatment probably fails because of the mis-application of conditioning theory principles.

response incompatible with anxiety occurs in the presence of the feared object or situation so that there is *complete or partial* suppression of anxiety responses, then the association between anxiety and the object or situation will be weakened. But if anxiety is only *partly* suppressed (and this is almost invariably the case in practice), then one could argue that the individual is still learning the old anxiety–situation connexion. Why weakening of the relationship rather than strengthening takes place is not made clear by the theory.

CONCLUSION

There are numerous problems in the theory and practice of behaviour therapy which remain unsolved, but what is quite clear is that learning theory has opened up a new approach to the understanding and treatment of neurotic disorders. It is entirely understandable that, at this relatively early stage, the techniques employed and the theories from which they derive are raw, un-developed and unsophisticated. Nevertheless, the evidence now emerging suggests that the laws of learning provide a genuine alternative approach to the appreciation of the origins of neurotic symptoms, and to their modification and change. Also, so far as one can say at this stage, behaviour therapy has at least as great a measure of success as psychotherapy, and is generally much more economical in time. The final verdict must, of course, rest upon the patient accumulation of experimental evidence, and upon the development of the theories of learning and their extension to the problems involved in treatment. More research is clearly needed and is, in fact, increasing in volume each year. However, in behaviour therapy as it is formulated at present, we have a really promising beginning in techniques which could assume a dominating role in the treatment of neurotic disturbance.

PERSONALITY AND SOCIAL PSYCHOLOGY

In the previous sections of this book there have been frequent references to the psychology of personality. Whenever the differences between people show up in a psychological study, there is a temptation to look for a relation between experimental results and type of personality, and this has led to the topic being studied from many points of view. Previous chapters have looked at the relations between personality and perception, thinking, heredity, early experience, reactions to drugs and the processes of learning. But the psychology of personality is a subject in its own right. It has been studied from the points of view of Freudian theory and child training; psychologists, and others, have invented innumerable typologies, and many tests have been devised to study personality traits. The method reported in the first chapter of this section is an experimental one which has great promise. It has been picked as one of the more exciting developments in this field.

In social psychology, too, there have been many new experiments and theories. The last two chapters of the book present two of the best known ways of studying the subject – looking at the behaviour of people in small groups, and comparing the behaviour of people from different cultures.

19. A NEW THEORY OF PERSONALITY

D. BANNISTER

It is likely that Personal Construct Theory will have a considerable future. It has given rise to an objective method for assessing differences in personality and has also given new ideas about the structure of personality. Dr Bannister is a pioneer in the use of the theory and its methods, and in this chapter he presents a primer on the subject.

PSYCHOLOGISTS AND PEOPLE

PROFESSOR G. A. KELLY of Ohio State University began work on what is now called Personal Construct Theory some two decades before it was published in a complete form in 1955. While cogitating on the problem of theories in psychology he noticed the interesting fact that each individual psychologist appears to propound not one but two theories of psychology. The first deals with the behaviour of what is variously called the organism, the subject or even people and indicates that these creatures are impelled by drives, incentives and appetites, respond mechanically to various stimuli in terms of their habit systems, are at the mercy of unconscious complexes or are jerking about at the behest of their central nervous system. The second theory deals with the behaviour of a different kind of creature known as 'the scientist' or more specifically 'the psychologist'. This creature is of quite another species; he operates by constructing theories from which he derives hypotheses, he puts these hypotheses to experimental test and modifies his theories according to the results. In general, he is trying to understand, predict and control his environment. The first set of notions is called a psychological theory and the second a description of scientific method, but both seem to be designed to account for some sort of human behaviour. Kelly records his original observation of these contrasting theories held by psychologists as follows:

One of my tasks in the 1930s was to direct graduate studies leading to the Masters Degree. A typical afternoon might find me talking to a graduate student at one o'clock, doing all those familiar things that thesis directors have to do – encouraging the student to pin-point the issues, to observe, to become intimate with the problem, to form hypotheses either inductively or deductively, to make some preliminary test runs, to relate his data to his predictions, to control his experiments so that he will know what led to what, to generalize cautiously and to revise his thinking in the light of experience.

At two o'clock I might have an appointment with a client. During this interview I would not be taking the role of the scientist but rather helping the distressed person work out some solutions to his life's problems. So what would I do? Why, I would try to get him to pin-point the issues, to observe, to become intimate with the problem, to form hypotheses, to make test runs, to relate outcomes to anticipations, to control his ventures so that he will know what led to what, to generalize cautiously and to revise his dogma in the light of experience.

At three o'clock I would see a student again. Likely as not he was either dragging his feet, hoping to design some world-shaking experiment before looking at his first subject to see first hand what he was dealing with or plunging into some massive ill-considered data-chasing expedition. So I would again try to get him to pin-point the issues, to observe open-mindedly, to become intimate with the problem, to form hypotheses – all the things that I had had to do at one o'clock.

At four o'clock another client! Guess what! He would be dragging his feet, hoping to design a completely new personality before venturing his first change in behaviour or plunging into some ill-considered acting-out escapade, etc. But this, of course, was not my hour for science; it was my hour for psychotherapy. And what I had done with that student back in the hour before, that was obviously not psychotherapy; it was science!

For Kelly, all men can be said to be 'scientists' in the sense that they have theories about their universe (not as systematic or sophisticated as the theories of professional scientists but theories nevertheless), and on the basis of these theories they have particular hypotheses (expectations) which are fulfilled or not fulfilled, and in the light of the outcome of their 'experiments' their views are modified. Thus the model man of Personal Construct Theory is 'man the scientist'.

A New Theory of Personality

MODEL MAN

All psychological theories seem to imply some sort of model man, some notion of what man essentially is. Thus psycho-analytic theories suggest that man is essentially a battlefield, he is a dark cellar in which a maiden aunt and a sex-crazed monkey are locked in mortal combat, the affair being refereed by a rather nervous bank clerk. Alternatively, learning theory and stimulus–response psychology generally seem to suggest that man is essentially a ping-pong ball with a memory. For Kelly, man is essentially 'a scientist'; he is in the predicting business. He is perpetually seeking to try and guess what happens next by construing and reconstruing his universe.

In Kelly's own words (1961):

Abstraction and generalization of human activity are not the exclusive prerogatives of professional psychologists. What they do any person may do. Indeed, every person does! Each individual the psychologists study abstracts and generalizes on his own, for he is even more vitally interested than they can ever be in the task of understanding himself and his relationship to other persons and values. Thus the psychology of personality is not simply a matter of disinterested psychologists assessing a disinterested organism but of psychologists, who happen to be professionally and casually interested in their chosen subject matter, assessing a non-professional psychologist, who, on his part, is intimately and urgently involved with the job of making sense out of the life upon which his existence depends.

MAN AS A PREDICTOR

The fundamental postulate of Kelly's theory is that '*a person's processes are psychologically channelized by the ways in which he anticipates events*'. Thus for him human behaviour is basically anticipatory rather than reactive. New avenues of behaviour open themselves to a person as he reconstrues the course of events surrounding him. Thus man is neither a prisoner of his environment nor a victim of his biography, he is neither pushed by external stimuli nor dragged along by his internal appetites.

Man tries to anticipate the future by erecting a conceptual framework, a series of related goggles through which he may view his universe. These goggles Kelly terms constructs. A construct is a bi-polar concept, a way of categorizing similarities and differences which we perceive in our environment. Thus *black–white*, *acid–alkali*, *friendly–hostile*, *light–heavy*, *like I am–like I would like to be* and so forth are constructs. They are the means by which we interpret our situation. Many of them may have clear verbal labels, for others our behaviour indicates we are perceiving a similarity/difference in some aspect of our situation, but we may have no explicit verbal label for it.

Kelly's notion of a construct differs from the traditional idea of a concept in many ways, but most significantly in two. Psychologists working on concepts and concept formation tended to behave as if each concept was a discrete entity, a kind of circular mental fence surrounding herds of physical things, but the question of the relationship between concepts is very inadequately explored. For Kelly, constructs are organized into a complex hierarchical network, each person has a personal *construct system*. Thus, for many of us, the construct *good–bad* may subsume and therefore be superordinate to the construct *intelligent–stupid*, since we may believe that *good* includes, among other things, *intelligent*, and *bad*, among other things, *stupid*. Secondly, concepts are traditionally treated as if they were merely labels or categories. For Kelly, constructs are essentially predictive instruments. Because of the network of relationships between X, Y and Z constructs, we expect of an element construed as an X, Y and Z types of behaviour. If we construe a man as *reliable* rather than *unreliable*, then if our construct of *reliable–unreliable* is closely linked with a network of constructs such as *punctual*, *trustworthy* and *affectionate*, then we are committed to a whole series of expectations about the behaviour of *reliable* people.

Thus Kelly's theory is centrally concerned with questions such as 'How do our personal construct systems develop and change?', 'How can they be measured?' and 'How can an understanding of a person's construct system lead to the effective understanding and prediction of his behaviour?' At the centre of his theory, Kelly has set up a series of postulates about the nature of constructs and construing processes a few of which are summarized in the following paragraphs.

A New Theory of Personality

CHARACTERISTICS OF CONSTRUING

A person anticipates events by construing their replications. We do not predict that what happened yesterday will happen tomorrow but we do expect that certain aspects of yesterday's events which we have construed will be replicated tomorrow. Just as when we listen to a piece of music and detect the recurrence of certain themes it does not lead us to predict that the notes will simply be repeated but it does enable us to structure the piece of music in our head (construe it, interpret it, understand it) so that we anticipate the replication of these themes.

It must be stressed at this point that all construct systems are *personal*. Thus a phrase like 'replication of events' must be taken to mean that the events perceived as replicated are particular to the subject. For example, in psychological experiments on learning, the subject may fail to construe as replicating events the reinforcements and non-reinforcements that the experimenter perceives and indeed arranges. The subject may perceive entirely different themes as replicated. Thus, when a subject fails to meet the experimenter's expectations it may be inappropriate to say that 'He has not learned' – rather one might say that 'What the subject has learned was not what the experimenter expected him to learn.'

Persons differ from each other in their construction of events. People can be seen as differing from each other not because there may have been differences in the events they have sought to anticipate but because there are different approaches to the anticipation of the same events. Thus we would look for explanations of the differences in individual behaviour, not in differences of experience as such but in terms of the differing subjective worlds which people inhabit as a result of the differing constructions which they have come to put upon events.

Individual constructs, construct sub-systems and whole construct systems have limited ranges of convenience. Most of us would find it difficult to construe an element like 'false teeth' as *religious–atheist*. It is not just that they are not religious or that they are not atheist – they do not appear to come within the range of convenience of the construct at all. 'Everything but *A* must

365

be not-*A*' may be *logically* true, but it is not *psycho*logically true.

A person's construction system varies as he successively construes replications of events. The construction one places upon events are working hypotheses which are about to be put to the test of experience. As our anticipations are hypotheses to be successively revised in the light of the unfolding sequence of events, a construction system undergoes a progressive evolution. The constant revision of personal construct systems is a function of incoming varying validational experience. Constructs are essentially *predictive*. Thus, when we construe a man as *honest* rather than *dishonest* we are essentially predicting that if we lend him money we shall get it back. When we construe a table as *solid* rather than *liquid* we are essentially predicting that if something is placed upon it it will 'stay on the surface' and not 'be submerged'. Constructs are not merely ways of labelling our universe, they are ways of trying to understand and anticipate it. Since every act of construing is simultaneously an act of prediction it follows that every act of construing may have one of three outcomes. The elements (objects, persons or whatever) which we construe as *X* may turn out to be *X* and we are validated. The elements may turn out to be the opposite of *X* and we are invalidated. The elements may turn out to be outside the range of convenience of our construct *X*–not-*X*. Thus, when the hopeful young man takes the young lady back to his flat he may construe her as *willing* rather than *unwilling* and he may be validated – an affair commences. He may be invalidated – she slaps his face and rings for the police. The element may turn out to be outside the range of convenience of the construct – 'she' turns out to be a transvestite. It is precisely because constructs are essentially predictions that our construct systems are in a continual state of change for each of us. As the evidence comes in we tend to modify the individual construct or parts of our construct system. The modification may be a minor one. We may simply shuffle the element from one pole of the construct to the other. A person we regard as *loving* behaves nastily and we now proceed to regard him (construe him) as *hating*. However, we may be wrong so persistently that we have to make some more major alteration, such as dispensing with the construct *loving–hating* and developing some other construct to view the element through. Or we may have to modify whole sub-systems within our construct system in order to get a truer (more predictive) view of the elements which confront us.

Kelly supplies a number of dimensions which are ways of differentiating types of change within construct systems. For example, he puts forward the idea that constructs or whole systems can be tightened or loosened. A tight construct is one which leads to unvarying predictions and is therefore brittle and liable to invalidation, but useful because it is precise. Or a construct may be loose, in which case it is liable to give multi-directional predictions, it is vague and woolly. This has the advantage that it is difficult to invalidate, but at the same time it is lacking in precision. Both scientists and mere men can be seen retreating rapidly from tight and precise constructs to woollier and vaguer (looser) constructs when the evidential going gets rough.

Even though only a few of the theory's principles have been given, it can be seen that Kelly is arguing that no man has ever yet reacted to 'a stimulus' – *he reacts to what he interprets the stimulus to be.* If a man has a construct of *Greek vase* he may find one lying on the ground. Lacking such a construct, what he has found is a *vase*; lacking such a construct, what he has found is a *lump of pot*; lacking such a construct, what he has found is *a thing*. Thus at the centre of the theory (as at the centre of all psychological theories) is an explanation of the fundamental phenomenon facing psychology – that two people may react entirely differently when they are in an identical situation. The explanation is simple, they are not in fact in 'an identical situation'. The situation of the two people may appear identical to a third observer through *his* construct system, but the two people (viewing the landscape through their particular and individual construct systems) are in different situations.

A MENTALISTIC SYSTEM ?

One of the frequent charges levelled against Personal Construct Theory is that it is too mentalistic. This partly arises from the fact that Kelly's assertion that all men are 'scientists' is taken too literally, and he is thought to be asserting that all men solve their problems by means of computers and formal experiments. This is absurd, since Kelly is not asserting that all men are good scientists or systematic scientists or academic scientists, merely that they can be construed as scientists in that they are attempting to understand, predict and control their universe by construing it and reacting to the fate of resulting expectations.

A more common source for the 'mentalistic' charge is that psychologists viewing the theory are perturbed by the disappearance of ancient notions such as 'emotion', 'motive', 'drive' and so forth. What Kelly does is to replace conventional ideas about emotion by the idea that *emotion is the awareness of the fact that our construct system is in a state of change or transition*.

Thus an 'emotion' like anxiety is defined as '*the awareness that the events with which one is confronted lie mostly outside the range of convenience of one's construct system*'. Using this type of abstraction we do not have to define anxiety in terms of specific concrete events or to view it as a kind of ginger pop bubbling about in our systems or to leave it vague as 'stress'. We can see it as the person's awareness that he is not fully able to comprehend the significance of the events with which he is faced; he is, in effect, faced with one of life's 'things that go bump in the night', something which is not properly construed and the outcome of which he cannot properly anticipate.

The emotion of guilt, which is invariably recognized by lay or common-sense psychology, which is both the gateway and the pitfall into psycho-analytic psychology and which is virtually totally ignored by learning theory, is defined as follows: '*guilt is the awareness of dislodgement of the self from one's core role structure*'. Core role constructs are those constructs which we use to conceptualize ourselves. They are the dimensions against which we measure ourselves and thereby the way in which we try to anticipate our own behaviour. If we find ourselves doing things which we would not have predicted on the basis of the kind of picture we have of ourselves, then these core role constructs are invalidated, and the whole network of constructs through which we view ourselves is in danger. We may become unpredictable to ourselves – a fate so fearful that religions are built around it and men kill themselves rather than sustain it.

Hostility is defined as '*the continued effort to extort validational evidence in favour of a type of social prediction which has already been recognized as a failure*'. Men (like some scientists) cannot always accept the validity of incoming evidence and modify their construing system. If the evidence threatens constructs which are superordinate and central to our system, then we have too much invested in them to be able to give them up. We may prefer to become 'hostile', i.e. to go on 'cooking' the evidence rather than risk the collapse and chaos for major sections of our view of the world. We would rather cling to invalid views of life than have life become meaningless for us.

CHARACTERISTICS OF THE THEORY

What has been written so far is in no sense a summary of the theory but merely an indication of some of its contentions. However, we can begin to see some of its major characteristics and the ways in which it differs from other extant psychological theories. For example, a central aspect of the theory is that it is *reflexive*. It is self-referring in that what the theory asserts applies to itself explicitly and implicitly. The theory accounts for the behaviour of the person making the theory. Personal Construct Theory is itself a way of construing and we can comment on its various aspects in terms of whether they contain tight or loose constructs and so forth. It can be argued that all psychological theories should be reflexive. Thus Oliver and Landfield (1963) say:

It is evident that if psychology, as a whole or in any of its branches, is concerned with the process of thought, it cannot, while it is dealing with the latter, avoid whatever problems accompany reflexivity. To derive conclusions from evidence, a man must think. Thus to assert that thought is of this or that nature, is to say something about the nature of the process whereby this conclusion has been derived.

Putting forward psychological ideas is itself a piece of human behaviour and we are facing a paradox if the ideas we put forward account for everything but our own behaviour in putting them forward. Theories in physics and chemistry do not need to be reflexive because the thinking of the physicist and the chemist is not the problem in hand, they are not called on to account for it. However, the psychologist is in no such happy position. He must account for his own activities as a psychologist in his theories and hypotheses. It can be seen that psychological theories to date have rarely, if ever, been reflexive. Granted it is possible at a joke level to assume that psycho-analysts writing long psycho-analytic papers are merely sublimating their sex instinct. Or learning theorists, writing long learning theory papers may show, in their duller moments, that they (and the reader) are suffering from a build-up of reactive inhibition. However, psychologists, in general, do not attempt to build reflexivity into their theories but calmly accept a paradoxical position.

We can also differentiate Personal Construct Theory from other extant theories in terms of its range of convenience. As has been mentioned Kelly argues that every single construct or construct system has a focus and range of convenience. The focus of convenience of a construct or theory is that group of elements which it was originally designed to make predictions about. The range of convenience is the maximum number of elements the theory can be stretched to cover. For example, the focus of convenience of Freudian theory can be said to have been originally middle-class Viennese neurotics. Granted the range of convenience of the theory is greater and people have sought to use it to account for the behaviour of men in primitive societies, phenomena such as war or art and so forth. However, it is noticeable that the theory begins to creak and become more vague and woolly (its constructs become looser), as its range of convenience is extended. Similarly, learning theory originally sought to account for the behaviour of animals such as rats and dogs in highly specific laboratory conditions – this was its focus of convenience. Currently, attempts have been made to extend its range of convenience to activities such as the therapy of neurotics, the failure of criminals to learn their lesson from going to prison and so forth. However, even the more optimistic learning theorists recognize how rapidly difficulties arise as soon as the focus of convenience has been left, and, indeed, there is a tendency to rush back to the original focus fairly frequently. The focus of convenience of Construct Theory was explicitly the field of interpersonal relationships and the way in which people construe each other, but it was specifically designed from the beginning to have a much wider range of convenience and it may be that this consciousness of the need for a wide range of convenience in a psychological theory will enable it to work more satisfactorily as its range of convenience is extended.

THE USES OF THEORY

Although a theory can be examined for its internal logical consistency and its ability to give superficially acceptable explanations of data, ultimately it must be put to the test of experiment. Theories, of course, are made elaborate and flexible so that they may ultimately account for many things which have not even been studied at the time the theory was constructed. Thus no single experiment or set of experiments can destroy a large and complex theory. However, in the long run, if a theory repeatedly produces wrong bets, i.e. it produces hypotheses and expectations which are repeatedly unfulfilled by actual experiment, then it must surely die. The proof of the theoretical pudding is always in the experimental eating.

Personal Construct Theory is not, as yet, commonly taught or accepted, and relatively little experimental work has been done with it so far. However, we can briefly view some of the experimental work it has inspired to see how it is working out in practice.

A NEW MEASURE OF PERSONALITY

The first thing to which Personal Construct Theory gave rise was a method of measurement. Obviously, if the theory hinges on the idea of constructs and the way in which constructs are built up, related and changed, then a primary task is to find ways of measuring constructs and constructs' inter-relationships. Thus, deriving it directly from his theory, Kelly devised the technique of repertory grid testing.

Kelly himself describes the technique as follows (1961):

Suppose I were to give one of you a card and ask you to write on it the name of your mother. Then I would give you another and ask you to write the name of your father. On a third you might write the name of your wife, and on a fourth the name of the girl you almost married – but didn't! We could continue until you had as many as twenty or thirty cards, each showing the name of a person important in your life.

Then suppose I should select three of these cards, perhaps the ones of your father, your mother and your boss or supervisor. Suppose I should ask you to think of some important way in which any two of them seem to be alike and in contrast to the third. What will you say? Perhaps you will say that your mother and your boss have always seemed to know the answers to the questions you asked, but that your father hesitated or told you to seek out your own answers.

Now if this is a distinction you can apply to your father, your mother and your boss, can you extend it also to the other persons you have named? You probably can. The important fact is that as you apply it to person after person you are not only characterizing those persons but you are also providing an *operational definition* of what you have in mind. Applied to enough persons this operational definition provides a more extensive definition of a particular channel of your thought than do words you may use to symbolize it.

Now suppose I select another three cards, perhaps the ones with the names of your mother, your wife and the girl you did not marry. What about them? Is there an important way in which two of them – any two – differ from the third? Perhaps you will respond immediately by saying that your wife and your mother are loving, but that the girl you did not marry turned out to be harsh.

And how will you extend this personal construct to the other persons who are important in your life? Let me suppose that each person you characterize as 'loving' is a person you have previously characterized as 'ready to answer your questions', and each person you characterize as 'harsh' is one you previously characterized as 'sending you off to look for your own answers'. Suppose this were true in case after case, to infinity. What could we say then? Would we then be ready to say that the two constructs were identical in everything but name?

Not quite! In our illustration the two constructs have been applied only to persons as whole entities. There is still the question of whether the constructs are applied identically to the separate acts of persons.

Moreover, we need also to make sure that both constructs occupy exactly the same range of convenience. That is to say, can the first construct in my illustration – the response–rejection construct – be applied to all the events to which the second construct – the loving–harsh construct – can be applied; and, of course, vice versa? If there are some events that can be classified by the person as responsive or rejecting but which he cannot treat in terms of lovingness or harshness, then the ranges of convenience of the two constructs are different and the constructs themselves are therefore not quite the same.

We can represent the data produced so far in a flat matrix with events – in this case the names appearing on the cards – ranged along the top from left to right, and with the constructs ranged along the side from top to bottom. The entries in the matrix are single digit binary numbers, indicating simply whether the event is regarded one way or the other in terms of the construct. For example, if you regarded your mother as loving, this particular datum would be represented in the matrix by the numeral '1' in the first cell of the second row – below *mother* and opposite *loving–harsh*. If you regarded your father as harsh the numeral '0' would be entered in the next cell, etc.

Now we may go on to expand the matrix until it is large enough to give us a stable idea of how the person construes his world. Starting with different triads of cards we can successively produce row after row of matrix entries.

This is not an interminable undertaking. Experience shows that only persons with the most complex or schizoid outlooks require more than twenty or thirty rows to express their repertory of constructs. Repertories used in everyday affairs are generally quite limited and especially, so it appears, among those who prefer to act rather than reflect.

As you can see, the matrix can be factor-analyzed to see to what extent the person is employing a variety of constructs, or only a few constructs masquerading under different names. We can examine the columns in the matrix to see which figures in his life are viewed as similar to others, or whether, indeed, there is any great variety perceived among them. For example, does the subject see himself as like his father?

Again, there are some men who can see complex differences among men, but only one-dimensional differences among women. There are some who have attempted to reduce all their interpersonal relations to the simple structure of one dimension – some military men, for example, and there are some who have done this in an effort to control the multi-dimensional confusion of their anxiety.

This technique of repertory grid testing has already been developed in a variety of ways using different statistical modes of analysis to make sense of the way in which a person sorts the elements with which he is faced. In the majority of cases the subjects have been sorting people known personally to them, but it has also been found possible to have them sort descriptions of situations, physical objects, lists of emotions and so forth, depending upon the type of construct which the investigator wished to explore. It has been used for purposes as varied as examining the way in which the thinking of severely disturbed schizophrenics is distorted and disorganized or the way in which children in their early construing gradually acquire the value systems of their parents. It is contributing substantially towards solving the old problem in psychology of 'vitality of material' versus 'precision of measurement'. Psychologists have often had to choose between two extremes. At one end they have been so concerned with precise quantification in measurement that they have been forced to concentrate on relatively fragmentary aspects of human behaviour (e.g. eye-blink conditionability, memory for rote-learned nonsense syllables, responses to standard lists of questions and so forth). At the other extreme they have sought to plunge deeper into the nature of human personality (as in projective tests which allow the subject to respond freely to a wide range of emotionally charged material), but this at the cost of abandoning quantitative measurement in favour of interpretative guesswork by the psychologist. Repertory grid technique has the advantage of quantifying in precise and statistically sophisticated form the responses of the subject while allowing him to deal with vital and meaningful material in terms of his personal life.

EXPERIMENTS IN PERSONAL CONSTRUCT THEORY

Purely by way of illustration, let us first consider the idea of 'threat' in human interpersonal relationships. Most of us have subjectively experienced psychological threat. We have been in the presence of people who 'make us uncomfortable'. Quite often the nature of the threat is not specific, it does not lie in any particularly hostile thing they have said or in any power they have over our actual future. From what then does this feeling of threat derive and what does it mean in terms of our personal psychology? This problem has been studied in terms of Personal Construct Theory by Landfield (1954, 1955). He assumed from the beginning that threat would have to do with our core role constructs – that is the constructs we apply to ourselves and the picture we have of ourselves. By using Repertory Grid Technique and getting his subjects to sort people significant in their lives on constructs such as *like I used to be* or *like I am now* as compared with constructs such as *like I would like to be*, Landfield built up a picture of the contrast between his subjects' past or present selves as seen by them and the ideal selves they pictured as desirable. He then had them identify people as threatening in terms of constructs such as *make me uncomfortable* and examined in detail how in other ways his subjects construed these threatening people. He discovered that the people they saw as threatening were often (at a statistically significant level) people whom they saw as like they used to be, but as sharply distinct from their ideal-self. It may be, then, that our behaviour is always in terms of some picture of ourselves towards which we are moving, and relationships with people who represent ourselves as we were or are, is in itself evidence of our failure to achieve ideals, and as such a threat to our general concept of what we are becoming. Later, Landfield returned to the problem and was able to throw some light on the disturbing subjective experience which we feel when in the presence of threatening people as he had now defined them. He found, interestingly enough, that an individual is disturbed in the presence of threatening people because he regards *himself* as less predictable in social relationships involving such people. In other words, it may be that our sense of uncertainty and unease derives not from any doubts as to how the threatening person may behave but grave doubts about what we may expect of ourselves in such circumstances. This line of work is obviously capable of considerable extension. For example, we might hypothesize that people who have a wide discrepancy between what they can see themselves to be and what they would like themselves to be are particularly open to experience of 'threat' and so forth.

Runkel and Damrin (1961) used Construct Theory to tackle the problem of the way in which students in training as teachers learn their subject. Construct Theory led them to look at the question of the complexity of the dimensions which their student teachers were using to view their work. In terms of Construct Theory it is easy to see that human beings may operate either a complex or a simple system in trying to make sense of their situation. For example, at one extreme a person may divide his acquaintances on almost one dimension: *nice–nasty* or *good–bad* or *likes me–doesn't like me,* and attempt to deal with all situations which they face in terms of some such single dimension. Granted they may have very many labels about people, but Repertory Grid Testing may show that all these labels are statistically equivalent and resolve themselves into one central dimension. Such people are themselves obviously going to produce rather rigid and stereotyped behaviour because, inevitably, they see themselves as being in the same situation over and over again. Runkel and Damrin faced their student teachers with a number of problems which might arise when they ultimately encountered pupils at school and asked them to rank order the kinds of information they would require in trying to solve these problems. By statistically analysing their responses it was possible to decide in each case whether the student teacher was viewing the problems through a number of different constructs or whether he was utilizing only one or two constructs with which to solve the problem. They tested student teachers at the beginning of their training, midway and towards the end of their training and found that initially student teachers approached their subject with a wide variety of dimensions for viewing it (relevant or irrelevant). Then, as training proceeded there was a general increase in their level of anxiety and they tended to narrow down until they were viewing the objects of their study through a very restricted range of constructs and then, as they gained more experience and became more confident, they began to elaborate these out again until they emerged at the end of their studies with a more complex way of viewing the field. There was some indication that the most successful teachers were those who most markedly showed curvilinear progress during training (a complex view, then simple and back to complex). It is perhaps significant that quite different types of 'cue utilization' experiments have shown that when people become anxious they restrict the number of cues of which they take note. Landfield's experiments suggest that this may be because they have restricted the actual number of dimensions through which they are prepared to view their environment, and some stimuli thereby disappear since there are less constructs available which could make their presence meaningful. The Runkel–Damrin finding obviously has implications for teaching people generally and trying to understand the process of mastering an area or learning a topic.

Sechrest (1962) studied the Freudian idea of transference using Repertory Grid Technique and Personal Construct Theory. The standard Freudian idea is that a patient in psychotherapy sees his therapist at some point as essentially like (playing the same role as) the patient's father or mother or at least someone from his early family situation. Sechrest took patients who were in therapy and had them sort the therapist along with members of their family and other figures against various constructs in a repertory grid test. When he subjected their sortings to statistical analysis they appeared to be perceiving their therapist much more as they perceived such figures as the family doctor, teachers and ministers of religion rather than perceiving them as substitute fathers or mothers. It was interesting that this pattern did not change during the course of therapy when patients were re-tested and the Freudian transference hypothesis was not supported. Obviously, Freudians might argue that the transference hypothesis relates to unconscious processes rather than those revealed by repertory grid tests. It must be pointed out that repertory grid tests do not involve a direct report and therefore do not preclude the operation of unconscious tendencies. In such tests the subject is almost invariably under the impression that what is important is his particular judgement of each person in relation to a particular category. In fact, it is the relationship between judgemental categories or constellations of persons which is actually being examined. Obviously, such work could be extended by checking in the first place whether the patient views model figures of the family doctor, minister, teacher-type favourably, and this might be an index of the way in which he will ultimately respond to the attentions of the therapist as such.

The use of both theory and technique in the field of clinical psychology where a systematic study of the individual case is required, appears to be steadily extending. Such uses are well exemplified by Fransella and Adams's (1965) study of an arsonist by means of a series of repertory grid tests administered during treatment. Figure 62 is a graphic illustration of the results of the third grid in the series.

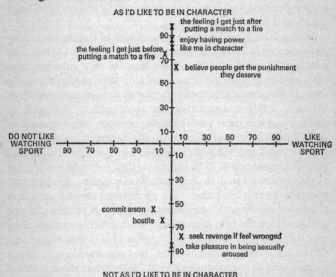

AS I'D LIKE TO BE IN CHARACTER

NOT AS I'D LIKE TO BE IN CHARACTER

Figure 62. Graphic illustration of Repertory Grid Technique.

The patient was asked to rank order photographs of people on constructs which had either been elicited from him or were thought to represent relevant aspects of his outlook. The resulting sorts were shown to lie (in statistical terms) mainly on one major axis *as I'd like to be in character* versus *not as I'd like to be in character* with a second independent axis (*do not like watching sport* versus *like watching sport*) as present but unimportant, in that virtually nothing is related to it.

One hypothesis under investigation at this point in the study was the commonly made assertion that for arsonists the act of

378

fire-raising is psychologically equivalent to sexual stimulation. For this patient the hypothesis is negated in that *takes pleasure in being sexually aroused* is a near polar opposite of '*fire-raising feelings*'. Also notable is the fact that the *like me in character* construct is negatively related to *commit arson*, although the man had a number of convictions for fire-raising. This may be the not unfamiliar case where we perpetrate an act, but because we hold our purpose to be unlike that of others who commit the same act we do not see ourselves in the same light. Indeed, the high positive relationship between ideal self, believing people get the punishment they deserve, like me in character, enjoy having power and (in previous grids) upright and righteous suggests that we have here (in his own eyes) not a criminal arsonist but a punisher of wrongdoers, a righteous burner of heretics. Aspects of his puritanical upbringing and his response to psychotherapy were consistent with this explanation of his behaviour. Fransella points out one possible extension of the finding that the patient who is a confessed fire-raiser does not see himself as (in character) an arsonist. It may be that the response of psychiatric patients to treatment is affected by the degree to which they see their symptom as a characteristic part of their personality or regard it as alien to their personality or view it as a kind of measles which attacked from outside, but has nothing to do with them as people. The essential feature of the type of clinical approach illustrated by this fragment, is that it seeks explanations of behaviour in terms of the patient's mode of viewing his world, not in terms of external events of alleged internal personality traits.

CONCLUSION

Many psychologists prefer to follow the English empirical tradition and shun theories altogether. This is puzzling since it is difficult to see how findings from different experiments are ever to be related or added to one another in any way unless they are derived from some common theoretical framework. The present position is that we have thousands of studies using different concepts and different operational definitions which represent so many mountainous piles of data which cannot be cross-referred.

In the more advanced sciences it is generally agreed that the most useful way of achieving and expressing an understanding of an area is to account for events by principles which are embodied into an overall theory of wide applicability. There seems no reason why psychology as a science should be an exception, and if we suffer unduly from bad theories this is no ground for rejecting theory as such.

Science is a competitive field in that all scientists are free (and obligated) to elaborate new theories which they hope will supersede older ones by proving more comprehensive, more predictively accurate and more fruitful of new insights. It is of crucial importance which theories a scientist chooses to work within, since a theory channels scientific work for better or for worse. A bad theoretical framework is a drain down which endless hard work may be poured. Thus the differences between Personal Construct Theory and other extant theories in psychology is not merely an academic issue. If Personal Construct Theory is misconceived, then many psychologists may dedicate large portions of their life to marching down an elaborate blind alley. If it is well conceived, then it may be that much of the psychological work being done in other theoretical frameworks is of very limited value. Only the practice of competing experimental work – the duelling code of science – can ultimately decide.

20. SMALL GROUPS

M. L. J. ABERCROMBIE

Social psychology is a difficult subject to study experimentally. The number of factors involved in any social situation is enormous, with the result that it is difficult to produce experimental results which have any generality. One of the more successful studies has been concerned with the psychology of small groups of people. Dr Abercrombie describes the various contributions, some coming from direct experiment, and some inspired partly by the techniques of 'group therapy'. Her own work on group discussions has inspired many educators to use her methods.

MAN is pre-eminently a social animal, and most of us spend most of our waking time interacting with other people. From the moment of birth, satisfactory psychological interaction of the infant with his mother (or any person who takes her place) is as essential for the development of his mental health as physiological interaction was previously for his viability as a parasite in the womb. Our ability to participate in many kinds of groups is conditioned by our experiences of this first group of two, and its early extensions to include the rest of the family and other people around the place. At present, this crucial development goes on 'naturally' – not haphazardly, because it is highly conditioned by tradition – but largely without conscious control; we are not, on the whole, aware of what other possibilities of behaviour are open to us as individuals, much less as a species.

Research on the way people behave in various kinds of groups may help us to behave more appropriately, not only the better to achieve the aims we already have set ourselves but also the better to think up new aims as yet undreamed of. The need to do this, whether on the scale of intimate personal relations, or at national and at global level, is clearly urgent.

Impoverished by ignorance and enchained by irrational fears, few of us lead our little lives as happily, or as fruitfully, as we would wish, and all of us are threatened with extinction by the forces that split the atom, manipulated with not much more understanding of what makes the cerebral cortex tick than the first man had when he split a stone to make an axe.

As we shall see, many factors affect the way each of us behaves in groups, mostly without our recognizing them. People who do recognize them can do quite a lot to modify the behaviour of others. Understanding the effects of different kinds of leadership, channels of communication, and group climates, may make it possible so to manipulate a given situation that a group will work more effectively towards a prescribed goal. This kind of human engineering, like the results of any other research, can obviously serve good social ends or bad. According to the orientation of the manipulator, whether it is good or bad that a group of workers should be helped to increase its output depends on what goods it makes and for whom; and if a committee is made to work more harmoniously, whether this is good or bad depends on what kind of resolutions it passes and what activities it initiates.

Perhaps one of the most useful results of the study of groups, and the safest one for the ultimate good of mankind, is the possibilities it gives of extending each person's understanding of his own behaviour, and thus empowering him with better control of his otherwise automatic and unthinking reactions. Two main sources of information are available for this purpose. One derives from reports of other people's behaviour, made by more or less 'objective' or 'scientific' methods, often involving the use of control (or at least comparison) groups. Notable recent contributions summarizing various aspects of this sort of work are Homans's classic *The Human Group* (1951), Cartwright's and Zander's *Group Dynamics* (1960), Sprott's introduction to the more general and sociological aspects (1958) and Klein's summary of communication studies (1956).

A second source of information comes from experiencing one's own behaviour in groups which are specially arranged to make each participant more effective in his behaviour outside the group. Among others, Slavson (1956), Frank and Powdermaker (1959) and Rosenbaum and Berger (1963) have surveyed this field, and Foulkes and Anthony (1965), Balint and Balint (1955) and Abercrombie (1960) have dealt with more specific aspects. Workers in this area tend to be therapeutically orientated rather than fact-finding; they tend to be less articulate (though not less vocal) than the experimentalists, and because their material is less amenable to pigeon-holing and their results to rigorous testing, they tend to get neglected by more conventional psychologists. It is, however, being increasingly recognized that the potentialities of applying this kind of work to the education of normal people (and not only to the mentally sick, or delinquent, for whom it has mostly been developed) are very great (Morris, 1965).

If a legitimate aim of psychology is to give each of us better control over our mental processes, a step in the right direction might be taken if these two approaches to self-knowledge could be combined. The kind of skills the group therapists have developed might be used in groups in order to facilitate the uptake of the information that the students of group dynamics have collected, and to make possible its efficient application to subsequent behaviour. This is no light task, and the hazards involved are commensurate with the potentialities it offers for mental growth. It is not without apprehension that I venture the bold but modest step of talking about both sources of information within the same few pages; in this essay I shall focus attention on those aspects of the study of group behaviour that seem to be most immediately relevant to this aim, of increasing the range of our reactions that might be subjected to more effective self-monitoring.

Part of the potentiality that groups have of improving self-awareness depends on the perception of individual differences among the participants, and this runs counter to much common thinking about groups. We tend to concentrate on the fact that a group consists of members who are behaving alike in certain important respects, and many of the terms used ('gang', 'clique', 'mob', 'following the crowd', 'mass movements' or 'herd instinct') have denigratory implications. We shall begin this essay, therefore, with a discussion of the ways people in groups tend to act alike.

First, however, let us be clear what we may mean by 'group'. A group may mean simply an aggregate, as a group of people waiting at a bus stop; in such a case each person has the same aim, to get on the bus, but there may be very little interaction between them, unless say, no bus arrives, or an accident is witnessed when, the commonality of their experience increasing, they start talking to each other. Many novels are histories of groups of people who have come together by chance and then interact, taking up various fairly well defined, but maybe changing roles; Golding's *Lord of the Flies* is a notable example and so is the film *12 Angry Men*, and Mary McCarthy's *The Group* tells of the continuing effects of joint experience at college, on the subsequent behaviour of members when the group has dispersed, and reassembles at intervals. Most laboratory studies are of a number of people in a single face-to-face meeting, or series of meetings. Field studies may be of larger, looser and more permanent groups, as in industry or housing estates.

It is clear that the term 'group' covers a large range of intensities of relationship between members; this essay will be concerned with groups small enough, and the members being long enough and in close enough contact, for each person to be aware of each of the others.

CONFORMING IN GROUPS

There is a great deal of evidence to show that people tend to conform in groups. People prefer to be with those like themselves, and having chosen their companions, become even more alike. Newcomb (1960) made a study of the behaviour of a group of seventeen men who were at first unacquainted, and lived together in a students' house for a year, at the only cost of giving an hour a week to the psychologists for investigation of their attitudes. It was found that long-lasting friendships were built on similarities; rather than change their attitudes, dissimilar people would break their incipient relationships. Moreover, as time went by, friends became more like each other in, for instance, their assessments of other people. This tendency to stick to the familiar is of course very obvious in ordinary life. An example of how easily habits can be built up was provided by an experience at an international conference on group work. Small groups of people, initially strangers, had been discussing professional matters for a few days, and then it became necessary for two groups to join together. Arranging the room to accommodate the newcomers, I took care to mix up the green chairs which my group had used, with the red ones brought in from the other group's room. As the people came in, they took their familiar seats, so this manoeuvre succeeded in mixing up the groups spatially, but it did not immediately achieve the aim of fusing them. Two conversations went on for some time, members of each group maintaining their relationship by talking across members of the other group.

This tendency to adapt oneself generally to other people is consistent with the human need to avoid discomfort, and is not unexpected. What is more surprising is that one's judgement on matters of 'fact' such as the relative sizes or weights of objects, is influenced by other people. In a classical experiment, Asch (1951) asked a group of eight people to match the length of a given line with one of three unequal lines. Unknown to one person (the 'subject') the other seven ('stooges') had been briefed by the experimenter to declare that certain lines matched even though they clearly did not. The subject was therefore faced with the extraordinary situation of a group unanimously contradicting the evidence of his senses. One-third of the choices made by the subjects were errors in the direction of the distorted opinions of the stooges (although a control group made virtually no errors). When those subjects who had made errors were cross-questioned, a few seemed to have suffered distortion of perception – the lines really had looked to them as the majority said they had looked; others suffered a disorder of judgement – they had been aware of a difference between their perceptions and those of the stooges, but had not trusted their own judgement; still others had suffered a disorder of action – though they recognized the disagreement, they had not liked to appear different from the others. An experiment by Seaborne (1963) was made in more life-like conditions and illustrates some of the difficulties that may occur when people are examining goods to see whether they are up to a required standard, a task which is common in industry. People were asked to pick out of a stack of cards those which were imperfect according to certain dimensions which were assessed with a notched gauge. A subject working at the same table as others, and on stacks of cards with the same proportion of sub-standard cards, would reject a similar number. But if his co-workers' stacks contained a higher proportion of sub-standard cards than his own, so that their reject rate was higher, then his proportion of rejects went up. The extra cards which he rejected in these conditions were not randomly picked but were borderline cases of the kind that might be rejected by himself and others in normal conditions. His judgement of where to draw the line between 'reject' and 'accept', even when it was made against an 'objective' standard, altered according to the number being rejected by his co-workers, and this without their attempting to influence his behaviour.

'DISSONANCE REDUCTION'

Festinger's ideas about 'cognitive dissonance' are of great value in helping to make comprehensive statements about these and other aspects of group behaviour. Festinger and Aronson (1960) state that 'the simultaneous existence of cognitions which in one way or another do not fit together (dissonance) leads to an effort on the part of the person to somehow make them fit better (dissonance reduction)'. Dissonance reduction seems to be the psychological analogue of the physiological mechanisms which maintain homoeostasis in the body.

Social interaction inevitably involves some dissonance – some disagreement with people like oneself. The magnitude of the dissonance will vary with the importance of the person expressing disagreement, and with the importance of the issue over which there is disagreement. Dissonance may be reduced in several ways (just as, in homoeostatic control, if one's temperature goes up it may be brought down by several mechanisms). The person may convince himself that the person disagreeing with him is unimportant; or the topic unimportant; or he may change his opinion, or attempt to change the other person's, or he may seek support from other people. Several laboratory experiments have been made that analyse the factors that affect which mechanism is likely to be used in certain prescribed conditions, and a remarkably interesting piece of field work also strengthens Festinger's thesis. The behaviour of a number of people who firmly believed that the world would end by a cataclysm was studied. On the night that the cataclysm was expected, most of the believers gathered in the home of one member to await a flying saucer which was to rescue them. When the prophecy was not fulfilled, the group was intensely disappointed and spent some hours trying to re-assure each other. They finally concluded that the explanation was that the world had been saved by their faith, which in this way they were able to retain. Other members had stayed in their own homes, and there, lacking social support, abandoned their faith. Whereas before the appointed day, the sect had made no attempt to attract public attention or proselytize, after the disap-pointment those who remained faithful attempted to convert new members, and gave Press conferences, that is, they sought support from outside. In various ways, predictable from Festinger's theory therefore, attempts were made to reduce dissonance.

Conforming to a group is only one method a person may take to reduce dissonance and whether he uses this or another depends partly on his personality. Crutchfield (1955) found that non-conformers, compared with conformers, were more effective intellectually, more mature in social relationships, more con-fident, less rigid, less authoritarian, more objective and realistic about their parents, and more permissive in their attitudes to child-rearing practices. Now one tends to think of such charac-teristics as fairly stable and unchanging, but the same person may behave more or less in these ways, according to the group-climate.

GROUP CLIMATES

The classic experiments of White and Lippitt (1960) show that children behaved differently according to whether their clubs had an autocratic, democratic or *laissez-faire* climate. The climate was established by the behaviour of the leaders who were trained to take these special roles. The leaders moved from one club to another each six weeks, and changed their leadership style as they did so. Thus each club, consisting of ten-year-old boys roughly equated for intellectual, physical and socio-economic status and personality characteristics, experienced three different climates under different leaders. Records were made of the behaviour of leaders and boys during each meeting.

Leaders taking the autocratic role tended to give orders, to make disruptive commands which cut across the activities of the boys, and to give non-objective criticism and praise, whereas those taking the other roles tended to control behaviour rather by making suggestions and giving information. The chief single difference between the democratic and *laissez-faire* leadership consisted in the amount of guidance given at times when it seemed necessary; the democratic leaders were more sensitive to the child's welfare and participated more fully in the life of the group than did the *laissez-faire* leaders. It is an interesting comment on the flexibility of behaviour that the leaders were able to play these different roles so well. The records of their behaviour in these respects show that they resembled each other more strongly in the same role than they resembled themselves in different roles.

Summarizing the main differences in the behaviour of the boys, the amount of work done was greatest in the autocratic climates and least in the *laissez-faire*; but motivation to work was greatest in the democratic climates, for the boys tended to go on working even when the leader had left the room. Work-orientated conversation among the boys was greatest in the democratic climates and least in the *laissez-faire*. Nineteen out of twenty boys preferred democratic leaders. Under autocracy, there was more discontent; the four boys who dropped out did so under autocratic régimes, though at times when there was no overt rebelliousness. In autocratic climates, the boys were more dependent on the leader, and more submissive to him, but more hostile and aggressive to each other. There was more originality, group-mindedness and friendly playfulness under democracy, and more readiness to share club property.

In this experiment it was the deliberate behaviour of the leader that caused differences in the climate of groups, other factors remaining constant. In less controlled conditions, of course, innumerable factors interact. In Deutsch's experiment (1949) the significant difference was made by giving different motivation to groups. Psychology students were given puzzles and human relation problems to work at in discussion groups. Some ('cooperative') groups were told that the grade that each individual got at the end of the course would depend on the performance of his group. Other ('competitive') groups were told that each student would receive a grade according to his own contributions. No significant differences were found between the two kinds of group in the amount of interest and involvement in the tasks, or in the amount of learning. But the cooperative groups, compared with the competitive ones, had greater productivity per unit time, better quality of product and discussion, greater coordination of effort and subdivision of activity, more diversity in amount of contributions per member, more attentiveness to fellow members and more friendliness during discussion.

When a group works together for a long period it develops a characteristic climate which may or may not be the best for its declared aims. Attending meetings of various scientific societies one is strongly aware of different sub-cultures reflected in the length of papers read, whether questions only are invited, or open discussion, whether the expression of non-conformist views is encouraged or inhibited, the facilities provided for informal conversation, and the amount of food and drink consumed communally. But the function of all these meetings is to disseminate information among the members. Designing a suitable climate is specially important when strangers meet for a short time with important work to do; Fremont-Smith (1961) has fruitfully paid attention to this in organizing interdisciplinary discussions among experts, and some of the complexities of arranging international conferences have been wisely discussed by Capes (1960). The main aim is to facilitate communication between members and careful attention is paid to group climate.

COMMUNICATION IN GROUPS

There has been a great deal of experimental work on different kinds of communication networks in groups, but as good discussions of it are easily available (Sprott, 1958; Klein, 1956) it will not be dealt with at length here. For our present purpose, the most relevant points are that different networks are optimal for different purposes. Thus in a situation where a group of five people has to solve a problem, and each has an essential piece of information, the task is done most quickly where there is a central member to whom each of the others has direct access.

In the diagram, each letter represents a person, and each line a communication link. Groups organized on the 'wheel' and 'Y' plans solved the problem more quickly than the 'circle' or the 'chain'.

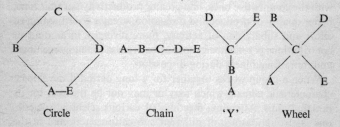

Circle   Chain   'Y'   Wheel

In the circle, no one member was regarded as a leader, but in the others, C tended to be so regarded. The circle people enjoyed themselves more than the others, because all could interact, both giving and receiving messages, whereas in the other systems the peripheral members had less to do, and in the wheel they needed only to send information to C, who needed to do nothing but collect it. When the task was changed, so that the information to be sent was ambiguous, the circle did best, because all the members could receive all the messages and could sort things out, whereas in the wheel C only received ambiguous messages which he could not check. The circle people had learned to cope with uncertainty (Klein, 1956).

It is notable that most of our institutions have communication networks more like the 'Y' or the wheel than like the circle, so that speed of performance of routine tasks may be gained at the cost of frustration and passivity for the peripheral members, and loss of adaptability at time of change.

Revans (1964) found a correlation between patterns of communication in hospitals and several indices of efficiency. In hospitals with low wastage of student nurses, slow turn-over of senior staff, and rapid discharge of patients, communication between the various groups of people was better than in those with higher student wastage, quicker staff turn-over and slower discharge of patients. In the former hospitals compared with the latter, the climate was more permissive and less authoritarian; the patients felt more able to question the nurses, the student nurses felt they could question their tutors, the sisters the matron, the matron the consultants and so on. There was ease of communication upwards as well as downwards.

Although in ordinary life the main barriers to free communication are such psychological bogeys as habit, or timidity, seemingly quite trivial things like spatial relationships also play their part. Sommer (1959) found that conversations occurred more frequently between people sitting at the corners of tables, than between those sitting opposite each other, or side by side. Communication between patients in a geriatric ward was improved when chairs were moved from a row against the walls, and put around little tables (Sommer and Ross, 1958). Foulkes (1965) pays special attention to the seating arrangements for his practise of group analytic psychotherapy. Ideally, the chairs should be similar, and placed in a circle. The positions taken by participants are significant – beside the therapist or opposite him, for instance, and pulling their chair in or withdrawing it from the circle.

GROUPS FOR CHANGING BEHAVIOUR

Although much of the experimental work on groups has been concerned with studying differences in behaviour according to current group structure, the importance of groups for facilitating more permanent changes has been long recognized. It was found easier, for instance, to cure alcoholics, to persuade people to eat more liver or to give their children more orange juice, in groups than singly.

The various kinds of group psychotherapy are all based on the assumption that the changes made in response to certain designed group structures are not transient, but carry over into behaviour outside the group; in fact, that in a group one can learn to behave better outside it. I shall not attempt to deal with strictly psychotherapeutic techniques but only to refer to some applications to the learning of normal people.

The value of groups for improving the understanding of social interactions by people who themselves are professionally concerned with human relationships is obvious, but the potentialities of this are by no means fully exploited. There are several possible lines to follow. One is the experiencing of group processes as a model for what goes on beneath the surface in ordinary life. Bion (1961) was one of the pioneers in this; his technique (erroneously called 'leaderless') forced the group to come to terms with conflicts over the authority–dependency relationship. It has obvious implications for education at all levels; modifications of it have been used for teachers in training (Morris, 1965).

Another line has been explored by E. and M. Balint (1955) in their teaching of psychotherapy. In groups of doctors learning about the psychological aspects of medical practice, the participants presented current cases, and in discussion of them it became clear that their treatment of the case was conditioned by personal attitudes which were not necessarily shared by other members of the group, and not necessarily the most effective possible. The differences of opinions in the group and the interpretations made by the conductor experienced in a supportive climate, helped to liberate the participants from too restricted a personal psychological framework. The potentialities of this kind of work for training in many professions are tremendous.

GROUPS FOR SCIENTISTS

Still another line has been taken (Abercrombie, 1960) of using a group situation for helping medical students to be more 'objective', to observe more accurately and comprehensively and to draw reasonable conclusions from their observations. Postulating that one might learn to make more valid judgements if one could become aware of some of the many factors that ordinarily influence them, a teaching situation was arranged to facilitate this. The approach was influenced by the transactional views on perception, and by Foulkes's method of group analytic psychotherapy. The method differed from the more therapeutically orientated uses of groups for training in human relations, in that the discussions were not entirely unstructured, but each was focused on a specific scientific topic – radiographs, for instance, or an account of an experiment. It was also more didactic in that statements about the processes involved in perception were deliberately introduced at appropriate times, in the hope that what was learned from a specific example would be more easily generalized. Within these limits, however, freedom of discussion was encouraged, and the conversation ranged widely, permitting the linking up of reactions towards scientific material with habitual ways of behaving in everyday life and thus encouraging the transfer of training. One of the most important features was that each student was confronted with a range of different interpretations of the same stimulus pattern. These different interpretations were made by people like himself – he was not comparing his effort with the 'correct' answer as is usually the case, but was forced to consider his own and other statements on their merits, and without the guidance of authority. It would appear, for instance, that what one student took for granted as a 'fact', another regarded as an inference of questionable validity, but then very soon, on another issue the tables would be turned. By analysing the ideas that each student associated with his judgement, it was possible to tease out some of the factors that had caused the differences between them. It was discovered that these factors ranged from minutiae of the immediate context (e.g. the precise typescript layout of a report of an experiment) to generalized and deep-seated attitudes concerned, for instance, with the extent to which you could take it for granted that researchers reported their work accurately.

At the end of a course of eight discussions the participants reacted more objectively to a test than did the other half of the class that had not yet had this course. They distinguished better between facts and inferences, made fewer false inferences, explicitly considered alternate hypotheses more frequently, and were less often inappropriately 'set' in their approach to a problem by previous experience of a similar one. It seemed that the experience of the discussions had helped them to be more flexible in their reactions to scientific material, and thus to attain greater objectivity.

'SYNECTICS'

We began this essay with a discussion of conformity in groups, so it is appropriate to end it with reference to one of the newest uses to which groups are being put – to help people to depart from conformity, and to encourage originality and inventiveness (see also p. 173).

The advocates of 'brain-storming' techniques (Osborn, 1953) for producing original ideas believe in the value of increasing spontaneous behaviour in groups. The participants are encouraged to express as many ideas as possible, the wilder the better, criticism must be withheld, and the need to combine different ideas together to make something new is emphasized. The practitioners of 'synectics' (Gordon, 1961) resemble the brain-stormers in encouraging spontaneity and a rich flow of ideas in groups, but they have, in addition, worked out methods for increasing the participants' understanding of what is going on. Their approach is based on the assumptions that invention in arts and in science involves the same fundamental processes which can be described, and that the descriptions can be used for teaching people to improve the creative output of both individuals and groups. Their groups consist of five or six people with diverse backgrounds and intellectual experiences, for the coming together of different analogical ways of thinking is regarded as essential. They stress the importance of such operations as making the familiar strange and the strange familiar. They recognize that the emotional aspects of the creative task are as important as the intellectual, and pay great attention to group climate.

In closing with these two examples of the use of group situations for the improvement of individual effectiveness, it may be noted that they attempt to give control of two kinds of behaviour which may seem to stand at opposite ends of a continuum. At one end is the scientist's need to see things as they are, objectively, veridically, and at the other the need to originate, to create something new. In both cases, the perception by participants of similarities and differences between their own behaviour and that of other members of the group is an important factor in learning. We are back again to conforming and non-conforming, and there would seem a promising future here for a link up with Festinger's ideas on dissonance reduction.

Although the last few years have seen an enormous expansion

of interest in group behaviour, our knowledge is still fragmentary and insecure, so that those who work with groups need faith as well as humility. Since he made the first stone tool, man has won increasing control over other animals and plants. Now the urgent need is for him to win better control over his own nervous system, and for this it is essential that he should understand how it interacts with those of other men.

21. CROSS-CULTURAL STUDIES

D. PRICE-WILLIAMS

One criticism of Freud's work was that his results may have been peculiar to the Viennese society from which most of his patients came. This criticism could only be substantiated by looking at other cultures, and many social anthropologists have tried to see if various patterns of child-rearing produce the different kinds of personality which Freudian theory would predict. Professor Price-Williams, who has studied tribes in Africa, shows how such cross-cultural studies have been extended to investigate the effects of culture on many other aspects of behaviour.

IN the same way that the study of individual differences shows to what degree a particular person is similar to or different from others, so cross-cultural studies focus on the similarities and differences of whole societies. Psychological cross-cultural studies provide an expansive background against which to plot information about any one society. For instance, when Freud's observations and inferences on the Oedipus complex were first propounded, the emphasis was placed on it as a universal biological phenomenon. The notion that it might be the product of a particular social structure operating in Central Europe, and that in other cultures there might be variants of the situation or even that it might not exist, did not occur to anybody at the time. It is, of course, no criticism of Freud that this cultural aspect was lacking; the data were supplied only considerably later by the anthropologist Malinowski (1927) who noted that among the Trobrianders of Polynesia the social structure was such that the young boy had the repressed wish to marry his sister and was jealous of the maternal uncle, while in European society the picture is jealousy of the father and erotic desires towards the mother. In European society the genitor and the pater are usually the same person, and there are strong prohibitions against incestuous relationships between a boy and his mother. In Trobriand society the genitor and pater are two different people, the mother's brother taking on the role of pater, and there is a taboo against the brother's relationship with his sister. While there is a similarity in principle between the Trobriand and the European model, the different relationships enable us to view the Oedipus complex as a function of a social and not a biological factor.

Apart from the advantage of utilizing the differences between cultures as a buffer against generalizing from a comparatively small sample of the earth's population, cross-cultural work has the further asset of seeking out situations and influences which are either difficult to find in our own culture or are just non-existent. For example, Zulus wean their children on a day set in advance; the weaning does not tail off gradually, but from this day the reliance on the mother's breast is terminated abruptly and permanently. This might conceivably be done by individuals in our own society, but it is not institutionalized. So that in the Zulu custom we are provided with an event which is rare, rather like finding an unusual specimen in the fields of botany and zoology. The event has more than just a curiosity value to the psychologist, because important issues related to theories about the effect of childhood experience on later life are bound up with the weaning experience. From this angle the Zulu case is more like a rare eclipse for astronomers; the theories can be tested empirically.

Unusual influences need not be related to social customs solely. They may be ecological, linguistic or occupational. Spatial perception can be studied in environments as markedly different as deserts and jungles. Linguistic differences in available words and phrases for the same object reveal much about perception and thinking. The Eskimoes, it is reported, have as many as thirty words for snow; some reindeer-herding people in Siberia have about the same number again for the patterns of reindeer hides; many West African tribes use only three to five colour categories. How do these varying linguistic stores affect the perception and thinking of these people? These are legitimate cross-cultural questions and ones to which we have partial answers.

PERCEPTION

Nativism versus *Empiricism*

One of the purposes of studying perception cross-culturally is that it enables us to discover the extent to which perceiving is structured by the nervous system (which is common to the entire human race), and to what extent it is influenced by experience. The issue of nativism *versus* empiricism can be approached experimentally through application of various visual illusions. Two of these illusions, the classic Muller–Lyer (Figure 63) and the horizontal–vertical (Figure 64) are provided here. One of the first comprehensive attempts to apply visual illusions on a cross-cultural basis was that of the Cambridge Anthropological Expedition to the Torres Straits at the beginning of the century. One of the members of the expedition, W. H. R. Rivers, displayed these two and other illusions to the natives in that area (Rivers, 1901)

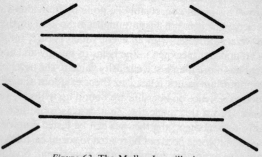

Figure 63. The Muller–Lyer illusion.

and compared the results with English adults and children. He found that the Murray Island inhabitants were less prone to the Muller–Lyer than Europeans, which he attributed to the fact that the natives limited their attention strictly to the task they were asked to perform, paying attention to the horizontal lines of the figure, while European observers tended to regard the figure as a whole with the arrows. On the other hand, the horizontal–vertical illusion was more marked among the Murray Island men which, together with the pronounced character of the illusion in children, made Rivers feel that the source of the effect was to be found in some physiological condition or at least in a psychological condition of a simple and primitive character. The Cambridge expedition, in this respect, was a pioneer attempt and we require considerably more data than that taken from two or three tribes.

A recent and more extensive approach has been carried out by North-western University, Illinois (Segall, Campbell and Herskovits, 1963; Campbell, 1964). Over a six-year period stimulus materials based upon the geometric illusions of the kind described were administered to samples of non-European children and adults, mainly in Africa, but including the Philippines, which were compared with South Africans of European descent and Americans in Illinois. There were thirty-nine items in all, which allowed for a comprehensive comparison between cultures. Rivers's finding with the Muller–Lyer is remarkably in agreement with these

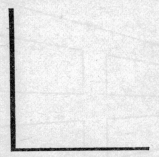

Figure 64. The horizontal–vertical illusion.

later and more extensive findings. If all the non-Europeans are compared with the Europeans, whether living in America or South Africa, the Europeans are much more prone to the illusion. If the illusion is measured by the percentage by which the upper line exceeds the lower line in Figure 63 * when they are judged equal by any observer, it is found that the Europeans lie between fourteen to eighteen per cent (Campbell 1964; Figure 1), while all the remaining non-European people, except the Senegalese,

* The tendency is to report that the lower line in the Muller–Lyer figure (Figure 63) and the vertical line in the horizontal–vertical illusion (Figure 64) are longer than their respective comparison lines. In the experimental situation the upper line in the Muller–Lyer and the horizontal line in the other illusion are extended until the observer judges the members of the pair to be equal. Exact percentage of the illusions can thus be calculated.

lie below the ten per cent level of error. The Bushmen are lowest at four per cent. The horizontal–vertical illusion has a different cultural distribution. Here we have the Batoro and Bayankole people of Africa, who both live in high open country, at the top end of the percentage illusion dimension, while the Bete people, of jungle environment, are at the bottom. The European samples are intermediate, together with the Zulu. In this matter the ecology of peoples is probably crucial, a point which we shall return to after describing another illusion. This is a different kind

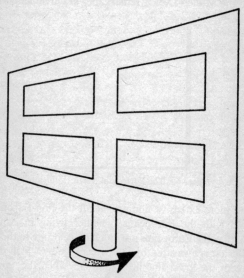

Figure 65. Rotating trapezoid.

from the geometric illusions and has its source in the 'transactionalist school' of perception which emphasizes the interaction between the perceiver and his environment (see p. 84). The illusion is generated by a figure cut in the form of a trapezoid which, when attached to a motor, revolves in a circle (Figure 65). Horizontal and vertical bars affixed to the trapezoid give the impression of a window. Most observers report the rotary figure as oscillating to and fro; seldom does it appear to them to revolve in a complete circle. Explanation of the phenomenon is given by the transactionalist school as a reconciliation by the observer of two sets of conflicting cues. On the one hand, the perceiver is accustomed to regarding longer retinal stimulations as coming from nearer objects. On the other hand, he regards this trapezoidal figure as a normal rectangular window. The longer edge of the figure is thus interpreted as being nearer and the window appears to oscillate rather than to rotate. The force of the illusion is thought to turn on the expectations which the observer brings to the figure. When the figure is altered to look less like a window by omitting the cross-bars, then the illusion is reduced. Similarly, it is reduced if it is presented binocularly rather than monocularly. The situation is thus perfect for showing the illusion to people who have had no experience with windows and who do not bring to it expectations of rectangularity. Allport and Pettigrew (1957) found such a case with Zulus, who do not live in towns and are not only not accustomed to conventional windows but also have a bias towards circularity, and not rectangularity, in their culture. Allport and Pettigrew then compared rural Zulu with urban Zulu and again with Europeans. The results were not entirely clear-cut as would be wished for any nativist–empiricist issue. Under optimal conditions for the illusion to be produced, that is monocularly at a longer distance, as many primitive Zulus reported the sway effect as urban Zulus and Europeans. However, under sub-optimal conditions (in which the effect is lessened) of binocular vision from a shorter distance, there was a tendency for the rural Zulus to report the effect less often than the urban Zulus. In particular, African subjects who held a preference for circles against a rectangle or trapezoid saw the illusion less often than those that expressed preference for rectangular figures.

The Role of Ecology

What lessons do these various cross-cultural studies on perceptual illusions contain? While there may not be completely unequivocal results supporting either side of the nativist–empiricist issue, the findings of both the early study of Rivers and the later North-western project indicate that there are functional differences in visual habits. If these habits are regarded culturally, then the clue to the differences might be sought in the varying habitats. This is not as simple to pin down as may appear, as within the same culture different occupations and interests may well have further influence, but certain broad trends can be distinguished. Campbell (1964) calls attention to what he calls the 'carpentered-world' hypothesis of the visual world of Western culture. 'We live in a culture in which straight lines abound and in which perhaps ninety per cent of the acute and obtuse angles formed on our retina by the straight lines of our visual field are realistically interpretable as right angles extended in space.' In a largely non-man-made environment, where the strict linearity of urban and Westernized features does not apply, there is less bias towards interpreting acute and obtuse angles as right angles extended in space. Campbell regards the cross-cultural findings on the Muller-Lyer and similar geometric illusions as well as the rotating trapezoid as supporting this idea. The horizontal–vertical illusion is similarly interpreted ecologically. The tendency here is to perceive the vertical line as longer than the horizontal, although both are of equal length. Campbell takes the ideal situation of a person who lives on a flat plain *versus* the person who lives in a rain forest. The former would have a much shorter retinal extension of vertical lines, that is lines that extended away from him, than those that crossed him from left to right. The latter who would have tree trunks and hanging vines extending vertically in front of him would be less likely to foreshorten the vertical. Europeans who had just as much familiarity with horizontal floors and vertical walls might provide intermediate cases. While the actual experimental data, as Campbell allows, do not completely fit this hypothesis, there is sufficient positive evidence to regard this line of thought as profitable. Being immersed in a single culture sometimes blinds one to the fact that apparently basic frameworks are in fact cultural artefacts. Two-dimensional representations of three-dimensional life as in drawings, photographs and motion pictures are examples of what we in our culture have mastered early in life and have grown accustomed to, so that we do not have to go through the inferential process of reconstructing the real world from the photograph. It can be quite otherwise with people not accustomed to such two-dimensional representations. Those that have attempted to show motion pictures to people totally unaccustomed to this type of representation have reported curious effects. Sellers (1941) who showed films to Nigerian audiences noted that a vertical 'tilt' shot of a building gave the impression that the building was sinking into the ground. Sellers inferred that his audiences were seeing the screen as flat, and not inferring a three-dimensional space. In an experimental situation Hudson (1960) compared literate and illiterate groups in South Africa in the perception of three-dimensional cues such as superimposition (one object partly obscuring another object), perspective and object size, in drawings and photographs. The literate sample perceived depth in the representations far more frequently than the illiterate group who had not been exposed to pictorial matter, and not one illiterate perceived a photograph as three-dimensional.*

COGNITION

In many ways it is extremely difficult to ascertain the thinking ability of non-European people, especially those in the under-developed regions of the world. Not only is it agreed by psychologists that formal tests of intelligence which have been constructed and standardized in Western society are inappropriate for evaluating results in these areas (Anastasi and Foley, 1949, 725–6; Cryns, 1962), but also tests of abstract reasoning, such as the Goldstein–Scheerer Cube test, have this difficulty of the bias of environmental factors (Jahoda, 1956). More fruitful approaches to cross-cultural cognition have consisted in comparing one particular cognitive process across various cultures, and investigating the special question of language.

Specific Cultural Elements

Choosing an element of a culture which can be examined from a cognitive point of view interests anthropologists as much as psychologists. Frake (1961) investigated the conceptual scheme of disease diagnoses in the Philippines. He describes his perplexity with the society's (the Subanun of Mindanao) diagnosis of an infectious swelling which he developed early in his field work.

* Compare the theory of illusions set out in Chapter 3.

He received a variety of names for his disease and was not able at first to perceive clarity in the diagnosis by Subanon people. Further interrogation, however, showed that different people were speaking at different levels of contrast. One person was contrasting skin diseases with all other kinds of external diseases. Another informed him that he had an 'inflammation' and not some other skin disease. Yet another refined the concept of inflammation as 'an inflamed quasi bite' and not some other kind of inflammation. It is clear from his account that a cognitive examination of Subanun diagnostic criteria involved a good knowledge of the underlying levels of contrast against which the disease concepts were operating. In a similar manner Hallowell (1942), investigating the psychological aspects of measurement among the Salteaux (an American Indian group) noted that there did not exist common units of distance which applied to all classes of linear measurement. Distance-away or distance-apart with reference to places or objects in space belonged to quite a different category to the length of an object which could be manipulated, like a piece of string or a canoe.

Comparative Thought Processes

Such anthropological descriptions, although of extreme interest for the psychologist (but not all psychologists take sufficient note of them) probably do not go far enough as analysis to satisfy the cognitive psychologist. An early attempt to stratify cultural thought along some psychological dimension was formulated by Carmichael who worked with Greenlanders (Carmichael, 1940). He gave his subjects a problem in the form of a narrative. In the story three men were discussing what they should do to a fourth man whom they all hated, and especially what they would do to him if he should suddenly at the moment enter. Whereupon the detested man does (in the narrative) enter, exhausted and cold, and the question is: What would the subjects do if they were in the place of the three men? Carmichael combed the answers not so much for the logical scheme underlying the answers but for the effect of social influences. He found features which reflected quick, confident and stereotyped responses, generalizations which reflected a cultural conventional way of thinking, of the same kind which Bartlett found in his study of remembering (Bartlett, 1932) and which Nadel found in the comparison of retention and communication between two African tribes (Nadel, 1937). When one turns to the question of logical thinking a convenient framework is that of the Swiss psychologist Piaget, who in many publications (see Flavell, 1963, for best summary) has postulated a number of levels through which children progress in their thinking. He has provided the impetus for several cultural studies. The writer has studied concepts of conservation of quantities with bush African children, and found that although there may have been an age delay with these children as compared with European children, the same sequence, from reliance on perceptual attributes to a proper understanding of what conservation implies, was detected. Jacqueline Goodnow (1962) investigated judgements of space, weight and volume with Chinese children in Hong Kong, with varying degrees of formal schooling. She compared these Chinese children with European children of comparable age living in Hong Kong. Variables like schooling and socio-economic status showed little effect on such judgements. Indeed Chinese children with low socio-economic status and semi-schooling did better than those children that had more schooling, and up to the age of eleven the Europeans do no better than the Chinese. On the other hand Peluffo (1962), who studied the differences between children born and resident in Genoa with those immigrating to Genoa from the underdeveloped parts of Southern Italy did find differences in conceptual understanding of substance, weight and volume. Such studies go beyond the simple question of whether there is any difference between subjects of different national and linguistic stock; they also ask whether there is any difference within the same country and language, due to impoverished economic environment and exposure to formal schooling. The advantage of employing Piaget's methods is that they are not of the paper and pencil kind; familiar objects such as glasses, bits of clay and stones – objects which are familiar to the culture – are used, and cross-cultural equivalence is better assured than by using more formal tests of abstraction and intelligence.

Other frameworks than that used by Piaget are possible. An

object-sorting task has been designed by Riley Gardner, consisting of seventy-three familiar objects which subjects are asked to cluster spontaneously into as many or as few groups as they prefer. An index of conceptual differentiation is made according to whether people form many groups, which represents a high degree of conceptual differentiation, or few groups, which represents a low degree. The use of this task in the United States with adults and with children has shown consistent differences in the manner in which objects are categorized. Application of this same test in Mexico (Mercado, Diaz Guerrero and Gardner, 1963) shows how unexpected light may be thrown on a culture through using a comparable technique across cultures. Whereas there were no differences between boys and girls in the American sample, there were found big sex differences in the Mexican population, boys performing at significantly higher levels of abstraction than girls. Such studies show that a major contribution of cross-cultural method lies not only in the gross comparison between cultures, but helps to illuminate the role of important variables such as sex, socio-economic status and the role of formal education.

Language and Thinking

Quite clearly any cognitive inquiry requires an examination of the linguistic features of the society being interrogated. Stimulated by the writings of Benjamin Lee Whorf (see Carroll, 1956) an important sub-field of psychology has emerged in the last few years aimed at understanding the influence of language – particularly languages not of the Indo-European stock – upon thinking. Much of this inquiry has been descriptive and inferential. For example, in the Hopi language there is no substantive noun for time and no tense system of past, present and future as in the English language. From considerations such as these Whorf questioned whether the Hopi thinking of time was similar to that of people who spoke of time events in the Indo-European languages. His thesis was that language acted as a mould to thought, forcing our thinking into the *a priori* linguistic categories; so that if a language exists which has, from our point of view, radically different ways of expressing time relationships, then thinking about it would be radically different also. Psychological experiments on this point are very difficult to carry out, as much of the thesis defies experimental design, but the Whorfian notion has stimulated some psychologists to probe into the question. Some idea of what has to be done is represented by a classic experiment by Brown and Lenneberg (1954), who worked with the English language throughout. The colour spectrum is divided into a small set of categories. There are, in fact, about seven and a half million 'just noticeable differences' in the colour solid, but in English we tend to use commonly only about eight colour names. In English some colours have a ready label, like red or green; others have to be eked out with two words, like 'royal purple' or 'shell-pink'. This difference in accessibility of labels has been called 'codability' by Brown and Lenneberg. The same colour in two different languages may be differentially codable. The contrast between the many terms used for snow in the Eskimo language with the almost single term of 'white' in the English language is a contrast in codability. To express shades of whiteness is easier if there exists in the language a range of terms to indicate them. The Brown and Lenneberg experiment consisted in initially finding out the codability factor for colours in the English language, and then correlating the colours for naming with their later recognition. In this the results proved positive; that is to say there did seem to be a relationship between the accessibility of linguistic terms and the psychological process of recognition. Particularly, the experiment showed the influence of language on the storage factor; simply, this means that it is easier to remember something if there is a term for it. This experiment was repeated in a cross-cultural framework with Zuni and English speakers. In Zuni orange and yellow are given a single term. In their recognition test, Zuni speakers frequently confused the orange and yellow colours. English speakers never made this error, while bilingual speakers of Zuni and English were intermediate.

An experiment with Navaho children further indicates the type of experiment in this field (Carroll and Casagrande, 1958). In the Navaho language verbs of handling involve different forms according to the kind of object being handled. A long flexible object, like a piece of string, has one verb form; a long rigid object, as a stick, has another verb form; and an object like a piece of paper or cloth which is flat and flexible has yet another verb form. Developmental psychologists have found with Euro-American children that objects are first distinguished on the dimensions of size or colour, and shape later. Contrasting, therefore, Navaho-speaking children with English- or American-speaking children, there should be a difference in the order of emergence of various concepts. Navaho children, if the peculiar emphasis on form in their language made any difference, should be able to distinguish form characteristics of objects earlier than American children. The experiments were arranged so that a child was shown a pair of objects in which the members differed significantly in two characteristics, and then was shown a third object which resembled the others in one characteristic only, and the child was asked which member of the original pair went best with the third object. For example, a yellow stick and a same-sized piece of blue rope was shown to the child; the child was then shown a yellow rope and asked to say which of the former two objects the yellow rope went best with. He could either choose on the basis of colour, that is he would choose the yellow stick, or he could choose on the basis of form, in which case he would choose the blue rope. Three groups were actually used in this experiment: Navahoes whose own language was dominant, Navahoes whose language was dominantly English, and white American children, speaking, of course, no Navaho at all. If the first two groups are compared alone, the results do seem to indicate that the linguistic factor is operative; the saliency for shape or form, although higher in both groups for shape over colour than the English group, is lower in the English-speaking Navahoes than the Navaho-speaking Navahoes. On the other hand, when the third group, the white American children from Boston, are considered, the overall impression is slightly marred by the fact that this group behaved like the Navaho-speaking Navahoes, a fact which has to be explained. The authors considered that early and continued practice with toys of the formboard kind tended to shift the importance of shape over colour in these fairly well-to-do children. Be that as it may, the Carroll and Casagrande experiment is of the kind needed to provide psychological and not just inferential evidence on this important issue.

SOCIALIZATION

The majority of older cross-cultural studies are those which have considered man in his cultural setting from the point of view of institutions. In this task the sister disciplines of social and cultural anthropology and of sociology have made heavy inroads into cross-cultural psychology. Many of the concepts used have stemmed from anthropologists; many of the methods employed are those which have been traditional in the social sciences. With the study of socialization we make a transition from the general processes of psychology, such as perception and thinking, towards accepting the individual as a social unit.

Universality versus Relativity

A simple inquiry of early work on socialization was to note whether 'growing-up' was more or less the same all over the world or drastically different. The notion had been held in psychological thought that the tribulations of adolescence were a feature of the muscular and glandular changes which occur during this period. The underlying assumption was that it was 'human nature' that adolescence should be a period of difficulty. It was part of the intentions of a cultural anthropologist like Margaret Mead to show by heavy and detailed documentation (Mead, 1928, 1930) that this model simply did not hold in the South Seas. In Polynesian society adolescence just did not have the sort of difficulties which European and American adolescents appeared to undergo. The emphasis, by psychologically minded anthropologists, on the cultural relativity of similar processes tended to shift attention away from the universal biological model towards the patterning of social institutions and their effect on the psychology of the individual.

Institutionalized Goals

Strictly speaking the term 'socialization' does not merely mean 'growing-up'; the term is properly used for the training of an individual towards certain sets of values which are dominant in any society. The units of socialization may be either descriptive or explanatory. That is to say the particular social unit taken for study may either be manifest in the society, like the emphasis placed on 'balance' in Balinese society (Belo, 1935), or the unit chosen may be explanatory in the sense that it is used to explain manifest behaviour in the individuals of the society. A variety of explanatory units exist, as they stem from different parent theories. Psycho-analytic theories tend to encourage usage of terms like orality and anality, which focus attention on the stages of nurturance by the mother and of preoccupations with toilet training, both of which are thought to be connected with later events in the individual's life. Achievement is a category which has issued from a different theoretical orientation and draws attention to the motive themes of a society and the effect of these on people: how achievement values are introduced to the child; the special institutions which encourage or discourage achievement, and so forth. With all such categories, in whatever way they are studied, there is the thesis that a longitudinal linkage exists whereby the values in a society are created and supported by events in childhood. Work on socialization has either been preoccupied with institutionalized values or actual individuals. The differing emphasis can best be described by indicating the methods used.

Methods

Anthropological observation has been the hallmark of early work on socialization. There has been a plethora of observational reports on varying aspects of childhood and puberty: dependence upon the mother, weaning, toilet training practices, early sexual behaviour with its restrictions and encouragements, aggressive behaviour, the tolerance of society for the child's independence, achievement themes, among others (see Child, 1954, for summary). Sometimes the observations are more narrowly psychological, concentrating on one aspect, as with the study of motor development in some African children (Géber, 1958). Many firsthand observational reports now exist from which the theoretically inclined psychologist finds sufficient data to build into his theories of child rearing. One school of thought (see Whiting, 1961, for summary) has utilized the ethnographic information collected in the Human Relations Area Files (which contain neatly categorized information pertaining both to social institutions and social processes such as child training) for engendering correlations between early events in childhood and adult practices. For example, it has been shown that exclusive mother and child sleeping arrangements are strongly associated with male initiation rites at puberty. This correlation has prompted different psychological interpretations. It is either taken to mean that sleeping arrangements increase the supposed Oedipal rivalry between the son and his father to an extent where open revolt at the time of puberty becomes dangerous to the maintenance of society, so that initiation rites have to be set up publicly to acclaim the youngster as an adult in his own right. Or it has been interpreted with respect to over-dependency on the mother; it is necessary to break this dependency sharply by some institutional practice at puberty. Or again while there may not be actual dependence on the mother there is an identification which must be broken. Further correlational studies appear to indicate the second or third interpretation rather than the first as being correct, but the evidence is still correlational. In this case the antecedent condition is ecological – sleeping arrangements; other correlational studies of the Whiting kind have selected personal behaviour as the antecedent and beliefs as the consequent condition. Spiro and D'Andrade (1958) established a connexion between parental treatment of children with attitudes towards supernaturals in the same society. Harsh parental treatment is associated with the belief that the spirit or supernatural world is also harsh and aggressive. On the other hand, gentle treatment of children is associated with the notion that gods can be propitiated. The specific argument is presented that people, who in their infancy and early childhood are treated kindly and with some indulgence by their parents or elders, grow up with the belief that supernatural forces or gods are not severe and aggressive beings like the Old Testament conception of Yahweh, but are beings that can be propitiated and perhaps controlled by ritual.

Although interesting and provocative, correlational studies probably do not meet the exact canons of experimentally minded psychologists who desire a more stringent observational design before drawing conclusions. Earlier the fact of sudden weaning among the Zulus was mentioned. This was taken as a central point for a comparative study by Albino and Thompson (1956). They compared Zulu children who had been weaned in the traditional fashion with urban Zulu children who had been weaned earlier and not abruptly. The authors kept track of the immediate changes following the weaning experience and noted that the traditional Zulu child went through various changes. At first he became negativistic and aggressive, and often ignored the mother. Then he tried to get the attention of his mother, which in turn was followed by increasing independence with no signs of anger or other forms of disturbance. In short there were transitory effects of the kind which might have been predicted from psycho-analytic theories of weaning, but they proved not to be lasting. What could be counted as more permanent effects in the experimental group of Zulu children were due to the readjustments of the organism to the experience of weaning. These readjustments varied from child to child; and showed themselves in different attitudes towards the mother. In some cases the child renounced the mother, in others there was renouncement plus hostility, in others again there was an attempt to regain affection. The authors considered that although abrupt weaning created a temporary disturbance in the child's emotional and social life, over a longer period it aided the development of the qualities of self-reliance and sociability. Succinctly, it was thought to be an adaptive transition rather than a cause of permanent damage.

PERSONALITY

With the latter example we move in the direction of the thesis that the adult personality is in some way moulded by the experiences which are undergone in childhood. As these experiences vary from culture to culture the relativistic notion has arisen that each society contributes towards its own special personality type. This has been expressed under various headings in the literature.

Cultural Personality Types

In a useful article Singer (1961) has marshalled the various ideas of personality and culture. In all of them there is contained the belief that each culture has a typical personality which is distinctive of that culture and which, therefore, can be contrasted with the typical personality of another culture. The key term 'typical', though, has different interpretations. Ruth Benedict emphasized a configurational personality which reflects the dominant *ethos* in the culture. Concentrating on the American Indian groups, literary and psychiatric typologies were constructed to call attention to the differing value patterns. Nietzsche's classical distinction of Apollonian and Dionysian types was attributed to the Zuni and Plains Indians respectively. While in later publications the Kwakiutl Indians were characterized as 'megalomaniac paranoid'. Benedict's personality typologies were impressionistic and built up from collective behaviour, such as rituals, rather than first-hand from actual individuals. The idea of a Basic Personality Structure, which we owe to Abram Kardiner, is a postulated personality type which is thought to mediate between what Kardiner called primary institutions such as family organization, subsistence techniques and child-rearing practices, and secondary institutions, by which Kardiner included art forms, folk-lore, mythology and religion. Under this scheme of cultural personality it is considered that once a set of nuclear trends could be identified, then the link between primary and secondary institutions could be made, and a causal sequence is implied in that the values inherent in the art and folk-lore of a society are influenced by early childhood techniques. This notion aims directly at the connexion between socialization and personality, and owes much to psychoanalytic theory. While both the models of Configurational Personality and a Basic Personality Structure reflect preoccupation with institutions, the third theory of a Modal Personality, originated by Cora Dubois, attempts to put over the view that an examination of actual individuals who share a common culture should reveal a set of common characteristics. As is implied by the usage of the statistical term 'mode', the implication is that although there may be different kinds of individuals in any one culture there is a most frequent type which can be contrasted with the most frequent type of modal personality of another culture.

National Character Typologies

This leads on to a historically older notion, namely, that different nations produce different characters, symbolized often by stock cartoons such as John Bull. The idea of a national character can degenerate into the stereotypes which one nation has of another, but some prominence has been given to it through the writings of anthropologists, sociologists and psychiatrists. Much has been written about the American, English, German, Russian, Japanese and Hindu characters, among other national groups. Inkeles and Levinson (1954) have made the logical point that what we call national character should really be equated with the idea of modal personality, in which case all that we have learned of the latter can be applied to the former. In practice, however, the idea of a national character has been mostly connected with child-rearing practices, so that, to give an extreme example, swaddling-techniques in childhood for the inhabitants of the area called Great Russia are postulated as being associated with impassivity and the control of rage in the adults. The insistence on toilet-training habits among Japanese people in relation to the Japanese character belongs to the same class. A difficulty with the concept of national character is that it is too embracing: Inkeles (1961) has shown that it can be defined as institutional pattern, as cultural theme, as action and as racial psychology. When differently defined the kind of picture that is drawn depicting the national characteristic involved and the methods whereby this is found out can also be different. When national character is identified with an institutional pattern the picture chosen as exemplar is that of the dominant institution, particularly, as Inkeles goes on to state, that concerned with politics or economics. When identified with a cultural theme attention is drawn to folk-ways; themes in books and films would be examples of this identification.

Methods

As with many other concepts in this field the validity of different personality and national character terms is based finally on the manner in which we can utilize them. Disregarding the analysis of child-rearing systems as constituting a special class of techniques, there are basically two methods generally employed (Inkeles and Levinson, 1954). The first is personality assessment of individuals, which leans heavily on the use of projective techniques. Rorschach and Thematic Apperception tests have been taken from Hindu, Javanese, Thai, Zulu and American Indians, and numerous other societies; the tests either being applied without any change to their original form or modified especially to fit in with the particular group studied. A genuine difficulty with this kind of personality test is that of confusing proper inference about personality characteristics with the factors of motivation and communication. Kaplan (1961) noted, with the Thematic Apperception Test responses from the records of Thai agricultural workers, that the subjects were not telling stories at all, but simply describing the picture and saying what appeared to be happening in them. Kaplan felt that one could not conclude from this that Thai people were literal-minded and that they lacked fantasy, only that the particular test did not elicit any fantasy material. This is not to dismiss all cross-cultural personality studies using projective techniques as being useless; only to mark that certain cultural factors completely outside personality enter into the inference that one might be led to draw from their application. Kaplan cautioned that one might be led into serious error if there was exclusive reliance placed on them. Many cross-cultural studies in the personality sphere also utilize interviews, questionnaires and other methods suitable for individual application.

The second method is to utilize collective adult phenomena – collective documents like folk-tales, films, popular journals; or collective behaviour, as in dramatic themes, or in rituals. In both of these groups dominant value patterns are traced which are supposedly spread among the individuals of the society. The collective behaviour and the themes which recur in documents are considered to be reflections of the tendencies of individuals making up the behaviour or producing the themes. The best-known case is that of Bateson and Mead (1942) in their study of the Balinese theme which is expressed in ceremonial dances. The female dancer transforms from a coquettish woman, leading on the responsive male, into a witch who violently frustrates the male. This theme or plot is found in other spheres of Balinese collective life and is found also in the relationship between mother and child. This is thought to reflect certain dominant personality tendencies in the Balinese individual.

CONCLUSIONS

Cross-cultural studies have both the advantage and disadvantage of belonging to a no-man's-land in which other disciplines, particularly cultural anthropology, have more salience than psychology. Different disciplines have their own language and their own theoretical framework. In the fields of perception and cognition the theoretical influence is basically psychological, with linguistics having a heavy bias. In the fields of socialization and personality the demarcation lines of disciplines are more difficult to lay down with complete clarity. Further cross-cultural work, which I have not had space to mention in this chapter, has been devoted to the study of dreams, emotions, expressive behaviour and, particularly, mental illness. Inasmuch as the world's the limit, there seems no stringency on what work can be done. A difficulty which faces the psychologist concerns the basis of comparison between cultures in the study of some psychological process. In order to assess, say, concept formation in two widely separate regions of the world, we have to be sure that the methods of interrogation can be equated for both regions. This is more difficult than it may superficially seem, for many psychological techniques are very sensitive to environmental influences, and to the way in which they are applied. The ability to create *transcultural* variables, so that they are measurable on an equivalent basis anywhere in the world, is a challenge which always faces cross-cultural research.

REFERENCES

ABEELEN, J. H. F. v. (1963). 'Mouse mutants studied by ethological methods'. *Genetica*, **34**, 79–94; 95–101; 270–86.

ABERCROMBIE, M. L. J. (1960). *The Anatomy of Judgment*. London: Hutchinson.

AINSWORTH, M. D., *et al.* (1962). *Deprivation of Maternal Care*. Geneva: World Health Organization.

ALBINO, R. C. and THOMPSON, V. J. (1956). 'The effects of sudden weaning on Zulu children'. *Brit. J. Med. Psychol.*, **29**, 177–210.

ALLPORT, G. W. and PETTIGREW, T. F. (1957). 'Cultural influence on the perception of movement: the trapezoidal illusion among Zulus'. *J. Abn. Soc. Psychol.*, **55**, 104–13.

ANAND, B. K. and BROBECK, J. R. (1951). 'Hypothalamic control of food intake in rats and cats'. *Yale J. Biol. Med.*, **24**, 123–40.

ANASTASI, A. and FOLEY, J. P. Jr. (1949). *Differential Psychology*. rev. edn. New York: Macmillan, 725–6.

ANDERSON, H. H. (1959). 'Creativity in perspective'. In Anderson, H. H. (ed.) *Creativity and its Cultivation*. New York: Harper & Row.

A.S.A.B. Symposium (1965). 'Learning and associated phenomena in invertebrates'. *Animal Beh. Supplement No. 1.*

ASCH, S. E. (1951). 'Effects of group pressure upon the modifications and distortion of judgments'. In Cartwright, D. and Zander, A. (eds.), *Group Dynamics* (1960). London: Tavistock.

ASERINSKY, E. and KLEITMAN, N. (1953). 'Regularly occurring periods of eye motility and concomitant phenomena during sleep'. *Science*, **118**, 273–4.

ATTNEAVE, F. (1959). *Applications of Information Theory to Psychology*. New York: Holt.

AVERBACH, E. and SPERLING, G. (1960). 'Short term storage of information in vision'. In Cherry, C. (ed.), *Information Theory*. London: Butterworth.

BALINT, E. and BALINT, M. (1955). 'Dynamics of training in groups for psychotherapy'. *Brit. J. Med. Psychol.*, **28**, 135–43.

BARRON, F. (1963). *Creativity and Psychological Health*. New York: Van Nostrand.

BARTLETT, F. C. (1932). *Remembering: a study in experimental and social psychology*. New York: Macmillan.

References

BASTOCK, M. (1956). 'A gene mutation which changes a behaviour pattern'. *Evolution*, **10**, 421–39.

BATESON, G. and MEAD, M. (1942). *Balinese character: A photographic analysis*. New York: New York Academy of Science.

BEECHER, H. K. (1955). 'The Powerful Placebo'. *J. Am. Med. Assoc.*, **159**, 1602–5.

BELO, J. (1935). 'The Balinese temper'. *Charact. Pers.*, **4**, 120–46.

BERKO, J. (1958). 'The child's learning of English morphology'. *Word*, **14**, 150–77.

BINET, A. and SIMON, Th. (1906). 'Misére Physiologique et Sociale'. *L'Année Psychologique*, **12**, 1–24.

BINET, A., SIMON, Th. and VANEY, F. A. (1906). 'Pedagogie Scientifique'. *L'Année Psychologique*, **12**, 233–74.

BION, W. R. (1961). *Experiences in groups*. London: Tavistock.

BLEWETT, D. B. (1954). 'An experimental study of the inheritance of intelligence'. *J. Mental Sci.*, **100**, 922–33.

BLOUGH, D. S. (1958). 'A method for obtaining psychophysical thresholds from the pigeon'. *J. exp. anal. Behav.*, **1**, 31–43.

BLUM, R. (ed.) (1964). *The Utopiates*. New York: Atherton Press.

BONJER, F. H. (1960). 'Physiological aspects of shiftwork'. Proc. 13th Int. Congr. Occ. Health.

BOWLBY, J. (1951). *Maternal Care and Mental Health*. Geneva: World Health Organization. Monograph Series 179.

BRADY, J. V. (1959). 'A comparative approach to the study of drug effects on the behaviour of higher animals'. In *Evolution of Nervous Control*. Washington, D.C.: American Association for the Advancement of Science.

BROADBENT, D. E. (1954). 'Role of auditory localization and attention in memory span'. *J. exp. Psychol.*, **47**, 191–6.

BROADBENT, D. E. (1956). 'Successive responses to simultaneous stimuli'. *Quart. J. exp. Psychol.*, **8**, 145–52.

BROADBENT, D. E. (1958). *Perception and Communication*. Oxford: Pergamon Press.

BROADBENT, D. E. and LADEFOGED, P. (1957). 'On the fusion of sounds reaching different sense organs'. *J. Acoust. Soc. Am.*, **29**, 708–10.

BROADBENT, D. E. and GREGORY, M. (1963a). 'Division of attention and the decision theory of signal detection'. *Proc. Roy. Soc. (London) Ser. B.*, **158**, 222–31.

BROADBENT, D. E. and GREGORY, M. (1963b). 'Vigilance considered as statistical decision'. *Brit. J. Psychol.*, **54**, 309–23.

418

References

BROADBENT, D. E. and GREGORY, M. (1964). 'Stimulus set and response set: The alternation of attention'. *Quart. J. exp. Psychol.*, **16**, 309–17.

BROADHURST, P. L. (1960). 'Studies in Psychogenetics'. In Eysenck, H. J. (ed.), *Experiments in Personality*. London: Routledge & Kegan Paul.

BROADHURST, P. L. and JINKS, J. (1963). 'The inheritance of mammalian behaviour re-examined'. *J. Heredity*, **54**, 170–6.

BROGDEN, H. E. and SPRECHER, T. B. (1964). 'Criteria of creativity'. In Taylor, Calvin W. (ed.), *Creativity: Progress and Potential*. London: McGraw-Hill.

BROWN, H. (1957). 'Day and night and three shift working'. *Personnel Mgmt.* **39**, 150–56.

BROWN, R. W. (1958). *Words and Things*. Glencoe, Illinois: Free Press.

BROWN, R. W. and LENNEBERG, E. H. (1954). 'A study in language and cognition'. *J. Abn. Soc. Psychol.*, **49**, 454–62.

BROWNFIELD, C. A. (1964). 'Hypotheses in deprivation research'. *Psychol. Bull.*, **61**, 304–13.

BRUNER, J. S. and GOODMAN, C. D. (1947). 'Value and need as organising factors in perception'. *J. Abnorm. Soc. Psychol.* **42**, 33–44.

BRUNER, J. S., GOODNOW, J. J. and AUSTIN, G. A. (1956). *A Study of Thinking*. London: Chapman & Hall.

BURKE, C. J. and ESTES, W. K. (1957). 'A component model for stimulus variables in discrimination learning'. *Psychometrika*, **22**, 133–45.

BURT, C. (1951). *The Backward Child* (1937). 1st edn. London: University of London Press.

BUSH, R. R. and MOSTELLER, F. (1951). 'A model for stimulus generalization and discrimination'. *Psychol. Rev.*, **58**, 413–23.

BUTLER, C. G. (1964). 'Pheromones in sexual processes in insects'. *Symp. Roy. Ent. Soc.*, **2**, 66–77.

CAMPBELL, D. T. (1964). 'Distinguishing differences of perception from failures of communication in cross-cultural studies'. In Northrop, F. S. C. and Livingstone, H. H. (eds.) *Crosscultural Understanding*. New York and London: Harper & Row.

CAPES, M. (ed.) (1960). *Communication or Conflict: Conferences, their Nature, Dynamics and Planning*. London: Tavistock.

CARMICHAEL, D. M. (1940). 'Some examples of constructive thinking among Greenlanders'. *Brit. J. Psychol.*, **30**, 295–315.

CARROLL, J. B. (ed.) (1956). *Language, Thought, and Reality: Selected writings of Benjamin Lee Whorf*. New York and London: Wiley.

References

CARROLL. J. B. and CASAGRANDE, J. B. (1958). 'The function of language classifications in behaviour'. In Maccoby, E. E., Newcomb, T. M. and Hartley, E. L. (eds.), *Readings in Social Psychology*, 3rd edn. New York: Holt, Rinehard & Winston.

CARTHY, J. D. (1958). *An Introduction to the Behaviour of Invertebrates*. London: Allen & Unwin.

CARTHY, J. D. (1965). *The Behaviour of Arthropods*. Edinburgh: Oliver & Boyd.

CARTWRIGHT, D. and ZANDER, A. (1960). *Group Dynamics*, 2nd edn. London: Tavistock.

CHERRY, E. C. (1953). 'Some experiments on the recognition of speech with one and with two ears'. *J. Acoust. Soc. Am.*, **25**, 975–9.

CHERRY, E. C. (1957). *On Human Communication*. London: Chapman & Hall.

CHERRY, E. C. and TAYLOR, W. K. (1954). 'Some further experiments upon the recognition of speech with one and with two ears'. *J. Acoust. Soc. Am.*, **26**, 554–9.

CHILD, I. L. (1954). 'Socialization'. In Lindzey, G. (ed.) *Handbook of Social Psychology*, Vol. 2. Cambridge, Mass.: Addison-Wesley.

CHOMSKY, N. (1957). *Syntactic Structures*. The Hague: Mouton.

CLARKE, A. D. B. and CLARKE, A. M. (1958). *Mental Deficiency: The Changing Outlook*. London: Methuen.

CLIFF, N. (1959). 'Adverbs as Multipliers'. *Psychol. Rev.*, **66**, 27–44.

COLQUHOUN, W. P. (1961). 'The effect of "unwanted" signals on performance in a vigilance task'. *Ergonomics*, **4**, 41–51.

CONNOLLY, K. J. (1964). 'Psychology and Genetics 1963'. *Bull. Brit. Psychol. Soc.*, **17**, 24–6.

COOK, L. (1964). 'Effects of drugs on operant conditioning'. In Steinberg, H. (ed.) *Animal Behaviour and Drug Action*, Ciba Foundation Symposium. London: Churchill.

CORNING, W. C. and JOHN, E. R. (1961). 'Effect of ribonuclease on retention of conditioned response in regenerated planarians'. *Science*, **134**, 1363–5.

COULSON, J. (1962). *Programmed Learning and Computer Based Instruction*. New York: Wiley.

CRANE, J. (1949). 'Comparative biology of salticid spiders at Rancho Grande Venezuela. Part 4. An analysis of display'. *Zoologica*, **34**, 159–214.

CROWDER, N. A. (1960). 'Automatic tutoring by intrinsic programming'. In Lumsdaine, A. A. and Glaser, R. (eds.) *Teaching machines and programmed instruction*. Washington, D. C.: National Education Association.

References

CRUTCHFIELD, R. S. (1955). 'Conformity and character'. *Am. Psychol.*, **10**, 191–8.

CRYNS, A. (1962). 'African intelligence: a critical survey of cross-cultural intelligence research in Africa south of the Sahara'. *J. Soc. Psychol.*, **57**, 283–301.

DAMRIN, D. E. (1961). 'Preferences for information about students'. *J. Ed. Psychol.*, **52**, 254–61.

DAVENPORT, D., CAMOUGIS, G. and HICKOK, J. F. (1960). 'Analyses of the behaviour of commensals in host-factor. I. A hesionid polychaete and a pinnotherid crab'. *Anim. Behav.*, **8**, 218–19.

DEMENT, W. (1960). 'The effect of dream deprivation'. *Science*, **131**, 1705–7.

DEMENT, W. and KLEITMAN, N. (1957). 'Cyclic variations in EEG during sleep and their relation to eye movements, body mobility and dreaming'. *EEG clin. Neurophysiol.* **9**, 673–90.

DETHIER, V. G. (1964). 'Microscopic brains'. *Science*, **143**, 1138–45.

DEUTSCH, J. A. (1955). 'A theory of shape recognition'. *Brit. J. Psychol.*, **46**, 30–7.

DEUTSCH, M. (1949). 'The effects of cooperation and competition upon group processes'. In Cartwright, D. and Zander, A. (eds.), *Group Dynamics*. London: Tavistock.

DIXON, N. F. (1956). 'Symbolic associations following subliminal stimulation'. *Int. J. Psycho-anal.*, **37**, 159–70.

DIXON, N. F. (1960). 'Apparent changes in the visual threshold. Central or peripheral?' *Brit. J. Psychol.*, **51**, 297–309.

DIXON, N. F. and HAIDER, M. (1961). 'Changes in the visual threshold as a function of subception'. *Quart. J. exp. Psychol.*, **13**, 229–35.

DIXON, N. F. and LEAR, T. E. (1963). 'Electroencephalograph correlates of threshold regulation'. *Nature*, **198**, 870–2.

DODWELL, P. C. (1960). 'Causes of behaviour and explanation in psychology'. *Mind*, **69**, N.S., 1–13.

DODWELL, P. C. (1964). 'Some factors affecting the hearing of words presented dichotically'. *Can. J. Psychol.*, **18**, 72–91.

DOLLARD, J. and MILLER, N. E. (1950). *Personality and Psychotherapy: an analysis in terms of learning, thinking and culture*. New York: McGraw-Hill.

DRESCHLER, R. J. (1960). 'Affect-stimulating effects of colours'. *J. Abn. Soc. Psychol.*, **61**, 323–8.

Editorial, (1964). 'Opiate addiction'. *Lancet*, i, 649–50.

References

EFRON, R. (1957). 'Stereoscopic vision. I. Theory of binocular temporal summation'. *Brit. J. Ophthalmol.*, **61**, 709–30.

EINDHOVEN, J. and VINACKE, W. E. (1952). 'Creative processes in painting'. *J. Gen. Psychol.*, **47**, 139–64.

ELLIS, N. R. (1963). 'The Stimulus Trace and Behavioural Inadequacy'. In Ellis, N. R. (ed.), *Handbook of Mental Deficiency*. New York: McGraw-Hill.

EPSTEIN, W. (1964). 'Experimental investigation of the genesis of visual space perception'. *Psych. Bull.*, **61**, 115–28.

EVANS, F. G. C. (1951). 'An analysis of the behaviour of *Lepidochiton cinereus* in response to certain physical features of the environment'. *J. Animal Ecol.*, **20**, 1–10.

EVANS, J., GLASER, R. and HOMME, L. (1960). *The Ruleg (Rule-Example) System for the Construction of Learning Programs*. University of Pittsburgh report.

EYSENCK, H. J. (1953). *Uses and Abuses of Psychology*. Harmondsworth: Penguin.

EYSENCK, H. J. (ed.) (1960). *Behaviour Therapy and the Neuroses*. Oxford: Pergamon Press.

EYSENCK, H. J. (ed.) (1963). *Experiments with Drugs*. Oxford: Pergamon Press.

FANTZ, R. L. (1961). 'The origin of form perception'. *Sci. Am.*, **204**, 66–72.

FERSTER, C. B. (1963). 'Essentials of a Science of Behaviour'. In Nurnberger, J. I., Ferster, C. B. and Brady, J. P. (eds.), *An Introduction to the Science of Human Behaviour*. New York: Appleton-Century-Crofts.

FERSTER, C. B. and SKINNER, B. F. (1957). *Schedules of Reinforcement*. New York: Appleton-Century-Crofts.

FESTINGER, L. and ARONSON, E. (1960). 'The arousal and reduction of dissonance in social contexts'. In Cartwright, D. and Zander, A. (eds.), *Group Dynamics*. London: Tavistock.

FISHER, A. E. (1964). 'Chemical stimulation of the brain'. *Sci. Am.*, **210**, 60–8.

FISHER, C. (1954). 'Dreams and perception'. *J. Am. Psycho-anal. Ass.*, **2**, 389.

FLAVELL, J. H. (1963). *The developmental psychology of Jean Piaget*. London: Van Nostrand.

FLESCHER, Irwin (1963). 'Anxiety and achievement of intellectually gifted and creatively gifted children'. *J. Psychol.*, **56**, 251–68.

References

FODOR, J. A., JENKINS, J. J. and SAPORTA, S. *Introduction to psycholinguistic theory*. New Jersey: Prentice Hall (forthcoming)

FOULKES, S. H. and ANTHONY, E. J. (1965). *Group Psychotherapy*, 2nd edn. Harmondsworth: Penguin.

FOULKES, W. D. (1962). 'Dream reports from different stages of sleep'. *J. abnorm. soc. Psychol.* **65**, 14–25.

FRAKE, C. O. (1961). 'The diagnosis of disease among the Subanun of Mindanao'. *Am. Anthrop.*, **63**, 113–32.

FRANK, J. D. and POWDERMAKER, F. B. (1959). 'Group psychotherapy'. In Arieti, S. (ed.), *American Handbook of Psychiatry*, **2**, 1362–74.

FRAENKEL, G. and GUNN, D. L. (1961). *The Orientation of Animals*. New York: Dover.

FRANSELLA, F. A. R. and ADAMS, B. (1965). 'An illustration of the use of repertory grid technique in a clinical setting'. *Brit. J. Soc. Clin. Psychol.*

FREMONT-SMITH, F. (1961). 'The interdisciplinary conference'. *A.I.B.S. Bull.*, **11**, 17–20.

FRENCH, J. D. (1957). 'The reticular formation'. *Sci. Am.*, May 1957.

FRIES, C. C. (1952). *The Structure of English*. New York: Harcourt, Brace; London: Longmans, Green.

VON FRISCH, K. (1954). *The Dancing Bees*. London: Methuen.

FUCHS, J. (1963). 'Physical alterations which occur in the blind and are illustrated in Ancient Egyptian works of art'. Proceedings of New York Academy of Sciences Conference on Photo-neuro-endocrine effects in Circadian Systems, with particular reference to the eye. June 1963.

FULLER, J. L. and THOMPSON, W. R. (1960). *Behaviour Genetics*. New York: Wiley.

GALTON, Francis (1869). *Hereditary Genius* (new edn, 1914). London: Macmillan.

GALTON, Francis (1883). *Human Faculty and its development*. London: Macmillan.

GARNER, W. R. (1962). *Uncertainty and Structure as Psychological Concepts*. New York: Wiley.

GÉBER, Marcelle (1958). 'The psycho-motor development of African children in the first year, and the influence of maternal behavior'. *J. Soc. Psychol.*, **47**, 185–95.

GETZELS, J. W. and JACKSON, P. W. (1962). *Creativity and Intelligence*. New York: Wiley.

GIBSON, E. J. and WALK, R. D. 'The visual cliff'. *Sci. Am.*, April 1960.

References

GIBSON, J. J. (1950). *Perception of the visual world.* Boston: Houghton Mifflin.

GLANZER, M. (1962). 'Grammatical category: a rote learning and word association analysis'. *J. verb. Learn. ver. behav.*, **1**, 31–41.

GOLDFARB, W. W. (1943). 'Infant rearing and problem behaviour'. *Am. J. Orthopsychiat.*, **13**, 249–65.

GOODNOW, J. (1962). 'A test of milieu effects with some of Piaget's tasks'. *Psychol. Monogr.*, **76**, 1–22.

GORDON, W. J. J. (1961). *Synectics: The development of creative capacity.* New York: Harper.

GREGORY, R. L. (1963). 'Distortion of visual space as inappropriate constancy scaling'. *Nature*, **199**, 678–80.

GREGORY, R. L. (1965). 'Seeing in depth'. *Nature*, **207**, 16–19.

GREGORY, R. L. and WALLACE, J. G. (1963). 'Recovery from early blindness'. *Quart. J. exp. Psychol.* Monograph Supp. 2.

GREGORY, R. L., WALLACE, J. G. and CAMPBELL, F. W. (1959). 'Changes in the size and shape of visual after-images observed in complete darkness during changes of position in space'. *Quart. J. exp. Psychol.*, **9**, 54–5.

GRUNT, J. A. and YOUNG, W. C. (1953). 'Consistency of sexual behaviour patterns in individual male guinea pigs following castration and androgen therapy'. *J. Comp. Physiol. Psychol.*, **46**, 138–44.

GUILFORD, J. P. (1950). 'Creativity'. *Am. Psychol.*, **5**, 444–54.

GUILFORD, J. P. (1956). 'The structure of intellect'. *Psychol. Bull.*, **53** (4), 267–93.

GUILFORD, J. P. (1959). 'Traits of creativity'. In Anderson, H. H., (ed.), *Creativity and its Cultivation.* New York: Harper & Row.

HADAMARD, J. (1954). *The Psychology of Invention in the Mathematical Field.* New York: Dover.

HALL, C. S. (1938). 'The inheritance of emotionality'. *Sigma Xi Quart.*, **26**, 17–27.

HALLOWELL, A. I. (1942). 'Some psychological aspects of measurement among the Salteaux'. *Am. Anthrop.*, **44**, 62–77.

HARKER, J. E. (1956). 'Factors controlling the diurnal rhythm of activity of *Periplaneta Americana*'. *J. exp. Biol.*, **33**, 224–34.

HARKER, J. E. (1960). 'Endocrine and nervous factors in insect circadian rhythms'. *Cold Spring Harbor Symp. Quant. Biol.*, **25**, 279–87.

HARLOW, H. F. (1959a). 'Learning set and error factor theory'. In Koch, S. (ed.), *Psychology: a study of a science*, Vol. 2. New York: McGraw-Hill.

HARLOW, H. F. (1959b). 'Love in infant monkeys'. *Sci. Am.*, **200**, 68–74.

References

HARLOW, H. F. (1961). 'The development of affectional patterns in infant monkeys'. In Foss, B. M. (ed.), *Determinants of Infant Behaviour*. London: Methuen.

HARLOW, H. F. and HARLOW, M. K. (1962). 'Social deprivation in monkeys'. *Sci. Am.*, **207**, 137–46.

HARLOW, H. F. and ZIMMERMANN, R. R. (1959). 'Affectional responses in the infant monkey'. *Science*, **130**, 421–32.

HARRIS, Th. 'Summary of investigation relating to reading'. *J. Educ. Res.*, **57**, 6, 283–327.

HASKELL, P. T. (1961). *Insect Sounds*. London: Witherby.

HEBB, D. O. (1949). *The Organization of Behaviour*. New York: Wiley.

VON HELMHOLTZ, H. (1923). *Physiological Optics* (trans. Southall). New York: Optical Society of America.

HERING, E. (1878). *Zür Lehre vom Lichtsinne*. Berlin: Springer.

HERMELIN, B. and O'CONNOR, N. (1964). 'Short-term memory in normal and subnormal children'. *Am. J. Ment. Defic.* **69**, 121–5.

HERON, W. (1957). 'The pathology of boredom'. *Sci. Am.*, January 1957.

HESS, E. H. (1958). 'Imprinting in animals'. *Sci. Am.*, March 1958.

HESS, W. R. (1954). *Das Zwischenhirn*, 2nd edn. Basel: Schwabe.

HETHERINGTON, A. W. and RANSON, S. W. (1940). 'Hypothalamic lesions and adiposity in the rat'. *Anat. Rec.*, **78**, 149–72.

HIGHNAM, K. C. (1964). 'Hormones and behaviour of insects'. *Viewpoints in Biol.*, **3**, 219–55.

HILGARD, E. R. (1964). 'Teaching machines and creativity'. *Programmed Learning*, **1 (2)**.

HIRSCH, J. (1962). 'Individual differences in behaviour and their genetic basis'. In Bliss, E. (ed.), *Roots of Behaviour*. New York: Harper.

HODOS, W. (1961). 'Progressive ratio as a measure of reward strength'. *Science*, **134**, 943–4.

HOLLAND, J. G. and SKINNER, B. F. (1961). *The Analysis of Behaviour: A Program for Self-instruction*. New York: McGraw-Hill.

VON HOLST, E. (1962). 'Electrically controlled behavior'. *Sci. Am.*, **206**, 50–9.

HOMANS, G. C. (1951). *The Human Group*. London: Routledge & Kegan Paul.

HOUSE, B. J. and ZEAMAN, D. (1963). 'The role of attention in retardate discrimination learning'. In Ellis, N. R. (ed.), *Handbook of Mental Deficiency*. New York: McGraw-Hill.

HOVEY, H. B. (1928). 'Effects of general distraction on the higher thought processes'. *Am. J. Psychol.*, **40**, 585–91.

References

HUBEL, D. H. and WIESEL, T. N. (1962). 'Receptive fields, binocular interaction and functional architecture in the cat's visual cortex'. *J. Physiol.*, **160**, 106–54.

HUDSON, L. (1962). 'Intelligence, divergence and potential originality'. *Nature*, **196**, 601–2.

HUDSON, L. (1963). 'Personality and scientific aptitude'. *Nature*, **189**, 913–14.

HUDSON, W. (1960). 'Pictorial depth perception in sub-cultural groups in Africa'. *J. Soc. Psychol.*, **52**, 183–208.

HURVICH, L. M. and JAMESON, D. (1957). 'An opponent-process theory of color vision'. *Psychol. Rev.*, **64**, 384–90, 397–404.

HURWITZ, H. M. B. and MILLENSEN, J. R. (1961). 'Maintenance of avoidance behaviour under temporally-defined contingencies'. *Science*, **133**, 284–5.

HUXLEY, A. (1954). *The Doors of Perception*. London: Chatto & Windus; Harmondsworth: Penguin.

INGRAM, T. T. S. (1960). 'Paediatric aspects of specific developmental dysphasia, dyslexia and dysgraphia'. *Cereb. Palsy Bull.*, **2**, 254.

INKELES, A. (1961). 'National character and modern political systems'. In Hsu, F. K. L. (ed.), *Psychological Anthropology: Approaches to Culture and Personality*. Homewood, Illinois: Dorsey Press.

INKELES, A. and LEVINSON, D. J. (1954). 'National character: the study of modal personality and sociocultural systems'. In Lindzey, G. (ed.), *Handbook of Social Psychology*, Vol. 2. Cambridge, Mass.: Addison-Wesley.

ITARD, J. M. G. (1801). *The Wild Boy of Aveyron*. (trans. G. and I. S. Humphrey, 1932). New York: Appleton–Century–Crofts.

ITTELSON, W. H. (1952). *The Ames demonstrations in perception*. Princeton: Princeton University Press.

JAHODA, G. (1956). 'Assessment of abstract behavior in a non-western culture'. *J. Abn. Soc. Psychol.*, **53**, 237–43.

JAKOBSON, R., FANT, C. G. M. and HALLE, M. (1951). *Preliminaries to Speech Analysis*. Cambridge, Mass.: M.I.T. Press.

JEVONS, W. S. (1871). 'The power of numerical discrimination'. *Nature*, **3**, 281–2.

JOYCE, C. R. B. (1961). 'Experiments with control substances'. *Ann. rheum. Dis.*, **20**, 78–82.

JOYCE, C. R. B. (1962a). 'Patient cooperation and the sensitivity of clinical trials'. *J. chron. Dis.*, **15**, 1025–36.

References

JOYCE, C. R. B. (1962b). 'Differences between physicians as revealed by clinical trials'. *Proc. Roy. Soc. Med.*, **55**, 776–8.

JOYCE, C. R. B. (1964). 'Drugs and personality'. *Trans. med. Soc. Lond.* **80**, 92–106.

JOYCE, C. R. B., *et al.* (1959). 'Potentiation by phenobarbitone of effects of ethyl alcohol on human behaviour'. *J. ment. Sci.*, **105**, 51–60.

JULESZ, B. (1960). 'Binocular depth perception of computer-generated patterns'. *Bell Tel. Syst. Tech. J.*, **39**, 1125–62.

JULESZ, B. (1964). 'Binocular depth perception without familiarity clues'. *Science*, **145**, 356–62.

KAPLAN, B. (1961). 'Personality study and culture'. In Kaplan, B. (ed.), *Studying Personality Cross-Culturally*. Evanston: Row, Peterson.

KELLY, G. (1955). *The psychology of personal constructs*. Vols. 1 & 2. New York: Norton.

KELLY, G. (1961). 'The abstraction of human processes.' *Proc. 14th Internat. Cong. Psychol. Copenhagen*, 220–9.

KISSEL, P. and BARRUCAND, D. (1964). *Placebos et Effet Placebo en médecine*. Paris: Masson.

KLEIN, J. (1956). *The Study of Groups*. London: Routledge & Kegan Paul.

KLEITMAN, N. (1963). *Sleep and Wakefulness*, rev. edn. Chicago: University of Chicago Press.

KLÜVER, H. and BUCY, P. C. (1939). 'Preliminary analysis of functions of the temporal lobes in monkeys'. *Arch. Neurol. Psychiat.*, **42**, 979–1000.

KOFFKA, K. (1935). *Principles of Gestalt psychology*. New York: Harcourt Brace.

KÖHLER, W. (1947). *Gestalt Psychology*. New York: Liveright.

KÖHLER, W. and WALLACH, H. (1944). 'Figural after-effects: an investigation of visual processes'. *Proc. Am. Phil. Soc.*, **88**, 269–357.

KRAVKOV, S. V. (1941). 'Colour vision and the autonomic nervous system'. *J. Opt. Soc. Am.*, **31**, 335–7.

LAMBERT, W. E. and JAKOBOVITS, L. A. (1960). 'Verbal satiation and changes in the intensity of meaning'. *J. Exp. Psychol.*, **60**, 376–83.

LANDFIELD, A. W. (1954). 'A movement interpretation of threat'. *J. Abn. Soc. Psychol.*, **49**, 529–32.

References

LANDFIELD, A. W. (1955). 'Self-predictive orientation and the movement interpretation of threat'. *J. Abn. Soc. Psychol.*, **51**, 434–8.

LASAGNA, L. *et al.* (1954). 'A study of the placebo response'. *Am. J. Med.*, **16**, 770–9.

LETTVIN, J. Y., MATURANA, H. R., McCULLOCH, W. S. and PITTS, W. H. (1959). 'What the frog's eye tells the frog's brain'. *Proc. Inst. Radio Engrs.*, New York. **47**, 1940.

LEVINE, S. (1962). 'The effects of infantile experience on adult behavior'. In Bachrach, A. J. (ed.). *Experimental Foundations of Clinical Psychology*. New York: Basic Books.

LIBERTY, P. G. Jr and JONES, R. J. (1962). *Age-mate perceptions of intelligence, creativity, and achievement*. Paper presented at Southwestern Psychological Association, U.S.A.

LIBERTY, P. G. Jr, JONES, R. J. and McGUIRE, C. (1963). 'Age-mate perceptions of intelligence, creativity and achievement'. *Perceptual and Motor Skills*, **16**, 194.

LINDAUER, M. (1961). *Communication among the Social Bees*. Cambridge, Mass.: Harvard University Press.

LINDEMANN, E. and FELSINGER, J. (1961). 'Drug effects and probability theory'. *Psychopharmacologia*, **2**, 69–92.

LINSCHOTEN, I. (1956). *Strukturanalyse der binokularen Tiefenwahrnemung*. Groningen: Wolters.

LORENZ, K. Z. (1952). *King Solomon's Ring: New Light on Animal Ways*. New York: Thomas Y. Crowell.

LUBY, E. D. *et al.* (1960). 'Sleep deprivation: Effects on behaviour, thinking, motor performance, and biological energy transfer systems'. *Psychosom. Med.* **22**, 182–92.

LUMSDAINE, A. A. and GLASER, R. (eds.) (1960). *Teaching machines and programmed learning*. Washington, D. C.: National Education Association.

LURIA, A. R. (1961). *The Role of Speech in the Regulation of Normal and Abnormal Behaviour*. Oxford: Pergamon Press.

McDOUGALL, W. (1924). *Outline of Abnormal Psychology*. London: Methuen.

McGHIE, A. and CHAPMAN, J. (1961). 'Disorders of attention and perception in early schizophrenia'. *Brit. J. Med. Psychol.*, **34**, 103–5.

McGINNIES, E. (1949). 'Emotionality and perceptual defence'. *Psychol. Rev.*, **56**, 244–51.

MACKAY, D. M. (1961). 'Interactive processes in visual perception'. In Rosenblith, W. A. (ed.) *Sensory Communication*. New York: Wiley, and M. I. T. Press.

References

McNemar, Q. (1933). 'Twin resemblances in motor skills and the effect of practice thereon'. *J. Genetic. Psychol.*, **42**, 70–97.

Mahut, H. (1958). 'Breed differences in the dog's emotional behaviour'. *Can. J. Psychol.*, **12**, 35–44.

Malinowski, B. (1927). *Sex and Repression in Savage Society*. London: Kegan Paul.

Manning, A. (1961). 'Effects of artificial selection for mating speed in *Drosophila melanogaster*'. *Anim. Behav.*, **9**, 82–92.

Mead, M. (1928). *Coming of Age in Samoa*. New York: Morrow.

Mead, M. (1930). *Growing up in New Guinea*. New York: Morrow.

Mercado, J., DiazGuerrero, R. and Gardner, W. (1963). 'Cognitive control in children of Mexico and the United States'. *J. Social Psychol.*, **59**, 199–208.

Michael, R. P. (1960). 'An investigation of the sensitivity of circumscribed neurological areas to hormonal stimulation by means of the application of oestrogens directly to the brain of the cat'. In *4th International Neurochemical Symposium*. Oxford: Pergamon Press.

Miller, G. A. (1962). 'Some psychological studies of grammar'. *Am. Psychol.*, **17**, 748–62.

Miller, N. E. (1957). 'Experiments on motivation'. *Science*, **126**, 1270–8.

Moray, N. (1959). 'Attention in dichotic listening: affective cues and the influence of instructions'. *Quart. J. exp. Psychol.*, **11**, 56–60.

Moray, N. and Connolly, K. J. (1963). 'A possible case of genetic assimilation of behaviour'. *Nature*, **199**, 358–60.

Morris, B. (1965) 'How does a group learn to work together?' In Niblett, N. R. (ed.) *How and Why do we Learn*. London: Faber & Faber.

Mowbray, G. H. (1953). 'Simultaneous vision and audition: comprehension of prose passages with varying levels of difficulty'. *J. exp. Psychol.*, **46**, 365–72.

Mowrer, O. H. (1950). *Learning Theory and Personality Dynamics*. New York: Ronald Press.

Nadel, S. F. (1937). 'A field experiment in racial psychology'. *Brit. J. Psychol.*, **28**, 195–211.

Newcomb, T. M. (1960). 'Varieties of interpersonal attraction'. In Cartwright, D. and Zander, A. (eds.), *Group Dynamics*. London: Tavistock.

Newell, A. and Simon, H. A. (1963). 'GPS, a program that simulates human thought'. In Feigenbaum, E. A. and Feldman, J. (eds.), *Computers and Thought*. New York: McGraw-Hill.

References

NEWELL, G. E. (1958). 'An experimental analysis of the behaviour of *Littorina littorea* under natural conditions and in the laboratory'. *J. mar. Biol. Ass. U.K.*, **37**, 241–66.

NEWMAN, H. H., FREEMAN, F. N. and HOLZINGER, K. J. (1937). *Twins: A Study of Heredity and Environment*. Chicago: University of Chicago Press.

NISSEN, H. W. (1951). 'Phylogenetic comparison'. In Stevens, S. S. (ed.), *Handbook of Experimental Psychology*. New York: Wiley.

O'CONNOR, N. (1956). 'The evidence for the permanently disturbing effects of mother child separation'. *Acta Psychol.*, **15**, 174–91.

O'CONNOR, N. (1965). 'Children in restricted environments'. In Newton, G. and Levine, S. (eds.), *Early Experience*. New York: Charles C. Thomas.

O'CONNOR, N. and HERMELIN, B. (1963). *Speech and Thought in Severe Subnormality*. Oxford: Pergamon Press.

O'CONNOR, N. and TIZARD, J. (1956). *The Social Problem of Mental Deficiency*. London: Pergamon Press.

OLDS, J. and MILNER, P. M. (1954). 'Positive reinforcement produced by electrical stimulation of septal area and other regions of rat brain'. *J. comp. physiol. Psychol.*, **47**, 419–27.

OLIVER, W. D. and LANDFIELD, A. W. (1963). 'Reflexivity: an unfaced issue of psychology'. *J. Indiv. Psychol.*, **20**, 187–201.

OSBORN, A. F. (1953, 1957). *Applied Imagination*. New York: Scribner.

OSGOOD, G. A. (1963). 'Psycholinguistics'. In Koch, S. (ed.), *Psychology: A Study of a Science*, Vol. 6. New York: McGraw-Hill.

OSGOOD, C. E. and SEBEOK, T. A. (eds.) (1954). 'Psycholinguistics: a survey of theory and research problems. Part 2'. *Supplement* to *J. Abn. Soc. Psychol.*, 49.

PAPPERT, S. (1961). 'Centrally produced geometrical illusions'. *Nature*, **191**, 733.

PARNES, S. J. and MEADOW, A. (1963). 'Development of individual creative talent'. In Taylor, C. W. and Barron, F. (eds.), *Scientific Creativity: Its Recognition and Development*. New York and London: Wiley.

PATRICK, C. (1935). 'Creative thought in poets'. *Arch. Psychol.*, **26**, 1–74.

PATRICK, C. (1937). 'Creative thought in artists'. *J. Psychol.*, **4**, 35–73.

PAVLOV, I. P. (1927). *Conditioned Reflexes* (Anrep, G. V. (trans)). London: O.U.P.

References

PELUFFO, N. (1962). 'Les notions et de causalité chez les enfants provenant de differents milieux physiques et socio-culturels'. *Arch. de Psychologie*, **38**, 275–91.

PENROSE, L. S. and PENROSE, R. (1958). 'Impossible objects'. *Brit. J. Psychol.*, **49**, 31.

PIAGET, J. (1959). Introduction in Gréco J. and Piaget, J. *Apprentissage et connaissance. Etudes d'epistémologie génétique*, vol. 7. Paris: Presses Univers. France.

PITTS, W. and McCULLOCH, W. S. (1947). 'How we know universals: the perception of auditory and visual forms'. *Bull. Math. Biophys.*, **7**, 127.

PRESSEY, S. L. (1950). 'Development and appraisal of devices providing immediate automatic scoring of objective tests and concomitant self-instruction'. *J. Psychol.*, **29**, 417–47.

PRITCHARD, R. M. (1958). 'Visual illusions viewed as stabilised retinal images'. *Quart. J. exp. Psychol.*, **10**, 77.

PRITCHARD, R. M. (1961). 'Stabilized images on the retina'. *Sci. Am.*, **204**, 72–8.

REVANS, R. (1964). 'Morale and effectiveness of hospitals'. *New Society*, **21**, 6–8.

RIVERS, W. H. R. (1901). 'Visual spatial perception'. Part I, Vol. II of Haddon, A. C. (ed.), *Reports of the Cambridge Anthropological Expedition to Torres Straits*. Cambridge: C.U.P.

RODGERS, D. and McCLEARN, G. E. (1962). 'Alcohol preference of mice'. In Bliss, E. (ed.), *Roots of Behaviour*. New York: Harper.

ROGERS, C. (1959). 'Towards a theory of creativity'. In Anderson, H. H. (ed.), *Creativity and its Cultivation*. New York: Harper & Row.

ROSENBAUM, M. and BERGER, M. M. (eds.) (1963). *Group psychotherapy and group function*. New York: Basic Books.

RUNKEL. P. J. and DAMRIN, D. E. (1961). 'Effects of training and anxiety upon teachers' preferences for information about students'. *J. Ed. Psychol.*, **52**, 254–61.

RUSHTON, W. A. H. (1962). *Visual Pigments in Man*. Liverpool: Liverpool University Press.

RYLE, G. (1949). *The Concept of Mind*. London: Hutchinson.

SCHAFER, R. and MURPHY, G. (1943). 'The role of autism in a visual figure–ground relationship'. *J. exp. Psychol.*, **32**, 335–43.

SCHOENFELD, W. N., CUMMING, W. W. and HEARST, E. (1956). 'On the classification of reinforcement schedules'. *Proc. Nat. Acad. Sci.* **42**, 563–570.

References

SCHRAMM, W. (1964). 'Research on Programmed Instruction'. Page 462 of Report on International Conference on Programmed Instruction and Teaching Machines, Pädagogische Arbeitstelle, Berlin, 1964.

SCOTT, J. P. (1958). 'Critical periods in the development of social behavior in puppies'. *Psychosom. Med.*, **20**, 42–54.

SCOTT, J. P. and FULLER, J. L. (1965). *Genetics and social behavior of the dog*. Chicago: Chicago University Press.

SEABOURN, A. E. M. (1963). 'Social effects on standards in gauging tasks'. *Ergonomics*, **6**, 205–9.

SEARLE, L. V. (1949). 'The organisation of hereditary maze-brightness and maze-dullness'. *Genet. Psychol. Monogr.*, **39**, 279–325.

SECHREST, L. B. (1962). 'Stimulus equivalents of the psychotherapist'. *J. Indiv. Psychol.*, **18**, 172–6.

SEGALL, M. H., CAMPBELL, D. T. and HERSKOVITS, M. J. (1963). 'Cultural differences in the perception of geometric illusions'. *Science*, **139**, 769–71.

SEGUIN, E. (1846). *Traitement moral, hygiéne et education des idiots et des autres enfants arriéres*. Paris: Ballière.

SELLERS, W. (1941). 'The production of films for primitive people'. *Oversea Education*, **13**, 221.

VON SENDEN, M. (1932). English translation by Heath, P., 1960. *Space and sight: the perception of space and shape in the congenitally blind before and after operation*. London: Methuen.

SHANNON, C. E. (1948). *The Mathematical Theory of Communication*. Urbana: University of Illinois Press.

SHANNON, C. E. and WEAVER, W. (1949). *The Mathematical Theory of Communication*. Urbana: University of Illinois Press.

SHEILDS, J. (1962). *Monozygotic Twins*. London: O.U.P.

SIDMAN, M. (1960). *Tactics of Scientific Research*. New York: Basic Books.

SIMON, C. W. and EMMONS, W. H. (1955). 'Learning during sleep'. *Psychol. Bull.* **52**, 328–42.

SIMON, C. W. and EMMONS, W. H. (1956) 'Responses to material presented during various levels of sleep'. *J. exp. Psychol.* **51**, 89–97.

SINGER, M. (1961). 'A survey of culture and personality theory and research'. In Kaplan, B. (ed.), *Studying Personality Cross-Culturally*. Evanston: Row, Peterson.

SKINNER, B. F. (1938). *The Behaviour of Organisms*. New York: Appleton–Century–Crofts.

SKINNER, B. F. (1948a). 'Superstition in the pigeon'. *J. exp. Psychol.*, **38**, 168–72.

References

SKINNER, B. F. (1948b). *Walden Two*. New York: Macmillan.

SKINNER, B. F. (1953). *Science and Human Behaviour*. New York: Macmillan.

SKINNER, B. F. (1954). 'The science of learning and the art of teaching'. *Harvard Ed. Rev.*, **24**, No. 2.

SKINNER, B. F. (1962). *Cumulative Record*. London: Methuen.

SLAVSON, S. R. (ed.) (1956). *The fields of group psychotherapy*. New York: International University Press.

SLUCKIN, W. (1964). *Imprinting and Early Learning*. London: Methuen.

SLUCKIN, W. and SALZEN, E. A. (1961). 'Imprinting and perceptual learning'. *Quart. J. exp. Psychol.*, **13**, 65–77.

SMALLWOOD, R. D. (1962). *A Decision Structure for Teaching Machines*. M.I.T. Press.

SOMMER, R. (1959). 'Studies in personal space'. *Sociometry*, **22**, 247–60.

SOMMER, R. and ROSS, H. (1958). 'Social interaction on a geriatrics ward'. *Brit. J. Soc. Psychiat.*, **4**, 128–33.

SPEARMAN, C. (1926). *The Abilities of Man*. London: Macmillan.

SPERLING, G. (1960). 'The information available in brief visual presentations'. *Psychol. Monogr.*, **74**, No. 11.

SPIRO, M. E. and D'ANDRADE, R. G. (1958). 'A cross-cultural study of some supernatural beliefs'. *Am. Anthrop.*, **60**, 456–66.

SPITZ, H. H. (1963). 'Field theory in mental deficiency'. In Ellis, N. R. (ed.), *Handbook of Mental Deficiency*. New York: McGraw-Hill.

SPROTT, W. J. H. (1958). *Human Groups*. Harmondsworth: Penguin.

TANNER, W. P. Jr and SWETS, J. A. (1954). 'A decision-making theory of visual detection'. *Psychol. Rev.*, **61**, 401–9.

TAUSCH, R. (1954). '*Optische Täuschungen als artifizielle Effekte der Gestaltungsprozesse von Gröben-und Formenkonstanz in der natürlichen Raumwahrnehmung*'. *Psychol. Forsch.*, **24**, 299–348.

TAYLOR, C. W. (1964). 'Some knowns, needs and leads'. In Taylor, C. W. (ed.), *Creativity: Progress and Potential*. London: McGraw-Hill.

TAYLOR, D. W., BERRY, P. C. and BLOCK, C. H. (1957). 'Does group participation when using brainstorming facilitate or inhibit creative thinking?' *Yale Univ. Industr. Admin. Psychol. Tech. Rep.*

TAYLOR, I. A. (1959). 'The nature of the creative process'. In Smith, P. (ed.) *Creativity: An Examination of the Creative Process*. New York: Hastings House.

TEUBER, H. L. (1960). 'Perception'. In Field, *et al.*, (eds.) *Handbook of Physiology*, Section 1: Neurophysiology. Washington, D.C.: American Physiological Society.

References

TEUBER, H. L., BATTERSBY, W. S. and BENDER, M. B. (1960). *Visual Field Defects after Penetrating Missile Wounds of the Brain.* Cambridge, Mass.: Harvard University Press.

THODAY, J. M. (1965). 'Geneticism and environmentalism'. In Meade, J. E. and Parkes, A. S. (eds.) *Biological aspects of social problems.* Edinburgh: Oliver & Boyd.

THOMAS, C., DAVIES, I., OPPENSHAW, D. and BIRD, J. (1963). *Programmed Learning in Perspective.* City Publicity Services.

THOMPSON, W. R. and MELZACK, R. (1956). 'Early environment'. *Sci. Am.,* **194**, 38–42.

THORPE, W. H. (1956) (2nd edn. 1963). *Learning and Instinct in Animals.* London: Methuen.

THOULESS, R. H. (1931). 'Phenomenal regression to the real object'. *Brit. J. Psychol.,* **21**, 239–59; **22**, 1–30.

THURSTONE, L. L. (1935). *The Vectors of Mind.* Chicago: University of Chicago Press.

TINBERGEN, N. (1951). *The Study of Instinct.* Oxford: Clarendon Press.

TITCHENER, E. B. (1908). *Lectures on the Elementary Psychology of Feeling and Attention.* New York: Macmillan.

TORRANCE, E. P. (1962). *Guiding Creative Talent.* Englewood Cliffe, N.J.: Prentice-Hall.

TORRANCE, E. P. (1963). *Education and the Creative Potential.* Minneapolis: University of Minnesota Press.

TREISMAN, A. M. (1960). 'Contextual cues in selective listening'. *Quart. J. exp. Psychol.,* **12**, 242–8.

TREISMAN, A. M. (1961). *Attention and Speech.* D.Phil. Thesis, Oxford University.

TRYON, R. C. (1940) 'Genetic differences in maze learning ability in rats'. *39th Yearbook Nat. Soc. Stud. Educ.* (Part I). Bloomington: Public School Pub. Co.

TURING, A. M. (1950). 'Computing machinery and intelligence'. *Mind,* **59**, 433–60.

VAN BRUNT, E. E., GANON, W. F. and SHEPHERD, M. D. (1963). 'Penetration of light into the brain of mammals'. New York Academy of Science Conference on Photo-neuro-endocrine effects in Circadian Systems, with particular reference to the eye. June 1963.

VERNON, M. D. (1962). 'Specific dyslexia'. *Brit. J. Ed. Psychol.,* **32**, 143–50.

VIGOTSKY, L. S. (1962). *Thought and Language.* Haufmann, E. and Vakar, G., (ed. and trans.). New York: Wiley.

References

WALLAS, G. (1931). *The Art of Thought*. London: Jonathan Cape.

WARREN, R. M. (1961). 'Illusory changes of distinct speech upon repetition – the verbal transformation effect'. *Brit. J. Psychol.*, 52, 249–58.

WASON, P. C. (1960). 'On the failure to eliminate hypotheses in a conceptual task'. *Quart. J. exp. Psychol.*, 12, 129–40.

WATSON, J. B. (1924). (Rev. edn., 1930). *Behaviourism*. New York: Norton.

WELLS, M. J. (1962). *Brain and Behaviour in Cephalopods*. London: Heinemann.

WERNER, H. (1956). 'Microgenesis and aphasia'. *J. Abn. Soc. Psychol.*, 52, 347–53.

WERTHEIMER, M. (1961). 'Psychomotor coordination of auditory and visual space at birth'. *Science*, 134, 1692.

WHITE, R. and LIPPITT, R. (1960). 'Leader behaviour and member reaction in three "social climates"'. In Cartwright, D. and Zander, A. (eds.), *Group Dynamics*. London: Tavistock.

WHITING, J. (1961). 'Socialisation process and personality'. In Hsu, F. L. K. (ed.), *Psychological Anthropology: Approaches to Culture and Personality*. Homewood, Illinois: Dorsey Press.

WILKINSON, R. T. (1962). 'Muscle tension during mental work under sleep deprivation'. *J. exp. Psychol.* 64, 565–71.

WILKINSON, R. T. (1965). 'Sleep deprivation'. In Bacharach, A. L. and Edholm, O. G. (eds.) *Sleep Deprivation*. London: Academic Press.

WOLPE, J. (1958). *Psychotherapy by reciprocal inhibition*. Stanford: Stanford University Press.

WORTHINGTON, A. G. (1962). *Meaningful components of a subliminal stimulus*. Ph.D. Thesis, University of London.

WYCKOFF, L. B. (1952). 'The role of observing responses in discrimination learning'. *Psychol. Rev.*, 59, 431–42.

WYRWICKA, W., DOBRZECKA, C. and TARNECKI, R. (1959). 'On the instrumental conditioned reaction evoked by electrical stimulation of the hypothalamus'. *Science*, 130, 336–7.

YNTEMA, D. B. and TRASK, F. P. (1963). 'Recall as a search process'. *J. verb. Learn. verb. Behav.*, 2, 65–74.

YOUNG, J. Z. (1964). *A model of the brain*. Oxford: Clarendon Press.

ZANGWILL, O. L. (1950). *An Introduction to Modern Psychology*. London: Methuen.

ZIMMERMAN, J. (1963). 'Technique for sustaining behaviour with conditioned reinforcement'. *Science*, 142, 682–4.

INDEX

(Italicised page numbers indicate references.)

436

Index

Index

Index